Challenging Southeast Asian Development

Over the course of the last half century, the growth economies of Southeast Asia – Indonesia, Malaysia, the Philippines, Singapore, Thailand and Vietnam – have transformed themselves into middle-income countries, and the poorer nations of the region are fast following suit. This book looks at how their very success has bred new challenges, created novel problems and generated fresh tensions.

The book critically interrogates the development 'success' narrative that is so often attached to the Southeast Asian region. It highlights the enduring and deepening nature of inequality; the creation of new forms of poverty, often invisible, that have run hand-in-hand with economic expansion; and the social, environmental and political trade-offs that have accompanied the growth bargain.This book is an important contribution to Southeast Asian Studies, Development Studies, Geography and Environmental Studies.

Jonathan Rigg is Professor of Geography at the National University of Singapore. His previous publications include *An Everyday Geography of the Global South* (2007), *Living with Transition in Laos: Market Integration in Southeast Asia* (2005), *Southeast Asia: The Human Landscape of Modernization and Development* (2003) and *Asian Cities, Migrant Labor and Contested Spaces* (co-edited, 2011), all published by Routledge.

Challenging Southeast Asian Development

Asian Development

The shadows of success

Jonathan Rigg

Routledge
Taylor & Francis Group

LONDON AND NEW YORK

First published 2016
by Routledge
2 Park Square, Milton Park, Abingdon, Oxon OX14 4RN

and by Routledge
711 Third Avenue, New York, NY 10017

Routledge is an imprint of the Taylor & Francis Group, an informa business

© 2016 Jonathan Rigg

The right of Jonathan Rigg to be identified as author of this work has been
asserted by him in accordance with sections 77 and 78 of the Copyright,
Designs and Patents Act 1988.

British Library Cataloguing in Publication Data
A catalogue record for this book is available from the British Library

Library of Congress Cataloging in Publication Data
Rigg, Jonathan, 1959– author.
Challenging Southeast Asian development: the shadows of success/
Jonathan Rigg.
pages cm
1. Economic development—Southeast Asia—Social aspects. 2. Poverty—
Southeast Asia. I. Title.
HC441.R547 2015
338.9—dc23
2015002756

ISBN: 978-0-415-71157-9 (hbk)
ISBN: 978-0-415-71158-6 (pbk)
ISBN: 978-1-315-68625-7 (ebk)

Typeset in Times New Roman
by Book Now Ltd, London

Contents

Figures

Tables

Boxes

Preface

This is not quite the book I set out to write.

The initial intention was to write a follow-up volume to my *Southeast Asia: the human landscape of modernisation and development*, published in 2003. That book was completed in the aftermath of the Asian financial crisis. As a result, debates over the roots of the crisis and what that meant for the Asian development 'model' dominated the opening chapters. While it was critical of some of the undercurrents of transformation in the region, the volume was, on balance, broadly positive and noted the degree to which economic expansion had made significant inroads into absolute poverty, which I took (and still take) to be no small achievement. I sense that many readers have viewed the book as a 'defence' of development-as-modernization in Southeast Asia, although I have always been a little uncomfortable with that view. Perhaps without my fully appreciating it, the cautionary caveats became lost in the general tenor of the text.

This volume is wider-ranging in its argument and far more critical in its tone. At first sight this is puzzling because the trends identified in the 2003 book have continued. It is not as if economic expansion has stuttered to a halt. All the countries of the region, with the exception of Cambodia and Myanmar, are now classified as middle-income economies, poverty has fallen, real incomes have grown, and many indices of human development have improved.

On reflection I think there are three core reasons why this book is so different from that earlier volume.

First of all, and as I set out in the opening chapter, addressing absolute or extreme poverty is probably the easy part of the development project. Dealing with the problems that accompany 'success' and which emerge as countries attain middle-income status are, I think, often more intractable. Policies have less purchase and the location of 'the problem' is less obvious. The connection between 'growth' and 'development' has been widening and this begs the question, 'Why?'.

The second reason is more personal. I began working in Southeast Asia in the early 1980s, in two villages in Northeast Thailand. At the time the villagers I worked with had little income, few consumer goods, only basic education, and limited access to health facilities. The problem as I saw it really was one of under-development and fostering and supporting economic growth seemed to me to be the self-evident answer. I sought, therefore, to understand the processes underway and what constituted the 'barriers' to growth. I have returned to the two villages several times since and these problems are now, for most inhabitants, historical artefacts; memories. Villagers are amazed when I show pictures that I took almost three decades ago when no one had a camera, let alone a mobile phone. But the problem of development has not gone away; it has been reworked in ways that are subtle and, generally, far harder to grasp as well as to address. The general problem of development in middle-income economies also has its local and personal manifestations and permutations.

Looking back over my published *oeuvre*, I do identify an increasingly critical tone in my writings. Books and papers on economic transition in the Lao PDR, market-based integration in the Greater Mekong Sub-region, and migration and development in Sri Lanka, for example, have all highlighted the problematic side-effects of economic growth and market integration. So the critical tone of this volume has not come completely out of the blue. Rather, it has provided me with an opportunity to bring these ideas together in the form of an extended, book-length and region-wide argument.

Finally, I am also sure that the sentiments on these pages reflect my engagement with other researchers. I have always been impressionable, and working with some of the finest scholars of development (many named in the Acknowledgements) has played a role in encouraging me to reflect on and think again regarding some of my beliefs and assumptions. So it is not just that the Southeast Asian region has changed; so too have I.

The argument here is meant to be region-wide; indeed, more than region-wide. I would like to imagine that the themes have resonance and relevance in other places too. But in the book itself, to provide me with the opportunity to empirically and geographically situate the arguments, I have drawn on analysis and discussion in certain countries, particular places, and on selected themes. I am conscious, for example, that while the Lao PDR features quite significantly there is scant discussion of Myanmar. There is far more on Vietnam than the Philippines, and a much more extensive reflection on the Thai experience than that of Malaysia. I have chosen to explore the issue of migration at some length, and have more 'rural' than 'urban' cases. These selections and preferences reflect those themes and places that I know best and have worked in for longest. The literature and my engagement and discussions with other scholars, however, tell me that the arguments themselves are neither particular nor peculiar to those countries and contexts.

I find myself, to my surprise and almost against my will, a critic of Southeast Asian development.

Acknowledgements

Each time I write a book there are more people to acknowledge. It is nice being able to thank people, although there is always the fear that someone, somewhere will be offended either because they haven't been mentioned or, possibly, because they have.

This book took root while I was Professor-at-large at the University of Western Australia's Institute of Advanced Studies, took shape during my final few months in the Department of Geography at Durham University in the UK, where I had been based for some two decades, and was completed after I arrived at the National University of Singapore's Department of Geography in mid-2013.

At the University of Western Australia I am grateful for the support of Susan Takao in the Institute of Advanced Studies and Matthew Tonts in the School of Earth and Environment. My annual visits to UWA over the last few years have been a wonderful break from a cold Durham and, more recently, a sticky Singapore.

At Durham I am indebted to colleagues who were far more than academic sparring partners. It is difficult to name names when, over twenty years, almost everyone has played a part in shaping my ideas, but I would particularly like to highlight and thank Peter Atkins, Louise Bracken, Harriet Bulkeley, Mike Crang, Alex Densmore, Chris Dunn, Antony Long, Cheryl McEwan, Colin McFarlane, Katie Oven, Rachel Pain, Joe Painter, Dave Petley and Marcus Power. There are also some former colleagues at Durham who, themselves, have moved on but whose ideas and work have influenced my own, in particular Emma Mawdsley, Liz Oughton, David Petley, Gina Porter and Janet Townsend. The Geography Department at Durham is truly an exceptional place to be a geographer.

Arriving at NUS in 2013 provided me with a needed injection of enthusiasm and expertise in all things Asian. The Department of Geography has been welcoming and the University without peer as a place to work on contemporary transformations in the Southeast Asian region. It is not easy moving jobs, cultures and continents after twenty years in one place but my new colleagues at NUS have made it as painless as it was possible for such a move to be. There are already too many people to name, but at the risk of offence I would like to thank: Tim Bunnell, Neil Coe, TC Chang, Dan Freiss, Jamie Gillen, Carl Grundy-Warr, Elaine Ho, Shirlena Huang, Lily Kong, Harvey Neo, Grahame Oliver, Choon Piew Pow, Kamal Ramdas, James Sidaway, Harng Luh Sin, Tracey Skelton, David Taylor, Eric Thompson, Bob Wasson, Brenda Yeoh, Henry Yeung and Alan Ziegler.

I have been fortunate to have supervised some 25 PhD students, most of whom have undertaken fieldwork in Southeast Asia, on development-related themes. Increasingly I find my ideas being fine-tuned through the work of these fine early career – and some now mid-career – researchers. There is nothing more satisfying than seeing a former PhD student writing more incisively and fluently than oneself. Those students whose work most obviously links to this volume, and in chronological order, are: Undala Alam, Fergus Lyon, Siriluck Sirisup, Mike Alderson, Anne Le Mare, Albert Salamanca, Guillaume Lestrelin, Hamzah Muzaini, Katie Oven, Jitsuda Limkriengkrai, Roy Huijsmans, Lata Narayanaswamy, Adeline Tengku Hamzah, Georgina Jordan, Wasana La-orngplew, Cat Button, Mohammad Ansari, Clare Collingwood, Honna Ruszczyk, Robert Cole and Keo Piseth.

Finally, there is an ever-growing number of scholars and researchers with whom I have been fortunate enough to work on assorted projects in various places. Increasingly my publications are multi-authored, reflecting this collaborative 'turn'. The following have most noticeably shaped my ideas in the pages that follow: Kate Gough, Mike Parnwell, Tony Bebbington, Dave Little, Cecilia Tacoli, Geoff Wilson, Deborah Bryceson, Raymond Bryant, Becky Elmhirst, Niels Fold, Jytte Agergaard, Irene Nørlund, Pietro Masina, Nancy Lee Peluso, Rodolphe de Koninck, Phil Kelly, Melissa Marschke, Sarah Turner, Steffanie Scott, Tania Murray Li, Jean Michaud, Peter Vandergeest, Rob Cramb, Andrew Walker, Phil Hirsch, George Curry, Tubtim Tubtim, Brian Shaw, Mark Beeson, Chusak Wittayapak, May Tan Mullins, Lisa Law, Ben Horton, David Simon, Bounthong Bouahom, Linkham Douangsavanh, Buapun Promphakping, Pham Van Cu, Luong Thi Thu Huong, Nguyen Tuan Anh, Dinh Thi Dieu, P. Hewage, Monchai Phongsiri, Mattara Sripun, Annuska Derks, Christine Padoch and Chaminda Kumara.

More specifically in terms of this book I would like to thank Erik Kuhonta for the time he took in clarifying some questions I had about inequality (his book *The institutional imperative* is the best critical analysis of inequality in Southeast Asia); Kearrin Sims at the University of Western Sydney for providing me with the opportunity to read his research on Laos; Tim Bunnell for pointing me in the right direction regarding his publications on estate workers in Malaysia; Anna-Klara Lindeborg for allowing me to use her photograph of rubber in northern Laos (I was fortunate to be the examiner for her PhD thesis *Where gendered spaces bend*, completed at Uppsala University); Annuska Derks for sending me her published work on migrants and bonded labour in Southeast Asia; Melissa Marschke for checking the discussion of sand mining in Cambodia in Chapter 6; and Manu Bhaskaran for permission to use his lead authored paper on inequality in Singapore.

At Routledge I would like to thank Dorothea Schaefter and Jillian Morrison for commissioning the book, and to Becky Lawrence, Emma Chappell and Sophie Iddamalgoda for keeping a weather eye on its progress, and a light hand on the tiller.

Over the years I have dragged my family to all sorts of places for extended stays; to Indonesia, the Lao PDR, Thailand, Vietnam and Australia. In each instance we knew we were coming back to the UK and sleepy Durham before too long. In 2013, however, we cut our ties with Durham and I took up a permanent position at NUS in Singapore. This has entailed leaving two children behind in London and taking two with us. It has been a big move for us all, but probably least for me. My office may be smaller and with a more industrial view, but the books that surround me are the same. I teach roughly the same material to similarly bright and engaged students, although I have much to learn about the minutiae of Singapore life, character and culture. My fieldwork is still Asia-based, but without the jet-lag. But for my family it has been all change. That they have embraced living in yet another new place with such enthusiasm is a source of pride to me.

I am eternally grateful to Janie, Joshua, Bella, Cesca and Sam for accompanying me on my adventures. This book is for them.

Jonathan Rigg
Department of Geography
National University of Singapore
March 2015

Acronyms, abbreviations and terms in Southeast Asian languages

3D work	Dirty, Dangerous and Demeaning (or, sometimes, Difficult)
3F states	countries that are Fragile, Failed and Fractious
3L work	Low pay, Low skill and Long hours
ABD	Accumulation by Dispossession
ADB	Asian Development Bank
ASEAN	Association of Southeast Asian Nations
AWD	Accumulation without Dispossession
BLES	Bureau of Labour and Employment Statistics (Philippines)
Bumiputera	literally, 'sons of the soil', to refer to the indigenous (mainly Malay) population of the country (Malaysia)
chao ban nok	rural folk (Thai)
charoen	progress (Thai)
chin thanakaan mai	reform or 'new thinking' (Lao)
CHNS	China Health and Nutrition Survey
CPF	Central Provident Fund (Singapore)
CPP	Cambodian People's Party
cyclo	pedicab (Vietnam)
Dayak	'tribal' peoples of Borneo
DFID	Department for International Development (UK)
doi moi	reform or 'renovation' (Vietnam)
ECOP	Employers' Confederation of the Philippines
ELCs	Economic Land Concessions (Cambodia)
EPZ	Export Processing Zone
FDWs	Foreign Domestic Workers
GMS	Greater Mekong Subregion
GPI	Genuine Progress Indicator
HES	Household Expenditure Survey (Malaysia)
ho khau	household registration system (Vietnam)
HYVs	High-Yielding Varieties (of rice)
ICCPR	International Covenant on Civil and Political Rights
ICERD	International Convention on the Elimination of all Forms of Racial Discrimination
ICESCR	International Covenant on Economic, Social and Cultural Rights

ILO	International Labour Organization
IOM	International Organization for Migration
khon pa	people of the forest, hill peoples or 'tribes' (Thai)
krismon	economic crisis (Indonesia)
LECS	Lao Expenditure and Consumption Survey (Lao PDR)
LECS 3	the third round of the Lao Expenditure and Consumption Survey
LPA	Labour Protection Act (Thailand)
MIC	Middle Income Country
MoM	Ministry of Manpower (Singapore)
MoU	Memorandum of Understanding
NEP	New Economic Policy (Malaysia)
NES	Nuclear Estate and Smallholder oil palm schemes (Indonesia)
OCWs	Overseas Contract Workers
ODI	Overseas Development Institute (UK)
Orang asli	literally, 'original people', to refer to the aboriginal peoples of Peninsular Malaysia
PPA	Participatory Poverty Assessment
PPP	Purchasing Power Parity
RTD	Right to Development (UN Declaration, 1986)
SD	Sustainable Development
sethakit phorpiang	sufficiency economy (Thai)
siwilai	civilized (Thai)
SHI	Social Health Insurance
SOE	State-Owned Enterprises
SPI	Social Protection Index
subak	Balinese irrigation societies
TFR	Total Fertility Rate
thuk nyak	poverty (Lao PDR)
UN	United Nations
UNDP	United Nations Development Programme
UNEP	United Nations Environment Programme
UPP	Urban Poverty Project (Indonesia)
WBG	World Bank Group
WCED	World Commission on Environment and Development
WEF	World Economic Forum
xe om	motorcycle taxi (Vietnam)
yaak chon, chon	poverty (Thai)

1 The shadows of success

A cautionary tale of Southeast Asian development

... even successful capitalist growth has always done damage to a significant portion of the population.

(Glassman 2004: 203)

Banyan's column on Singapore's economic model concluded that 'nobody has come up with an alternative'. Here are a few: cease the uncritical reverence for GDP growth figures; reduce protectionism at Singaporean firms by weaning them off their addiction to cheap foreign labour; do not use monetary incentives and propaganda to increase the fertility rate but instead bring about a pro-family environment; govern with a dose of Rawlsianism; recognise that development comes at the expense of natural and cultural heritage; and bring back Singapore's early *kampung* spirit, which emphasises community over consumption.

(Ching Hu, Paris. Letter to *The Economist*, 23 February 2013)

We believe that the central challenge we face today is to ensure that globalization becomes a positive force for all the world's people ... only through broad and sustained efforts to create a shared future, based upon our common humanity in all its diversity, can globalization be made fully inclusive and equitable ...

(UN General Assembly at the launching of the Millennium Development Goals initiative)

Setting the scene

The headline story of the Southeast Asian region is one of success, a story that has been told and retold for over a quarter of a century, so much so, and so many times that it has lost its ability to impress or enthral. Asia's miraculous growth is shrugged off as routine, even mundane and the 'Asian Century' has become a hackneyed phrase useful only to make the point that the fulcrum of economic activity has shifted (back) to Asia – hardly particularly insightful. We have grown weary of the growth thesis, almost to the point of distraction.

In 1993, the World Bank famously selected eight High Performing Asian Economies (HPAEs) for special attention, of which four were Southeast Asian (World Bank 1993); 15 years later, the Commission on Growth and Development identified 15 'success stories', five of which were Southeast Asian (CGD 2008); and more recently still, in 2011, the 'Tracking development' project (van Donge *et al.* 2012) selected four sets of paired Southeast Asian and African nations – Indonesia and Nigeria, Malaysia and Kenya, Vietnam and Tanzania, and Cambodia and Uganda – so that the policies that had generated growth in the Southeast Asian members of each twin might be identified and extracted for wider communication (Table 1.1).

These three major studies, which themselves draw on many narrower and less ambitious projects, reflect a dominant thread in our understanding of development: that everything follows from the achievement of high and sustained economic growth and the challenge is to identify the policies that will generate and support growth. This is not caprice. Reductions in poverty and improvements in material well-being are closely tied to economic expansion, even though the causalities (i.e. the policies that lead to economic growth) are not quite as clear as intuitively they might seem, nor, as later chapters will argue, is the relationship between growth and poverty alleviation necessarily immutable.

There were scholars who questioned the development 'success' of Southeast Asia right from the earliest years of the economic 'miracle'. We can see this reflected in critical views of Thailand's development experience, even when the Kingdom was the fastest growing large economy in the world and poverty rates were declining steeply. Peter Bell, for example, wondered whether

> there is reason . . . to question the use of the term 'development' at all when applied to this pattern of economic growth [in Thailand] as it violates important values of equity, economic democracy, ecological balance, and human decency.
>
> (Bell 1992: 61)

And similarly, Mike Parnwell and Daniel Arghiros suggested that despite Thailand's "undoubted economic, social and welfare achievements, the notion of 'success' and the accomplishment of 'development' have both to be qualified" (1996: 2). In the wake of the financial crisis these voices became more numerous and strident. Jim Glassman (also quoted at the start of this chapter) observed that industrialization in Thailand was "predicated heavily on marginalization of the peasantry, 'feminization' of manufacturing labour, and fragmentation of labour and political opposition" (2004: 205). At the populist end of the spectrum, the promotion by the King of Thailand of the 'sufficiency economy' (*sethakit phorpiang*) likened building an economy to building a house: "we must bear in mind how much weight a house can bear before we begin to build it" (Thai Chamber of Commerce 2010: 9). These countervailing views of Thailand's economic progress also find their echoes in work on the other middle- and high-income countries of the region – Indonesia, Malaysia, the Philippines, Singapore and Vietnam. There are two missing elements – sub-plots, as it were – to this story of Southeast Asian development success.

First of all, the success story narrative, usually tightly tied to the achievement of economic expansion, tends of gloss over the individuals, sectors and regions that have been 'left behind'. It is this sub-plot that has received the greatest attention, most obviously in debates over inequality and the need to generate pro-poor,

Table 1.1 Normalizing Southeast Asian developmental success

Report	Source and date	Identified Southeast Asian economies	Success 'story' recounted
The East Asian miracle	World Bank (1993)	Indonesia, Malaysia, Singapore, Thailand (4 out of 8)	"East Asia has a remarkable record of high and sustained economic growth. … What caused East Asia's success? In large measure the HPAEs [High Performing Asian Economies] achieved high growth by getting the basics right" (World Bank 1993: 1 and 5)
The growth report: strategies for sustained growth and inclusive development	Commission on Growth and Development (2008)	Indonesia, Malaysia, Singapore, Thailand, Vietnam (5 out of 15)[a]	"Since 1950, 13 economies have grown at an average rate of 7 percent a year or more for 25 years or longer. … This report is about sustained, high growth of this kind: its causes, consequences, and internal dynamics.… Growth is not an end in itself. But it makes it possible to achieve other important objectives of individuals and societies" (CGD 2008: 1)
"Tracking development in South-East Asia and Sub-Saharan Africa"	van Donge *et al.* (2012)	Four paired Southeast Asian and African countries, of which the former are Cambodia, Indonesia, Malaysia and Vietnam	"The [project] identifies a clear cluster of policies that explain the main differences in the development trajectories of sub-Saharan Africa and South-East Asia. The pivotal element therein is raising farm incomes and increasing the supply of public goods in the rural sector . … This appears to require macroeconomic stability as a necessary, but not sufficient, factor" (van Donge *et al.* 2012: S20)

Note
a In fact there are 13 identified countries, although the report adds India and Vietnam as economies that "may be on their way to joining this group" (CGD 2008: 19). It is worth noting that of the 15, 11 are Asian.

shared or inclusive growth. For Sen (2012: 7), it is in this regard – in the real conditions that people face and the social inequalities that underpin them – that the concentration on the rate of GNP growth as the key indicator has had the most damaging effect.

Second, there are the problems and tensions that have arisen *from* growth. Economic expansion, whether directly or indirectly, has led to an array of social, environmental, political and economic side-effects. Sometimes these have also been the very sources of growth. Whether they can be regarded as negative side-effects is not always clear, although that case will be developed in the chapters that follow. These are the handmaidens of growth, all too often left at the margins as inevitable but short-term 'costs' to be shouldered for the greater good and in the interests of 'the nation'. As a report on social cohesion in Singapore put it – and this could be applied region-wide – "the unrelenting pursuit of growth has major ramifications on [Singapore's] society, creating new divergences and deepening some existing fault lines in the country" (Hassan 2013: 6). Some of these outcomes may not have been planned as such, but they were expected; others have emerged to the surprise of policy-makers and scholars alike.

Producing poverty and destitution in contexts of prosperity and growth

Where do the poor live in Southeast Asia?[1]

It is often assumed that the challenge of poverty in Southeast Asia lies with – and in – the region's poorest countries. However, as Table 1.2 shows, there are, today, far more poor people living in middle-income than in low-income countries in the region, even using the (very low) $1.25 international poverty line. The difference becomes starker still if a more generous $2.00 line is used (Table 1.2). This distribution of the poor between low- and middle-income countries is *new*: in 2005, across developing Asia, 69 per cent of the poor lived in low-income countries; in 2008 the figure was 19 per cent. Over 80 per cent of Asia's poor, therefore, were living in middle-income countries by 2008 (Wan and Sebastian 2011: 29). This is not because a new stock of poor people has suddenly revealed itself in middle-income countries. It reflects the transition of formerly low-income countries to middle-income status even while their poverty challenge has remained to be comprehensively addressed (see Table 1.3). This is the regional incarnation of a 'new geography' of global poverty, one where we need to pay attention to the partially obscured poor in what may well be rapidly growing – and therefore 'successful' – countries (Sumner 2012). As Evans writes in her think piece, "hard to reach and chronic poverty will continue to persist [even] in rapidly growing middle-income countries" (Evans 2010: 2).

This concern for the poor in middle-income countries shifts the terms of the debate, and more than geographically, from the so-styled 'bottom billion' (Collier 2007) living in low-income countries, to the poor living in middle-income countries.[2] The assumption until quite recently was that the large majority of the global poor suffered from poverty because they were living in '3F' states – countries that are

Table 1.2 Proportion and numbers of poor by country in Southeast Asia, $1.25 and $2.00 poverty lines (latest available)

	$1.25-per-day poverty line		$2.00-per-day poverty line	
	Headcount (%)	*No. of poor (millions)*	*Headcount (%)*	*No. of poor (millions)*
Low-income countries				
Cambodia	27.2	4.1	55.0	8.3
Lao PDR	31.8	2.0	64.0	4.1
Myanmar	–	–	–	–
Timor Leste	37.4	0.4	72.8	0.8
Total:		6.5		13.2
Middle-income countries				
Indonesia	18.6	43.1	50.6	117.4
Malaysia	0	0	2.2	0.6
Philippines	16.7	15.6	41.1	38.4
Thailand	0.2	0.1	9.7	6.6
Vietnam	12.6	11.1	37.8	33.3
Total:		69.9		196.3
High-income countries				
Brunei Darrusalam	0	0	0	0
Singapore	0	0	0	0
Total:		0		0

Sources: Wan and Sebastian (2011: 6, 10); Timor Leste from World Bank data (downloaded from: http://data.worldbank.org/country/timor-leste. There are no current data on poverty in Myanmar which correspond to the international poverty lines used here. The UNDP has published data indicating that 25 per cent of the population were living in poverty in Myanmar in 2010 but this is on the basis of a very low poverty line (see http://www.mm.undp.org/ihlca/01_Poverty_Profile/index.html).

Note: All income/consumption estimates calculated in terms of purchasing power parity (PPP). Headcount poverty rates based on latest year: Cambodia (2009), Indonesia (2011), Lao PDR (2008), Malaysia (2009), Philippines (2009), Thailand (2010), Timor Leste (2007), Vietnam (2008).

fragile, failed and/or fractious. As Sumner (2010) argues, the large majority of the poor today live in middle-income, usually stable, and often economically successful states:

> [T]here is *a new* 'bottom billion' who are living in the MICs [middle-income countries]: most of the world's poor – three-quarters, or almost one billion poor people – now live in MICs. Indeed, about two-thirds of the world's poor live in stable MICs. This is not just about India and China as the percentage of global poverty accounted for by the MICs minus China and India has risen considerably from 7 per cent to 22 per cent.
>
> (Sumner 2010: 26 [emphasis in original])

This applies equally to the countries of Asia. Furthermore, this changing geography of poverty raises a series of important questions: has there been a shift from an international political economy of poverty where differences are largely between countries to one where it is intra-state inequalities that are paramount? In the process, have the causalities of poverty also shifted from those associated with 3F states to those related to the distribution of growth? And finally, what does this mean for both international development policy and for national development policy?

When the poor were concentrated among low-income countries it was usual to see poverty as a problem of low growth and underdevelopment (Table 1.3). The solution was clear: encourage growth. The persistence of poverty in rapidly growing middle-income countries, however, reflects something rather different, and arguably more intractable.[3] The question in these countries is: why do we not see an eradication of poverty in the context of rapid growth? The standard answer is that it is because growth has been unequal and this, in turn, has informed the policy debate over how to support and generate pro-poor growth. The growing inequalities that have accompanied rapid growth led Edward (2006) to qualify Dollar and Kraay's (2002) oft-repeated claim that "growth is good for the poor", by adding the rider "*but it is much better for the rich*" (2006: 1682 [emphasis in orginal]).[4] The importance of addressing the inequality that seems to be a growing feature of economic growth in developing Asia is political, as much as it is moral and humanitarian: "Rising inequalities in Asia pose a clear and present danger to social and political stability and, therefore, the sustainability of the growth process itself" (Ali and Juzhong Zhuang 2007: 9). This applies, therefore, as much to high-income Singapore as to middle-income places like Thailand and Malaysia, and low-income countries such as the Lao PDR. Between 2001 and 2008, the poorest three deciles of Singapore's resident working population saw their real incomes *fall*, while for the next two deciles up the income ladder, their incomes stagnated (Bhaskaran *et al.* 2012: 2). Income growth was concentrated in the richest half of the population.

Table 1.3 The changing framing of development problems and solutions in Asia

	Problem	*Solution*	*Positions*
Poverty in low-income countries (Cambodia, Lao PDR, Myanmar)	Low growth and underdevelopment	Encourage growth	"Growth is good for the poor ..." (Dollar and Kraay 2002)
Poverty in middle-income (Malaysia, Philippines, Thailand) and high-income (Brunei, Singapore) countries	Distribution of growth	Promote pro-poor development (inclusion)	"Growth is good for the poor ... *but it is much better for the rich*" (Edward 2006: 1682)
	The governance and politics of growth, and the recognition that capitalist growth is harmful to (some) people's interests	Promote social and spatial justice	"[S]ome significant rethinking is required within international development regarding the forms of politics that are presumed to be pro-poor" (Hickey 2009: 474)

The challenge of achieving pro-poor growth is highly important, as the next chapter will explore, but it goes beyond the question of the economics of anti-poor growth. It is also about the governance and politics of growth (Sumner 2012: 875). This book argues that the core issue is not just that the poor have somehow missed out on growth – which is then taken to mean that the policy challenge is how to achieve 'inclusion' – but that, and counter-intuitively, the poor have also been, relatively and sometimes absolutely speaking, *harmed* by growth. So inclusion addresses only part of the challenge. We also need to understand how and why capitalist growth is harmful to (some) poor people's interests. In the main, practitioners have been good at demarcating and describing what poverty is like, but rather less good at explaining why there are poor people in the first place. This, then, leads us away from *characterizing* poverty, to *explaining* poverty.

Why are the poor, poor?

> Development got human (via poverty reduction), it got social (via social capital), and it even got political (via the rubrics of empowerment, good governance and even 'equity').
>
> (Hickey 2010: 1139)

For international development organizations, the poor are measured in absolute terms, using economic indices, on the basis of which a population group is identified that falls beneath some 'international' poverty line (as in Table 1.2). This creates a poverty agenda where growth is pursued to generate income to 'lift' these people above such a line, and therefore out of poverty. While the poverty agenda has taken due heed of the problem of inequality-widening growth, this is viewed through the lens of market forces. Globalization is seen to have driven inter- and intra-country inequality due to technological change, wide variations in human capital in the form of education, and the operation of the market.

There are well-known shortcomings with the economics of poverty, and these tend to follow three lines of argument. First of all, and most widely articulated, is the argument that standard, economic approaches to poverty fail to get to grips with the multidimensional nature of poverty. The experience of being poor is, to be sure, related to lack of income but it also encompasses vulnerability to ill-health and natural hazards, lack of empowerment and having a 'voice' in society, and lack of opportunity (World Bank 2001). These can be seen to be both causes and effects. The second shortcoming relates to the way in which such an approach standardizes the poor, omitting to take account of the very different experiences of poverty. There is no 'stock' of poor who can be understood and treated in a uniform, singular manner (Rigg 2012). Furthermore, poverty is not only multi-dimensional but the poor themselves are a highly diverse group, so multi-dimensionality is both within group and between group. As Amartya Sen observes in his book *Poverty and famines*:

A small peasant and a landless labourer may both be poor, but their fortunes are not tied together. In understanding the proneness to starvation of either we have to view them not as members of the huge army of 'the poor,' but as members of particular classes, belonging to particular occupational groups, having different ownership endowments, and being governed by rather different entitlement relations. Classifying the population into the rich and the poor may serve some purpose in some context, but it is far too undiscriminating to be helpful in analysing starvation, famines, or even poverty.

(Sen 1981: 156)

The third and final shortcoming relates to the need to see poverty in temporal perspective. There is an important dynamic to poverty and a surprising degree of turbulence in the poor population between generations, across seasons, and in relation to the life course (Krishna 2010, 2011; Krishna and Shariff 2011). As panel studies have shown, while there is an entrenched population of chronically poor, there is usually a much larger group of occasionally or sometimes poor: the transient poor.

These issues are all important and this book does not seek to suggest otherwise. However, the focus on the economics of poverty and inequality distracts our attention from the socio-politics of inequality and, therefore of (relative) poverty (Nissanke and Thorbecke 2006: 1338–1339). There is little doubt that economic growth, if translated into income growth, for individuals is income poverty reducing, but there are many instances where such a neat translation does not occur. This then opens up not so much an economic question about the distribution of growth often framed in terms of how best to 'reach' the poor, but a socio-political question (Green and Hulme 2005: 868).[5] The socio-political question takes us a step back from considering why individuals and households do not have access to resources, to considering a more fundamental question about why individuals and households do not have the entitlements (Sen 1981) that would enable them to access such resources. These entitlements may be structured in poverty-creating ways due to customary practices, or they may be directly associated with policies and development interventions. Poverty may, therefore, be both 'old' – an inheritance of the past – and 'new' – a product of contemporary processes of transformation and the policies that underpin such processes. This is a concern that runs through the discussion in Chapter 3.

To begin to understand the persistence of poverty in rapidly growing 'developing' Asia it is worthwhile considering four dimensions of poverty (Table 1.4), which offer different – but not mutually exclusive – ways of thinking about poverty and the poor.

Four dimensions of poverty and the poor

The more usually highlighted dimensions of poverty are designated Poverty 1.0 and Poverty 2.0 in Table 1.4. There are some people living meagre lives in absolute poverty (whether designated as those living below the $1.25- or $2-a-day poverty lines) in Southeast Asia, even in middle-income countries such as Malaysia and Thailand (see Table 1.2). These individuals and households are sometimes characterized as 'trapped' in inherited poverty: the small number of poor living below the $2-per-day poverty line in Malaysia, for example, might fall into this category.[6] They are the Orang Asli of Pahang and Dayak groups living in the more remote areas of East Malaysia (Kuhonta 2011: 95). "Growth without social, economic, or political transformation", Sumner suggests, "might begin to explain the continuing levels of absolute poverty in the MICs" (Sumner 2010: 27).

Much larger numbers of poor, however, live in relative poverty in Southeast Asia – these are designated the unequal poor (2.0 Poor) in Table 1.4. The persistence of poverty in the middle-income economies of Asia lies largely in the uneven and unequal nature of economic expansion. To understand these poor requires us to study the non-poor because it is in relation to the rich that they emerge. The 2.0 Poor, while they find their incomes rising and living conditions improving in real terms, are unable to fulfil their aspirations to become fully contented consumers. They are frustrated in this desire. That so many Southeast Asians have acquired a degree of material prosperity but remain dissatisfied requires us to turn our attention to the cultural and social bases of poverty and social exclusion: what are those resources that attendant society deems the acquisition, consumption and display of as being important, and the absence of to be indicative or emblematic

Table 1.4 Understanding the persistence of poverty in Asia: four approaches

Type of poverty	Character	Measurement	'Solution'
1.0: The residual poor	'Traditional' poverty: lack of food, health facilities, education, clean water, and other 'basic' needs. Lack of income	Absolute and usually in monetary terms (either income or consumption). Allows inter-country comparison based on $1.25 or $2 poverty 'lines'	Economic growth
2.0: The unequal poor	Poverty created by the unequal distribution of growth and the failure of some people's incomes to keep pace with the general rate of growth, leading to *relative* decline	Calculated in terms of income, but relative to median income. In most richer countries the poor are those earning less than 50 or 60 per cent of the median income	Pro-poor, shared or inclusive growth (neo-liberal solution); redistribution (more radical answer)
3.0: The produced poor	'Impoverishment' – poverty that is created by processes of development	Overlooked by policy makers; invisible to or seen to be undeserving by the wider public	Politicisation
4.0: The invisible and unreported (uncounted) poor	Transnational migrants, both registered and unregistered	Uncounted and therefore, unmeasured	Recognition and inclusion

of poverty? And why are some individuals and groups excluded from accessing such resources?

More paradoxically and contentiously, Poverty 3.0 is poverty created by development – through a parallel process of 'impoverishment'. For its critics (see Li 2007; Green 2006), inclusive liberalism, like the post-Washington consensus, changes little: for the most vulnerable, modern capitalism remains disempowering and impoverishing. Their poverty is created by the structural violence of the operation of the market economy. This is explored in more detail in Chapter 3, but for Farmer (2004: 307), "structural violence is violence exerted systematically – that is, indirectly – by everyone who belongs to a certain social order ... . In short, the concept of structural violence is intended to inform the study of the social machinery of oppression". Thus market integration, while it may generate economic growth and raise incomes in absolute terms also does *systematic harm* to some groups and individuals; as Mosse puts it, "the poverty of certain categories of people is not just unimproved by growth or integration into (global) markets, but deepened by it" (2010: 1161).

There is also a fourth group of poor in Southeast Asia, designated here the uncounted or invisible poor (4.0 Poor). These poor include many millions of transnational migrant workers who service and support the needs of the emerging middle classes in MICs like Brunei, Malaysia and Singapore. These constitute both registered overseas contract workers (OCWs) or 'guest' workers (see Yeoh 2006) but also many women and men who work beneath the radar of the state as undocumented migrants, and who are particularly at risk. More egregious still, they include modern-day bonded labourers – effectively slave workers, in the view of some analysts. Such categories of people often lack any significant ability to shape the political debate: they are, as a class, rendered unpoliticized and their condition, as an issue, depoliticized. They have little or no political representation, and therefore have no voice. And because they do not count, they are not counted – hence their designation here as the uncounted or invisible poor. It becomes more complex, however, when groups occupy one class position in their place of work (say, as domestic workers in Singapore or construction workers in the Middle East), and another in their place of residence (say, in villages in the Philippines or Thailand). These poor and their life and working conditions are explored in Chapter 4.

In the main, Southeast Asian countries have been very good at generating growth and reducing Poverty 1.0; they have been rather less good at addressing Poverty 2.0, but nonetheless the success of the growth agenda has made this, until recently, less urgent. It is with regard to Poverty 3.0 and Poverty 4.0 where the achievement of success really does have to be qualified, and it is here that the emerging development challenge lies. The source of the challenge lies not in the exhortation 'must do better', but rather in the need to change the grounds and terms of the debate. The reason for the persistence, even expansion of Poverty 3.0 and Poverty 4.0 is because the definition and categorization of the poor have, often quite deliberately, hidden the poor from view. The need, then, is first to shift the agenda; only then will these poor become visible and their needs and rights subject to consideration and addressing.

From poverty to well-being and human flourishing

A point made above is that the essence of what it means to be poor is socially constructed – an observation that can be traced back to Adam Smith and, indeed to the Bible and the Buddhist scriptures. This provides a further reason to pay attention as much to the successful middle-income countries of the region as to the low-income nations. It is when we move beyond the 'obvious' manifestations of poverty – hunger, lack of access to clean water and basic medical care, inadequate education – that how we understand the conditions of the poor and appreciate the persistence of these conditions become both conceptually and empirically more challenging. These poor are often not 'obviously' poor; why they might be constructed as such is none too clear; and how their poverty should be 'addressed' in policy terms is uncertain and contested. In a real sense, addressing absolute poverty is the easy part of the development challenge.

The sense that poverty does not adequately capture the relationship between economic growth, development, and human progress can be seen in work on 'well-being'. Chambers' (2004) concern to view development as more than just the proliferation of material goods and amenities through economic expansion, but *good change* encapsulates this desire to bring together 'objective' and 'subjective' well-being (Gough *et al.* 2006), sometimes discussed in terms of human 'flourishing' (Kleinig and Evans 2013) or human 'progress' (Kubiszewski *et al.* 2013).[7] As Deneulin and McGregor (2009: 7) write:

> Development is ... not about what people have but about what they are able to do and to be with what they have, such as living long and healthy lives, being educated, having a voice to participate in decisions which affect their lives.

In Thai, wellbeing has been variously translated as 'live well, eat well' (*yuu dii kin dii*) and 'live well, have happiness' (*yuu dii mii sukh*). This then pays attention to the quality of living, and not just to the achievement of a certain level of consumption. 'Flourishing', or 'doing well' in subjective and objective terms, show close associations with these two Thai terms.

The analytical and experiential gap between income and welfare (or well-being) is graphically illustrated in Figure 1.1, drawing on the work of Jones and Klenow (2010).[8] There is, as the graph shows, a mismatch between per capita income and welfare in some Asian countries. In the rich European countries illustrated, well-being 'exceeds' income per capita, while in Singapore and the Asian MICs the reverse is the case: in these countries, in aggregate terms, it seems that people are income rich but well-being poor. As Jones and Klenow write:

> [M]any economists have noted [that] GDP is a flawed measure of economic welfare. Leisure, inequality, mortality, morbidity, crime, and a pristine environment are just some of the major factors affecting living standards within a country that are incorporated imperfectly, if at all, in GDP.
>
> (2010: 2)

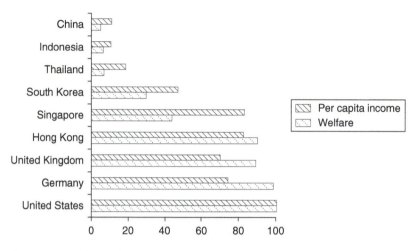

Figure 1.1 Welfare and per capita income (2000)

Source: data extracted from Jones and Klenow 2010: 22

This issue of how we measure progress and assess development in fast (economically) growing countries such as those in Southeast Asia will be returned to in the final chapter.

When the terms of the poverty debate are extended from measures of income/consumption to subjective issues such as the capacity to aspire (Appadurai 2004; and see Bunnell and Goh 2012; Bunnell and Harris 2012),[9] human freedom (Sen 1999), human dignity, happiness, justice, life satisfaction, and individual agency, two key shifts in the debate occur. To begin with, and most obviously, the debate is widened considerably, from the economic to the social, from the measureable (income) to the less measurable (values), and from possessions to capabilities.[10] This is a challenge from a policy point of view because it takes us away from the easily measureable and assessed. In light of this, it is not surprising that many states have shied away from embracing the well-being challenge. The second shift in the debate is that the separation of means and ends becomes fuzzier. The well-being 'turn' in poverty studies has, itself, been criticized for its individualizing tendencies (Deneulin and McGregor 2009: 4). The terms of discussion are about how individuals can aspire, achieve happiness and dignity, and have control over their lives. Some critics see this emerging from a Western concern with the sanctity of the individual, rather than the health of wider society (Christopher 1999) and future generations.[11] When US President George Bush Senior famously told the Rio Conference on Environment and Development in 1992 that "the American way of life is not negotiable", he was doing far more than just making a statement regarding the interests of the USA versus those of the rest of the world. He was also, implicitly, rendering an idea of development that emphasizes the here-and-now over the future and the interests of individual Americans rather than wider society.

The concern to resituate the poverty debate in a wider frame that stretches beyond objective well-being is fundamentally different from the earlier discussion about the politics and political economy of poverty. The latter is about causality; the concerns summarized here are about definitional questions and issues of framing. That said, the two are related in so far as the object of study (the definitional concern) has a large bearing on where and how we look to ascertain causality.

Judging development

The widening of the human development debate from poverty (income/consumption) to well-being has been important in bringing into sharper focus some of the negative consequences – 'costs' – of modernization processes. These range widely from the dissolution and dislocation of the family and the household explored in Chapter 5, to heightened levels of crime and anti-social behaviour, intergenerational tensions, and drug abuse. Looking across the piece, these concerns regarding the side-effects of modernization can be corralled under the term 'fractured societies'. Referring back to Chambers' (2004) desire to view development as 'good' change, the focus on such concerns permits us to question whether the modernization processes evident across Southeast Asia – and reflected in rapid economic expansion and rising aggregate incomes – can be counted as 'development'. In this way, we see the opening up of an explanatory (in academic and policy terms) and experiential (in terms of people's engagement with change) gap between the performance and achievements of development as economic expansion, and development as good change. The argument here is that while in the earlier stages of development, the gap between development-as-growth and development-as-good-change was quite small, this has progressively widened. The chapters that follow seek to illuminate the content of this widening gap, in its social (Chapter 5), environmental (Chapter 6) and political (Chapter 7) guises.

The way development is presented in the previous paragraph makes a common although problematic distinction. It sees development defined in terms of economic growth having certain outcomes or costs (as well as benefits). However, many of these things usually counted as 'costs' should be conflated *with* development. They do not follow *from* the process; they are part *of* the process. Thus environmental degradation, rather than being seen as a 'price worth paying' in the context of rapid economic growth, should be viewed as an elemental part of the process. This was the core point that Amartya Sen developed in his important book *Development as freedom* (1999; and see Corbridge 2002). It is not a question of whether, for example, social and political freedoms are conducive (or not) to economic growth (with economic growth termed 'development') they are *constitutive components of development*. In his book *How Asia works*, Studwell then takes Sen's view and links it back to issues of well-being: "The miseries visited on ordinary people by a lack of attention to institutional progress deserve attention in their own right. Economic development is the subject of this book, but economic development alone is not a recipe for human happiness" (2013: xxiv).

The market imperative and the neoliberal development project: pinning down some terms

The core reason why, so often, development in terms of policy and practice becomes translated into policy and practice to support economic growth, rather than policy and practice to improve human well-being, is because development is deeply tied to the tenets of the market economy. These are so pervasive and deep-seated that they have become naturalized.

There are a number of linked – and often contested – terms used through this book which come under the broad heading the 'market imperative'. It is worth setting out how these are used and what they mean in terms of the discussion that follows. These terms are:

- the market imperative and market dependence;
- market integration and marketization;
- commoditization;
- capitalism and capitalist relations;
- market reform;
- liberalism and neoliberalism;
- the Washington consensus and post-Washington consensus.

Market integration or, rather unattractively, *marketization* refers to the process by which people and places are integrated into the market, leading to an intensification of market relations. This can occur through the extension of the market into previously un- or under-marketized areas by, for example the building of roads or the activities of traders or other commercial agents; or it may occur through resettlement, whether planned or spontaneous – in effect bringing the people to the market, rather than the market to the people. It is important to emphasize, however, that Southeast Asia was never completely unmarketized and notions that 'the market' intruded into a space of pure subsistence relations is, in most places and cases, fanciful. Historical study has shown that the market was at work surprisingly early in Southeast Asia's history (see Rigg 1994). Furthermore, resettlement was a feature of the pre-colonial as well as the colonial and post-colonial periods. More often than not, therefore, marketization and market integration refer to an intensification of market relations. We might usefully think of this as the *market imperative*, leading to greater *market dependence*.

Part of this process of market integration involves the *commoditization* of labour and resources which were previously un- or under-commodified. Reciprocal labour exchange, for example, is transformed into wage labour, while water and wildlife become items with an exchange value – in effect, marketable products. This process may be linked to the act of enclosure by which ownership is marked out, enabling commodification. The last half-century has, therefore, not only seen an intensifying integration of people and places into the market sphere; it has also seen the extension of market value to new products, resources and activities (see Nevins and Peluso 2008).

While the market has had a long-presence in Southeast Asia, *capitalism* and *capitalist relations* are more recent. Capitalism is the (social) system by which the ownership of the means of production and distribution is held by a capitalist class, underpinned by the profit motive. Markets can exist independently of capitalism, and capitalism does not equate with the 'free' market. There has also been a rich debate about Asian capitalism(s) which has sought to identify the specificities of capitalism in the region, and how capitalism in Asia/Southeast Asia requires a rethinking of models which in large part are built on the Western experience (see Crawford 2000; Tipton 2009). Storz *et al.* (2013) see this effort at defining Asian capitalism falling into four areas: the paths of capitalist change, the institutions of capitalism, institutional change, and innovation in capitalist systems. Sometimes the terms used betray the views of commentators: 'ersatz capitalism', 'crony capitalism' and 'pariah capitalism', for instance, implies capitalism that has been somehow distorted from an ideal type. In a similar but more finely hewn manner, Hall (2004) notes in his paper on market dependence in smallholder commodity production in Southeast Asia that capitalism can take markedly different forms. He also makes a case for the necessity of clarifying what form(s) capitalist relations take in any particular context, rather than using it as a catch-all without adequate specification.

For the transition economies of Southeast Asia (the Lao PDR and Vietnam, and to some extent Cambodia and Myanmar), it is common to see reference made to *reform* – the process by which the economies of the formerly communist/ socialist countries of the region have been 'marketized'. While most scholars find little difficulty writing of reform or using the local term for the process (*doi moi* [renovation] in Vietnam, *chin thanakaan mai* [new thinking] in the Lao PDR), Gainsborough (2010) finds 'reform' problematic in the case of Vietnam and prefers instead to use the word 'marketization' instead (see above). This is for three reasons: the emphasis that reform places on change, rather than on continuity (and there is much that has not changed in countries like Vietnam); the assumption that reform is driven from the top, by elite policy-makers; and the impression of policy coherence that the term implies (a reform 'agenda').

Neoliberal is perhaps the most problematic and contested of the terms outlined here. This is mainly because it is used to refer to so many different things. It is, at the same time, a macro-economic doctrine, a set of policy prescriptions, an economic project, a mode of regulation, and a political and ideological credo (see Bakker 2010: 716; Ferguson 2010). Some scholars, therefore, in using the term are referring to a set of economic practices and policy prescriptions; others, however, use the term to denote a political mode of thinking. As McCarthy and Prudham (2004: 276) say, "defining neoliberalism is no straightforward task, in part because the term 'neoliberalism' stands for a complex assemblage of ideological commitments, discursive representations, and institutional practices, all propagated by highly specific class alliances and organized at multiple geographical scales".

In the context of this book, but only in a pure sense, neoliberalism is seen to accord with David Harvey's definition:

> Neoliberalism is a theory of political economic practices proposing that human well-being can best be advanced by the maximization of entrepreneurial freedoms within an institutional framework characterized by private property rights, individual liberty, unencumbered markets, and free trade. The role of the state is to create and preserve an institutional framework appropriate to such practices.
>
> (2007: 22)

The trouble is that all countries deviate from this 'ideal' prescription, to a greater or lesser extent, and furthermore they do so more in Asia than in probably any other region of the world (Rigg 2012). The experience of Asia has been one not of neoliberal orthodoxy (as Harvey sets out) but of policy heterodoxy (Rodrik 2007) or eclecticism (Wade 2004). There is an awful lot in Asia's development policies and practices which are self-evidently *not* neoliberal. Of these, the most commented on is the significant role played by the state in Asia's modernization, encapsulated in the notion of the *developmental state* (Rigg 2012: 62–69). So the 'rolling back' or 'retreat of the state' argument does not have as much purchase in East and Southeast Asia as it does in some other regions. And there are many other ways, large and small, where policies and pronouncements cannot be equated easily with Harvey's clearly demarcated neoliberal project.

That said, for Harvey, neoliberalism has been 'naturalized' in the sense that it has a taken-for-granted quality; as a doctrine – and notwithstanding its uneven development around the world – 'there is no alternative'.[12] This macro-economic doctrine, reflected in a set of very widely accepted economic tenets, is then also reflected in a certain political rationality. This has been made possible, in the case of Singapore, by what Liow (2012) calls the actions of the 'neoliberal development state'. The Singapore state is in the business of creating neoliberal citizen subjects who embody the neoliberal qualities of self-reliance, personal responsibility and individual entrepreneurship.

Finally, neoliberal policies are often encapsulated in another key term with wide exposure, namely the *Washington consensus*.[13] The policies that constitute the Washington consensus are, in Williamson's original formulation, fiscal 'discipline', growth-motivated public expenditure, tax reform, interest and exchange rate liberalization, trade liberalization, the encouragement of foreign direct investment, privatization, deregulation and individual property rights (Vestergaard 2004; Williamson 1990, 2000). Following the Asian financial crisis, the Washington consensus was recast into the slightly less austere *post-Washington consensus*, but for its critics this was still informed by the neoliberal doctrine.

The structure of the book

Following this introductory chapter, the core of the book falls into two halves of three chapters each. The three chapters in the first half examine the case for 'inclusive/exclusive development' in Southeast Asia.

Chapter 2 reviews the region's record in terms of the distribution of growth – in other words, patterns of inequality, measured in economic terms. It explores *why* inequality is important and also seeks to understand what policies and other factors underpin the different levels of inequality that we see across the region. As the chapter argues, there is no immutable association between growth and inequality. The discussion is quite dense and data rich, but this is necessary to set down the economic markers that provide the context for the later chapters, which explore the human dimensions of development drawing on ethnographic evidence.

The following two chapters move beyond the economic data to pay attention to the social groups that lie behind these figures. Chapter 3 focuses on the 'produced poor': those groups and individuals, whether poor in absolute or in relative terms, who have found their living conditions squeezed by casualization, undermined by dispossession, or otherwise compromised by the processes and policies of market-led growth. This is followed by a consideration, in Chapter 4, of the 'unreported' and 'uncounted' poor. This focuses on transnational migrants who are so important to some Southeast Asian countries' development projects and yet do not figure in their poverty data and socio-economic surveys, and are not worthy of equal consideration in so many other regards. Taken together, these three chapters seek to look beneath the headline data on economic growth to ask questions about the distribution of that growth, the links between growth and development, and the hidden geographies of poverty and economic expansion.

The second half of the book takes, respectively, a social, environmental and political cut through the region's recent development record. Chapter 5 examines how the market imperative has reworked the family and household with a particular focus on how the emergence of multi-sited households has created a care puzzle or conundrum. The requirement and desire to engage with the market economy to generate income and raise material well-being has required that household members migrate to work in other places; but in migrating to such work in order to secure material progress the household is at risk of failing in its caring role. Chapter 6 examines the case for the region's 'sustainable' development, in environmental terms, utilizing the theme of environmental violence to link the case studies presented, from sand mining in Cambodia to enclosing the commons in the uplands of mainland Southeast Asia. The essence of this chapter is to highlight the illogics of liberal environmentalism. The final core chapter, Chapter 7, is on the politics of development – with a small 'p' – in the Southeast Asian region. The discussion here links the everyday with the structural politics of development, revealing how the Right to Development has been curtailed by the policies and processes – and the very success – of market-led growth.

The concluding chapter of the book returns to some of the themes paraded in this introduction. For instance, the key question of what constitutes development, and how we should track and record it; the structural factors that have been intrinsic to the growth process in the region; the trap, which it is so easy to fall into, of equating development with economic growth; and the question of how – and whether – it is possible to construct a 'better' capitalism.

A chasing of the wind?

At the beginning of 2014 the World Bank released a document entitled *Prosperity for all: ending extreme poverty*. This document restated the position of the Board of Governors of the World Bank Group (WBG) that the "WBG would focus on ensuring that the benefits of prosperity are shared by shifting from a focus on average economic growth to promoting income growth amongst the bottom 40 percent of people" (World Bank 2014). That the World Bank felt the need to make such a statement in 2014 in itself is remarkable. It shows the degree to which – notwithstanding all the many thousands of critical reports, papers and books – the development agenda remains coincident with the growth agenda. Furthermore, and as this book will argue, there is a growing mismatch between the growth and development agendas, and their respective outcomes.

At the end of October 2014, as this book was being finalized for submission, it was said that Chinese ministers had few worries about economic growth of 7.3 per cent in the third quarter of 2014. This was slightly below the target of 7.5 per cent growth for the year but, Vice-Premier Zhang Gaoli said, "within our forecast range". That so much appeared to be riding on one figure, and how close it might have come to an earlier projection, is instructive. The figure tells us nothing about the distribution of that growth, between social groups, economic sectors or geographical spaces. It also tells us nothing about how the growth was generated. Was it, for example, based on non-sustainable resource exploitation; on the dispossession of land; and on the expansion of casual factory work? It is these sorts of questions that need to be asked if we wish to understand why Southeast Asia's 'miracle' growth is not, often, being translated into development.

Further reading

For work on new geographies of poverty, the studies of Andy Sumner (2010, 2012) have probably done most to encourage a delinking of the poverty from the underdevelopment debates and to recognize the growing concentration of the poor in middle-income countries. It is worth while reading his work against the architect of the 'bottom billion', Paul Collier (2007).

Amartya Sen has done most to resituate many of those factors that have traditionally been seen as means of achieving (or impeding) development as desirable ends – or as constitutive of development, as he puts it. His book *Development as freedom* (1999) is key, but also see his short paper (2012) in the *New York Review of Books* where he compares the development outcomes of economic expansion in India and China.

The debate over the structural violence of neoliberal development is returned to in later chapters, but issue 46(7) of *The Journal of Development Studies* (2010) focuses on the 'government of chronic poverty'. In particular, look at David Mosse's (2010) agenda setting piece in this issue of *JDS*.

Notes

1 "Where do the poor live?" is the title of Sumner's 2012 paper in *World Development*.
2 In 1990, 93 per cent of the world's poor lived in low income countries; by 2007–8, 72 per cent were living in middle-income countries (Sumner 2010).
3 From an international-aid perspective it also raises the question of whether aid should be channelled to poor countries, or to poor people. If the latter, then more attention needs to be directed at middle-income countries such as Indonesia where the majority of the poor are now to be found. This was one of the key arguments used to try (unsuccessfully) and prevent the British government from ending its aid programme to India, announced in November 2012. The UK Development Secretary Justine Greening explained: "Having visited India I have seen first-hand the tremendous progress being made. India is successfully developing and our own bilateral relationship has to keep up with 21st Century India. It's time to recognise India's changing place in the world" (http://www.dfid.gov.uk/Documents/publications1/press-releases/Greening-announces-new-development-relationship-with-India.pdf). India may be an emerging power but in 2010 one-third of the population were living on less than $1.25 a day, and two-thirds on less than $2 a day (http://data.worldbank.org/indicator).
4 Rather than one-to-one growth, at best Edward sees it as 'one-to-two' growth so that every 2 per cent expansion in the economy leads to a 1 per cent growth in the consumption of the poor (2006: 1682). In 2013, Dollar and Kraay (with Kleineberg) released an update to their 2002 paper, coming to much the same conclusion and entitled 'Growth still is good for the poor' (Dollar *et al.* 2013).
5 In the same vein as Adam Smith in the eighteenth century and Marshall Sahlins more recently, Green and Hulme write: "Poverty is not a natural fact, but a social experience. The category of the poor is similarly socially constructed" (2005: 869).
6 Some scholars would not see such people as necessarily poor (see Note 5); in this line of thinking, the poor are created through their connection and articulation with the market, but on adverse and deleterious terms.
7 "We can think of human flourishing in terms of living well, an activity and achievement that is likely to have both subjective as well as objective dimensions" (Kleinig and Evans 2013: 556).
8 Jones and Klenow (2010) calculate welfare based on consumption, leisure, inequality and mortality.
9 For Appadurai (2004: 59), the capacity to aspire is cultural capacity that connects culture and the future-oriented logic of development.
10 Sen's capabilities approach was famously framed in the UNDP's first (1990) *Human Development Report* in the guise of 'choices'. This, as Deneulin and McGregor point out (2009: 10), shifts Sen's work rather too close to the neoliberal position that people should have the means and powers to achieve their desires. For Sen, capabilities are about the freedom to pursue the functionings that they value.
11 Christopher (1999: 142) argues that "Western concepts of psychological well-being may be deeply shaped by our [Western] culture's individualistic moral visions".
12 "The uneven geographical development of neoliberalism, and its partial and lopsided application from one country to another, testifies to its tentative character and the complex ways in which political forces, historical traditions, and existing institutional arrangements all shaped why and how the process [of neoliberalization] actually occurred on the ground" (Harvey 2007: 27).
13 The term 'Washington consensus' was coined by John Williamson in 1990. The term encapsulates the policy framework that came to be seen by mainstream, orthodox (or neoliberal) economists and institutions as lying at the heart of an economic framework that would promote economic growth. It was a *Washington* consensus because the three key institutions promoting this economic orthodoxy were based in Washington: the World Bank, the International Monetary Fund and the US Treasury.

References

Ali, I. and J. Zhuang (2007). Inclusive growth toward a prosperous Asia: policy implications. ERD Working Paper No. 97. Manila, Asian Development Bank.

Appadurai, A. (2004). The capacity to aspire: culture and the terms of recognition. *Culture and public action.* V. Rao and M. Walton. Stanford, MA, Stanford University Press: 59–84.

Bakker, K. (2010). "The limits of 'neoliberal natures': debating green neoliberalism." *Progress in Human Geography* 34(6): 715–735.

Bell, P. F. (1992). Gender and economic development in Thailand. *Gender and development in Southeast Asia.* P. v. Esterik and J. v. Esterik. Toronto, Canadian Council for Southeast Asian Studies: 61–81.

Bhaskaran, M., H. S. Chee, D. Low, T. K. Song, S. Vadaketh and Y. L. Keong (2012). Inequality and the need for a new social compact. *Singapore Perspectives 2012: Singapore inclusive – bridging divides.* Singapore, Institute of Policy Studies, Lee Kuan Yew School of Public Policy: 1–41.

Bunnell, T. and D. P. S. Goh (2012). "Urban aspirations and Asian cosmopolitanisms." *Geoforum* 43(1): 1–3.

Bunnell, T. and A. Harris (2012). "Re-viewing informality: perspectives from urban Asia." *International Development Planning Review* 34(4): 339–347.

CGD (2008). *The growth report: strategies for sustained growth and inclusive development.* Washington DC, World Bank.

Chambers, R. (2004). Ideas for development: reflecting forwards. IDS Working Paper 238. Brighton, UK, Institute of Development Studies.

Christopher, J. C. (1999). "Situating psychological well-being: exploring the cultural roots of its theory and research." *Journal of Counseling & Development* 77(2): 141–152.

Collier, P. (2007). *The bottom billion: why the poorest countries are failing and what can be done about it.* Oxford, Oxford University Press.

Corbridge, S. (2002). "Development as freedom: the spaces of Amartya Sen." *Progress in Development Studies* 2(3): 183–217.

Crawford, D. (2000). "Chinese capitalism: cultures, the Southeast Asian region and economic globalisation." *Third World Quarterly* 21(1): 69–86.

Deneulin, S. and J. A. McGregor (2009). The capability approach and the politics of a social conception of wellbeing. WeD working paper 09/43. Bath, UK, Wellbeing in Developing Countries, University of Bath.

Dollar, D. and A. Kraay (2002). "Growth is good for the poor." *Journal of Economic Growth* 7(3): 195–225.

Dollar, D., T. Kleineberg and A. Kraay (2013). Growth still is good for the poor. Policy Research Working Paper no. 6568. Washington DC, World Bank.

Edward, P. (2006). "Examining inequality: who really benefits from global growth?" *World Development* 34(10): 1667–1695.

Evans, A. (2010). *Aid effectiveness post-2010 – a think piece on ways forward.* London, Overseas Development Institute.

Farmer, P. (2004). "An anthropology of structural violence." *Current Anthropology* 45(3): 305–325.

Ferguson, J. (2010). "The uses of neoliberalism." *Antipode* 41(S1): 166–184.

Gainsborough, M. (2010). *Vietnam: rethinking the state.* London, Zed Books.

Glassman, J. (2004). *Thailand at the margins: internationalization of the state and the transformation of labour.* Oxford, Oxford University Press.

Gough, I., J. A. McGregor and L. Camfield (2006). Wellbeing in developing countries: conceptual foundations of the WeD programme. WeD Working Paper 19. Bath, University of Bath.

Green, M. (2006). "Representing poverty and attacking representations: perspectives on poverty from social anthropology." *The Journal of Development Studies* 42(7): 1108–1129.

Green, M. and D. Hulme (2005). "From correlates and characteristics to causes: thinking about poverty from a chronic poverty perspective." *World Development* 33(6): 867–879.

Hall, D. (2004). "Smallholders and the spread of capitalism in rural Southeast Asia." *Asia Pacific Viewpoint* 45: 401–414.

Harvey, D. (2007). "Neoliberalism as creative destruction." *Annals of the American Academy of Political and Social Science* 610: 22–44.

Hassan, N. (2013). Developing an analytical framework on social cohesion in Singapore: reflections from the framing of social cohesion debates in the OECD and Europe. Working Paper No. 17. Singapore, EU Centre in Singapore.

Hickey, S. (2009). "The politics of protecting the poorest: moving beyond the 'anti-politics machine'?" *Political Geography* 28(8): 473–483.

Hickey, S. A. M. (2010). "The government of chronic poverty: from exclusion to citizenship?" *Journal of Development Studies* 46(7): 1139–1155.

Jones, C. I. and P. J. Klenow (2010). Beyond GDP? Welfare across countries and time. NBER Working Paper 16352. Cambridge, MA, National Bureau of Economic Research.

Kleinig, J. and N. Evans (2013). "Human flourishing, human dignity, and human rights." *Law and Philosophy* 32(5): 539–564.

Krishna, A. (2010). *One illness away: why people become poor and how they escape poverty*. Oxford, Oxford University Press.

Krishna, A. (2011). Characteristics and patterns of intergenerational poverty traps and escapes in rural north India. Working paper no 189. Manchester, UK, Chronic Poverty Research Centre, IDPM, University of Manchester.

Krishna, A. and A. Shariff (2011). "The irrelevance of national strategies? Rural poverty dynamics in states and regions of India, 1993–2005." *World Development* 39(4): 533–549.

Kubiszewski, I., R. Costanza, C. Franco, P. Lawn, J. Talberth, T. Jackson and C. Aylmer (2013). "Beyond GDP: measuring and achieving global genuine progress." *Ecological Economics* 93: 57–68.

Kuhonta, E. M. (2011). *The institutional imperative: the politics of equitable development in Southeast Asia*. Stanford, CA, Stanford University Press.

Li, T. M. (2007). *The will to improve: governmentality, development, and the practice of politics*. Durham, NC and London, Duke University Press.

Liow, E. D. (2012). "The neoliberal-developmental state: Singapore as case study." *Critical Sociology* 38(2): 241–264.

McCarthy, J. and S. Prudham (2004). "Neoliberal nature and the nature of neoliberalism." *Geoforum* 35(3): 275–283.

Mosse, D. (2010). "A relational approach to durable poverty, inequality and power." *Journal of Development Studies* 46(7): 1156–1178.

Nevins, J. and N. L. Peluso (2008). Introduction: commoditization in Southeast Asia. *Taking Southeast Asia to market: commodities, nature, and people in the Neoliberal age.* J. Nevins and N. L. Peluso. Ithaca, NY and London, Cornell University Press: 1–24.

Nissanke, M. and E. Thorbecke (2006). "Channels and policy debate in the globalization-inequality–poverty nexus." *World Development* 34(8): 1338–1360.

Parnwell, M. J. G. and D. A. Arghiros (1996). Uneven development in Thailand. *Uneven development in Thailand.* M. J. G. Parnwell. Aldershot, Avebury: 1–27.

Rigg, J. (1994). "Redefining the village and rural life: lessons from South East Asia." *The Geographical Journal* 160(2): 123–135.

Rigg, J. (2012). *Unplanned development: tracking change in South East Asia.* London, Zed Books.

Rodrik, D. (2007). *One economics, many recipes: globalization, institutions, and economic growth.* Princeton, NJ and Oxford, Princeton University Press.

Sen, A. (1981). *Poverty and famines: an essay on entitlement and deprivation.* Oxford, Clarendon Press.

Sen, A. (1999). *Development as freedom.* New York, Alfred A. Knopf.

Sen, A. (2012). "Quality of life: India vs. China." *The New York Review of Books* 12 May.

Storz, C., B. Amable, S. Casper and S. Lechevalier (2013). "Bringing Asia into the comparative capitalism perspective." *Socio-Economic Review* 11(2): 217–232.

Studwell, J. (2013). *How Asia works: success and failure in the world's most dynamic region.* London, Profile Books.

Sumner, A. (2010). Global poverty and the new bottom billion: what if three-quarters of the world's poor live in middle-income countries? Working Paper no. 349. Brighton, UK, Institute of Development Studies.

Sumner, A. (2012). "Where do the poor live?" *World Development* 40(5): 865–877.

Thai Commerce of Commerce (2010). *Sufficiency economy: 100 interviews with business professionals.* Bangkok, Amarin Publishing.

Tipton, F. B. (2009). "Southeast Asian capitalism: history, institutions, states, and firms." *Asia Pacific Journal of Management* 26(3): 401–434.

UNDP (1990). *Human development report 1990.* New York, Oxford University Press.

van Donge, J. K., D. Henley and P. Lewis (2012). "Tracking development in South-East Asia and sub-Saharan Africa: the primacy of policy." *Development Policy Review* 30: s5–s24.

Vestergaard, J. (2004). "The Asian crisis and the shaping of 'proper' economies." *Cambridge Journal of Economics* 28(6): 809–827.

Wade, R. (2004). *Governing the market: economic theory and the role of government in East Asian industrialization.* Princeton, NJ and Oxford, Princeton University Press.

Wan, G. and I. Sebastian (2011). *Poverty in Asia and the Pacific: an update.* Manila, Asian Development Bank.

Williamson, J. (1990). What Washington means by policy reform. *Latin American adjustment: how much has happened?* J. Williamson. Washington, DC, Institute for International Economics.

Williamson, J. (2000). "What should the World Bank think about the Washington Consensus?" *The World Bank Research Observer* 15(2): 251–264.

World Bank (1993). *The East Asian miracle: economic growth and public policy.* Oxford, Oxford University Press.

World Bank (2001). *World development report 2000/2001: attacking poverty.* Oxford, Oxford University Press for the World Bank.

World Bank (2014). *Prosperity for all: ending extreme poverty.* World Bank Group, Spring Meetings. Washington DC, World Bank.

Yeoh, B. S. A. (2006). "Bifurcated labour: the unequal incorporation of transmigrants in Singapore." *Tijdschrift voor economische en sociale geografie* 97(1): 26–37.

2   Generating growth, sustaining growth, delivering inequality

> The central point to appreciate here is that while economic growth is important for enhancing living conditions, its reach and impact depend greatly on what we do with the increased income.
>
> (Amartya Sen in *New York Review of Books*, 12 May 2012, p. 1)

Introduction: the growth of inequality and interest in inequality

From an emphasis on growth in the 1980s, to pro-poor growth in the 1990s and 2000s and, most recently, to 'inclusive' or 'shared' growth (or 'shared prosperity'), there has been a continuing shift in focus towards the quality of growth and, in particular, to its distribution within and between population groups whether they are defined in terms of class, gender, generation, ethnicity, occupation or geographical location. While poverty has declined across developing Asia (see Figure 2.6), this would have been even steeper had growth been more equally distributed. Furthermore, and notwithstanding the rhetoric of pro-poor and inclusive growth, the evidence is that the net poverty impact of growth has actually *worsened* in recent years. Four-fifths of developing Asia's population live in countries where inequality deepened in the final decade of the twentieth century and the first decade of the twenty-first century (ADB 2012: xi). It seems that in some countries the 'growth with equity' narrative of the 1980s has been turned on its head.

This must be counted as significant if we are interested in human development; it is also important politically because deep-seated and enduring inequality is politically problematic. It also, however, raises something of a puzzle: why, with our better data for identifying policies for intervening and tools for targeting, do we see the holy grail of pro-poor growth becoming, in many instances, seemingly ever more distant? Is there something about the shift from low-income to middle-income status that makes pro-poor growth harder to achieve? Or is it something about the policies and processes of late capitalism? Are there, at the same time, success stories among the countries of Southeast Asia and what distinguishes them from those that have failed to achieve pro-poor growth? Given Simon Kuznets' hypothesis that the relationship between growth and inequality would take the shape of an inverted U, it was expected that, as developing economies matured, inequalities would narrow – that, in time, the benefits of growth would, in that famous phrase, 'trickle down' under the inescapable forces of economic gravity, to the poor. Dollar and Kraay's highly cited and contentious paper "Growth is good for the poor" (2002; and see Lübker *et al.* 2002 and Amann *et al.* 2006 for two critiques) essentially makes the argument – reflected in the title – that governments should focus on achieving growth because poverty reduction will surely follow: "we simply emphasize that growth on average does benefit the poor as much as anyone else in society, and so standard growth-enhancing policies should be at the center of any effective poverty reduction strategy" (Dollar and Kraay 2002: 219).[1] There are many scholars and policy-makers who continue to adhere to this view (e.g. Warr 2005).

This chapter will not provide a detailed account of patterns, geographical and temporal, of the progress of inequality across the countries of Southeast Asia. There are a number of recent and readily accessible reports which do just that;[2] rather, the emphasis here is on the 'why' and 'what' of inequality. In particular, the chapter focuses on the following two questions: what is it about market-led development in an era of globalization that sustains, deepens and/or creates inequality? And: why should we care?

Clearly, and as a starting point, a measure – a degree – of inequality is inevitable, in all societies; it may even be desirable. That said, stark differences in the depth and pattern of inequality between countries indicate that the nature of inequality is shaped in market economies by much more than just the operation of the market. Writing of inequality in the USA, Joseph Stiglitz observes that "American inequality didn't just happen. It was created. Market forces played a role, but it was not market forces alone. … our growing inequality is a distinctly American 'achievement'" (2012: 28).

This point can be made for all countries, whether with regard to those that have 'achieved' deeply unequal growth, like the USA, or those that have accomplished a measure of pro-poor or inclusive economic expansion. As the chapter will set out, the countries of Southeast Asia have markedly different inequality signatures and while geographical and historical context surely matter, policies and institutions can – and do – also play a defining role. So, following on from the central aim of the chapter to explore the links between market relations and inequality is the important question of how states can promote pro-poor or inclusive development through policy interventions and through the operation of the institutions of government. Markets, the functioning of markets and – with respect to the discussion here – the inequality signatures that emerge are shaped by policies and these, in turn, by politics. The injustices of economic development need to be seen not as 'natural' market outcomes but arising from the institutions, policies and programmes that have been put in place. While Gupta (2012; and see page 104 this volume) may regard the premature death of 140 million Indians as structural violence, here such outcomes are viewed as structural injustice.

Developing a conceptual framework for inequality

The starting point for this chapter is, rather perversely, the distributional end-point of growth, namely distributional inequality. This, though, can be tracked back, as well as forwards. The backward-looking questions are: how does distributional inequality come to be manifested, and how has this been produced and reproduced over time? The forward-looking questions are: what are the implications of inequality, and why should we be concerned?

Distributional inequality is an outcome – or manifestation – of structural and procedural inequalities. Structural inequalities include, for example, class, gender, generational, spatial and ethnic cleavages. Procedural inequalities go some way to sustaining and deepening inequality and can be seen in the uneven coverage of legal provisions, embedded discrimination, participatory exclusions, and networks that deliver advantages to certain societal groups. (Both of these facets of inequality will be explored in Chapter 3.) These manifestations of inequality can, in turn, be linked back to what are termed in Table 2.1 'root contexts', which are here divided into three: geo-historical settings, market processes and the policy milieu. Taken together these encapsulate much of what shapes contemporary geographies of inequality. One point that arises from this is that we need to pluralize inequality, just as poverty has been pluralized (see Sen 1981). Looking to the fourth column in Table 2.1, 'implications', this highlights why addressing inequality is so important. High levels of inequality lead to economic inefficiency and socio-economic injustices. This lies at the core of Amartya Sen's *Development as freedom* (1999: xii) in which he argues that "development consists of the removal of various types of unfreedoms that leave people with little choice and little opportunity of exercising their reasoned agency", adding that the "removal of substantial unfreedoms ... is *constitutive* of development" [emphasis in original].

Table 2.1 Beyond inequality: building a conceptual framework

Root contexts	Manifestations	Outcome	Implications
Geo-historical settings	*Structural (in) equalities*		*Economic (in) efficiency*
E.g. colonialism, histories of migration and settlement, and marginal regions and environments	E.g. class, gender, generation, occupational, spatial and ethnic divides)	DISTRIBUTIONAL (IN)EQUALITY	E.g. reduced investment in human capital formation, proneness to economic crisis, cronyism)
Market processes			
E.g. market integration, FDI, globalisation, commoditisation and integration)	*Procedural (in) equalities*		*Socio-economic (in)justice*
Policy milieu	E.g. unequal legal provisions and protections, networks of privilege, participatory exclusions and elite capture, and discriminatory cultural norms)		E.g. high(er) levels of poverty, violence, crime and mental illness, and greater political tensions)
E.g. social protection, universal health care, policies of urban/rural bias and progressive tax regimes)			

Why inequality matters

> The debate [over globalization and inequality] tends to be conducted by each side as if its case was overwhelming, and only an intellectually deficient or dishonest person could see merit in [the] other's case.
>
> (Wade 2004: 568)

Why does inequality matter? This may seem obvious given the degree to which pro-poor growth has become accepted as a 'good thing' in many quarters. However, the broad acceptance of the positive attributes of growth with equity means that it is all too easy to lose sight of the reasons why such a view has come to be accepted in the first place.

It used to be held that greater inequality was the 'price' for high economic growth: a degree of inequality was not only inevitable, it was suggested, but also necessary for the effective functioning of markets (Berg and Ostry 2011). For many neoclassical economists in the 1980s and 1990s, it was therefore accepted (and acceptable) that high economic growth with greater inequality was better for the poor than the opposite, namely low economic growth and greater equality. The difficulty with this position is that the empirical evidence does not offer any clear link between growth rates on the one hand and trends in inequality on the other (Ravallion 2013: 8). It is hard not to come to the conclusion that doctrinal predilections during the high point of the Washington consensus led many to this view.

The relationship between growth and inequality is more complex than hitherto thought (see below) and the justification for enduring high inequality on the basis that this delivers growth is therefore problematic. This has gradually become more widely accepted and, as a result, many scholars, most development institutions and, increasingly, many governments have come to regard deepening inequality as a threat both to the sustainability of growth and to national stability (ADB 2012: vi). There comes a point where inequality becomes destructive of growth, not to mention corrosive in social and political terms.

The issue of sustainability urges attention be paid to the economic costs or burden of unequal growth; stability, however, raises concerns that are more political and social in nature. As the Asian Development Bank's President Haruhiko Kuroda put it in a forward to the 2012 report *Confronting rising inequality in Asia*, the "social and political consequences of an Asia left to divide itself by wealth can no longer be ignored" (ADB 2012: vi). While it may useful to see the relationship having, in this way, discrete economic and socio-political dimensions, as set out in Table 2.2, these are often linked: political elites, for example, are able to protect their economic interests through promoting policies that entrench or encourage inequality.

While it may be that the balance of opinion has shifted to regard inequality as problematic, the nature of the relationship between growth and inequality remains disputed. Shin (2012; and see Kefi and Zouhaier 2012; Li and Zou 1998) posits in his review of the economic literature that this relationship – between income inequality and economic growth – can be both positive and negative, and each can be plausibly argued theoretically and demonstrated empirically. He concludes

Table 2.2 Reasons to care: the logics of equal growth

Economic

Unequal societies are less efficient. The economies of unequal societies do not function efficiently because policies become shaped by power geometries rather than on the basis of efficiency. Elites may use their economic power to protect their interests in the guise of rent-seeking or various corrupt practices, while the poor and dispossessed may use their political influence (based on numerical weight) to push for populist policies, which may be equally damaging to long-run growth

Unequal societies are more prone to economic instability and crisis. Heightened levels of rent-seeking and corruption, characteristic of unequal societies, raise the risk of economic instability and crisis

Unequal societies do not realise the economic potential of their populations. Inequality means that the human resources of a country are not fully utilised and realised – for example, if women are not educated or if the poor are unable to invest in developing their human capital

---

Social

Unequal economies produce and perpetuate unequal societies. Inequality of income tends to be reproduced in other dimensions of inequality, such as health and education such that levels of human development and broader measure of well-being are compromised

Unequal societies have higher levels of poverty. At a given level of income, unequal societies will have a greater number of poor than those societies that are more equal. Unequal growth dampens the impact of economic expansion on poverty reduction

Unequal societies are more violent. Generally, the incidence of crime and violence is greater in unequal societies

---

Political

Unequal societies are less democratic. The concentration of wealth and therefore power means that such societies are less democratic, in a broad sense

Unequal societies are politically unstable. With a large section of the population who feel they are not getting their 'fair' share of the cake, there is a heightened risk of political instability. In particular, an expanding middle class – more likely when growth is equally distributed – tends to lead to greater stability

---

Sources: distilled from Stiglitz (2012); ADB (2012); Fajnzylber *et al.* (2002).

that there is reason to suggest that the nature of the relationship is tied to level of development: in the early stages of economic development, inequality has a negative effect on growth (i.e. greater inequality, less growth), but in the later stages of development inequality has a positive effect (greater inequality, higher growth). This temptingly simple transition relationship, though, is disputed on the grounds that it is necessary to distinguish between the ignition of growth on the one hand, and its sustainability on the other. Berg and Ostry (2011) argue that high inequality has a negative effect on the long-run growth prospects of a country and that this applies in rich(er) as well as poor(er) countries. It is one thing to start the growth process; it is quite another to sustain it.

The reason for thinking that deep-seated and long-lasting inequality will, in the longer run, impact negatively on sustainability rests on the belief that unequal societies are less efficient, more prone to crisis and instability, and do not fully meet their potential (Table 2.2 and Figure 2.1). Inequality leads to reduced private investment in human capital formation thus inhibiting the full realization of a country's potential: the poor and the near-poor lack the means to further their education or stay healthy and this, in the end, will impact on economic growth (Berg and Ostry 2011). Debates over the 'middle-income trap' – which has particular resonance in Asia – partly emerge from this interest in how countries make the transition from middle income to high income (see Box 2.2). While the poor may, in this way, be trapped in low-return work, at the other end of the wealth spectrum, the rich are able to protect their interests through promoting policies that distort the efficient operation of the economy. In more extreme cases, this can take the form of rent-seeking or corruption, which raise the risk of economic instability and crisis.

In their influential paper "Distributive politics and economic growth", Alesina and Rodrik state that their "main conclusion is that inequality is conducive to the adoption of growth-retarding policies" (1994: 465). This is, essentially, because unequal societies have to put in place redistributive populist policies that are growth impeding. The political economy of inequality can work either, or both, ways: if political power is more equally distributed than economic power, then the poor(er) may agitate for redistribution through populist policies which will be growth-retarding; and, in their turn, economic elites may seek to use their wealth and influence to buy votes and shape policies to their benefit but against the national interest. Income inequality, then, is not just a proxy for other factors in explaining the achievement of sustainable growth; it is a robust indicator, in itself, of growth duration (Berg and Ostry 2011: 13)

It is worth reiterating, however, that the relationship between growth and inequality is complex and even when a relationship is demonstrated empirically one way or the other this should not be interpreted as implying causality (ADB

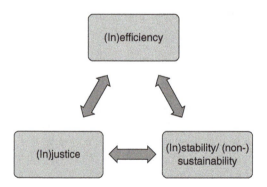

Figure 2.1 The inequality triangle

2012). The debate has far from run its course and data and methodological limitations remain severe.[3] So, for example, Warr (2005) in his discussion of pro-poor growth in Asia argues that there has been excessive attention paid to inequality in the pro-poor growth debate, and insufficient attention paid to growth:

> The resulting literature distracts attention from the central objective of reducing poverty because it has little to say about which forms of economic growth and which policy regimes are best at reducing poverty. … *Growth that is most effective at reducing poverty does not necessarily coincide with growth that reduces inequality.*
>
> (2005: 16 [emphasis added])

In this way, Warr rehearses the neoliberal view that we should start by paying attention to growth, and not to equality/inequality.

The debate over the links between economic growth and inequality remains very much alive; there is less contention, however, when it comes to the social and political costs of excessive levels of inequality. This forms the third corner of the triangle of factors depicted in Figure 2.1, namely: (in)justice.

If we are serious about poverty reduction, then we should be concerned about pro-poor growth for the simple reason that growth distributed equally will reduce poverty faster than growth distributed unequally. While there has been some dispute over whether global inequality fell during the 1990s (Ravallion 2013) or rose (Wade 2004), it does seem to have risen during the 2000s and the "future evolution of overall inequality will be crucial to the trajectories of overall poverty measures" (Ravallion 2013: 7). The poverty-reducing effects of growth in different contexts of equality/inequality are striking. In the most unequal countries, a 1 per cent increase in incomes reduced poverty by just 0.6 per cent; in the most equal countries it generated a 4.3 per cent reduction in poverty (Economist 2013: 12; and see Ali 2008: 16). As Figure 2.2 shows with regard to Indonesia and the Lao PDR, poverty reduction in those two countries would have been markedly better had inequality not deepened between the 1990s and 2000s. In the case of Indonesia, rather than 16 per cent of the population living below the poverty line, the figure would have been just 6 per cent.[4] These are big differentials and, in Indonesia's case, amount to 20 million people remaining in poverty.

The case for pursuing growth with equity (or equity with growth) extends beyond its greater poverty-reducing effects. There is growing evidence, admittedly mostly from the rich world where supporting statistics are broader and more robust, that societies where income is unequally distributed tend to be less healthy whether measured in terms of life expectancy, obesity or infant mortality; more violent as reflected in higher levels of homicide, crime and imprisonment; display greater social problems such as mental illness, teenage births and drug abuse; and have poorer educational outcomes (Wilkinson and Pickett 2009).[5] Indeed, it is remarkable the degree to which problems with a social gradient are more pronounced – by a factor of between two and ten – in more unequal societies (Wilkinson and Pickett 2013: 176–177). This even applies to the richest 5–10 per cent who similarly show worse outcomes than do their equivalent in more equal societies.

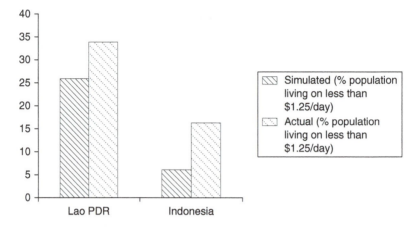

Figure 2.2 Actual and simulated poverty rates in Indonesia and the Lao PDR, 1990–2008 (%, $1.25 per day)

Note 1: simulated poverty is the incidence of poverty at $1.25 per capita per day had levels of inequality in the final year remained the same as they were for the initial year in the 1990s. In both countries, levels of inequality increased.
Note 2: data extracted from World Bank's PovcalNET in March 2012.

Source: ADB 2012: 41.

So, for a compelling set of reasons – economic (growth-related), social and political – since the late 1990s there has been a significant shift towards (re-) emphasizing growth with equity, what has become known as pro-poor growth.

Pro-poor and inclusive (or shared) development

The commonsensical view of pro-poor growth is that it is growth that benefits the poor (i.e. reduces poverty). Where differences emerge are between those who argue for an *absolute* approach to pro-poor growth and those who take a *relative* view. The former argue that any growth that benefits the poor is pro-poor. This essentially focuses the debate on poverty reduction and is sometimes also said to be 'weak' on the grounds that any reduction in poverty, however small, is pro-poor (Kakwani *et al.* 2003: 420). The latter, relativist approach contends that for growth to be pro-poor it must not just benefit the poor, but benefit the poor *more than* it benefits the non-poor. This is sometimes said to be a 'strong' interpretation of pro-poor growth.

- *A weak, absolute approach:* "growth is pro-poor if the poverty measure of interest falls" (Kraay 2006: 199; see also Ravallion 2005; Warr 2005).
- *A strong, relative approach:* "economic growth may be called pro-poor if the poor enjoy the benefits of growth proportionally more than the non-poor" (Son and Kakwani 2008: 1049; see also Krongkaew and Kakwani 2003).

There are potential difficulties with both of these approaches to pro-poor growth. It is conceivable, with regard to the first definition, for example, that a pattern of growth which delivers a 5 per cent increase in income to the non-poor and 0.1 per cent to the poor would still be regarded as 'pro-poor'; as regards the latter definition, it is plausible here that a contraction in the economy that benefitted the poor over the non-poor would be pro-poor, even when the poor are absolutely improverished.[6]

Of course, underpinning both approaches to the definition of pro-poor growth is the long-standing issue of how we define 'the poor' – using what measure(s) and on the basis of what poverty 'line'. There are weighty methodological challenges both with regard to identifying and measuring the poor[7] as well as a set of more fundamental questions as to the way in which the development industry and social relations create the poor in the first place.

There have been attempts to address the shortcomings of the weak/absolute and strong/relativist interpretations of pro-poor growth by combining elements of each. Ravallion (2005: 6), for example, calculates the rate of pro-poor growth as the "ordinary rate of economic growth times a 'distributional correction'", with this correction based on the ratio of the actual change in poverty to the change that would have been observed under conditions of distribution neutrality such that the growth incidence curve is flat. Partly to move the debate on from this rather unproductive conversation between economists (and especially between Kraay and Ravallion on the one hand, and Kakwani and Son on the other), some scholars and practitioners prefer to write about 'inclusive' or 'shared' growth, rather than pro-poor growth. As both terms imply, these foreground the distributional aspects of growth, but are subtly different from the pro-poor growth discussion.

Shared growth refers to the combination of a growth agenda with wealth sharing instruments such as broad-based public education and universal health care that provide the opportunity for all members of society to share in and benefit from growth (Page 2006: 525–6). This is, therefore, about democratizing opportunity such that even the poor have the wherewithal – not least, the human capital – to participate in the modern economy. It is prospective to the degree that attention is paid not only to poverty and well-being today, but to the future ability of marginalized groups to engage fully with the development process.[8] *Inclusive growth*, similarly, directs our attention to both the pace and the pattern of growth. Once again, growth (pace) is of central importance but this is allied to a concern for the way in which that growth is imprinted across sectors, geographical spaces, and population groups. As with shared growth, the emphasis is on ensuring that growth benefits the poor(er), many of whom are to be found in certain sectors (agriculture) and regions (rural, marginal and lagging areas) (Ali and Son 2007; Kanbur and Rauniyar 2010).

The important thread that runs through both of these approaches is the assumption that, left to market forces alone, growth will not be pro-poor, in the strong sense of the term (see Table 2.3). This therefore creates an imperative for public policy interventions that rebalance the benefits of economic expansion towards the poor. Kanbur and Rauniyar's (2010) paper on inclusive

Table 2.3 Development that assists the poor(er): the definitional swamp

Term	Meaning	Sources
Pro-poor growth (strong)	Growth is pro-poor if the poor benefit from growth to a greater extent than the non-poor	Son and Kakwani (2008); Krongkaew and Kakwani (2003)
Pro-poor growth (weak)	Growth is pro-poor if the poverty rate falls	Kraay (2006); Ravallion (2005)
Shared growth	Growth that is combined with wealth distributing mechanisms that widen opportunities for the poor	Page (2006)
Inclusive growth	Growth that is concerned both with the pace of economic expansion and with ensuring that the pattern of expansion is broadly distributed between groups, sectors and geographical spaces	Ali and Son (2007)
Inclusive development	Growth that delivers not just economic gains for the many, but also non-economic progress and improvements in well-being	Kanbur and Rauniyar (2010)
Shared prosperity	A focus on the income growth of the bottom 40 per cent of a country's population: growth is necessary but particular attention should be paid to the less well off	World Bank (2014)

Note: the meanings briefly summarized above are themselves open to some dispute but are here provided for guidance.

development in Asia rather effectively communicates the muddled flavours that constitute this debate:

> [I]f inequality in the overall distribution falls with growth, this would have some claim to be labeled 'inclusive growth'. If there is growth and a fall in overall inequality, poverty will fall, so in this case growth will be 'pro-poor' as well. But if there is growth and an increase in inequality, then we could have the case that poverty falls because the growth effect dominates the inequality effect. In this case, growth is 'pro-poor', in the sense that poverty has fallen; but it is not 'inclusive', in the sense that inequality has risen. *These are not just definitional games. The recent experience of most fast-growing economies, in Asia and elsewhere, precisely matches this stylized pattern.*
>
> (Kanbur and Rauniyar 2010: 439, emphasis added)

Clearly, then, there is a continuing debate over what, exactly, constitutes pro-poor growth; Table 2.3 provides a summary of these definitional contortions. A point on which the large majority of scholars and policy-makers tend to agree, however, is on the importance of addressing inequality and the need to understand the roots of unequal growth and the means – the policy interventions – that might foster shared growth. It is to these issues that the chapter now turns, with reference to the Southeast Asian experience.

Patterns of unequal growth in Southeast Asia

In the 1980s, it was often said that the growth economies of East Asia[9] had achieved the holy grail of development namely, growth with equity:

> The HPAEs [High Performing Asian Economies] enjoyed much higher per capita income growth at the same time that income distribution improved by as much or more than in other developing economies .... The HPAEs are the only economies that have high growth *and* declining inequality . ... As a result of rapid, shared growth, human welfare has improved dramatically.
> (World Bank 1993: 3–4, emphasis in original)[10]

This was significant because it was – and remains – so rare. It was, furthermore, partly on the basis of this claim (and not just the HPAEs' rapid economic growth) that the appellation 'miracle' was bestowed. Even in the 1980s, however, not all of the HPAEs were achieving balanced growth and the claim may have been "exaggerated, if not erroneous" (Jomo 2006: 3) even at the very time it was conferred.[11] It seems that the highly unusual growth–equity relationship among the East Asian first-tier newly industrialized countries (Japan, South Korea, Taiwan), possibly an outcome of some very particular historical conditions, was extended to the growth economies of Southeast Asia (Indonesia, Malaysia, Thailand) without due consideration to the equity side of the equation. Moreover, during the 1990s and the first decade of the twenty-first century, inequality widened in many countries of Asia, and sometimes dramatically so. The puzzle is that even while the evidence for the inequality-widening effects of global integration has become more persuasive, and even as the evidence for the corrosive effects of inequality has become more convincing, key institutions – and not least the World Bank – have continued to make the case for global market integration on the basis that this is the best means to reduce poverty. This position is promulgated particularly strongly for the 'new globalizers' of the global South (World Bank 2002). Problematically, a case is made for the inequality-neutral effects of globalization: "Within countries, globalization has not, on average, affected inequality..." (World Bank 2002: 2).[12]

There are, as Box 2.1 sets out in summary form, a number of factors that make measuring inequality an art rather than a science. Nonetheless, the statistical picture of trends in growth and inequality for the countries of Southeast Asia over the last 20–25 years shows that, at a regional level, and *pace* the World Bank, inequality *has* risen. On a population basis for the seven countries in Table 2.4 for which we have data,[13] two-thirds live in countries where, at the end of the first decade of this century, the poorest quintile earned a smaller share of national income than they did in the early 1990s. In the three countries, namely Malaysia, the Philippines and Thailand, where the quintile ratios improved, in two of these three (Malaysia and the Philippines) this was only by a very small amount and in the third (Thailand) it improved from a previously high level, and remains highly unequal (Table 2.4). While country experiences are markedly different – and these differences are explored in greater detail later in this chapter – the evidence is that rather than narrowing with economic growth and globalization, inequalities based

Table 2.4 Inequality in Southeast Asia

	Population (2012, millions)	Gini coefficient of income[a]				Gini coefficient of wealth[b]	Quintile ratios[c]		Inequality level[d] (L, M, H)	
		Initial year	Final year	1990s	Latest	2000s	1990s	2000s	1990s	2000s
Cambodia	14.8	1994	2008	0.383	0.379	0.71	5.8	6.1	M	M
Indonesia	247.2	1990	2011	0.292	0.389	0.76	4.1	6.6	L	M
Lao PDR	6.5	1992	2008	0.304	0.367	–	4.3	5.9	L	M
Malaysia	29.3	1992	2009	0.477	0.462	0.73	11.4	11.3	H	H
Philippines	95.8	1991	2009	0.438	0.430	0.72	8.6	8.3	H	H
Thailand	64.4	1990	2009	0.453	0.400	0.71	8.8	7.1	H	H
Singapore	5.3	1990	2005	0.436	0.522	0.89	–	–	H	H
Vietnam	88.8	1992	2008	0.357	0.356	0.68	5.6	5.9	M	M

Sources: Data extracted from ADB (2012: 47, 67); Jomo (2006: 6–7); Davies *et al.* (2009); and World Bank development indicators.

Notes

a The Gini coefficient of income is a measure of the distribution of income, consumption or expenditure between households. The Gini ranges from 0 (perfect equality, every household has the same income, expenditure or consumption) to 1 (perfect inequality, when all income accrues to one household). Sometimes the coefficient is multiplied by 100. *Italic* indicates a worsening Gini coefficient (greater inequality).

b The Gini coefficient of wealth refers to the distribution of the net worth or the value of physical and financial assets minus liabilities. Wealth inequalities are generally much higher than income inequalities.

c The quintile ratio (based on either income or expenditure) is the ratio of the total income/expenditure of the richest 20 per cent of the population to that of the poorest 20 per cent. Thus for Cambodia in the 1990s, the richest 20 per cent received 5.8 times more than the poorest 20 per cent. *Italic* indicates a deterioration in the ratio of income/expenditure (growing wealth disparities) of the richest quintile compared to the poorest.

d Inequality level estimated on the basis that a Gini coefficient of ≤0.3 is low; 0.3–0.4 is medium; and ≥0.4 is high.

on income have widened. All of the countries of the region for which we have data exhibit medium or high levels of income inequality.

Box 2.1 **The challenges of measuring and assessing inequality**

On the face of it, it would seem fairly straightforward to measure inequality. It would be a measure of the difference in incomes between members of a population. As with measuring poverty, however, there are a series of practical challenges, statistical simplifications and methodological assumptions that sit behind the data, such as those data presented in Tables 2.4 and 2.5. These are summarized below under the headings 'choices', 'challenges' and 'unknowns', and even this list is far from exhaustive.

Choices

- *Income or expenditure.* Should we measure what people earn or what they consume/spend? Consumption/expenditure is a better indicator of well-being but harder to collect; most available data remain recorded in income, not consumption terms and generally inequality based on income is significantly higher than inequality measured in consumption/ expenditure terms.
- *Gross or net income.* Should income be assessed after or before taxation and other transfers and should publically funded investment be included in the calculation?
- *Income or wealth.* Should we be measuring income inequality or wealth inequality, with the latter based on an individual or household's net worth (assets minus debts or liabilities)? Generally, wealth inequalities are much greater than income inequalities (see Table 2.4) but are hard to calculate in many poorer countries.
- *Individual or household.* Should we use the household or individual as the unit of analysis? Invariably it is the household, but we increasingly know that the household is internally differentiated and cannot be treated as an 'individual by another name'.
- *Income or non-income measures.* Inequality is usually measured in terms of income or expenditure but it may be that non-income factors (say, education or health) are better measures of human well-being. These, furthermore, are forward-looking and help distinguish between equality of opportunity and equality of outcome.
- *National or international poverty lines.* Should estimates of inequality be based on national or international (say, $2 per day) poverty lines? The former pay greater attention to national context, while the latter permit cross-country comparison.

(Continued)

(Continued)

Challenges

- *How to factor in costs of living.* Costs of living vary across space, and particularly between rural and urban areas; the marked differences that exist in poverty estimates *using the same data sets* are often associated with how variations in living costs are factored in.
- *How to account for different survey methods.* The raw socio-economic data from which living standards, poverty and therefore inequality are calculated often use different survey methods with different degrees of coverage. Moreover, national survey methods and coverage usually change over time so that comparing across survey periods is also problematic.

Unknowns

- *Statistical manipulation.* It has been suggested that some countries engage in statistical manipulation to massage the poverty statistics in ways that are favourable to the ruling government (see Jomo 2006: 29, fn 8 regarding Malaysia's poverty estimates).

It is possible to demonstrate the impact of this (unequal) distribution or pattern of growth on poverty through calculating the growth elasticity of poverty. This is a simple measure of how effectively growth is translated into poverty reduction by calculating the percentage change in poverty for each 1 per cent growth in per capita GDP. Pro-poor growth would show a growth elasticity of poverty greater than one; anti-poor growth would be reflected in a figure of less than one. As Table 2.5 shows, for only a single country during one period between 2002 and 2008 was growth pro-poor (Indonesia between 2002 and 2005). Furthermore, in only three of the seven countries did the growth elasticity of poverty improve between 2002–5 and 2005–8, and in every instance it continued to remain anti-poor in character. We can therefore come to two conclusions about the growth/equity experience of Southeast Asia. First, growth was generally unequal even during the heyday of the Asian miracle; and, second, that inequalities have further deepened over the course of this century.

The impact of this in terms of poverty rates can be seen by looking at two countries that have experienced rising levels of inequality over the decade before and the decade since the year 2000, namely Indonesia and the Lao PDR. Figure 2.3 shows that annual expenditure has been growing progressively faster for richer than for poorer quintiles in both countries. It is this that lies behind the striking difference in actual and simulated poverty levels in Figure 2.2.

The evidence presented and the discussion thus far has focused on *income* (or consumption) inequality. A focus on income, just as Chapter 1 noted with regard to poverty, does not capture the full scope of inequality. Inequalities in access to health

Table 2.5 GDP growth and poverty reduction (based on $2/day poverty line)

	2002–5			2005–8		
	GDP per capita growth	Poverty reduction	Growth elasticity of poverty[a]	GDP per capita growth	Poverty reduction	Growth elasticity of poverty
Cambodia	32.1	7.6	0.24	25.9	12.1	0.47
Indonesia	11.0	13.2	*1.20*	15.2	9.0	*0.59*
Lao PDR	14.3	6.5	*0.45*	15.8	3.2	*0.20*
Malaysia	11.7	2.2	0.19	12.0	5.4	0.45
Philippines	10.1	−1.3	−0.13	10.3	2.9	0.28
Thailand	16.2	3.6	*0.22*	11.1	1.5	*0.14*
Vietnam	21.1	18.2	*0.86*	20.8	10.1	*0.49*
Simple average	16.6	7.1	*0.43*	15.9	6.3	*0.40*

Source: based on Wan and Sebastian (2011: 36).

Notes: *italic* indicates countries where the impact of growth on poverty has declined (worsened) during the two periods.

a The growth elasticity of poverty is a simple measure of how effectively growth is translated into poverty reduction. The figure shows the percentage change in poverty reduction for each one per cent growth in per capita GDP.

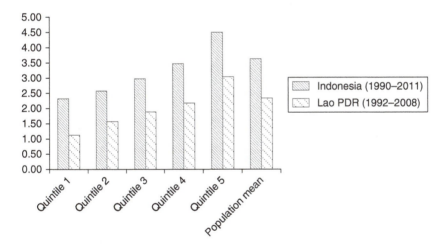

Figure 2.3 Growth incidence of expenditure by quintile, Indonesia and Lao PDR (annual growth of mean per capita expenditure by quintile)

Note: growth incidence bars show the distribution of income (or expenditure) growth between two periods across income groups.

Source: ADB estimates using PovcalNet extracted from ADB 2012: 49.

and education, inequality of opportunity to engage directly in politics, inequalities in power between the genders, discrimination on grounds of race – these are, arguably, as important as income inequality and are likely to become more so as countries become more prosperous. Later chapters in this book will pay particular attention to these facets of inequality: the inequality that arises from who people are, where they live, and what they do – rather than inequality based on what they earn and consume.

Digging down: inequality across four countries

To supplement the general discussion so far with some more detailed analysis of country experiences, the chapter turns to take a closer look at Indonesia, Malaysia, Thailand and Vietnam. This permits us to begin to understand the contextual factors that might have played a role in creating the very different inequality signatures of these four countries.

In general, we can say the following about inequality trends in these countries since data were first collected:

- *Indonesia:* low levels of inequality, but rising over the course of this century;
- *Malaysia:* initially high but, from the 1980s, falling levels of inequality;
- *Thailand:* consistently high and increasing levels of inequality;
- *Vietnam:* (assumed) initially low levels of inequality, but rising over the course of this century.

As a first cut, Figure 2.4 shows the trend of the Gini coefficients for Indonesia, Malaysia, Thailand and Vietnam. Time series vary (they are particularly short

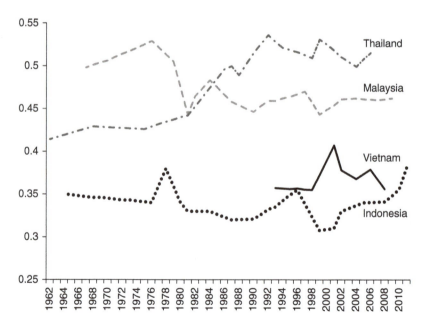

Figure 2.4 Gini coefficient of income inequality, Indonesia, Malaysia, Thailand and Vietnam (1962–2011, selected years)

Source: data extracted from Kuhonta (2011), supplemented by Jomo (2006) and World Bank data.

for Vietnam) and there are also sometimes quite sharp discrepancies in the coefficients from different sources, the challenge of which is elaborated in Box 2.1. Even so, there are significant differences in levels of income inequality between the four countries and also in terms of how their inequality profiles have progressed over time.

In Thailand, inequality has remained high and almost every study (e.g. Jomo 2006; Krongkaew and Kakwani 2003) has remarked on the enduring character of inequality in the country (Figure 2.4). A range of reasons has been suggested: a regressive tax system that taxes consumption rather than income and therefore hurts the poor and near-poor; policies, such as sectoral protection policies, that are biased in favour of industrial activities and urban areas and against farmers and rural areas (the very areas and sectors where poverty is concentrated); over-concentration of activity and wealth in Bangkok, the Bangkok extended metropolitan area and the Eastern Seaboard; and limited expenditure on health and education which might have, respectively, protected vulnerable populations and improved the opportunities for the poor and near-poor by raising their human capital, thus permitting them to engage productively in the growth sectors of the economy.

Malaysia, at least to begin with, also shared some of these policy characteristics and, indeed, during the 1970s had higher levels of inequality than Thailand. During the late 1970s and into the 1980s, however, inequality decreased, only to rise again more recently (although not to previous levels) (Figure 2.4). Of particular note when it comes to understanding inequality in Malaysia is the ethnic dimension, and particularly levels of wealth and poverty among the Malay and Chinese (and, to a lesser extent, Indian) populations. As Figure 2.5 shows, in 1970, Chinese incomes were well over double those of the Bumiputera population.[14] Escalating ethnic tensions which culminated in communal riots in 1969 made it politically imperative that policies be put in place to redress the ethnic imbalance. To some degree coincidentally, these also addressed spatial inequalities in the guise of rural/urban and agriculture/non-agriculture divisions because Malays, at that time, predominantly lived in rural areas and engaged in farm-based pursuits. Through the New Economic Policy (NEP), a series of policies driven by political necessity began to redress the balance through supporting farming and rural livelihoods, positively discriminating in favour of Malays in terms of access to higher education, and subsidizing Malay businesses and entrepreneurs. All this had the outcome, through the 1980s and 1990s, of relatively raising the incomes of Malays, of farmers and of those in rural areas, and served to narrow inequalities even though the proximate driver was the need to redress inequalities between ethnic groups. In 1970, the income of Malays was 65 per cent of the national figure; by 2004 it had risen to 84 per cent. During the 1990s, however, this coincidence of interests began to break down as the remaining poor in rural areas saw their incomes decline in relative terms so that in 2004 they were lower, relatively speaking, than they had been in 1970 (see Figure 2.5).

It is Indonesia, however, where the dampening – or redistributive – effects of policy on inequality have been most surprising (Figure 2.4). From the 1960s through to the early 1990s, inequality remained low and only really increased significantly from the mid-to-late 1990s. It has been suggested that the decision

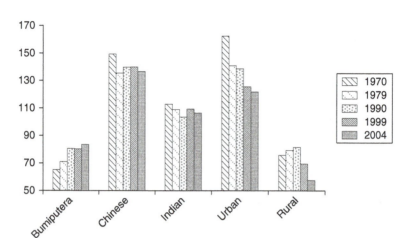

Figure 2.5 Incomes by ethnic group in Malaysia, 1970–2004 (percentage of mean income across all ethnic groups)

Note: *Bumiputera* ('sons of the soil') is the term used to refer to Malays and other indigenous groups in Malaysia. The Malays are numerically dominant in this designation.

Source: calculation based on income data extracted from Jomo 2006: 29.

to allocate much of the windfall of the oil boom to sustained investments in irrigation, new rice technologies, crop support and input subsidization schemes, universal primary level education, a nation-wide family-planning programme, roads and other physical infrastructure in peripheral as well as central island locations, and health facilities across the archipelago, helped to narrow inequalities by diverting state resources to rural and peripheral regions and to farmers (see Booth 2000; Asra 2000; Jomo 2006). As Asra writes: "during the two decades from 1976 to 1996 Indonesia experienced a significant increase in real average consumption, a consistent decline in poverty incidence and a relatively insignificant change in inequality of consumption" (2000: 104). By the late 1990s, however, these poverty-reducing and inequality-stabilizing investments began to falter. Indonesia's *krismon* (financial crisis) did not help, but perhaps more important in terms of relations between groups was the way in which the easy gains of the 1970s and 1980s (primary health care, primary education, basic needs) were not being carried into broad-based investments in upper secondary- and tertiary-level education, which would have done much to broaden the ability of those from less privileged backgrounds to access better paying jobs in the modern economy.

Last of the four countries is Vietnam. The most important aspect of the Vietnam inequality story is its progressive transformation beginning in 1986 from a command to a market economy. Notwithstanding the data concerns noted more than once in this chapter but which are all the more acute for Vietnam, it does seem that inequalities have widened with this transition. Intuitively one would expect this, notwithstanding the World Bank's claim that Vietnam has achieved global integration with "no significant change in inequality" (World Bank 2002: 6). As Melanie Beresford, who observed Vietnam's transformation from the very beginning of *doi moi* (renovation), writes:

> The rise of structural inequality along class (and gender) lines does not imply immiseration. It implies that inequality in Vietnam is increasingly based on new mechanisms of capital accumulation in which control over the means of production – whether indirectly, through management of state-owned assets, including land, or directly through private ownership – is confined to a small proportion of the population while strong redistributive mechanisms are absent.
>
> (2008: 238)

Market reforms have bestowed three premiums on certain groups and individuals which, taken together, have served to deepen inequalities that had previously been corrected under the socialist system. First, a location premium: people living in remote areas and especially in upland regions (often inhabited by ethnic minorities) have seen their relative incomes fall. Those living close to the centres, often coastal, of economic dynamism have done rather better. Second, a connection premium: those with the right connections (access to what Beresford calls public–private networks), when finance is tight, rules are constraining and information limited, have had preferential access to employment and investment opportunities. And third, an education premium: those with upper secondary or tertiary education, especially from prestigious secondary schools and universities, have been better placed to take advantage of the opportunities that reform has created.

The short inequality storylines or vignettes set out above provide some hint at the intersection of market processes, policies and inequality.

Sources of inequality: the 'why' and 'how' questions

If the relationship, as suggested earlier in this chapter, between growth, development and inequality is unclear then what might be the mix of factors that has contributed to unequal growth and, in light of that, how might – in policy terms – equal growth be pursued? Multilateral institutions such as the World Bank and the International Monetary Fund (IMF) have made the case that globalization has not only been the primary driver of growth but has also done so in a manner that has narrowed within and between country inequalities, or at least not widened them (World Bank 2002). Globalization has, therefore, delivered on its promise of development.

With reference to the Southeast Asian region the argument here is quite the reverse: modernization has tended to widen inequalities and, moreover, this is intimately tied to the nature of global market integration. It is important to emphasize that this is *not* to suggest that real standards of living, defined in income/expenditure terms, have deteriorated for the poor. As Figure 2.3 shows for Indonesia and the Lao PDR, even in the context of unequal growth the poorest quintiles in each country's population have still seen their real incomes rise.

For those adhering to a weak interpretation of pro-poor growth, this would still be counted as pro-poor (see above).

The association of openness/globalization with inequality and/or growth is not straightforward, as experience shows. The World Bank, no less, has acknowledged that countries with the same level of openness show "massive" differences in inequality (World Bank 2002: 48). How, though, does globalization lead to a widening of inequalities and what are the factors or interventions that might dampen this tendency?

The key processes that have driven the rise in inequality are the same as those that have driven growth, namely market reforms and technological change. Market reforms have opened up productive spaces for investment and growth and, by association, higher incomes for some of those linked to these growth sectors. More specifically, the ADB (2012: ix–xx) notes that the forces of globalization tend to bias growth in three ways: towards capital over labour; spatially, towards those areas that are more favourably endowed or have enhanced infrastructure; and in human terms, towards those people with skills that can be productively deployed in the context of a modernizing economy. We can see this being echoed in the country storylines in the previous section. Overall, labour's share of national income in the countries of Southeast Asia has been falling while relative returns to skilled labour have been rising; at the same time, globalization has endowed those areas with better access, more favourable locations or superior infrastructure with the lion's share of economic activity. The *World Development Report 2009: reshaping economic geography* accepts that development is inherently unequal, particularly in terms of its spatial dimension:

> [E]conomic growth is seldom balanced. Efforts to spread it prematurely will jeopardize progress. Two centuries of economic development show that spatial disparities in income and production are inevitable. A generation of economic research confirms this: there is no good reason to expect economic growth to spread smoothly across space. The experience of successful developers shows that production becomes more concentrated spatially.
>
> (World Bank 2009: 5–6)

Those individuals who cannot ride this wave of technological change are marginalized either in agriculture or in low-skill, low-return non-farm activities. The failure of a number of countries of Southeast Asia to progress from middle to high income, termed the 'middle-income trap', is linked to this failure, but multiplied many times over (Box 2.2). Writing of the 'tiger' economies of Southeast Asia, Yusuf and Nabeshima say that the

> underlying worry is that [their slowing economic performance] presages the beginning of a downward trend, the harbingers of which are lower rates of investment, persistently low rates of total factor productivity, and low levels of innovativeness ... a creeping economic sclerosis or what some observers are calling the *middle-income trap*.
>
> (2009a: 3, emphasis in original)

Box 2.2 **The middle-income trap in Southeast Asia**

Across the world, there are 28 countries which by 1987 had attained middle-income status but, in 2012 still remained, seemingly marooned, in this middle-income category. Having rapidly made the transition from low income to middle income, in the process escaping the poverty trap, 35 years of further growth have failed to propel these countries into the high-income category of advanced economies. It is this failure which has puzzled – and concerned – development economists and policy-makers who have sought to understand the stickiness of development in the transition from middle income to high income.

At its simplest level, the 'middle-income trap' refers to countries that experience a 'growth slow-down' when they achieve middle-income status (Eichengreen *et al.* 2013). More concretely, the term is used to describe a situation where a country lacks the human capital and state vision to upgrade from the stage of industrialization where technology is absorbed through foreign investment (classically represented by FDI-driven, low-cost, low-wage, labour-intensive manufacturing), to the stage where a domestic private sector emerges that can create technology (Ohno 2009). The trap – or "glass ceiling" as Ohno (2009: 28) calls it – is, therefore, the apparent inability of a country to move up the value chain where complex technologies provide the means to generate high-value-added products which, in turn, can justify higher wages. They are caught between low-income countries, with which they cannot compete on wage cost grounds as the labour market tightens and wages rise, and high-income countries, with which they cannot compete in terms of skills and technology and therefore on productivity grounds. Successfully negotiating this transition is critical to progressing from middle-income to high-income status. As Eichengreen *et al.* (2011: 17) write, "it is worth recalling that only a small group of countries successfully completed this transition in the second half of the 20th century, while a much larger group ... are still struggling to escape the middle-income trap". In summary, the term 'middle-income trap' has become an 'empirical generalization' to describe the stalling that seems to afflict countries as they move up the ladder from middle to high income (Warr 2011: 4).

Of the 28 countries which were classed as middle income in 1987 and which still remained middle income in 2012 (Zhuang *et al.* 2012: 9; and see Eichengreen *et al.* 2013), three are to be found in Southeast Asia: Indonesia, Malaysia and Thailand (Table 2.6) . In Southeast Asia, only one country has successfully made the transition from middle to high income: Singapore, a city state of little more than 5 million people representing just 1 per cent of the Southeast Asian region's total population.[15] Since 1987 Indonesia, the Lao PDR, Timor Leste and Vietnam have also made

(Continued)

(Continued)

the transition from low income to middle income and there is the question therefore of whether they, too, might become trapped like their richer regional neighbours.

Table 2.6 Stages of growth in Southeast Asia, 1987–2011

	Low income	Lower middle income	Upper middle income	High income
Singapore				1987–present
Brunei Darrusalam				1987–present
Malaysia			*1987–present*	
Thailand		*1987–2009*	*2010–present*	
Vietnam		*1987–2008*	*2008–present*	
Philippines		*1987–2011*		
Indonesia	1987–2002	2003–present		
Timor Leste	2002–2006	2007–present		
Lao PDR	1987–2009	2010–present		
Cambodia	1987–present			
Myanmar	1987–present			

Source: World Bank data accessed at http://data.worldbank.org/about/country-classifications/a-short-history.

Notes: countries in *italic* are those trapped in middle-income status. In 2002 Timor Leste (East Timor) attained independence from Indonesia.

The more radical view of this process is that the forces of globalization exert downward pressure on wages as investment seeks out those locations where labour is cheapest. The progressive shift of low-wage activities in the Asian region in the light of prevailing wage rates tends to support this interpretation of how global capital operates in an internationalizing context. It has variously been termed 'immiserizing growth', 'competitive austerity', the 'race to the bottom', and a 'not-so-friendly-to-labour' mode of industrialization or, alternatively, 3D development (dirty, dangerous, demeaning) or 3L development (low skill, low pay, long hours). Even Joseph Stiglitz who, as chief economist at the World Bank was at the heart of the globalization project, would seem to accept the logic of the immiserizing growth thesis: "With capital highly mobile – and with tariffs low – firms can simply tell workers that if they don't accept lower wages and worse working conditions, the company will move elsewhere" (Stiglitz 2012: 61).[16]

This interpretation of the way in which globalization has perpetuated poverty is intuitively convincing and theoretically sound, but is not obviously borne out empirically, at least not at a national level (although it might be in particular sub-national circumstances). The evidence is that real incomes, even for those engaged in low-skill work, have improved over the course of the last three decades or so and this is reflected in steep falls in absolute poverty using the $1.25-a-day international benchmark (see Figure 2.6a). In that sense, to term growth in Asia 'immiserizing' is misleading. Nonetheless, there are large numbers of poor living between the $1.25 and $2.00 poverty lines, and economic growth between 1990 and 2010 has made less-dramatic inroads into the $2-a-day poverty rates (Figure 2.6b). The middle-income trap thesis, furthermore, suggests that growth in real incomes may be levelling off as low-wage industrialization reaches its limits.

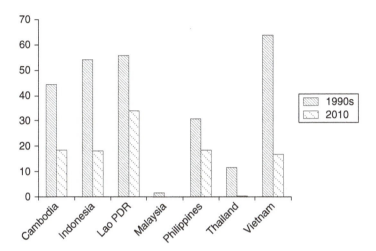

Figure 2.6a Proportion of the population below the $1.25 poverty (PPP), 1990s and 2010 (%)

Note: 1990s data are from the following years: Cambodia (1994), Indonesia (1990), Lao PDR (1992), Malaysia (1992), Philippines (1991), Thailand (1990), Vietnam (1993). Data for Brunei, Myanmar and Timor Leste are not available.

Source: ADB 2013.

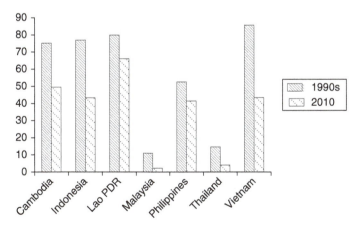

Figure 2.6b Proportion of the population below the $2.00 poverty (PPP), 1990s and 2010 (%)

Note: 1990s data are from the following years: Cambodia (1994), Indonesia (1990), Lao PDR (1992), Malaysia (1992), Philippines (1991), Thailand (1990), Vietnam (1993). Data for Brunei, Myanmar and Timor Leste are not available.

Source: ADB 2013.

The fact that levels of globalization/openness and levels of inequality are highly varied is in no small part due to policies that have been instituted to 'correct' for some of the biases and trends noted above. Markets, in short, do not operate in a political and social vacuum. As the *2009 World Development Report* goes on to say, the "most successful nations also institute policies that make basic living standards more uniform across space" (2009: 6). For the World Bank, it seems, while it is not the role of government to intervene in the operation of market forces, it is the role of government to pick up the pieces.

Sometimes these policies are generated from the bottom up as governments respond to worker agitation or to the actions of non-governmental and other civil society organizations. Tran (2007), for example, makes a case for such bottom-up processes in Vietnam. She shows how minimum wage action by workers in foreign-invested factories in Vietnam between 2005 and 2006 led to a series of critical (i.e. supportive of workers) pieces in *The Laborer*, a union newspaper in Ho Chi Minh City. These, in turn, encouraged central labour unions and then the state to take notice, leading to a 40 per cent increase in the minimum wage in 2006 and to the introduction of a revised strike law by the end of that year.

In Kuhonta's (2011) study of the politics of equitable development in Southeast Asia, in which he focuses on Malaysia, Thailand, the Philippines and Vietnam, he makes a claim for the primacy of institutions in the explanatory mix: "The central thesis of this study is that institutional power and capacity, along with pragmatic ideology, are crucial to the pursuit of equitable development" (2011: 4). For him, strong institutions – by which he means institutionalized political parties allied to interventionist states – provide the political ballast to ensure that public interests take precedence over private interests. He then explores and sustains his thesis through a detailed analysis of the contrasting experiences of Malaysia and Thailand.

In Malaysia, following the communal riots of 1969, the government's *laissez-faire* mind-set was replaced by a raft of policies (embedded in the New Economic Policy) that systematically addressed the relative underdevelopment and impoverishment of Malays and extracted them from rural areas and agriculture and encouraged them into the modern economy. This was made possible partly because of the fear that the country might implode if the ethnic divide, reflected in sharply differing levels of wealth and poverty (see Figure 2.5), was not addressed and partly because the government, led by the United Malays National Organization, was able to bring political vision and institutional capacity to bear. But it was done in such a way that the Chinese population, so critical to the modernization of the country and the growth agenda, were not felt to be completely marginal to the country's future. Just as there was a racial bargain at independence, so this was recalibrated in the wake of the 1969 riots.

The contrast with Thailand could not be more striking. Here, the rural poor were only thrown morsels of comfort in the guise of a few uncoordinated interventions – many roads, to be sure (but arguably for security rather than local development reasons), but only halting investment in other areas. The reason, and here the contrast with Malaysia is stark, is that there was no driving political imperative to redress the balance between rural and urban, and agricultural and industry. Moreover, even if there had been such an imperative, one wonders whether Thailand, at that time, had the institutional capacity to challenge the deep fissures in society and economy. As Kuhonta writes, the "political institutions that might break through a conservative veneer" (2011: 123) as had happened in Malaysia, were absent in Thailand. This was only challenged by Thaksin Shinawatra's short-lived rise to power in 2001 (see p. 219 this volume).

Kuhonta's (2011) study highlights that achieving equitable development is about difficult trade-offs: between public and private interests, between rich and poor, between rural and urban, and sometimes between ethnic groups as well. For these trade-offs to be addressed in a progressive manner requires a degree of political power, bureaucratic capacity and institutional discipline. But these difficult choices need to be made in a spirit of pragmatism – nothing "too radical or destabilizing" (2011: 41). Kuhonta's focus on institutions is echoed in Jomo's (2006) examination of the growth–inequality–poverty nexus in East and Southeast Asia. Jomo concludes:

> These experiences suggest that poverty alleviation and the reduction of income inequality can not only accompany, but may even be conducive to rapid growth and industrialization. Income inequality however tends to worsen with economic liberalization, especially in the absence of effective provisions for redistribution. Furthermore, the fact that income inequality in Taiwan and Korea declined in the initial stages of growth, and worsened as the two economies liberalized, turns the Kuznets hypothesis on its head. However, the unique circumstances of post-war asset redistribution (including land reforms) suggest that initial conditions, rather than subsequent growth itself, may better explain these Northeast Asian exceptions.
>
> (Jomo 2006: 10)

The headline point is that focusing purely on the economic question – which is certainly an important one – of the inter-relationships between inequality, poverty and growth will only get us so far. The varied inequality experiences of the countries of Southeast Asia can only be interpreted and explained by taking seriously the shaping roles of historical conditions, political exigencies, institutional capacities and the policies that have been put in place and (which is different) then set in train. To quote Stiglitz again, "inequality is, to a very large extent, the result of government policies that shape and direct the forces of technology and markets and broader societal forces" (2012: 82). He thus highlights the point that inequality does not emerge out of a set of economic forces that are beyond governments' ability to mould, but out of a set of policy decisions and priorities and over which governments have control. Liberalization may be inequality widening but this can be tempered when governments have the capacity and will to address the challenge of inequality.

Conclusion

This chapter has shown the degree to which development transformations in Southeast Asia have deepened economic inequalities. It has also made a case for the centrality of market processes – the market imperative – in shaping those outcomes. This is not to argue that a more equitable, pro-poor development is impossible in the context of market-led transformation, but to highlight the necessity and centrality of policies focused on mitigating the inequality-deepening effects of market integration, and protecting the weakest and most vulnerable. Looking across the piece and the temptation is to conclude that the countries of the region have failed to blunt the negative tendencies of marketization. The policies, laws and regulations that have emerged; the ways those policies, laws and regulations have been enacted (implemented); and the institutions that exist to support and inform those tasks, have all been found wanting. These interventions, or the lack of them, all have distributive consequences and these have been either sub-optimal in economic terms or injudicious or undesirable in social terms. And the reason for this, more often than not, lies in the sphere of politics.[17]

What the chapter has not done, however, is explored how particular social groups become implicated in these processes and the specific mechanisms that lead to their exclusion and, in this way, to the deepening patterns of inequality that have been sketched out. It is all too easy to overlook the individuals that lie behind the aggregate statistics that have largely informed this chapter. Global inequality – between-country inequality – drives the transnational migration streams that have become such a feature of the Southeast Asian landscape, while within-country inequality helps to explain rural–urban movements and the concentration of poverty, vulnerability and ill-being in certain geographical and social spaces. It is this more detailed interrogation which is the concern of the next chapter.

In the 1950s and 1960s when most of the countries of Southeast Asia established national development-planning agencies and systematically began to pursue 'development', the problems they faced were those of underdevelopment, reflected in high levels of poverty and low levels of human development and material consumption. While levels of poverty remain high in countries like Cambodia, the Lao PDR and Myanmar (see Figures 2.6a and 2.6b), most countries are now middle income, and poverty is no longer a product of underdevelopment, but a function of inequality. This, arguably, has changed – or, in some countries is changing – the nature of the poverty challenge facing these countries, placing the need to address inequality ahead of the necessity to foster growth. As Wilkinson and Pickett say, "standards of health and social well-being in rich societies may now depend more on reducing income differences than on economic growth without redistribution" (2009: 5). To be sure, most of Southeast Asia is not yet rich, but increasingly the challenge of transformation is not about generating growth but about the quality of that growth and its distribution. In development terms, less may very well be more.

Further reading

For a data rich overview of inequality in Asia see the Asian Development Bank's *Asian development outlook 2012: confronting rising inequality in Asia* (http://www.adb.org/sites/default/files/pub/2012/ado2012.pdf) (ADB 2012).

The debate over the links between growth, poverty and inequality is extensive. Dollar and Kraay's paper (2002) is perhaps the best known and one of the most cited papers that makes the case for focusing on growth before equity; growth, they claim, helps the poor as much as it helps the non-poor. As a counterpoint, see Wade's (2004) paper; he argues that inequality is rising with global integration and the assumption that openness leads to balanced growth is, to his view, based on shaky evidence.

Although it focuses on the USA, Joseph Stiglitz's *The price of inequality* (2012) sets out clearly and with authority the case against US-style growth and why it is so corrosive. As chief economist at the World Bank between 1997 and 2000, during the years of the Asian financial crisis, he had a large hand in shaping the post-Washington consensus. Kuhonta (2011) provides the most detailed political economy interrogation of inequality in Southeast Asia (focusing on Malaysia and Thailand, complemented by an analysis of the Philippines and Vietnam). His central conclusion is that we need to look at the quality and nature of institutional interventions if we are to understand (in)equality. Jomo's (2006) downloadable (http://www.un.org/esa/desa/papers/2006/wp33_2006.pdf) report produced for the UN echoes Kuhonta's argument.

Two short 'briefing' notes on pro-poor growth, what it means and how it can be supported, have been produced by the ODI (2008) and DFID (2004). For a discussion of inclusive growth see Kanbur and Rauniyar (2010).

Data on poverty, income and inequality are problematic in their collection and calculation. The easiest to access are from the World Bank's online data bank. See: http://data.worldbank.org/.

Notes

1   In stating this, Dollar and Kraay are not making a case for trickle-down economics but rather arguing that the benefits of growth for the poor accrue *at the same time* as they do for the non-poor. It is not jam tomorrow for the poor, but jam today.
2   See for example: ADB (2007) (http://www.adb.org/sites/default/files/pub/2007/Key-Indicators-2007.pdf), ADB (2008) (http://www.adb.org/sites/default/files/pub/2008/December-2008.pdf), ADB (2012) (http://www.adb.org/sites/default/files/pub/2012/ado2012.pdf) and ADB (2013) (http://www.adb.org/sites/default/files/pub/2013/devasia14.pdf).
3   For example, in Alesina and Rodrik's (1994) paper they use land ownership and income distribution as measures of inequality. Both have their shortcomings.
4   This assumes, of course, that economic growth trajectories would have been the same under different levels of equality/inequality. This, as noted, continues to be contested.
5   Using the Gini index of income inequality and homicide (1965–95) and robbery (1970–94) rates across 39 countries, Fajnzylber *et al.* (2002) demonstrate empirically a strong and positive correlation between inequality and violent crime. In his more ethnographic study, Kramer (2000) similarly argues that high levels of inequality

fosters a climate where social exclusion and the absence of social capital nurture violence and crime.

6 It might also conceivably lead to sub-optimal outcomes for *both* the poor and non-poor: a pattern of growth that raised the incomes of the poor by 2.0 per cent and the non-poor by 1.5 per cent would be preferred over one that raised incomes of the poor by 2.5 per cent and the non-poor by 3.0 per cent.

7 Which are not rehearsed here, but see Maxwell's (1999) summary of the 'fault lines' that characterize the poverty debate.

8 Ali (2008: 19) therefore calls such poverty "doubly pernicious" because these individuals and groups are not only poor or near poor but trapped in that condition.

9 The World Bank's HPAEs were: Hong Kong, Indonesia, Japan, Malaysia, Singapore, South Korea, Taiwan (China) and Thailand.

10 This is a claim that has also been made at a global level: "Since 1980 world inequality has ... stopped increasing, and may have started to fall" (World Bank 2002: 7).

11 "Contrary to the claims of the World Bank, the East Asian economies do not demonstrate any clear relationship between export-oriented industrialization and better income distribution" (Jomo 2006: 43).

12 Although they add to this the rider that "behind the average there is much variation". This same report states:

> A widespread anxiety is that global integration is leading to heightened inequality within countries. Usually, this is not the case. Most of the globalizing developing countries have seen only small changes in household inequality, and inequality has declined in such countries as the Philippines and Malaysia. ... As Vietnam has integrated it has had a large increase in per capita income and no significant change in inequality.
>
> (World Bank 2002: 4, 6)

13 This table excludes Brunei, Myanmar, Singapore and Timor Leste; data on quintile ratios for Singapore are not available.

14 Namely, Malays and other indigenous groups (such as the *orang asli*).

15 Brunei Darussalam is also high income but has achieved this on the basis of being oil rich, and on these grounds is discounted here.

16 The globalization of manufacturing has created a "treadmill of export-led growth [that] tends to preclude sustained improvements in the overall conditions and opportunities available to the majority of working people" in countries like Indonesia, Malaysia and Thailand (Hart-Landsberg and Burkett 1998: 103). Other scholars who have argued this include: Bell (1992 [on Thailand]); Mehmet and Tavakoli (2003 [on East Asia]); Knorringa and Pegler (2006 [in general]); Stiglitz (2012 [in general]); and Carmody (2013 [on India]).

17 "Our hypothesis is that market forces are real, but that they are shaped by political processes. Markets are shaped by laws, regulations, and institutions. Every law, every regulation, every institutional arrangement has distributive consequences ..." (Stiglitz 2012: 52).

References

ADB (2007). *Key indicators 2007: inequality in Asia.* Manila, Asian Development Bank.

ADB (2008). *Tackling Asia's inequality: creating opportunities for the poor.* Manila, Asian Development Bank.

ADB (2012). *Asian development outlook 2012: confronting rising inequality in Asia.* Manila, Asian Development Bank.

ADB (2013). *Key indicators for Asia and the Pacific 2013.* Manila, Asian Development Bank.

Alesina, A. and D. Rodrik (1994). "Distributive politics and economic growth." *The Quarterly Journal of Economics* 109(2): 465–490.

Ali, I. (2008). "Inequality in developing Asia." *Asian Development Review* 25(1/2): 15–21.

Ali, I. and H. H. Son (2007). "Measuring inclusive growth." *Asian Development Review* 24(1): 11–31.

Amann, E., N. Aslanidis, F. Nixson and B. Walters (2006). "Economic growth and poverty alleviation: a reconsideration of Dollar and Kraay." *European Journal of Development Research* 18(1): 22–44.

Asra, A. (2000). "Poverty and inequality in Indonesia." *Journal of the Asia Pacific Economy* 5(1–2): 91–111.

Bell, P. F. (1992). Gender and economic development in Thailand. *Gender and development in Southeast Asia.* P. v. Esterik and J. v. Esterik. Toronto, Canadian Council for Southeast Asian Studies: 61–81.

Beresford, M. (2008). "Doi Moi in review: the challenges of building market socialism in Vietnam." *Journal of Contemporary Asia* 38(2): 221–243.

Berg, A. G. B. and J. D. Ostry (2011). Inequality and unsustainable growth: two sides of the same coin? IMF Discussion Note. Washington DC, International Montary Fund.

Booth, A. (2000). "Poverty and inequality in the Soeharto era: an assessment." *Bulletin of Indonesian Economic Studies* 36(1): 73–104.

Carmody, P. (2013). "A global enclosure: the geo-logics of Indian agro-investments in Africa." *Capitalism Nature Socialism* 24(1): 84–103.

Davies, J. B., S. Sandström, A. B. Shorrocks and E. N. Wolff (2009). The level and distribution of global household wealth. NBER Working Paper Series, Working Paper 15508. Cambridge, MA, National Bureau of Economic Research.

DFID (2004) What is pro-poor growth and why do we need to know? Pro-Poor Growth Briefing Note 1, London: Department for International Development.

Dollar, D. and A. Kraay (2002). "Growth is good for the poor." *Journal of Economic Growth* 7(3): 195–225.

Economist, The (2013) "The poor: not always with us." *The Economist,* 1 June.

Eichengreen, B., K. Shin and D. Park (2011). When growing economies slow down: international evidence and implications for China. NBER Working Paper no. 16919. Cambridge, MA, National Bureau of Economic Research.

Eichengreen, B., K. Shin and D. Park (2013). Growth slowdowns redux: new evidence on the middle-income trap. NBER Working Paper no. 18673. Cambridge, MA, National Bureau of Economic Research.

Fajnzylber, P., D.Lederman and N. Loayza (2002). "Inequality and violent crime." *Journal of Law and Economics* 45(1): 1–39.

Gupta, A. (2012). *Red tape: bureaucracy, structural violence, and poverty in India.* Durham, NC, Duke University Press.

Hart-Landsberg, M. and P. Burkett (1998). "Contradictions of capitalist industrialization in East Asia: a critique of 'flying geese' theories of development." *Economic Geography* 74(2): 87–110.

Jomo, K. S. (2006). Growth with equity in East Asia? DESA Working Paper 33. New York, United Nations.

Kakwani, N., H. H. Son, S. K. Qureshi and G. M. Arif (2003). "Pro-poor growth: concepts and measurement with country case studies [with comments]." *The Pakistan Development Review* 42(4): 417–444.

Kanbur, R. and G. Rauniyar (2010). "Conceptualizing inclusive development: with applications to rural infrastructure and development assistance." *Journal of the Asia Pacific Economy* 15(4): 437–454.

Kefi, M. K. and H. Zouhaier (2012). "Inequality and economic growth." *Asian Economic and Financial Review* 2(8): 1013.

Knorringa, P. and L. E. E. Pegler (2006). "Globalisation, firm upgrading and impacts on labour." *Tijdschrift voor economische en sociale geografie* 97(5): 470–479.

Kraay, A. (2006). "When is growth pro-poor? Evidence from a panel of countries." *Journal of Development Economics* 80(1): 198–227.

Kramer, R. C. (2000). "Poverty, inequality, and youth violence." *Annals of the American Academy of Political and Social Science* 567: 123–139.

Krongkaew, M. and N. Kakwani (2003). "The growth–equity trade-off in modern economic development: the case of Thailand." *Journal of Asian Economics* 14: 735–757.

Kuhonta, E. M. (2011). *The institutional imperative: the politics of equitable development in Southeast Asia*. Stanford, CA, Stanford University Press.

Li, H. and H.-F. Zou (1998). "Income inequality is not harmful for growth: theory and evidence." *Review of Development Economics* 2: 318–334.

Lübker, M., G. Smith and J. Weeks (2002). "Growth and the poor: a comment on Dollar and Kraay." *Journal of International Development* 14(5): 555–571.

Maxwell, S. (1999). *The meaning and measurement of poverty. ODI poverty briefing.* London, Overseas Development Institute.

Mehmet, O. and A. Tavakoli (2003). "Does foreign direct investment cause a race to the bottom?" *Journal of the Asia Pacific Economy* 8(2): 133–156.

ODI (2008). Pro-poor growth and development: linking economic growth and poverty reduction. ODI Briefing Notes no. 33. London, Overseas Development Institute.

Ohno, K. (2009). "Avoiding the middle-income trap: renovating industrial policy formulation in Vietnam." *ASEAN Economic Bulletin* 26(1): 25–43.

Page, J. (2006). "Strategies for pro-poor growth: pro-poor, pro-growth or both?" *Journal of African Economies* 15(4): 510–542.

Ravallion, M. (2005). *Pro-poor growth: a primer.* Washington DC, Development Research Group, World Bank.

Ravallion, M. (2013). How long will it take to lift one billion people out of poverty? Policy Research Working Paper no. 6325. Washington DC, World Bank.

Sen, A. (1981). *Poverty and famines: an essay on entitlement and deprivation.* Oxford, Clarendon Press.

Sen, A. (1999). *Development as freedom.* New York, Alfred A. Knopf.

Shin, I. (2012). "Income inequality and economic growth." *Economic Modelling* 29(5): 2049–2057.

Son, H. H. and N. Kakwani (2008). "Global estimates of pro-poor growth." *World Development* 36(6): 1048–1066.

Stiglitz, J. (2012). *The price of inequality.* London, Allen Lane.

Tran, A.N. (2007). "Alternatives to the 'race to the bottom' in Vietnam: minimum wage strikes and their aftermath." *Labor Studies Journal* 32(4): 430–451.

Wade, R. H. (2004). "Is globalization reducing poverty and inequality?" *World Development* 32(4): 567–589.

Wan, G. and I. Sebastian (2011). *Poverty in Asia and the Pacific: an update.* Manila, Asian Development Bank.

Warr, P. (2005). "Pro-poor growth." *Asian-Pacific Economic Literature* 19(2): 1–17.

Warr, P. (2011). "A nation caught in the middle-income trap." *East Asia Forum* 3(4): 4–6.

Wilkinson, R. and K. E. Pickett (2009). "Income inequality and social dysfunction." *Annual Review of Sociology* 35(1): 493–511.

Wilkinson, R. and K. Pickett (2013). "Richard Wilkinson and Kate Pickett reply to three reviews of The Spirit Level: why equality is better for everyone." *Work, Employment & Society* 27(1): 175–177.

World Bank (1993). *The East Asian miracle: economic growth and public policy.* Washington DC, World Bank and Oxford University Press.

World Bank (2002). *Globalization, growth and poverty: building an inclusive world economy.* Washington DC, World Bank and Oxford University Press.

World Bank (2009). *World development report 2009: reshaping economic geography.* Washington DC, World Bank.

World Bank (2014). *Prosperity for all: ending extreme poverty.* Washington DC, World Bank Group, World Bank.

Yusuf, S. and K. Nabeshima (2009). *Tiger economies under threat: a comparative analysis of Malaysia's industrial prospects and policy options.* Washington DC, World Bank.

Zhuang, J., P. Vandenberg and Y. Huang (2012). *Growing beyond the low cost advantage: how the People's Republic of China can avoid the middle-income trap.* Manila, Asian Development Bank and the National School of Development.

3 The produced poor
Another world of poverty and development

[T]he transition narrative corresponds closely to a popular desire to leave behind the insecurities of subsistence production, and enjoy the fuller life that better food, housing, education and health care can offer. Yet the sad truth is that this desire is frustrated, especially for the poorest people, who are routinely dispossessed through the very processes that enable other people to prosper. Far too many of them cannot even access a living wage, because their labour is surplus to capital's requirements. Whose responsibility is it to attend to the welfare of surplus populations?

(Li 2010a: 87)

Introduction: placing the produced poor

It has already been remarked that, notwithstanding rapid growth, there are still many millions of poor people in developing Asia. This applies not just to less developed countries like the Lao PDR and Cambodia, but also Malaysia and, even, Singapore. In Chapter 1 it was noted that we can see these poor existing in four ways, as:

- the *residual poor* – those who have been 'left behind' in the wake of economic transformation;
- the *unequal poor* – those whose poverty is linked to the unequal distribution of growth and their 'falling behind' in relative terms;
- the *produced poor* – those whose poverty is linked to the very processes that have generated growth, or the 'immiserated' poor, who are highlighted in Tania Li's quote above;
- the *unreported poor* – those people who are poor but, for various reasons, are not counted as such – the 'invisible' poor.

This chapter focuses largely on the third of these four categories or populations of poor, the produced poor. Chapter 4 will pay attention to the final category, the invisible poor, although, as will become clear, these two categories not infrequently intersect. Furthermore, it is these two sets of poor who have tended to be overlooked in economic and policy-related analyses. The story of poverty reduction which has played such a prominent place in Asia's wider narrative of development success is one where the analytical stage is occupied by the first category of poor: the residual, or absolute poor. More latterly, the second category, the unequal poor, has become an increasing source of concern as was outlined in the previous chapter. But the third and fourth populations of poor, the produced and unreported poor, are often silent characters in this play, and are usually situated off-stage, out of sight. As Lawrence Lien, a Nominated Member of Parliament in Singapore has said: "As a society, we like to hide our problems and the marginalised. We need to stop hiding poverty" (Rigg 2013).

The reasons for this paradigmatic short-sightedness are often political. Many of these poor are politically marginal, or are constructed in such a way that they become so. The growing inequality mentioned in the previous chapter may also have played a role in pushing these poor out-of-sight, because such is the gap between rich and poor that decision-makers have lost the ability to grasp, even to imagine, what it is like to be poor. Finally, a large number of the unreported poor – addressed in the next chapter – are legal, licit and illegal migrant workers who, as non-nationals, are not recorded in the first place and, furthermore, are objects of little public (and therefore political) interest and concern.

Recording, ignoring or creating? An excursion into the poverty data

For many in government, poverty data record the poor. In that sense they are seen to reflect a certain reality of poverty. Kishore Mahbubani, Dean of the Lee Kuan Yew School of Public Policy at the National University of Singapore, has written about the 'eradication' of poverty in Singapore:

> There are no homeless, destitute or starving people in Singapore. *Poverty has been eradicated* …. Remarkably, the poorest five per cent of households have about the same levels of ownership of homes, television sets, refrigerators, telephones, washing machines and video recorders as the national average.
> (Mahbubani 2001, emphasis added)[1]

For Mahbubani, it would seem, the poverty challenge has been addressed in Singapore and is now something of only historical interest or as a lesson for other countries who might wish to emulate the city state.

But who and what governments and institutions count and, by association, who and what they do not count is based on a set of methodological decisions, some seemingly quite arbitrary but others carefully calibrated and calculated, often for political reasons and exigencies. Usually this is linked to where the poverty line is drawn – where the poverty cut-off point lies. Mahbubani's claim that there are no poor in Singapore, for example, is partly linked to the fact that Singapore has no poverty line and has proven reluctant to introduce one (Ng 2013; Asher and Nandy 2008).[2] Analysts are forced to use other measures to identify the poor and the socially excluded such as the monthly household income threshold of

S$1,500, which is the point at which financial assistance programmes come into play. Another approach is to take the Minimum Household Expenditure and multiply this by 1.25, which results in around 10 per cent of Singaporean households falling below this threshold. Or, third, simply taking the poor as those earning less than half the median income, as many richer countries do, which would amount to around 20–30 per cent of the population (Hassan 2013: 7). But even these approaches do not accurately reflect the number of poor residing in the country because migrant workers, many earning less than S$1,500 per month, are not included in such calculations and are ineligible for support.[3] They may not be Singaporeans, but their underclass status and relatively impoverished condition in the richest country in the world is nonetheless very real (Box 3.1).

Box 3.1 Wealth, poverty and inequality in Singapore

As the so-styled 'world's most successful economy', it might be imagined that, of all the countries of the region, Singapore is one where growth and development really have coincided in a positive fashion. And yet in September 2013 a seminar entitled "Building an inclusive society: understanding and empowering the poor in Singapore" attracted several hundred participants from academia, civil society, the media and government. Four statements highlight the paradox of Singapore's growth experience:

- In 2012 Singapore was counted as the wealthiest country in the world in terms of per capita income measured at purchasing power parity.[4]
- In 2012, Singapore was the most unequal of the OECD economies with an income gap after tax and transfers between the top and bottom deciles of 7.9.[5]
- Officially there are no poor in Singapore, because there is no poverty line.
- The stated mission of the People's Action Party, in power ever since independence, is "To build a fair and just society where the benefits of progress are spread widely to all".

Inequality is not only high, but increasing. Certainly this has been a feature of many countries over this century, but in Singapore the increase has been significantly greater. Between 1996 and 2012 the real wages of the top decile of the population increased from S$7,322 to S$10,718 per month; for the bottom decile they declined from S$793 to S$791. If this decile is broken down by occupational group the data are even more striking: in the decade between 1996 and 2006, the median monthly starting pay for cleaners and labourers *fell* from S$860 to S$600. This widening in inequality began at the turn of the century but accelerated from 2004. That year also marked the beginning of what became known as the 'growth at any/all costs' strategy. Indeed, the two are linked. The growth at all costs strategy justified putting in place policies that would push down the wages of the least well paid and, in particular, migrant workers and more generally lead to a casualization of work.

Singapore has a Social Protection Index (SPI) that is markedly low given the country's wealth.[6] Spending on social protection amounts to just 3.5 per cent of GDP; in Japan it is 19 per cent and for South Korea, 8 per cent (ADB 2013: 14–15). The closest Singapore comes to a poverty line is the Absolute Household Expenditure on Basic Needs (AHEBN). This amounts to around S$10 per person per day to meet all expenditure needs from housing and utilities to food, transport, health and education.

From this we can arrive at a fifth statement to add to the Singapore growth/development paradox:

- Singapore may statistically have no poverty but ethnographically there are many thousands of poor people.

In other countries of the region, the question is not whether, but where to draw the poverty line. Using data from Malaysia's 2004/05 Household Expenditure Survey, Mok *et al.* (2013: 102) arrive at four very different estimates of poverty in Malaysia (Figure 3.1), giving headcount rates across the country that vary by a factor of three, from 7.4 per cent to 22.0 per cent. These marked differences are linked to whether poverty is measured on the basis of income or consumption (the latter leads to generally higher poverty rates), which percentile groups are used as reference points (in this case, the tenth or twentieth percentiles), and

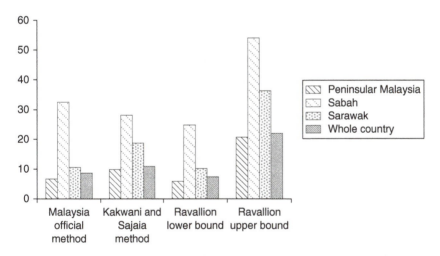

Figure 3.1 Four estimations of poverty in Malaysia, 2004/05 (head count poverty, %)

Notes
1 data are taken from the 2004/05 Household Expenditure Survey (HES).
2 Ravallion's lower bound estimation of poverty is the food poverty line, with no allowance made for non-food expenditure; this is close to the official definition of 'hard core' poverty in Malaysia (Begum *et al.* 2011). The upper bound estimation also includes an allowance for non-food expenditure and this is based on those households whose food expenditure just meets the food poverty line.

Source: data extracted from Mok *et al.* 2013.

what methods are employed to estimate the poverty line. Regarding the latter, Malaysia's definition of the 'hard core' poor makes no allowance for non-food expenditure, and it is on this basis that Hatta and Ali (2013: 53) can claim, rather like Mahbubani in Singapore, that "Malaysia can effectively declare victory in its fight against poverty", with hard core poverty in 2009 standing at just 0.9 per cent.[7] As soon, however, as allowance is made for non-food expenditures, the poor quickly begin to emerge from the statistical miasma.

Not only does the drawing (or not drawing) of the poverty line create a certain reality of poverty which is determined by a set of decisions made by 'experts' often guided by political exigencies but, and more importantly, it changes the *texture* of poverty as well as the numbers of poor. There is a gulf between the measurement of poverty (which is a technical challenge) and the condition of the poor (which is an experience) (Harriss-White 2006: 1241). As Hilgers writes:

> [T]he production of such abstract data performs reality and has major economic and social consequences. ... This process plays a major role in the ways in which societies are perceived and, as a corollary, in the ways in which people and institutions will act on and within a society.
>
> (2013: 81)

This highlights the important questions of what (or who) governments count, and what (or who) governments do not count and the logics that underpin these calculations. Returning to the case of Singapore, the fact that there is no poverty line is a largely political decision but one which has significant implications for policy, institutional action and public perception.

It is suggested here that if we begin to unearth and examine the conditions of the produced poor and, in the next chapter the unreported poor, then – and in a profound and not just an incidental way – another world of poverty comes into view and, as a result, another world of development.

The produced poor

A general point made in the opening chapter of this book is that market integration – or capitalism – harms as well as helps people. Of course, that has been said in a rhetorical or discursive sense for many years. Here I mean it in a real sense: capitalist relations and processes create poor people. As Harriss-White writes:

> [P]overty cannot be eradicated; on the contrary poverty is continually being created and recreated under the institutions of capitalism. ... States may... seek to mitigate poverty, but in order to do so effectively the processes which create poverty must be openly understood and the – sometimes perverse – consequences of the various mitigating strategies on these poverty-creating processes must be recognised.
>
> (2006: 1241)

For this argument to have credibility, however, and not just to appear to be political posturing or arising from ideological partiality, it needs to be grounded in examples that demonstrate the selectively harmful effects of the very processes and policies that have also produced prosperity.[8] Table 3.1 provides such an inventory. Clearly this table encompasses a wide range of effects, but they all emerge from the manner of the operation of the market economy and its intersection with the state, state policies, society and everyday living. There are clear connections between the three processes, but they are distinguished one from the other in the context of this chapter as follows:

1 *dispossession* – the taking, sometimes by force, of the resources (especially land) of the poor;
2 *displacement* – the removal of people, often against their will, from their spaces of living, work and social interaction (e.g. through resettlement);
3 *casualization* (or *precarization*) – the restructuring of modes of work into forms that lack security of employment and income and the various protections that come with formal, secure employment.

In those instances where these problems become so self-evident and visible that they can no longer be ignored, states and their supporters tend to employ four explanatory or justifying devices. They claim:

1 'This is beyond our control – it arises from the unavoidable forces of globalization'.
2 'This is a cost that has to be borne, and the benefits (for the many) far outweigh the costs (to the few)'; or 'it is for the common good'.
3 'Programmes to ameliorate these harmful effects have been put in place'.
4 'This is just a few agitators at work and does not reflect the majority view'.

In the next chapter, attention is paid to two other, associated processes, namely:

1 *exclusion* (or *social exclusion*) – the marginalizing processes that prevent individuals or groups from participating fully in social and economic life;
2 *disempowerment* – the processes that lead to a reduction in the agency, autonomy, and 'power' of groups or individuals to control and shape their lives. This is also addressed in Chapter 7.

With such a range of possible case studies there is a danger of simply lining them up, with the hope that sheer weight of numbers and breadth of effects will convince. The approach here, however, will be to take one or two examples relating to the five processes identified in Table 3.1 (denoted in italics), explore these in some detail, and then draw together how each, individually and then collectively, can be seen to be inextricably linked to the policies and practices of neoliberal development, or the market imperative.

Table 3.1 An inventory of capitalism's harmful effects

Processes	Examples	Sources
Dispossession	*Accumulation by dispossession in Sulawesi*	Li (2002, 2010a, 2010b, 2012)
	Land grabbing in the Lao PDR	Hall *et al.* (2011); Kenney-Lazar (2012); La-orngplew (2012); Barney (2007; 2009); Andriesse and Anouxay Phommalath (2012); Laungaramsri (2012)
	Dispossession of land for Special Economic Zones and industrial estates	Levien (2013)
	'Everyday' or 'intimate' dispossession of coconut planation land in Davao Oriental, the Philippines	Adam (2013)
	Dispossession of lands in the colonial economies of Malaya, Vietnam, the Dutch East Indies and the Philippines to make room for large-scale estate crop production	Laungaramsri (2012); Cleary (2003)
	Dispossession of lands in Indonesia for oil palm	See Chapter 7
Displacement	*Displacement of plantation workers to make way for Putrajaya, Malaysia*	Bunnell (2002, 2004); Bunnell *et al.* (2010)
	Resettlement of minority hill peoples in the Lao PDR	Hall *et al.* (2011: 46-50); Rigg (2005); Evrard and Goudineau (2004); Baird and Shoemaker (2007); Ducourtieux *et al.* (2005); High *et al.* (2009); Vandergeest (2003) Sims (2013)
	Households displaced by urban development in Luang Prabang, Lao PDR	Viratkapan and Perera (2006)
	Slum evictions in Bangkok, Thailand	Paling (2012); Springer (2013); Un and So (2011);
	Land grabbing and evictions in Phnom Penh, Cambodia	LICADHO (2009); Brickell (2014) Harms (2014)
	Clearing 'wastelands' in Vietnam's urban centres	
Casualization and precarity	Precarity in Asia	Hewison and Kalleberg (2013); papers in *American Behavioral Scientist* (57[3 and 4] 2013)
	Precarity and informalization in Indonesia and Vietnam	Arnold (2013); Cling *et al.* (2011); Tran (2011)
	Casualization of taxi driving in Bangkok, Thailand	Hickey (2013)

Note: examples in *italics* are explored in greater detail in the text of this chapter.

Dispossession

Work on dispossession often begins with Harvey's *The new imperialism* (2003) and his development of the notion of 'accumulation by dispossession', or ABD. Harvey takes Marx's primitive accumulation which provides the pre-conditions for the transition to capitalism (and capitalist accumulation), and shows how the same set of processes and predatory practices – land grabbing, the extension of private property rights, the commodification of labour – continue to underpin expropriations under conditions of advanced capitalism. For Levien (2013), Harvey's economic focus is too restrictive and he widens ABD to also include the state logics that drive the process, thus leading him to write of 'regimes of dispossession':

> A regime of dispossession is thus a socially and historically specific constellation of political, economic and ideological forces that underpin a relatively consistent pattern of dispossession. It involves (typically) a state that is willing to coercively expropriate resources from one class for another for a set of purposes that it seeks to legitimize through claims to the public good.
> (2013: 402)[9]

There has been debate over whether the experiences of the countries of East and Southeast Asia actually provide evidence, not of accumulation by dispossession (ABD) but, rather, accumulation *without* dispossession (AWD) (Box 3.2). This alternative view is rooted in the fact that industrialization in East and some countries of Southeast Asia has generally occurred while populations have retained access to their land. A second quite distinctive feature of the debate on ABD (or AWD) as it has evolved in the Southeast Asian context is the degree to which small producers are enthusiastic participants in the process (Hall 2012). This has led scholars of the region to write of "enclosure from below", "dispossession from below" (Li 2010a, 2010b) or "intimate dispossession" (Adam 2013), highlighting the point that poor villagers are both dispossessed and dispossess. It is this puzzle which threads its way through Tania Murray Li's work on upland Sulawesi.

Box 3.2 **Accumulation *by* dispossession or accumulation *without* dispossession? The Asian debate**

It has been suggested that dispossession has more resonance and explanatory purchase in the context of Africa and Latin America than it does in Asia. As Hart (2002, 2006) has explored, the situation in the East Asian first-generation newly industrialized countries and more latterly in the Asian late developers such as Vietnam and, most notably, China has not been one of dispossession: these countries have had – and maintained during rapid industrialization – relatively egalitarian land ownership profiles. Industrial accumulation in East and Southeast Asia has not occurred through ABD

(Continued)

(Continued)

but by accumulation *without* dispossession or AWD (Hart 2006; and see Arrighi *et al.* 2010; Hall 2012). AWD has been based on the continuing role of small farms in releasing labour power for industrialization, cross-subsidizing capitalist growth, reworking gender and generational relations to free young men and, especially, young women, to work in the factory sites of the global economy. To be sure, there is – and was under colonial regimes – pernicious landlessness and dispossession in East and Southeast Asia. The establishment of large-scale estates in the 'empty' lands of Vietnam, Malaya, the Philippines and the Dutch East Indies (Indonesia) led to dispossession on a very large scale indeed. Nonetheless, the key to understanding accumulation in Asia is not through how producers (peasants) have been separated from their means of production (land), but how their *continuing* connections permit accumulation (Glassman 2006: 615).

Li (2002, 2007, 2010a, 2010b, 2014) began her work in the hills of Lauje in Sulawesi in 1990. Shortly thereafter, farmers began to experiment with cocoa. The crop entered an agrarian context where land was a collective, lineage resource and where swiddening predominated. Cocoa, as a tree crop, replaced all swidden fields and a process of enclosure, privatization, commoditization and unequal accumulation led to the creation, in a remarkably short time, of a class of landless hill farmer. While there was turbulence and a degree of randomness in the process, generally co-heirs were squeezed out and senior men benefited, while women and younger men lost out. Then, in a second stage of this agrarian transformation, more successful farmers accumulated land from the less successful. Notions of capitalism being violently inserted into Lauje space do not ring true in the case that Li describes; but dispossession did occur, capitalist relations were at the centre of events, and ultimately it led to the unravelling of subsistence security for many in the Lauje hills. In her book *Land's end,* Li writes:

> In these highlands ... capitalist relations emerged by stealth. No rapacious agribusiness corporations grabbed land from highlanders or obliged them to plant cacao. No government department evicted them. Nor was there a misguided development scheme that disrupted their old ways.
>
> (2014: 9)

As Hall says in general terms and which is borne out in Li's study from Sulawesi, we need "to determine the implications of specifically capitalist social relations in this specific situation at this specific time", adding that to "assume that capital and the state relentlessly push primitive accumulation while 'we' resist it will not get one very far; indeed, it may set one off in the wrong direction" (Hall 2012: 1205).

Li's work in Sulawesi provides an insight into everyday processes of dispossession, showing how it may be enacted from below by smallholders who can become either victims or beneficiaries. Debates on 'land grabbing' (Hall 2013: 95–105; Kugelman and Levenstein 2009), or the global enclosure movement as it is also called, provide, however, a rather less ambiguous portrait of the effects of the insertion of capitalist relations into rural contexts.

Laos, along with Myanmar, Cambodia and parts of Indonesia, is often paraded as a land resource frontier – a place where there are 'empty' lands ready to be exploited and, sometimes, to be settled. The logic of the global enclosure movement is that there are large expanses of unpopulated and under-used land in these countries, and that these spaces can be drawn into market relations with few untoward effects. At a regional level, the land frontier continues to expand in Southeast Asia (Hall 2009; De Koninck *et al.* 2011) and much of this has been driven by boom crops, a process which

> embodies a series of characteristics that the WDR [the World Bank's *2008 World Development Report*] consistently praises as highly positive: the production of high-value crops, intensified land use, integration into world markets and commodity chains, and the involvement of agribusiness.
>
> (Hall 2009: 605)

Scholars have noted the contradiction between the growth-, export- and income-generating effects of such agricultural developments on the one hand, and their negative impacts on environment, land tenure security and rural poverty on the other (see Hall 2009; McMichael 2009; Akram-Lodhi 2008). The impetus and general support that agribusiness, governments and multilateral agencies have given to the expansion of high value, export crops in frontier areas of Southeast Asia (and elsewhere) raises questions about the beneficiaries of such developments. Regarding the expansion of oil palm in Sabah, Bernard and Bissonnette write that "the current large-scale land conversion to oil palm plantations can hardly be legitimized by socio-economic development aims" (2011: 145). Certainly, agriculture is being developed; but is this agriculture *for development*, the sub-title of the World Bank's (2007) influential report or, rather, agriculture *for economic expansion*? The expansion of oil palm and its effects is returned to in greater detail in Chapter 7.

Of the countries of Southeast Asia, it is possibly the Lao PDR where debates over the developmental effects of large-scale land enclosure or land grabbing have been most vociferous. Field studies in Laos by scholars such as Barney (2007, 2009), Baird (2014), Kenney-Lazar (2012), Andriesse and Anouxay Phommalath (2012), La-orngplew (2012) and Laungaramsri (2012) reveal common threads in the way that such frontier spaces and people are characterized: that land is unused or inefficiently used; that upland people are 'backward' and poor because of their adherence to traditional livelihoods; that their style of living does not contribute to national development; and that the best means to develop both the people and the land resource is through marketization.[10] The ADB and the Lao government, furthermore, have been instrumental in this characterization of large areas of the country as 'empty' and 'undeveloped', thus creating a frontier space – a fictive frontier – that capital can exploit through the transfer of land in the form of land-scale land concessions (Delang *et al.* 2013; Barney 2009).[11] It has been variously suggested that between 2 and 3.5 million hectares of land or up to 15 per cent of the country's total land area are under agri-business land concessions (see Kenney-Lazar 2012: 1023) comprising contracts with over 1,000 companies, some 40 per cent of which are foreign-owned (Laungaramsri 2012: 464) (Figure 3.2).[12]

The literature on land enclosure in the Lao PDR tends to focus on three key development problematics: first, on the assumption that the land being enclosed or grabbed is unsettled and unused; second on the means by which land is enclosed; and third, on the livelihood effects of the process. The literature is recent but – and this is notable – is almost uniformly critical, albeit to varying degrees.

The Lao PDR may be thinly populated but even the uplands are patently not empty of people. Frontier capitalism, however, is founded on the operational assumption that these lands are underused even if they are not unpopulated, this in turn being linked to the 'primitive' livelihood systems that predominate. The subtle morphing of unpopulated into underused, and then underused into under-productive, often underpinned by notions of backwardness, are all too clear. Drawing on her work on rubber concessions in southern Laos, Laungaramsri writes that the "making of the frontier reflects the manipulative imagery and

Figure 3.2 Rubber concessions in northern Laos (photo: Anna-Klara Lindeborg [permission granted])

construction of a subsistence economy in the uplands that is instrumental to resource expropriation by transnational capitalism" (2012: 477). It has been expedient for those agencies and corporations seeking to enclose land so that it can be made available for capital to operate in areas where upland peoples lack secure tenure, have traditionally been shifting cultivators and, even better, where they are – as in the Lao case – minority groups who lack power.

Given that 'empty' lands are rarely empty, to make space available for capital requires clearing such land of people. As Susanna Hecht says, "forests without people are an invitation to plunder" (personal communication, CIFOR workshop, October 2013). This underpins the logic of dispossession: only by dispossessing, uprooting and resettling people can land be possessed by capital. There is a corollary effect to 'turning land into capital' when that land is occupied; and that is to turn 'people into labour':

> [T]he system of issuing large-scale economic land concessions to foreign investors from other Asian countries such as Vietnam, China, Thailand and others … not only involves the expropriation and enclosure of land and resources … but also driving semi-subsistence farmers into labour markets.
>
> (Baird 2011: 12)

For, having uprooted people from their traditional lands, settling them in villagers and thereby connecting them – in a physical sense – to the mainstream, these settlers can then be drawn into market relations. Only in this way can minority peoples, partially separate and separated from the market, contribute to the national development project. We therefore see in the Lao PDR, and also in upland Vietnam, in Malaysian and Indonesian Borneo, in Cambodia, and in West Papua both a land and a labour process in train:

Land effects:	Depopulation $\rightarrow$ Expropriation $\rightarrow$ Enclosure $\rightarrow$ Capitalization
Labour effects:	Displacement $\rightarrow$ Resettlement $\rightarrow$ Incorporation $\rightarrow$ Proletarianization

In Baird's (2011) study he describes how minority groups in Banchieng in southern Laos' Champasak province have been displaced to make way for large-scale rubber concessions. These indigenous ethnic peoples – Jrou, Souay, Brou and Brao – are then hired back as casual wage labour on their former lands. New forms of labour discipline are imposed and those who do not adhere to these regimens of work are sacked. Precarity is the outcome (see p. 70 this volume).

The effects of land enclosure have not always been inimical to the interests of upland dwellers in Laos. That said, the frequency with which studies show that the livelihoods of the poor are compromised by the process is striking. Delang *et al.*'s (2013) study of the Bolaven Plateau, for example, found that those forced to relocate were provided with insufficient compensation for their loss of land and crops, and that any new land allocated was either of poorer quality or already settled. This is a common refrain for most resettlement schemes, in Laos and beyond. Delang *et al.* conclude by arguing that "the people living on the Bolaven Plateau are at best bypassed by the benefits of the foreign investment pouring into the region, and at worst the victims of such investment" (2013: 160).

Of course, the process, just as in the Lauje uplands of Sulawesi, is not a simple story of dispossession of the weak by the strong. Uplanders have often enthusiastically embraced the new economic forms which have colonized the hills of Laos; they have been far from powerless bystanders, but often active participants (Barney 2009: 153–156; La-orngplew 2012). Social differentiation in the uplands has been such that some individuals and even some villages have evidently benefitted in material terms and not infrequently in other ways too (Lindeborg 2012).[13] The Lao government, at both local and national levels, has also not been impervious to the numerous studies and reports as to the negative effects of land concessions on livelihoods and the often cavalier way they have been instituted (see Delang *et al.* 2013). In some instances, however, rural producers have simply been pushed to the margins, left to eke out a living on smaller plots with attendant problems of land degradation, declining yields and a livelihood squeeze, sometimes resulting in a more profound displacement from the land (Lestrelin 2010; Chapter 6 provides a more detailed discussion of the operation of the environment–development nexus in Laos, see page 180).

This last point links the discussion here with the next section on displacement and a later discussion on precarity. One narrative in this anti-developmental story is of rural dispossession designed so that land can be more efficiently and productively used, leading to the erosion of rural livelihoods and increases in the poverty and vulnerability of upland minorities. A second narrative, however, pays attention to the reshaping and redeployment of unproductive people as labour in the wider national development project and, therefore, national interest.

Displacement

Development not infrequently involves displacement, if not dispossession. This may be displacement from land or from established ways of living, and it is often done in the name of development. This is the point that Escobar makes when he writes that "Over the first development decades, few took notice that the level of violence entailed by development was not secondary and temporary but actually long lasting and structural ... this violence is not only endemic but constitutive of development" (2004: 16; and see Sargeson 2013). We can see the articulation of development with displacement in the case of Malaysia's new capital, Putrajaya.

Planning for Putrajaya began in 1993 when 4,400 hectares were ear-marked for development. In a manner resonant of capitalism's creation of the Lao resource frontier (see above), this was portrayed as a 'greenfield project' but in fact encompassed four plantation estates supporting 2,400 people of which the largest was Perang Besar with 177 resident families made up of some 1,500 people (Bunnell 2002: 282). The estate was run down as plans for Putrajaya progressed and Perang

Besar was finally closed in 1995, leaving its workers and their families without shelter and without employment. As Bunnell explains, the placing of these Tamil ('Indian') workers at the margins of the Malaysian political economy can be traced back to British colonial policies and practices of racial segregation and the construction of a colonial economy fractured according to racial group (Malay, Chinese, Indian, Other). "Nonetheless", he writes,

> Putrajaya and the social and spatial exclusion associated with it *are* bound up with the physical and discursive construction of specifically high-tech futures [which are] legitimised by authoritative discourses of technology and globalisation that posit 'high-tech' as a national necessity.
>
> (Bunnell 2002: 284, emphasis in orginal)

Bunnell later followed up these relocated Tamil plantation workers to their new flats in four-storey blocks in Dengkil's Taman Permata, on the southern outskirts of Putrajaya. But while Putrajaya and its sister city Cyberjaya are meant to showcase Malaysia's bright present and even brighter future, for the Tamil population uprooted from the empty, 'greenfield' site to make way for this high-tech city their engagement has been as cheap labour, pruning bushes, cutting lawns and watering fringes. Bunnell *et al.* (2010: 1267), through interviews, piece together the views of these Malaysians living at the edge of Wawasan (Vision) 2020: "we live like refugees because we are Tamils"; "nothing is possible for Indians in Malaysia – everything is possible for Malays"; we have been "discarded like rubbish".

In Malaysia such displacements often taken on a racial tone, because of the embedded, racialized nature of the Malaysian political economy (see p. 39 this volume). If the Tamils had been Malays, or so the argument goes, their treatment would have been very different: "The arbitrariness of the law … [reveals] … the violence inherent in juridical notions of citizen subject grounded in ethnic privilege" (Bunnell *et al.* 2010: 1270). But the story cannot be entirely understood through the lens of ethnic privilege. Indian knowledge workers and entrepreneurs are a central part of the Putra/Cyberjaya story and, at the same time, there are also many Malays who have found themselves displaced by development. Furthermore, these relocated Tamils *have* found work in the new cities; it is just that it is low skilled, low paid and non-unionized. Even a Cybercity, after all, needs its cleaners and gardeners.

Land grabbing and displacement in urban contexts

Most work on land grabbing and displacement has a rural and agricultural tinge. Clearly, hundreds of thousands of hectares of land have been grabbed, enclosed and converted to tree crops such as rubber and oil palm (see p. 213) in Southeast Asia. The sheer areas involved demand our attention. Land grabbing, however, also occurs in urban contexts and the numbers of people affected, if not the areas of land, can indeed be very large (see Table 3.1 for examples).

Among Southeast Asia's urban centres, Phnom Penh, arguably, reveals the most potent intersection of social and economic inequalities, opaque legalities and political ambiguities. In order to create a modern capital comprising rudiments of the world (if not global) city, thousands of poor have been evicted from informal settlements close to Phnom Penh's core, and displaced to peri-urban sites which were, until very recently, rural and agricultural. In 1997, the proportion of the urban poor living in the city centre as opposed to outer districts was around 50/50; in 2009 the balance was 30/70 (Percival and Waley 2012: 2880). It has been calculated that between 1990 and 2009, some 133,000 people, or 10 per cent of the city's population, were evicted from the centre of Phnom Penh, most of these low-income families (LICADHO 2009: 1).

Much of this has been forcible displacement (Paling 2012: 2892). The motivation for eviction has partly been due to a desire on the part of the city planners to create a certain type of city; the urban poor, previously so visibly a part of the urban fabric, are not part of this vision and have been displaced from the centre to the peripheries, hidden from view at the margins of the city along with thousands of migrant factory workers. Also at work, however, are simple economics and the logics of capital accumulation. As Cambodia has recovered from its past and the economy has expanded, so urban land prices have risen. Poor residents in Phnom Penh have, therefore, become targets for dispossession as the value of the land on which they reside – but over which they have disputed or tenuous formal rights – has escalated.

Scholars and activists have tended to interpret the operation of the legal framework for land in Phnom Penh in two, quite different, ways. On the one hand, there are some (e.g. Un and So 2011) who highlight the weaknesses and limitations of land law and land titling. This creates a legislative space which the rich and connected can exploit to take control of land, displacing the poor, weak and unconnected in the process. Un and So argue that "inadequate land titling and Land Laws, compounded by the absence of a functioning land management institution following the 1989 land reform, set the stage for [the] intensification of land conflicts" (2011: 307–8). The explanation here focuses on the *absence* of a clear legal framework and, in the process, highlights the need for a strengthening of legislation and, importantly, an increase in the state's capacity to implement and oversee the legislation. It is Cambodia's weak political and civil society which permits such urban land grabbing and eviction.

An alternative explanation is provided by Springer (2013) who highlights the way in which the 2001 Land Law and associated titling are being used to evict those who lack title to the land their occupy and therefore cannot clearly demonstrate ownership. Here land conflicts are seen to lie not in the absence of land laws, but in their *strengthening*. Traditionally, even in urban contexts, people claimed usufruct rights to land, based on occupation and use and confirmed and recognized through community agreement. The legalization and formalization of land ownership has exposed people who occupy land on the basis of such traditional rights to eviction: "Evictees have virtually no recourse, as their 'ownership' claims are not reflected in official documentation or legal entitlement but in traditional understandings relating to occupation, community consensus, and actual use" (Springer 2013: 610).[14]

The exposure of the poor and weak to eviction in this manner is intimately bound up in the emergence and intensification of capitalist relations in Cambodia and the wider neoliberal turn in Cambodia and more generally (see Brickell 2014 for a paper on the 'intimate politics' of eviction in Phnom Penh). Land titling has been a key policy thrust across the poorer world, supported by the World Bank and popularized most famously through the work of De Soto (2000; and see Hall 2013: 114–125).[15] The justification for land titling lies in a desire for justice, founded on the premise that secure ownership rights will deliver security to smallholders, enable them to gain access to formal finance, and encourage them to invest in their land. Proponents of land titling do not blindly see it applying in all cases – it is seen to work best where land is *de facto* private property but rights are not formalized. It then becomes a means of protecting the poor, along the lines suggested by Un and So (2011). But if there are failures or gaps in governance such formalization may harm rather than help the poor, as Springer (2013) argues. A 2009 report of Cambodian League for the Promotion and Defense of Human Rights (LICADHO) sets out the governance failures that create such an anti-development space:

> The Cambodian military continues to be involved in evictions, in contravention of the law, as well as heavily implicated in land grabbing for their own benefit. The Cambodian courts continue to act on behalf of rich and powerful interests, ignoring the evidence, the Land Law and other relevant legislation, enforcing eviction where ownership remains undecided and imprisoning those who dare to protest. And to underline the fact that these evictions are really about grabbing valuable land – rather than actual development – many sites from which people have been evicted in recent years remain largely untouched by their new owners. The government, meanwhile, says there is no problem.
>
> (LICADHO 2009: 2)

A distinction is made in the literature between 'access' (see Ribot and Peluso 2003) and 'property' (see Sikor and Lund 2009). It is possible for individuals to have access to land (for example), and to derive benefit from that access, without necessarily having property rights to it. At the same time, it is occasionally true that individuals have property rights but are denied full access.[16] What links the two is legitimization, which is often seen as politico-legal in nature but in many traditional contexts is socio-cultural. Understanding what has happened in Phnom Penh, and also in other instances of land grabbing and eviction/displacement, is linked to the way that the nature of the legitimation process has changed. From being rooted in customary practice – which will, of course, have its own exclusions and violences (against women, female-headed households, ethnic minorities, the unmarried …) – legitimization becomes institutionalized in new ways, through legal codes, for instance. This process of legitimization requires that we pay attention to the architectures of power.

Casualization, informalization and precarity[17]

> Members of [Bangkok's] urban lower class face precarious housing and work situations …. Their employment is unstable, and they constantly face the threat of eviction … Thailand's social security arrangements are not geared to deal with the urban lower class … if these workers become unable to work due to injury or illness, they experience a sudden loss of income.
>
> (Endo 2014: 1)

The Tamil estate workers of Perang Besar, discussed in Bunnell's study of Malaysia (Bunnell 2002; Bunnell *et al.* 2010), were not only physically displaced, they also found themselves in a new, even less secure, employment context. The casualization – or sometimes 'flexibilization' and, more recently, 'precarity' – of work is seen to be one of the defining features of late capitalism as countries are forced to compete with each other for mobile capital.[18] This competition has led to the progressive dismantling of employment which used to be progressing, or so it seemed, towards (more) permanent, formal, unionized and pensioned working patterns. Instead, work has increasingly become fixed-term or part-time, non-formal, non-unionized, casual and unregulated. It has become, in short, precarious, with few benefits and protections leading to the creation of a new class, the 'precariat'.[19]

The terms 'precarity' and 'precariat' are linked most obviously to the work of Guy Standing and, in particular, his book *The precariat: the new dangerous class* (2011). The term 'precarity' links the adjective 'precarious' with the proletariat and, in Standing's (2011, 2013, 2014) view, is a class "in the making". Globalization is said to have fractured traditional class structures and led to the emergence of a new class, distinct from the old working class. For Standing, the precariat

> consists of people who have minimal trust relationships with capital or the state, making it quite unlike the salariat. And it has none of the social contract relationships of the proletariat, whereby labour securities were provided in exchange for subordination and contingent loyalty, the unwritten deal underpinning welfare states.
>
> (2013: 2)

The invention of this new precariat class has not been without its critics, however. Munck (2013), for example, finds that while it might capture some of the vulnerabilities and insecurities associated with emerging working patterns and practices in the global North, it has little traction when it comes to understanding work in the global South where ideas of marginality, informalization and social exclusion are more apposite. It is seen to be Eurocentric, particularly in so far as it misconstrues the nature of class-making in the global South with its focus on the decline of Fordism and the welfare state. It is also, he claims, politically problematic.

These criticisms do warn against the uncritical use of the term in contexts such as Southeast Asia. That said, it is regarded as valuable in terms of the discussion in this chapter for three reasons. First, and in contradistinction to the criticisms noted above, it permits us to think differently about class-making in the global South. Globalization is leading to a multiplicity of proletarian forms, one of which (and it may or may not be distinct) is the precariat. Second, it highlights the way in which labour incorporation processes in the global South are forging new forms of vulnerability, allowing us to connect work on accumulation by/without dispossession (see p. 61) with notions of precarity. And third, it allows us to view improverishment in rural areas and farming with insecurity in urban areas and industry. We can, as it were, follow the money and the people from the uplands of mainland Southeast Asia to the factories of Vientiane and Phnom Penh.

There is a fourth valuable attribute of the precarity debate: it helps us to understand the puzzle of the growing gap between wealth and well-being in the fast-growing economies of Southeast Asia. Standing writes:

> A feature of the precariat is not the level of money wages or income earned at any particular moment but the lack of community support in times of need, lack of assured enterprise or state benefits, and lack of private benefits to supplement money earnings.
>
> (2013: 5)

It is these factors, not income or prosperity *per se*, which are important when it comes to understanding why populations that are richer in income terms – which they undoubtedly are across the Southeast Asian region – can, at the same time, be more vulnerable. Furthermore, the emergence of such work as normal is intimately tied to the nature of global market integration with its emphasis on flexible working. The outcome is that economic growth has often not translated into security; indeed, quite the reverse (Box 3.3). Working-class exploitation has increasingly become a "privilege rather than a curse" (Arnold and Bongiovi 2013: 290).

Box 3.3 The precarious business of taxi driving in Bangkok

In mid-1992, the taxi industry in Bangkok was liberalized and availability of taxis went from famine to feast. The reforms lifted the quota on the number of taxis on Bangkok's roads, effectively allowing the market to determine the balance between supply and demand. Shortly before liberalization the cost of getting a taxi on the road in Bangkok was around 600,000 baht or US$24,000; a few months later it was 2,000 baht or US$80. Between 1992 and 1993 the number of new taxis registered in Bangkok more than tripled from 5,906 to 19,468.

(Continued)

(Continued)

The large majority of taxi drivers are Thai male migrants, many of these originating from the poor Northeast. This is a continuation of a pattern that can be traced back to the 1970s and 1980s when *tuk-tuks* (motorized three-wheeler taxis) dominated and, earlier still, to a period when *saamlors* (pedicabs) were the main means of public, short-distance travel around the city.

Hickey (2013) argues that this process of (neo)-liberalization has resituated risk from the taxi companies to taxi drivers. To make a living in a newly hyper-competitive market required that drivers work significantly longer hours. She writes:

> [T]he structural intensification of risk for drivers accomplished through the deregulation of the taxi supply was accompanied by a parallel 'down-streaming' of accountability, and the discursive relocation of blame for failure away from the internal logic of the system and directly onto the groups and individuals who do not, or cannot, successfully compete in the new arena.
>
> (2013: 10)

Taxi driving in Bangkok has always been casual. Hickey's point, however, is that the pre-1992 quota system created a degree of security. The reforms, as she puts it, made it easier to become a taxi driver, but harder to be one (2013: 9).

The *2013/14 Global competitiveness report* published by the World Economic Forum (WEF) sets out the logic that shapes a globally competitive, flexible labour force. This comes under the "Seventh pillar: labour market efficiency":

> The efficiency and flexibility of the labor market are critical for ensuring that workers are allocated to their most effective use in the economy and provided with incentives to give their best effort in their jobs. *Labor markets must therefore have the flexibility to shift workers from one economic activity to another rapidly and at low cost, and to allow for wage fluctuations without much social disruption.*
>
> (Schwab and Sala-i-Martín 2013: 6–7, emphases added)[20]

A significant but frequently overlooked character of this trend towards increasing precarity is that it reverses the direction that employment conditions took through much of the twentieth century, where increasing formalization of work was normal and, furthermore, was expected to advance as countries advanced. The informal economy, 'discovered' in Kenya by the International Labour Organisation (ILO) in 1972, was thought to be a product and a reflection of underdevelopment, and thus would gradually disappear as development proceeded. The Kenya report coined the term 'informal sector' and described the sector and its role and significance in the following terms:

> The problem with employment is that the statistics are incomplete, ... omitting a range of wage earners and self-employed persons, male as well as female, in what we term 'the informal sector'. ... from the vantage point of central Nairobi, with its gleaming skyscrapers, the dwellings and commercial structures of the informal sector look indeed like hovels. For observers surrounded by imported steel, glass and concrete, it requires a leap of the imagination and considerable openness of mind to perceive the informal sector as a sector of thriving economic activity...
>
> (Quoted in Bangasser 2000: 9)

The puzzle is that in many countries of Asia, while labour legislation has become more comprehensive in scope, the actual experience of work has become less secure. A process of informalization has occurred in the context of modernization and development. Chang (2011) calls this the informalization of the formal sector. "Contrary to many expectations", Chang writes, "that growing national wealth or poverty reduction could resolve the problem of the growing informal sector in developing countries, the bigger the economy grew, the bigger became the population that came to work informally" (Chang 2009: 165). In some cases, the hazards and health risks of work as well as its insecurity have also increased (Hewison and Kalleberg 2013). The ILO now no longer writes about the informal 'sector' with the implication that this sector will disappear and become subsumed within the formal sector, but the informal 'economy' (Chen 2007: 1). The informal, in effect, has colonized the formal.

This process of informalization occurs in different ways and countries have their own distinctive informalization pathways. Chang (2009) picks out three such pathways which, he suggests, have broad purchase (Table 3.2). The first (Pathway A) – and the pathway we are most familiar with – comprises the classic informal sector of garbage-pickers, shoe-shiners and roadside newspaper-sellers. The second (Pathway B) involves the relocation or resituating of formal sector work in an informal context. This might, for example, involve the outsourcing of some of the stages of production from the formal sector to homeworkers. Pathway C, meanwhile, is the informalization of the formal sector. This pays attention to the way in which workers in modern factories, for example, are employed on terms that are in essence informal when viewed in terms of the security they bestow and the benefits they offer.

Clearly, these categories are blurred, but the key point is that while Pathway A was expected to evolve out of existence, Pathways B and C have evolved and grown in importance. The ILO's shift from writing of the informal sector to the informal economy is indicative of another shift: from focusing on informal *enterprises,* to informal *working arrangements* within the formal economy (Chen 2007). The persistence and growing prevalence of the informal economy is evident across

Table 3.2 Informal sector to informal economy

Pathway	Type	Characteristics and context	Focus
Pathway A	Informal sector expansion	This comes closest to the ILO's original designation of the informal 'sector': street vendors, cobblers, recyclers, garbage pickers, domestic workers, pedicab drivers, home workers... this informal sector pathway is highly visible	Enterprises in poorer, less developed countries
Pathway B	Informal labour in the formal sector	This occurs when work which used to be undertaken in the formal sector is contracted out and therefore leaves the ambit of the formal, regulated sector. It includes agency working, casual work, out-sourced activities and the self-employed. It is less visible than Pathway A	Employment relationships, often in more advanced economies of the region
Pathway C	In-fact informal labour	This involves the informalisation of the formal sector as workers are employed part-time, on fixed term contracts and without the employment benefits that come from formal sector employment. It is characteristic of much work in export-oriented factories and in EPZs. It is less visible than Pathway A	Employment relationships in advanced and developing economies

Source: adapted from Chang (2009: 170).

the region (Table 3.3). As Figures 3.3a and 3.3b show, informal employment in Thailand dominates most sectors and, furthermore, has remained the dominant form of employment.[21] During the two decades from 1980, as surplus labour left agriculture to enter the non-farm economy and as the informal sector of the non-farm economy became increasingly formalized, so Thailand saw a gradual decline in informal employment, broadly in line with what commentators at the time thought would occur with development.[22] Since the turn of the Millennium, however, this trend has stabilized, perhaps even reversed. In 2000, 58 per cent of employment was informal; in 2012 the figure was 63 per cent.

Table 3.4 is an attempt, problematically didactic admittedly, to show how the emergence of the precariat is, descriptively, taking different routes in the global North and global South. In the North the precariat is emerging from the changing circumstances of the proletariat in an era of globalization and post-Fordism. This also applies to a smaller proportion of the salariat.[23] Enterprise and state benefits continue to exist, although they are being eroded as labour market 'reforms' and austerity measures bite. In the global South, however, the precariat is emerging from the (clumsily termed) informalariat and self-relariat. The precariat here probably never enjoyed enterprise (or for that matter state) benefits and while community support has been eroded family support remains significant (see p. 138).

Table 3.3 The size and evolution of the informal economy in Southeast Asia

Country	Size of the informal economy (% total employment)			Informal economy trend	Data notes
	Earliest date (year)	Middle date (year)	Latest date (year)		
Indonesia	25% (1971)	42% (1990)	66% (2010)	Expanding	Based on data recording informal employment; here presented as a percentage of total employment
Philippines	57.6% (1980)	49.3% (2000)	41.5% (2010, BLES) 77% (2006, ECOP)	Expanding	Estimates of the informal sector vary because there is no informal sub-sector category in the country's labour statistics. The ECOP estimate is much higher because it includes the 'underemployed', most of whom work in small and micro-industries
Thailand	77% (1980)	58% (2000)	63% (2012)	Expanding	Informal employment is now defined as employment outside the social security system. This includes home workers and casual and contract labourers as well as farmers and street vendors; it also includes a relatively small number of professionals, such as doctors
Vietnam	–	–	82% (2007)	Expanding	Labour market data for Vietnam are "insufficient in scope, poor in quality, and piecemeal in sources" (Arnold 2013: 472). In an ILO and Vietnamese government study, the informal sector is defined as "all private unincorporated enterprises that produce at least some of their goods and services for sale or barter, are not registered (no business licence) and are engaged in non-agricultural activities" (Cling et al. 2011: 5)

Sources: Offreneo (2013); Chang (2009); Hewison and Tularak (2013); Tjandraningsih (2013); Arnold (2013); Cling et al. (2011).

Notes: BLES = Bureau of Labour and Employment Statistics (Philippines); ECOP = Employers' Confederation of the Philippines.

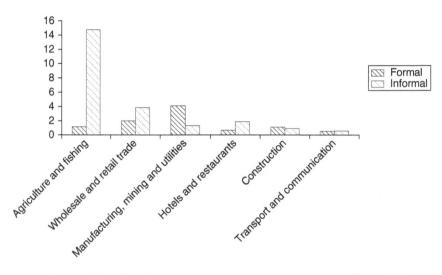

Figure 3.3a Formal and informal employment in Thailand, by sector (millions, 2009)

Source: Hewison and Woradul Tularak 2013: 447.

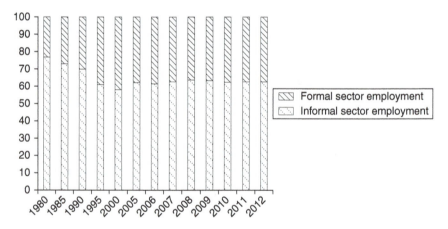

Figure 3.3b Formal and informal employment in Thailand, per cent of total employed
population, 1980–2012

Sources: Hewison and Woradul Tularak 2013: 450, ILO 2013 and NSO 2012.

Table 3.4 misrepresents the transition path as regards work and employment
in the global South in two ways. To begin with, it seems to imply that people are
moving from working in the informal sector to working in the informal economy.
In fact many are those in the growing informal economy are new entrants to the
labour market, who were never employed in the informal sector. At the same time,
the informal sector has not been 'developed' out of existence; it remains an important

part of the economies of most countries in the global South (and in Southeast Asia) and provides work and livelihoods for many tens of millions (see Chhachhi 2014). The background point, and this applies to global North and South alike, is that it is the beggar-my-neighbour policies that emphasize labour market flexibility (as reflected in the quote extract from the *2013/14 Global competitiveness report* reproduced above) which are driving the creation of the precariat.

Table 3.4 The changing composition of social income in the global North and global South

Global North	Pre-modern era		Pre-globalization era			Globalization era
	Self-relariat		Proletariat	Salariat		Precariat A
Subsistence or self-production	***		×	×		×
Family and transfers support	***		*	**		*
Community support and transfers	***		*	×		*
Money wage	×	⇒	**	***	⇒	***
Enterprise benefits	×		*	***		*
State benefits and public transfers (welfare)	×		*	***		**
Private, asset-based benefits (savings, investments)	×		*	***		**

Global South	Pre-modern era		Pre-globalization era		Globalization era
	Self-relariat		Informalariat		Precariat B
Subsistence or self-production	***		***		*
Family and transfers support	***		**		**
Community support and transfers	***		**		*
Money wage	×	⇒	×	⇒	**
Enterprise benefits	×		×		*
State benefits and public transfers (welfare)	×		×		*
Private, asset-based benefits (savings, investments)	×		×		*

Source: composition of social income adapted from Standing (2013: 5); table extended from Rigg and Oven (2015).

Notes: *, **, *** = increasing importance for sustaining livelihoods; × = generally absent as a livelihood-sustaining feature.

Of course, not everyone in either the global South or in Southeast Asia engages in precarious work and not everyone, as a result, lives an insecure existence. Both precarity and insecurity are differentiated according to age, gender, family responsibilities, ethnicity, education level and country context (Arnold and Bongiovi 2013). Across the globe, women are more likely to be in informal employment than men and, when men are so employed, it is also often on better terms. In the case of Vietnam, discussed below, the fact that more than 60 per cent of workers in industrial estates and export processing zones are young (aged between 20 and 35 years old) female migrants from poor provinces (Tran 2011: 60) plays a large part in explaining their vulnerability and the precariousness of the work they pursue. It is also clear that the neat – or apparently neat – delineation of the formal and informal sectors that the ILO set out more than four decades ago is becoming increasingly indistinct as the boundaries between formal and informal sectors, work and employment conditions become blurred. It is evident, in short, that increasingly the "informal nature of work is neither a problem of certain groups of workers in specific sectors, nor that of developing countries alone" (Chang 2009: 176).

Precarity in Vietnam

Vietnam is a country which only comparatively recently – from the mid-1980s – made the transition from a command to a market economy, and large numbers of workers continue to remain employed in state-owned enterprises (SOEs). Nonetheless we see in Vietnam, over a remarkably short period, how a liberalizing economy has led to work becoming more informal and, with this, more precarious.

It has been estimated that over 80 per cent of employment in Vietnam is informal; this includes both the classic informal economy including garbage-pickers, itinerant salespeople and roadside stallholders (as well as farmers), and the informal-formal economy such as factory and construction work. The increasing precarity of formal sector work is reflected in the growth of workers on fixed-term or verbal contracts, or with no contracts whatsoever. According to Arnold, in 2009 in a survey of formal sector workers in Vietnam, over 70 per cent were without permanent contracts (2013: 475).[24] One of the background reasons for the extension of precarity in Vietnam and elsewhere in Asia is because of the way in which the growth in employment in the formal sector is so tightly bound up with migration. In Vietnam, migrants usually maintain a rural *ho khau* (or registration, as in China) which denies them some of the rights that come with an urban *ho khau* (Nguyen *et al.* 2012); but even in countries of Asia where there is no such household registration system, migration is a process that opens up a non-regulated and only partially legible space where the informalization of the formal economy can be pursued and enacted. (This is explored in more detail in the next chapter.)

With the introduction of *doi moi* in Vietnam in 1986 and its extension thereafter, we see the progressive dismantling of the former socialist system with its subsidies, rationing, putative guarantees and universal access to health care, education and other social services. A key debate is whether these elements of the former system were more honoured in the breach than in the observance. For Kerkvliet (2005, 2009), it was the failure of the socialist system to deliver an adequate standard of living which led to the spontaneous emergence of a market economy *before* the advent of *doi moi*. There are elements of Vietnam's experience of the informalization of the formal economy which are echoed elsewhere: the absence of effective unions; the way in which migration has drawn 'peasants' into the industrial workplace; and the role of footloose capital in shaping a wider institutional context that has promoted flexible working.

Vietnam also has its own particularities, however, notably a number of socialist-era hangovers. While state guarantees and subsidies may largely be a feature of the past, the *ho khau* system of household registration remains in place. To be sure, it does not restrict mobility in the way that it did, but it does limit the ability of migrants to engage fully and easily with urban living. As the UNDP stated:

> Viet Nam's household registration system presents a systemic institutional barrier for internal migrants in accessing both basic and specialized Government services ... reform of this system is needed so that the registration status of citizens is decoupled from their access to social services, giving equal access to everyone ...
>
> (2010: 7)

In addition, trades unions and the media often operate as they did during the pre-*doi moi* period. This means that on occasion workers can use this legacy of a socialist past to challenge employers in a manner that would not be possible in other countries. A case in point would be the example discussed in the last chapter (Tran 2007; see p. 46 this volume) where workers, in their struggle for a living wage, were successfully able to gain the support of pro-labour newspapers, labour unions and through these, the Ministry of Labour.

Factories without a working class

For Chang (2011), one of the outcomes of this latter-day informalization process is what he terms the 'paradox of East Asian development' where the region has become the global factory or workshop of the world, but without the emergence of a classic working class. Instead, new forms of informal labour, in the manner described above, have been shaped.

The question which has not been addressed yet in any detail is how the extension of precarity can be linked to the advance of capitalism and, in particular, to globalization. The argument is that when capital and economic activity – financing, production, distribution and consumption – are globalized, then regulation, whether by governments or labour movements, becomes compromised. Flexible labour is seen as an essential component for success in a neoliberal, global market place and as a key generator of employment, growth and economic development. To quote the World Economic Forum's *Global competitiveness report* again, "labor markets must ... have the flexibility to shift workers from one economic activity to another rapidly and at low cost" (Schwab and Sala-i-Martín 2013: 6–7). The logics of flexible specialization have not only helped to generate economic growth and corporate profits; they have also produced the army of disposable workers who work in the global factory (Chang 2009).[25] Once again, rapid economic expansion, such as that which many Asian countries have experienced and exemplified, has not reduced precarious work, as one might expect, but amplified and accentuated it (Arnold and Bongiovi 2013: 290).

Social protection

The traffic is not entirely one way, however. While there may have been an informalization of work in the manner described above, and with it growing precarity, at the same time social protection measures have been progressively introduced in several Southeast Asian countries.

Social protection takes three forms (ADB 2013; and see Ananta 2012; Zin 2012). The first, and most significant, is social insurance usually through contributory schemes that protect people during times of illness and unemployment, and in retirement. For those who are unable to participate in such contributory schemes, there is a second form of social protection, in the form of social assistance or welfare payments (whether in cash or in-kind) to support individuals or households living in constrained circumstances, often taken to mean in poverty. Typically, this is through elderly, child and disability benefit, health assistance, disability benefit, and disaster relief. The third form of social protection is through what is sometimes known as workfare: labour market programmes that help people to access employment through training, skills development and cash or food-for-work programmes so that they can make the transition from welfare to work.

Welfare regimes in Asia have taken a significantly different tack from welfare in (especially) Europe. In wider East Asia – in Hong Kong, Singapore, South Korea and Taiwan – welfare has been 'productive'. It was introduced at a lower level of development than in Europe, and has been used as a tool for achieving national economic development, rather than as a social support system. Kwon (2005, 2009) terms these countries 'developmental welfare states', where welfare has been subordinated to the demands of development and where minimizing dependence on the state has been, hitherto, a guiding principle. Social welfare programmes, moreover, have been targeted at the employed, largely industrial workforce. They have had the effect, therefore, not of protecting the vulnerable but of widening inequalities between, on the one hand, those working in the agricultural and informal sectors and, more latterly, the informal economy (see above) and, on the other, those employed in formal work. What, of course, this has meant is that the growing informalization of the economy, discussed above, has sometimes taken people out of the welfare net or, more commonly, prevented them from accessing it in the first place.

The Asian financial crisis of 1997–9 brought into sharp focus the precarity of the lives and livelihoods of many working in the modern sectors of the economy in Southeast Asia, and led to an examination of welfare provision and national welfare regimes. As Gough (2001) notes in his study of welfare in five countries, four in Southeast Asia (Indonesia, Malaysia, Philippines and Thailand) and one in East Asia (South Korea), responses to the welfare challenge have differed. But of these, only South Korea has opted to move towards inclusive public provision of welfare.

In 2005 the Asian Development Bank developed and published a social protection index (SPI) for Asia, which has subsequently been refined (ADB 2013). This index is essentially a measure of the proportion of GDP allocated to social protection which, for Southeast Asia, ranges from 0.5 per cent in Cambodia to 4.225 per cent of GDP in Singapore. Reflecting on the performance of Southeast Asia in relation to the rest of Asia, the ADB concludes:

> The SPI for Southeast Asia is below average, at 0.095 [0.099 if Timor Leste is included], even though the region includes one high-income country, Singapore, and several large middle-income countries, such as Indonesia, Malaysia, the Philippines, and Thailand. The SPIs for these five countries range from 0.169 for Singapore to 0.044 for Indonesia. Even though this region's average GDP per capita is above average, its spending on social protection as a share of GDP is only 2.6%. … This low rate might be due to a relative lack of commitment to expanding social protection, the importance attached to other development priorities, or a historical legacy of past practices.
>
> (ADB 2013: xiv and 22)[26]

Of the three forms of social protection noted above, for Southeast Asia it is social insurance – i.e. contributory schemes – that dominates. Indeed, it does so to a greater degree than any other region in the Asia-Pacific. This tends to limit the coverage of social protection to those who are in or have been in permanent employment. While the poor may be covered by social assistance schemes, the marginal but non-poor are vulnerable to being excluded from both social insurance (because they are not part of a contributory scheme) and social assistance (because they are non-poor). This potentially large group the ADB terms the "missing middle" (2013: 83). It is partially to address this lacuna that Indonesia, Thailand and Vietnam have introduced universal health insurance schemes.

When it comes to the depth of coverage, Southeast Asia again performs poorly. The ADB is generally moderate in its criticisms of national governments but nonetheless says that "the depth of Southeast Asia's labor market programs, at 0.228, is much less than that for social insurance". "Worse, however", the Bank continues, "the depth of social assistance is *abysmal*, at about 7% of poverty-line expenditures, leading to small social assistance benefits" (ADB 2013: 42, emphasis added). While there is a link between development status (reflected in GDP/capita) and social protection, the systems that we see in place in Southeast Asia are very clearly the result of quite deliberate political decisions. Nowhere is this clearer than in Singapore.

Singapore has a mandatory savings scheme (the Central Provident Fund or CPF) for people in employment, with no social risk pooling. There are other social protection programmes for vulnerable groups, such as Workfare and ComCare, but these are stringently means-tested and provided, when awarded, at a low level. Even so, there are questions about the sustainability of Singapore's social protection system given an ageing population, and also questions about its ability to protect the most vulnerable in society. Arguably, if Singapore is not to experience a sharp expansion of the numbers of elderly (particularly) living in *de facto* poverty[27] then it will have to introduce a more equitable social protection system. As Asher and Nandy (2008: 58) say, "ultimately, social sector policies exhibit a revealed preference concerning the vision of the society". They continue by suggesting that "adherence to social Darwinism [by the Singapore state] and [a] desire to perpetuate socio-political control are additional factors preventing the development of a much-needed multi-tier social protection system".

Health insurance in Vietnam

Vietnam began the process of introducing universal health coverage, or social health insurance (SHI) in 1992, when the country was still low income. This initial foray included a contributory compulsory scheme for public and SOE employees and those in the private formal sector, and a non-contributory scheme for certain social beneficiary groups, such as war veterans and the disabled. Two years later, in 1994, a voluntary scheme was opened up to non-formal workers, including farmers, and in 2003 the non-contributory element of the scheme was extended to include households defined as poor and to some ethnic minority groups. In 2005, children under six came under the aegis of the non-contributory scheme. Finally, in 2008, a new Health Insurance Law collected all these various initiatives together in to a single, nation-wide programme (Palmer 2014: 385).

In general, analysts have been favourably impressed by Vietnam's achievements and particularly with the fact that universal coverage was considered and, to some extent, addressed early on during the transition process and that this has then been progressively extended over time. It is thought that by 2012 or so around 60 per cent of the population were covered in one way or another by SHI. This commitment to broad-based health provision can be linked to the country's socialist origins. Nonetheless, the livelihood risks of ill-health for vulnerable groups remain very significant indeed.

To begin with, there is a large currently uninsured population (Ekman *et al.*, 2008: 260) of whom many are migrants who lack an urban *ho khau*. Without such a registration these migrants are denied access to social protection, leaving them institutionally vulnerable (Le 2009; Le *et al.* 2011). Palmer's recent (2014: 386) study of inequalities in Vietnam's universal health care coverage found that while state employees, students, ethnic minorities and the officially designated poor are well covered (ranging from 70 to 90 per cent), for farmers and the self-employed – both very large groups – coverage is only around 40 per cent and 23 per cent respectively.

Furthermore, there are significant costs even for those who are covered: accessing public health providers in some areas (especially remote, rural areas) is difficult and costly; and there are various medical, non-medical, out-of-hospital and 'informal' costs. The poor find these costs prohibitive even for quite minor illnesses, while "for catastrophic illness that requires a hospital admission the out-of-pocket expenses … are large even for those with health insurance" (Sepehri *et al.* 2006: 614). There is also evidence that inequalities in health care access are widening both in terms of access and quality of provision (Giang 2008). For the poor whose main, often only asset is their labour, an accident or illness can cause them to sell whatever assets they do have and/or become indebted to a debilitating degree (see Box 3.4). Short-term illnesses can, in this way, result in the compromising of families' and individuals' long-term prospects (Krishna, 2010). It is worth noting that Vietnam has, by comparison with other countries in the region – notably, Cambodia, the Lao PDR and Myanmar – an impressive SHI scheme; in these other places, the effects of illness, infirmity or injury can, indeed, be catastrophic.

Box 3.4 On a wing and a prayer

We met Mr Viet in Hanoi's Dong Da district at the end of September 2010. At the time, he was 57 years old and worked as a motorcycle taxi driver. Two decades earlier he had left his natal village in Nam Dinh's Xuan Truong district to travel the 120 km to Hanoi. He arrived in the city early in Vietnam's reform process and two years later he had taken up *cyclo*[28] driving. When, in 1994, the city authorities banned *cyclos* from the city (except in the Old Quarter), Mr Viet became a *xe om* (motorcycle taxi) driver. The other drivers in the area where he worked in Dong Da district were also from his commune, nine drivers in all. After 20 years working in the city he was still 'temporarily' in Hanoi and lived in a small rented room with three other migrant men, surrounded by drying washing and with a peeling Spice Girls poster on one wall (Figure 3.4). Mr Viet's income had risen, but so too had his expenses. In 1992, as a *cyclo* driver, he earned around 500,000 VND (US$25) a month; in 2010, driving a motorbike, he made 1.5 million VND (US$75) to 2.0 million VND (US$100). But rental and food costs in Hanoi had increased even more steeply, and when he had paid his bills had only a small amount left to send home. He was also getting too old for a job suited to younger men. He worked from five in the morning to eleven at night and that was hard, he told us, for someone in their late fifties.

Mr Viet did own nine units of land and a one-storey house on a 360 m^2 residential plot in his village. The farm was managed by his wife and his village was one where most of the working-age population had left, and those who had not were supported by those who had.[29] As the eldest son, Mr Viet felt a responsibility to maintain his patriline, binding him to his

(Continued)

(Continued)

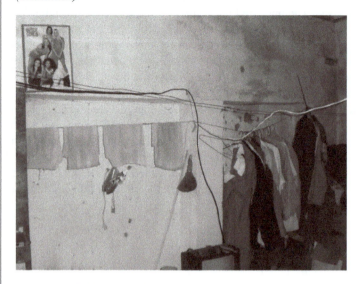

Figure 3.4 Mr Viet's rented room (shared with three other migrant men)

homeland even while his village could not sustain a livelihood for him, his wife and his daughters: it took a lot of rice and a lot of time, Mr Viet told us, to earn the money to buy the things needed for a reasonable existence. His work in Hanoi, however, was risky and a serious accident could undermine all his industry at a stroke. He recognized that he had been lucky in maintaining his health and avoiding accidents. After all, his labour was all he could offer.

(Extracted and condensed from Rigg *et al.* 2014)

Conclusion

This chapter has focused on Southeast Asia's 'new' poor, leading the discussion away from the 'old' poor whose condition, across much of the region, has been largely addressed. There are, now, relatively few Southeast Asians living in absolute poverty, at least when that is drawn at the $1.25-a-day line. None, it seems, in Brunei, Malaysia and Singapore; and just 100,000 in Thailand. For the region as a whole there were 70 million people living on less than $1.25 a day in 2010, or 13 per cent of the total population.[30] On current projections this figure will quickly reduce further: in 2015, 6.9 per cent of the population of the region will be living on less than $1.25 a day; in 2020, 2.5 per cent; in 2025, 1.3 per cent; and in 2030, 0.8 per cent (ADB 2014: 33). Of course, there are many who are relatively poor, as Chapter 3 explored and many more than 70 million subsisting between the $1.25- and $2.00-a-day poverty lines.

This chapter, however, has focused its attention on the emergence of a population of *new* poor who have been created by the very same processes that have generated growth. These poor need to be understood less in terms of their position above, below or close to some poverty line, but rather in terms of the relations and processes that have served to mark them out as vulnerable, precarious or dispossessed. The fact of their poverty or non-poverty is of less significance than the articulations of society and economy that have created their relations of existence. These individuals and households, in Amartya Sen's (1999) terms, have substantial 'unfreedoms'. These, moreover, are not inheritances of the past but have been produced by development and by the policy decisions taken by governments.

There has been a tendency to focus attention on the failures of development interventions. The assumption is that if only we could shape and fine-tune policies in ways that were more 'pro-poor' then this would address the poverty and development problems and inadequacies that exist. What, though, if the problem lies not with policies but, more fundamentally, with the processes of market development?

Gillian Hart (2001) draws a distinction between Big D and Little d development, the former being the interventions that drive the development project, and the latter as the historical processes of social and economic transformation, sometimes termed immanent development. This chapter has directed attention at the *successes* of Big D development. It is the very success of the policies that have been pursued in Southeast Asia, and which have generated rapid growth and economic expansion and led to sharp falls in absolute poverty across the region, which have shaped the failures that are recounted here. The expansion of oil palm and rubber across hundreds of thousands of hectares of the region has boosted exports, raised foreign exchange, contributed to economic expansion, and created employment; it has also, though, forced people off their land, undermined subsistence production systems, and created new forms of vulnerability. Similarly, the enormous expansion of factory work has been, by many measures and accounts, an enviable development success story. It has also, though, engendered – along with higher incomes – a greater precarity of existence for the workers in those factories.

Hall *et al.* (2011) in their important book *Powers of exclusion* note the surprising failure of many neoliberal commentators to see beyond – or beneath – the economic growth outcomes of the policies that are pursued:

> Remarkably, the depth of capitalism's exclusionary effects often goes unacknowledged by development experts of a neo-liberal persuasion who advocate intensified market dependence as a means to reduce poverty that is co-produced with wealth. Alternatively, they may recognise the poverty but highlight the benefits awaiting the expelled population when they move to town, or envisage the provision of 'safety nets' or shift scales to observe the public benefits of economic growth in terms of the greatest good for the greatest number.
>
> (Hall *et al.* 2011: 11)

At times, negative development outcomes are the product not of state policies, but of the actions of international and multilateral organizations. The term 'crimes of globalization' has been coined to encapsulate such outcomes. Friedrichs and Friedrichs (2003; and see Ezeonu 2008; Ezeonu and Koku 2008), for example, use the example of Thailand's Pak Mun Dam, funded by the World Bank, to argue that the "World Bank's mode of operation is intrinsically criminogenic" (p. 26). The suffering experienced by protesters and those villagers negatively impacted by the dam can be laid at the doors of the institution. This is not to say that the World Bank adopts policies with the intent of doing harm, but critics argue that it is complicit in such 'crimes'. This is, as it were, Galtung's structural violence (see page 104) but brought to the international stage.

There is another facet to the Southeast Asian success story, one that often lurks in the shadows: the story of migrant labour and the stories of migrant labourers. These are the women and men who have, often, provided the human ballast that has underpinned growth. This group provides the entry point for the next chapter.

Further reading

There is a great deal of literature on displacement, exclusion and dispossession, both empirical and conceptual. The challenge is to know which conceptual framework to use to make sense of the empirical material. Perhaps the best region-wide, integrative book on how new populations of poor and socially excluded are being produced in the context of economic transformation is Hall *et al.*'s (2011) *Powers of exclusion: land dilemmas in Southeast Asia* (which is also relevant for the next chapter). This can be combined with the discussion of accumulation by dispossession in David Harvey's *The new imperialism* (2003) and Hart's (2006) work on accumulation without dispossession.

For case study material on dispossession see Tania Li's (2002, 2007, 2014) exploration of upland Sulawesi; Baird (2011) and Barney (2009) on land grabbing in Laos; Paling (2012) and LICADHO (2009) on urban evictions in Phnom Penh; and Bunnell (2002) and Bunnell *et al.* (2010) on plantation workers displaced to make way for the 'high-tech' Putraja in Malaysia.

The best collection of papers on precarity in Asia is to be found in a special issue of the *American Behavioral Scientist* (57[4], 2013) edited by Hewison and Kalleberg on "Precarious work in South and Southeast Asia" where there are separate papers on Indonesia (Tjandraningsih 2013), the Philippines (Ofreneo 2013), Thailand (Hewison and Tularak 2013) and Vietnam (Arnold 2013). Arnold and Bongiovi's paper in the previous issue of the same journal (*American Behavioral Scientist* 57[3], 2013) provides a general overview of the informalization of the formal economy. Standing's *The precariat: the new dangerous class* (2011) is the fullest treatment of precarity at a general level, but also see his shorter interventions (Standing 2008, 2012, 2013, 2014). Munck (2013) provides a critique of the approach with particular reference to the global South.

A good, albeit dry, overview of social protection in Asia Pacific is provided by the Asian Development Bank (ADB 2013) but this can be complemented with Palmer's (2014) more detailed study of universal health insurance in Vietnam.

Notes

1 Mahbubani has restated his view that Singapore has 'eradicated' poverty on a number of occasions (see http://www.mahbubani.net).
2 In September 2013 Hong Kong introduced its first poverty line, set at half the median income. Like Singapore, Hong Kong has a highly unequal distribution of income with a Gini coefficient of 0.537. The result is that in one of the richest countries in the world, 19.6 per cent of the population or 1.31 million people fall below this relative poverty line, or 1.01 million (or 15.2 per cent of the population) after transfers (Ngo 2013; and see Rigg 2013).
3 So a distinction needs to be made between Singaporean households and households in Singapore. The former are Singaporean citizens and permanent residents; the latter include temporary migrants working in Singapore but who are largely unaccompanied by their families.
4 The measure of Singapore as the wealthiest country in the world (at US$56,532, with Norway in second place) is taken from Knight Frank and Citi Bank's *Wealth report 2012* (http://www.thewealthreport.net/The-Wealth-Report-2012.pdf).
5 See http://www.singstat.gov.sg/Publications/publications_and_papers/household_income_and_expenditure/pp-s19.pdf.
6 The SPI is calculated by dividing total expenditure on social protection by the number of intended beneficiaries of social protection programmes (ADB 2013). See Chapter 4 for more details of social protection programmes in the region.
7 Hard core poverty can be equated to the residual poor mentioned in the opening section of this chapter.
8 This is not, it should be noted, a view held only by those on the radical margins of the development debate. As noted in Chapter 2, Joseph Stiglitz argues that in a world of mobile capital and low barriers to trade "firms can simply tell workers that if they don't accept low wages and worse working conditions, the company will move elsewhere" (2012: 61). Ravi Kanbur (former Director of the World Bank's *World Development Report*) with Indraneel Dasgupta similarly suggest that "a prior increase in the incomes of capitalists, or, more generally, rich individuals, sets in motion community and competitive market processes which subsequently…can reduce workers' earnings as well as welfare" (Dasgupta and Kanbur 2002: 19).
9 This Levien (2013) then empirically grounds and explores in the context of industrial estates in India.
10 Li's (2014) account of change in upland Sulawesi reveals a very similar tendency. When she visited the desa headmen in their offices they informed her that "the forests were dense, and the highland population was sparse, semi-clothed, residing in trees and under rocks, and prone to use poisoned blowpipes against strangers" (p. 23). The coastal elite talked about the "deficiencies of the [upland] people, whom they characterized as lazy, uneducated, and lacking in enterprise" (p. 39).
11 This also sometimes happens in urban contexts. Harms (2014), for example, writes of how peri-urban land in Vietnam's Ho Chi Minh City is defined as empty 'wasteland' or *khai pha* to make it available for New Urban Zone development. Harms points out that thousands of households live in these 'empty' spaces.
12 Dwyer (2013), while not disputing that land is being enclosed in the hills of Laos, argues that to get a full appreciation we need to pay attention to the 'micro-geopolitics' of the process. "Southeast Asia's transformation from battlefield to marketplace", he writes, "is far slower and incomplete, is more locally grounded, and is more domestically

controlled that has been widely argued" (p. 24). This echoes the point made with reference to Tania Li's work on Sulawesi noted earlier in the chapter.

13 See the responses to Holly High's paper in *Critical Asian Studies* (High *et al.* 2009).

14 Hall (2013: 120–1) makes much the same point, but at a generic level.

15 Perhaps the most successful land-titling project in Southeast Asia has been in Thailand, partly funded through a World Bank loan that ran from 1984 to 1992. The project completion report states:

> The direct impact of the project has been the provision of title deeds to a large number of eligible land owners .... Although it is too early for the full economic impact of land titling to be felt, preliminary results ... indicate a significant increase in land prices ... easier access to and increased levels of commercial bank lending. Total farm assets also increased substantially as a result of the project.
>
> (World Bank 1993b: v)

16 An example might be when property rights over protected land prevent it being freely used or developed.

17 For a recent set of papers dealing with these issues see the special issue of *Development and Change* (2014, 45[5]) on "The 'labour question' in contemporary capitalism".

18 For a general introduction to precarity (and geography) see Waite (2009).

19 A wide range of terms are used to describe this process, which can be arrayed under the blanket term 'informalization': agency work; casual, casualization; contract, contractualization; flexible, flexibilization; informal, informalization, formless; non-standard; out-sourced, out-sourcing; precarious, precarity; and unregulated, non-regulated.

20 The report continues:

> The importance of [ensuring flexibility] has been dramatically highlighted by events in Arab countries, where rigid labor markets were an important cause of high youth unemployment, sparking social unrest in Tunisia that then spread across the region. ... Efficient labor markets must also ensure clear strong incentives for employees and efforts to promote meritocracy at the workplace, and they must provide equity in the business environment between women and men.
>
> (Schwab and Sala-i-Martín 2013: 7)

21 The Thai National Statistical Office undertakes informal employment surveys. These can be downloaded from http://web.nso.go.th/.

22 In addition, a change in the definition of the minimum age of employment from 13 to 15 years in 1998 took out of the calculation a large number of family-employed workers so there are also definitional issues at work here.

23 The salariat being those in stable, full-time employment.

24 Hewison and Tularak (2013: 445) make the same point regarding factory work in Thailand, a fact revealed during the floods of 2011 (see p. 176).

25 This is not just a feature of developing countries; the same arguments can be deployed for advanced economies as well.

26 In the ADB report, Timor Leste (East Timor) is grouped under the Pacific region rather than Southeast Asia.

27 I use *de facto* here because at the present time Singapore has no poverty line (see p. 55).

28 Bicycle rickshaw.

29 We also visited his wife in Nam Dinh.

30 Myanmar has been excluded from this calculation as comparable poverty figures for the country are not available.

References

Adam, J. (2013). "Land reform, dispossession and new elites: a case study on coconut plantations in Davao Oriental, Philippines." *Asia Pacific Viewpoint* 54(2): 232–245.

ADB (2013). *The social protection index: assessing results for Asia and the Pacific.* Manila, Asian Development Bank.

ADB (2014). *Key indicators for Asia and the Pacific 2014 – poverty in Asia: a deeper look.* Manila, Asian Development Bank.

Akram-Lodhi, A. H. (2008). "(Re)imagining agrarian relations? The World Development Report 2008: Agriculture for development." *Development and Change* 39(6): 1145–1161.

Ananta, A. (2012). "Sustainable and just social protection in Southeast Asia." *ASEAN Economic Bulletin* 29(3): 171–183.

Andriesse, E. and A. Phommalath (2012). "Provincial poverty dynamics in Lao PDR: a case study of Savannakhet." *Journal of Current Southeast Asian Affairs* 31(3): 3–27.

Arnold, D. (2013). "Social margins and precarious work in Vietnam." *American Behavioral Scientist* 57(4): 468–487.

Arnold, D. and J. R. Bongiovi (2013). "Precarious, informalizing, and flexible work: transforming concepts and understandings." *American Behavioral Scientist* 57(3): 289–308.

Arrighi, G., N. Aschoff and B. Scully (2010). "Accumulation by dispossession and its limits: the Southern Africa paradigm revisited." *Studies in Comparative International Development* 45(4): 410–438.

Asher, M. G. and A. Nandy (2008). "Singapore's policy responses to ageing, inequality and poverty: an assessment." *International Social Security Review* 61(1): 41–60.

Baird, I. G. (2011). "Turning land into capital, turning people into labor: primitive accumulation and the arrival of large-scale economic land concessions in the Lao People's Democratic Republic." *New Proposals: Journal of Marxism and Interdisciplinary Inquiry* 5(1): 10–26.

Baird, I. G. (2014). "Political memories of conflict, economic land concessions, and political landscapes in the Lao People's Democratic Republic." *Geoforum* 52: 61–69.

Baird, I. G. and B. Shoemaker (2007). "Unsettling experiences: internal resettlement and international aid agencies in Laos." *Development and Change* 38(5): 865–888.

Bangasser, P. E. (2000). The ILO and the informal sector: an institutional history. Employment Paper 2000/9. Geneva, International Labour Organisation.

Barney, K. (2007). Power, progress and impoverishment: plantations, hydropower, ecological change and community transformation in Hinboun District, Lao PDR. Toronto and Washington, DC, YCAR Papers and Rights and Resources Initiative.

Barney, K. (2009). "Laos and the making of a 'relational' resource frontier." *The Geographical Journal* 175: 146–159.

Begum, R. A., R. A. Begum, C. Siwar, R. Abidin and J. J. Pereira (2011). "Vulnerability of climate change and hardcore poverty in Malaysia." *Journal of Environmental Science and Technology* 4(2): 112–117.

Bernard, S. and J.-F. Bissonnette (2011). Oil palm plantations in Sabah: agricultural expansion for whom? *Borneo transformed: agricultural expansion on the Southeast Asian frontier.* R. De Koninck, S. Bernard and J.-F. Bissonnette. Singapore, Singapore University Press: 120–151.

Brickell, K. (2014). "'The whole world is watching': intimate geopolitics of forced eviction and women's activism in Cambodia." *Annals of the Association of American Geographers* 104(6): 1256–1272.

Bunnell, T. (2002). "Multimedia utopia? A geographical critique of high-tech development in Malaysia's multimedia super corridor." *Antipode* 34(2): 265–295.

Bunnell, T. (2004). Cyberjaya and Putrajaya: Malaysia's 'intelligent' cities. *The cybercities reader.* S. Graham. London, Routledge: 348–353.

Bunnell, T., S. Nagarajan and A. Willford (2010). "From the margins to centre stage: 'Indian' demonstration effects in Malaysia's political landscape." *Urban Studies* 47(6): 1257–1278.

Chang, D.-O. (2009). "Informalising labour in Asia's global factory." *Journal of Contemporary Asia* 39(2): 161–179.

Chang, D.-O. (2011). The rise of East Asia and classes of informal labour. Power-Point presentation at Sawyer Seminar Colloquium. Chapel Hill, NC.

Chen, M. A. (2007). *Rethinking the informal economy: linkages with the formal economy and the formal regulatory environment.* Geneva, United Nations Department of Economic and Social Affairs.

Chhachhi, A. (2014). "Introduction: the 'labour question' in contemporary capitalism." *Development and Change* 45(5): 895–919.

Cleary, M. (2003). "Land codes and the state in French Cochinchina c. 1900–1940." *Journal of Historical Geography* 29(3): 356–375.

Cling, J. P., M. Razafindrakoto and F. Roubaud (2011). *The informal economy in Viet Nam.* From http://www.ilo.org/wcmsp5/groups/public/—asia/—ro-bangkok/—ilo-hanoi/documents/publication/wcms_171370.pdf.

Dasgupta, I. and R. Kanbur (2002). How workers get poor because capitalists get rich: a general equilibrium model of labor supply, community, and the class distribution of income. Working Papers 27. Ithaca, NY, Cornell University, Department of Applied Economics and Management.

De Koninck, R., S. Bernard and J.-F. Bissonnette (Eds) (2011). *Borneo transformed: agricultural expansion on the Southeast Asian frontier.* Singapore, Singapore University Press.

De Soto, H. (2000). *The mystery of capital: why capitalism triumphs in the West and fails everywhere else*, New York, Basic Books.

Delang, C. O., M. Toro and M. Charlet-Phommachanh (2013). "Coffee, mines and dams: conflicts over land in the Bolaven Plateau, southern Lao PDR." *The Geographical Journal* 179(2): 150–164.

Ducourtieux, O., J.-R. Laffort and S. Sacklokham (2005). "Land policy and farming practices in Laos." *Development and Change* 36(3): 499–526.

Dwyer, M. B. (2013). "Micro-geopolitics: capitalising security in Laos's golden quadrangle." *Geopolitics*: 1–29.

Ekman, B. E., T. L. Nguyen, H. A. Duc and H. Axelson (2008). "Health insurance reform in Vietnam: a review of recent developments and future challenges." *Health Policy and Planning* 23(4): 252–263.

Endo, T. (2014). *Living with risk: precarity and Bangkok's urban poor.* Singapore and Kyoto, NUS Press and Kyoto University Press.

Escobar, A. (2004). "Development, violence and the new imperial order." *Development* 47(1): 15–21.

Evrard, O. and Y. Goudineau (2004). "Planned resettlement, unexpected migrations and cultural trauma in Laos." *Development and Change* 35(5): 937–962.

Ezeonu, I. (2008) "Crimes of globalization: health care, HIV and the poverty of neoliberalism in Sub-Saharan Africa." *International Journal of Social Inquiry* 1(2): 113–134.

Ezeonu, I. and E. Koku (2008). "Crimes of globalization: the feminization of HIV pandemic in Sub-Saharan Africa." *The Global South* 2(2): 112–129.

Friedrichs, D. O. and J. Friedrics (2002) "The World Bank and crimes of globalization: a case study." *Social Justice* 29(1/2): 14–36.

Giang, T. L. (2008). *Social health insurance in Vietnam: current issues and policy recommendations.* Bangkok, International Labour Organisation, Subregional Office for East Asia.

Glassman, J. (2006). "Primitive accumulation, accumulation by dispossession, accumulation by 'extra-economic' means." *Progress in Human Geography* 30(5): 608–625.

Gough, I. (2001). "Globalization and regional welfare regimes: the East Asian case." *Global Social Policy* 1(2): 163–189.

Hall, D. (2009). "The 2008 World Development Report and the political economy of Southeast Asian agriculture." *The Journal of Peasant Studies* 36(3): 603–609.

Hall, D. (2012). "Rethinking primitive accumulation: theoretical tensions and rural Southeast Asian complexities." *Antipode* 44(4): 1188–1208.

Hall, D. (2013). *Land.* Cambridge, Polity Press.

Hall, D., P. Hirsch and T. M. Li (2011). *Powers of exclusion: land dilemmas in Southeast Asia.* Singapore and Honolulu, National University of Singapore Press and University of Hawaii Press.

Harms, E. (2014). "Knowing into oblivion: clearing wastelands and imagining emptiness in Vietnamese new urban zones." *Singapore Journal of Tropical Geography* 35(3): 312–327.

Harriss-White, B. (2006). "Poverty and capitalism." *Economic and Political Weekly* 41(13): 1241–1246.

Hart, G. (2001). "Development debates in the 1990s: culs de sac and promising paths." *Progress in Human Geography* 25: 605–614.

Hart, G. (2002). *Disabling globalization: places of power in post-apartheid South Africa.* Berkeley, University of California Press.

Hart, G. (2006). "Denaturalizing dispossession: critical ethnography in the age of resurgent imperialism." *Antipode* 38(5): 977–1004.

Harvey, D. (2003). *The new imperialism.* Oxford and New York, Oxford University Press.

Hassan, N. (2013). Developing an analytical framework on social cohesion in Singapore: reflections from the framing of social cohesion debates in the OECD and Europe. Working Paper No. 17. Singapore, EU Centre in Singapore.

Hatta, Z. A. and I. Ali (2013). "Poverty reduction policies in Malaysia: trends, strategies and challenges." *Asian Culture and History* 5(2): 48–56.

Hewison, K. and A. L. Kalleberg (2013). "Precarious work and flexibilization in South and Southeast Asia." *American Behavioral Scientist* 57(4): 395–402.

Hewison, K. and W. Tularak (2013). "Thailand and precarious work: an assessment." *American Behavioral Scientist* 57(4): 444–467.

Hickey, M. (2013). 'Itsara' (freedom) to work? Neoliberalization, deregulation and marginalized male labor in the Bangkok taxi business. ARI Working Paper Series No. 204. Singapore, Asia Research Institute.

High, H., I. G. Baird, K. Barney, P. Vandergeest and B. Shoemaker (2009). "Internal resettlement in Laos." *Critical Asian Studies* 41(4): 605–620.

Hilgers, M. (2013). "Embodying neoliberalism: thoughts and responses to critics." *Social Anthropology* 21(1): 75–89.

ILO (2013). *Thailand: a labour market profile.* Geneva, International Labour Organization.

Kenney-Lazar, M. (2012). "Plantation rubber, land grabbing and social-property transformation in southern Laos." *The Journal of Peasant Studies* 39(3–4): 1017–1037.

Kerkvliet, B. J. T. (2005). *The power of everyday politics: how Vietnamese peasants transformed national policy.* Singapore, Institute of Southeast Asian Studies.

Kerkvliet, B. J. T. (2009). "Everyday politics in peasant societies (and ours)." *Journal of Peasant Studies* 36(1): 227–243.

Krishna, A. (2010). *One illness away: why people become poor and how they escape poverty.* Oxford, Oxford University Press.

Kugelman, M. and S. L. Levenstein (Eds) (2009). *Land grab? The race for the world's farmland.* Washington DC, Woodrow Wilson International Center for Scholars.

Kwon, H.-J. (2005). "Transforming the developmental welfare state in East Asia." *Development and Change* 36(3): 477–497.

Kwon, H.-J. (2009). "The reform of the developmental welfare state in East Asia." *International Journal of Social Welfare* 18: S12–S21.

La-orngplew, W. (2012). Living under the rubber boom: market integration and agrarian transformations in the Lao Uplands. PhD, Durham University.

Laungaramsri, P. (2012). "Frontier capitalism and the expansion of rubber plantations in southern Laos." *Journal of Southeast Asian Studies* 43(3): 463–477.

Le, B. D. (2009). Social protection for rural-urban migrants to large cities in Viet Nam. *Regional trends, issues and practices in urban poverty reduction: social protection in Asian cities.* UNESCAP. Bangkok.

Le, B. D., G. L. Tran and T. P. T. Nguyen (2011). Social protection for rural-urban migrants in Vietnam: current situation, challenges and opportunities. Research Report 08. Brighton, UK, Center for Social Protection, Institute of Development Studies.

Lestrelin, G. (2010). "Land degradation in the Lao PDR: discourses and policy." *Land Use Policy* 27(2): 424–439.

Levien, M. (2013). "Regimes of dispossession: from steel towns to special economic zones." *Development and Change* 44(2): 381–407.

Li, T. M. (2002). "Local histories, global markets: cocoa and class in upland Sulawesi." *Development and Change* 33(3): 415–437.

Li, T. M. (2007). *The will to improve: governmentality, development, and the practice of politics.* Durham, NC and London, Duke University Press.

Li, T. M. (2010a). "To make live or let die? Rural dispossession and the protection of surplus populations." *Antipode* 41: 66–93.

Li, T. M. (2010b). "Indigeneity, capitalism, and the management of dispossession." *Current Anthropology* 51(3): 385–414.

Li, T. M. (2012). "Why so fast? Rapid class differentiation in upland Sulawesi." *Revisiting rural places: pathways to poverty and prosperity in Southeast Asia.* J. Rigg and P. Vandergeest (eds). Singapore and Honolulu: National University of Singapore Press and University of Hawaii Press: 193–210.

Li, T. M. (2014). *Land's end: capitalist relations on an indigenous frontier.* Durham, NC and London, Duke University Press.

LICADHO (2009). *Land grabbing and poverty in Cambodia: the myth of development.* Phnom Penh, Cambodia, Cambodian League for the Promotion and Defense of Human Rights.

Lindeborg, A.-K. (2012). *Where gendered spaces bend: the rubber phenomenon in northern Laos.* PhD, Uppsala University.

Mahbubani, K. (2001). "Following Singapore's lead on the road of development." *Earth Times,* 15 January.

McMichael, P. (2009). "Banking on agriculture: a review of the World Development Report 2008." *Journal of Agrarian Change* 9(2): 235–246.

Mok, T. P., G. Maclean and P. Dalziel (2013). "Alternative poverty lines for Malaysia." *Asian Economic Journal* 27(1): 85–104.

Munck, R. (2013). "The precariat: a view from the south." *Third World Quarterly* 34(3): 747–762.

Ng, I. Y. H. (2013). "Social welfare in Singapore: rediscovering poverty, reshaping policy." *Asia Pacific Journal of Social Work and Development* 23(1): 35–47.

Ngo, J. (2013). 1.3 million Hongkongers live in poverty, government says, but offers no solution. *South China Morning Post*, 28 September.

Nguyen, T. A., J. Rigg, L. T. T. Huong and D. T. Dieu (2012). "Becoming and being urban in Hanoi: rural-urban migration and relations in Viet Nam." *The Journal of Peasant Studies* 39(5): 1103–1131.

NSO (2012). *The informal employment survey 2012*. Bangkok, National Statistical Office.

Ofreneo, R. E. (2013). "Precarious Philippines: expanding informal sector, 'flexibilizing' labor market." *American Behavioral Scientist* 57(4): 420–443.

Paling, W. (2012). "Planning a future for Phnom Penh: mega projects, aid dependence and disjointed governance." *Urban Studies* 49(13): 2889–2912.

Palmer, M. G. (2014). "Inequalities in universal health coverage: evidence from Vietnam." *World Development* 64: 384–394.

Percival, T. and P. Waley (2012). "Articulating intra-Asian urbanism: the production of satellite cities in Phnom Penh." *Urban Studies* 49(13): 2873–2888.

Ribot, J. C. and N. L. Peluso (2003). "A theory of access." *Rural Sociology* 68(2): 153–181.

Rigg, J. (2005). *Living with transition in Laos: market integration in Southeast Asia*. London, RoutledgeCurzon.

Rigg, J. (2013). Prosperity and poverty in affluent states. *Straits Times*, Singapore, 18 October.

Rigg, J. and Oven, K. (2015) "Building liberal resilience? A critical review from developing rural Asia." *Global Environmental Change* 32: 175–186.

Rigg, J., T. A. Nguyen and T. T. H. Luong (2014). "The texture of livelihoods: migration and making a living in Hanoi." *The Journal of Development Studies* 50(3): 368–382.

Sargeson, S. (2013). "Violence as development: land expropriation and China's urbanization." *The Journal of Peasant Studies* 40(6): 1063–1085.

Schwab, K. and X. Sala-i-Martín (2013). *The Global Competitiveness Report 2013–2014*. Geneva, World Economic Forum.

Sen, A. (1999). *Development as freedom*. New York, Alfred A. Knopf.

Sepehri, A., S. Sarma and W. Simpson (2006). "Does non-profit health insurance reduce financial burden? Evidence from the Vietnam living standards survey panel." *Health Economics* 15(6): 603–616.

Sikor, T. and C. Lund (2009). *Access and property: a question of power and authority. The politics of possession: property, authority, and access to natural resources*. Oxford, Wiley-Blackwell: 1–22.

Sims, K. (2013). *Raising homes for a rising Asia: development-induced-displacement and regionalism in Laos*. David C Lam Institute for East-West Studies. Hong Kong, Hong Kong Baptist University.

Springer, S. (2013). "Violent accumulation: a postanarchist critique of property, dispossession, and the state of exception in neoliberalizing Cambodia." *Annals of the Association of American Geographers* 103(3): 608–626.

Standing, G. (2008). "Economic insecurity and global casualisation: threat or promise?" *Social Indicators Research* 88(1): 15–30.

Standing, G. (2011). *The precariat: the new dangerous class*. London, Bloomsbury.

Standing, G. (2012). "The precariat: from denizens to citizens?" *Polity* (Basingstoke) 44(4): 588–608.

Standing, G. (2013). "Defining the precariat: a class in the making." *Eurozine*, 19 April.

Standing, G. (2014). "Understanding the precariat through labour and work." *Development and Change* 45(5): 963–980.

Stiglitz, J. (2012). *The price of inequality.* London, Allen Lane.

Tjandraningsih, I. (2013). "State-sponsored precarious work in Indonesia." *American Behavioral Scientist* 57(4): 403–419.

Tran, A. N. (2007). "Alternatives to the 'race to the bottom' in Vietnam: minimum wage strikes and their aftermath." *Labor Studies Journal* 32(4): 430–451.

Tran, A. N. (2011). "The Vietnam case: workers versus the global supply chain." *Harvard International Review* 33(2): 60–65.

Un, K. and S. So (2011). "Land rights in Cambodia: how neopatrimonial politics restricts land policy reform." *Pacific Affairs* 84(2): 289–308.

UNDP (2010). *Internal migration and socio-economic development in Viet Nam: a call to action.* Hanoi, Vietnam, United Nations Development Programme.

Vandergeest, P. (2003). "Land to some tillers: development-induced displacement in Laos." *International Social Science Journal* 175(March): 47–56.

Viratkapan, V. and R. Perera (2006). "Slum relocation projects in Bangkok: what has contributed to their success or failure?" *Habitat International* 30(1): 157–174.

Waite, L. (2009). "A place and space for a critical geography of precarity?" *Geography Compass* 3: 412–433.

World Bank (1993a). *The East Asian miracle: economic growth and public policy.* Oxford, Oxford University Press.

World Bank (1993b). *Project completion report: Thailand. Land Titling Project.* Report No. 11896. From http://www-wds.worldbank.org/external/default/WDSContentServer/WDSP/IB/1993/05/21/000009265_3960925180627/Rendered/PDF/multi_page.pdf

World Bank (2007). *World development report 2008: agriculture for development.* Washington, DC, World Bank.

Zin, R. H. M. (2012). "Malaysia: towards a social protection system in an advanced equitable society." *ASEAN Economic Bulletin* 29(3): 197–217.

4   The unreported and uncounted

Tracking the living and lives of
Southeast Asia's transnational
migrants

Introduction: placing migration

That the world is becoming increasingly integrated is clear, whether in terms of
investment flows, higher education, cultural practices, political institutions, or
trading norms. That said, this does not, as Friedman contentiously put it, mean
that *The world is flat* (2005). It is not, in every sense. Place still matters – where
we are born, love, work and die – in shaping people's prospects. Indeed, these
flows of capital, knowledge, people and technology occur *because* the world is
not flat. It is the very unevenness of the world that drives processes of integration and far from equalizing difference, integration often further accentuates
such differences. Of these flows one stands out in terms of its visceral human
dimensions: migration.

Much human movement is internal (or domestic) as people migrate to access
employment, education or land, whether permanently or as temporary sojourners.
The movement of approaching half-a-billion country dwellers to urban work in
China since the 1980s constitutes the largest labour flow in history (Zhao 1999).
Because a significant proportion of these migrants do not relinquish their rural
homes, China also sees the annual movement of more than 250 million workers as they return to their natal villages to celebrate the lunar New Year. Across
the globe, the UNDP put the figure for internal movements in its 2009 *Human
Development Report: Overcoming barriers – human mobility and development*
at 740 million (UNDP 2009: 21). In addition to these internal movements there
is a somewhat smaller, but also highly significant, international flow of people –
estimated at 214 million by the UNDP. In total, there are some one billion people,
or around one-in-seven of humanity, who have moved – largely – because the
opportunities in one place are better than they are in another.[1]

These movements are often developmental in their motivations and sometimes
also in their outcomes: people move because this, they hope, will bring higher
incomes, better prospects, more robust livelihoods, and greater freedoms. The
World Bank in its 2009 *World Development Report: Reshaping economic geography* largely views international and domestic labour migration as a positive or, at
worst, a benign process. Writing of the human resource links between Singapore
and Malaysia, the report states:

Prosperity [in Singapore] spilled over into neighboring Malaysia. Malaysia's manufacturing-led prosperity in turn helped more than 2 million Indonesians who streamed in to fill jobs in construction and services. … [Singapore] the 'little red dot' on a map – as reportedly derided by a neighboring president – has transformed itself, integrated its neighborhood, and overtaken Britain, its former colonizer.

(World Bank 2009: 14)

In a book on cross-border labour migration in the Greater Mekong sub-region, Jalilian and Reyes (2012: 92) contend that the balance of costs and benefits of migration in economic terms is positive; that such movements benefit sending and receiving countries and, importantly, migrants themselves. They also say, however, that Lao and Cambodian migrants' hopes for a better life are "often crushed, given the demeaning treatment they are subject to once in Thailand". The tendency to 'balance' the costs and benefits of migration, especially when financial imperatives and economic necessities take centre stage, will, almost inevitably, arrive at the conclusion that migration is a beneficial process. The downside is de-emphasized in the light of the imperatives of national economic development and individual and household material progress.

Despite the undoubted economic logics that may often underpin migration, it is also self-evident that such movements are not unproblematically developmental. This is clear in the conditions of work and employment that overseas contract workers face; in the level of labour unrest in facilities dominated by migrant workers; in states' ever more stringent and draconian attempts to control and 'discipline' guest workers; and in the terrible risks that people take to access what they hope will be a better life. Taking just four months at the tail end of 2013 and the start of 2014:

- In October 2013, more than 360 African migrants hoping to access a brighter future in Europe drowned as their overcrowded boat caught fire and sank off the Italian island of Lampedusa.
- In November 2013, Amnesty International released a sharply critical report claiming that abuse was so widespread and on such a scale in Qatar's construction sector as that country prepares for the 2022 football World Cup, that it had become "routine" (Amnesty International 2013).
- In December 2013, the first riots in Singapore for more than 30 years were triggered by the death of an Indian migrant worker in a traffic accident and involved largely South Asian migrant workers.
- In January 2014, police opened fire on striking Cambodian garment workers, mostly migrants from rural areas, killing three. The workers were demonstrating for an increase in the minimum wage to US$160 a month.

While this book is about Southeast Asia, an interview that I conducted in 2007 in a village in Sri Lanka's dry zone reflects the risks that some migrants take when they leave home. Sanduni first left for Dubai in 1998 as a young 26-year-old wife and mother, to work as a housemaid. This two-year trip itself she counted a success given its motivation (to earn money to support her family), although in her absence Sanduni's husband turned to drink and frittered away the income that she had so carefully saved and then remitted to him for safe keeping. On her return, relations with her husband deteriorated and in 2006 Sanduni felt compelled, through economic necessity, to leave again for a second trip to Dubai. This was disastrous. Sanduni was sexually assaulted by her new employer, became pregnant, and had to return home after four months to give birth to a daughter. Her husband rejected the child, the couple separated, and Sanduni herself was ostracized, shunned by her fellow villagers (Hewage *et al.* 2011: 213).

The focus in this chapter is not on domestic (internal) movements, important though they are, or on emigration; the chapter is, instead, concerned with exploring transnational labour sojourning. The literature refers to both 'international' and 'transnational' labour migration. The use of 'transnational' emphasizes the degree to which migrants maintain ties, links and associations with their places of origin: emotional, familial, economic, religious and cultural. While sometimes migrants may become permanently resident in their destinations, even taking on the citizenship of their adopted countries, in the discussion here the focus is on migrant sojourners – temporary migrants – who form the large majority of such transnational flows in the Southeast Asian region.

Determining the scale of movement in Southeast Asia

Data on migration and mobility, both intra- and trans-national, are poor. National censuses often do not pick up short-term movements and population registers are either lacking or provide only rudimentary coverage: "For the most part, migration data remain patchy, non-comparable and difficult to access" (UNDP 2009: 28; and see Newland 2009: 10). In an assessment of the situation for Asia, Kundu writes that "studies on internal migration are seriously constrained by the fact that no international organization systematically collects or tabulates even the basic demographic information . . . in a cross sectionally and temporally comparable manner" (Kundu 2009, 14). The same is true of transnational movements where there is often a significant underestimation of the scale of migration flows across international borders, with large numbers of irregular migrants (see Table 4.1).

Notwithstanding these caveats, however, we do know that socio-economic and political transformations over the last 40 years, and particularly over the last two decades, have served to create a vital landscape of human mobility. This is particularly striking in the Southeast Asian region where political rapprochement, the growing permeability of borders, the easing of frictions of distance as roads are built and upgraded and personal transport expands, deepening inequalities between and within countries, the logics of globalization, and growing needs have all played their part in spawning a mobility revolution.

Kelly (2011: 486; and see Kaur 2010) suggests that there are two general circuits of transnational movements in the Southeast Asian region, one centred on Thailand which lies at the core of a mainland Southeast Asian human resource

Table 4.1 The scale of movement in Southeast Asia's mainland and insular migration circuits

Circuit	Country of origin	Numbers (date)	Comments
Mainland Southeast Asia Thailand	Myanmar Lao PDR Cambodia	1,111,541 100,046 267,638	Irregular transnational migrants are thought to exceed the figures for regular migrants. Migrants constitute around 10 per cent of the Thai workforce
	Regular Irregular	1,479,225 (2012) ~2,000,000	
	Total	~3,500,000 (2012)	
Insular Southeast Asia Malaysia	Indonesia Bangladesh Nepal India Burma Vietnam Philippines Thailand Pakistan Cambodia Other countries	1,150,000 266,000 223,000 144,000 123,000 115,000 25,000 18,000 15,000 10,000 10,000	Migrants make up 37 per cent of the manufacturing workforce, 28 per cent of construction and 28 per cent of agriculture. In total, migrant workers constitute around a quarter of the Malaysian workforce of 12 million
	Regular/legal Irregular	2,358,000 (2010) 800,000 (2009)	
	Total	3,158,000 (2009/10)	
Singapore	Philippines	163,000 (2009)	Large majority of migrants are regular and constitute around 36 per cent of the Singapore workforce
	Regular Irregular	1,967,000 (2010) –	
	Total	1,967,000 (2010)	
Brunei Darussalam	Regular Irregular	143,300 –	Migrants were projected to make up 33 per cent of the total population of Brunei of 436,500 in 2011
	Total	143,300 (2011)	

Sources: Kelly (2011); Martin (2009); Kaur (2010); Chanda (2012); Huguet *et al.* (2012); Azim (2002); MAP foundation website (http://www.mapfoundationcm.org/eng/).

economy; and the other centred on Malaysia, Singapore and Brunei which likewise have become pivotal destination sites for insular Southeast Asia. Both these cores exert an economic gravitational pull on neighbouring countries, attracting migrants to the employment opportunities that exist.

When it comes to pinning down the scale of movements – beyond noting that they are significant – there is, however, a good deal of room for error (Table 4.1). Not only are systems for recording regular (i.e. legal) movements poor but a large number of movements are undocumented, unregistered and, often, 'illegal' – or 'irregular'. Some of these registered flows are of skilled, managerial and professional workers; but far more numerous is the migration of low-skilled workers concentrated in agriculture, low-skilled manufacturing, construction and the more poorly remunerated service sector jobs, most notably domestic work. While the situation varies between countries, we can make four statements that have general validity and purchase: (i) such workers are hired on a temporary basis; (ii) they do not enjoy the same rights as citizen employees and are barred from achieving citizenship; (iii) they are low paid, work long hours often in poor and sometimes dangerous or degrading conditions; and (iv) they are situated at the margins of mainstream society. They are classically 'socially excluded' but are also indispensable elements of the labour system as it has evolved in the Southeast Asian region.

In addition to these two Southeast Asia-focused migration circuits there is also a flow of migrants from Southeast Asia to other parts of the world, and particularly to East Asia and the Middle East. Here the numbers are rather better known because it is that much harder to slip into a distant country than it is to ghost across a land border in Southeast Asia.

The triple paradox of the transnational labour migrant

Transnational labour migrants are both 'regular' and 'irregular'. At a crude level, regular labour migrants are legally employed and have full documentation while irregular migrants are working illegally, without full documentation. The International Organization for Migration (IOM) defines an irregular migrant as a "person who, owing to unauthorized entry, breach of a condition of entry, or the expiry of his or her visa, lacks legal status in a transit or host country".[2] The IOM goes on to state that the "term 'irregular' is preferable to 'illegal' because the latter carries a criminal connotation and is seen as denying migrants' humanity".[3] Stated thus, the distinction between regular and irregular appears unambiguous. However, for some countries, irregular labour migration is so 'regular' – or normal – that it has become 'licit'. Furthermore, and as discussed below, just because a labour migrant has full documentation does not make that person immune to abuse. Thus *de facto*, whether viewed in terms of how irregular migrants are officially regarded or regular migrants are treated, the distinction is rather more blurred than the regular/irregular, documented/ undocumented division suggests.

The reason for this blurring of regular/irregular is not simply because the authorities are lax, lacking in capacity, corrupt or incompetent. Some countries have come to rely on irregular migrants as critical components in their labour forces and therefore the authorities have been intentionally accommodating of irregular migrants. Li (2012) writes, in her study of Chinese migrant workers in Israel, but which is more broadly germane:

> All the relevant groups have an interest in maintaining current [permissive] arrangements. Israel needs migrant workers to fill up the low end of the domestic manual labour market; foreign workers expect to earn higher incomes through working in Israel; the local authorities in the sending area are willing to see the economic betterment of the migrants' families; and

the intermediates make profits from running their businesses. In the end ...
all of the factors interact and result in a permissive situation that allows this
particular combination of illegal but licit activities to persist in transnational
labour migration.

(Li 2012: 94)

Seen this way, and the legality or otherwise of a particular transnational movement
is de-emphasized because it seems, at least superficially, that it is in everyone's
interest for the process to continue. The knots that authorities tie themselves in
to juggle these sometimes conflicting aims – of leniency in the interests of the
economy on the one hand, and vigilance in terms of security and social stability
on the other – is reflected in how the Thai government dealt with undocumented
transnational migrants until 2010. Up until that year, undocumented or illegal
migrants from neighbouring countries could register as 'irregular workers'. This
gave them no rights to remain in Thailand, indeed it confirmed their status as illegal migrants and merely suspended their deportation for a set registration period
(Pearson and Kusakabe 2012: 14). But this, of course, also made them available
to employers to work in the unskilled and poorly paid sectors of the economy.

The reality is that while migrants may often be needed, rarely are they wanted,
and seldom are they welcomed. Furthermore, times change and migrants are vulnerable to the shifting sands of public and political opinion. More often than not,
the 'rights' of migrants are shaped by political considerations which go much
further than the legality or illegality of an individual's presence in a particular country.
This creates what is termed here the triple paradox of the transnational migrant.

First, migrants are often critical components in national development, essential for processes of capitalist accumulation; at the same time, however, they are
often only given a grudging welcome at best, and their presence is conditional.
Migrants face public opprobrium and thinly disguised xenophobia and prejudice
(Arnold and Pickles 2011; Pearson and Kusakabe 2012). Following the first riots
in more than three decades in Singapore by labour migrants from South Asia, one
reader of the *Straits Times* wrote to the newspaper saying that "foreign workers
are here to make a living and they should do just that, instead of creating trouble",
while a second said that "foreign workers need to know that they cannot import
their culture or their way of life here [to Singapore]", adding "kudos to the authorities for adopting a tough and resolute stance against the rioters" (*Straits Times*,
10 December 2013). As in Singapore, migrants in Thailand form the mainstay of
the country's low-wage and low-skill workforce, critical to continuing capitalist
accumulation. Yet they are "seen at the same time as a threat to its social order,
national security and even to the health of its people" (Derks 2013: 225).

Partly reflecting such public views, most countries have policies and laws that
seek to limit migrant numbers, control their employment, channel their activities,
and maintain a degree of surveillance over their daily lives. This then creates a
second paradox: laws are put in place ostensibly to protect migrant workers but, in
practice, these laws become a means by which employers can restrict and exploit
their workers. "Sovereign power simultaneously adopts labor laws to regulate

the market", Lee writes, "while wilfully withdrawing itself from subcontracted sweatshops, export processing zones, and the informal economy that hire undocumented immigrants in order to sustain and reproduce the hypercapitalist order" (2010: 60–61).

This is reflected in the scores of factories that have sprouted up in and around the Thai border town of Mae Sot, close to the border with Myanmar (Burma), since the late 1990s and early 2000s. By 2004 there were some 125,000 registered Burmese migrant workers in Tak province (of which Mae Sot is a part), although Pearson and Kusakabe state that the actual figure was three times this, or 375,000 (2012: 4). Arnold and Pickles (2011) not only highlight the racialized discrimination that occurs but also the shockingly low wages paid and conditions endured.[4] Mae Sot, they contend, "is a quintessential example of a garment-producing center that attracts employers keen on squeezing or sweating labor" (2011: 1610). In 2008 the provincial minimum wage was set at 147 baht per day; the rate paid to Burmese workers was around 70 baht or some US$2, and this included overtime. In the same year a survey of factories in the Mae Sot area found that only *one* out of more than 400 was paying the minimum wage, and the average daily wage was around 40–70 per cent of the minimum (Pearson and Kusakabe 2012: 94; and see Kusakabe and Pearson 2010). More recently, a survey undertaken by MAP Foundation in 2012 (MAP 2012: 6) found that for Burmese migrant workers without documentation, their average wage was 46 per cent of the minimum wage of 251 baht per day; for those with a migrant workers card it was 62 per cent, and for migrants with a temporary passport it was 89 per cent (Table 4.2).

Table 4.2 The wages of work: Burmese migrant workers in Thailand (2012)

	Migrants without documentation (n = 195)	*Migrants with migrant workers ID card (n = 137)*	*Migrants with temporary passport (n = 161)*
Wages			
Average wage per day (baht)	115	156	224
Minimum wage (baht)	251	251	251
Average wage as % of minimum wage	46%	62%	89%
% earning less than 100 baht per day	48%	22%	2%
Hours of work (% respondents)			
8–9 hours per day	53%	60%	77%
10–12 hours	22%	16%	14%
>12 hours	25%	24%	9%
Conditions			
Experience of accidents at work	18%	18%	23%
Wish to change job	59%	39%	25%

Source: data extracted and recalculated from MAP (2012: 6). The respondents were interviewed in Mahachai, Mae Sot and Chiang Mai. The minimum wage in 2012 was 251 baht per day.

Workers live in dormitories where they have limited freedoms, work long hours (10 hours or more, see Table 4.2), and are subject to sexual harassment. While Arnold and Pickles may suggest that the justification for the 'intolerable' conditions lies in racialized discrimination that can be tracked back over centuries of cross-border warfare and friction, the wider explanation for the conditions and for the presence of approaching 150,000 migrant Burmese in Mae Sot and the surrounding area lies in the operation of the cross-border and wider regional human resource economy. The higher-level explanation of why these factories exist and the conditions that obtain there can be found in the logics of the global factory. However, and it is a very significant 'however', we also need to see workers' conditions of employment being shaped by national policies regarding labour practices, as well as by the quite particular intersections of historical contingencies and social norms that pertain nationally and locally. Finally, even in factories such as those of Mae Sot there is scope for resistance and agency, a point returned to later in this chapter.

The third paradox also emerges from the legal context that exists in most destination countries: migrants are, by definition, mobile and yet their daily mobility becomes tightly circumscribed. Derks (2010b: 930) writes of the "politics of immobilisation" and quotes the words of a Cambodian fisherman, Thou, on a Thai trawler in Rayong:

> Living here means that we don't have rights. We don't have much freedom. We have no clear timeframe. When we work for them [fishing-vessel owners], it is all up to them. When they want us to stop, for several months, for years, it is up to them.[5]

Studies (e.g. Kusakabe and Pearson 2010) of female migrants in the garment factories on Thailand's western frontier with Myanmar also note the degree to which they find themselves controlled in their activities and restricted in their movements. Factory owners often prevent their workers from leaving the factory and dormitory compound and registration documents restrict migrants to their province of employment. The seizure of migrants' passports and other documents by employers is commonly employed to (illegally) limit their mobility.

The right to freedom of movement is enshrined in the UN Declaration and also in many countries' constitutions, and the presence of tens of millions of transnational migrants across the world is testament to people's ability and willingness to cross international borders. The actual lived experience of 'guest' workers, however, is one of constrained movement and controlled daily living where, if they are undocumented, they face the ongoing threat of deportation and, even when documented, have to abide by certain rules. In Singapore they are summarily repatriated should the business cycle demand it (Yeoh and Huang 2010: 223).

The bare life of the transnational labour migrant

These [migrant] narratives...abound with stories of stabbings, murders, rape, deportation, confinement, physical abuse, confidence games, outright cheating, suicides, suicides under suspicious circumstances, unsafe working conditions, illness, and more.

(Gardner 2010: 198, on Indian guest workers in Bahrain)

I argue that death and suffering within the context of transnational labor migration, as illustrated by the case of Thai workers in Singapore, is best understood as an immense human struggle to make the Agambenian 'bare life' bearable. Surviving a bare life is the major characteristic of being an overseas migrant workers.

(Kitiarsa 2014: 3)

The work most often used to conceptualize the vulnerable position of the irregular migrant is Giorgio Agamben's influential *Homo sacer: sovereign power and bare life* (1998).[6] The protagonist in Agamben's book is *homo sacer*, the sacred man of ancient Rome who can be killed and yet cannot be sacrificed. *Homo sacer* were individuals who were banned and deprived of all rights, and who could be killed with impunity: their killing was not, legally speaking, murder.[7] The apparent contradiction of a 'sacred' man being killed with impunity but not sacrificed has been noted and debated, but Agamben uses it as a way of opening up a space of 'indistinction' between sacred and profane, religious and juridicial (p. 74).

In the third section of *Homo sacer*, Agamben ties the sacred man to the political history of modernity, from 'ethnic cleansing' in Serbia and Hitler's National Socialist eugenics programme, to refugees and, most substantially, to the condition of the Jews in Nazi Germany. He also draws in Foucault's work on biopolitics.[8] Agamben writes:

The Jew living under Nazism is the privileged negative referent of the new biopolitical sovereignty and is, as such, a flagrant case of a *homo sacer* in the sense of a life that may be killed but not sacrificed. His killing therefore constitutes ... neither capital punishment nor a sacrifice, but simply the actualization of a mere 'capacity to be killed' inherent in the condition of the Jew as such.

(1998: 114)

The killing of these categories of people could occur without sacrifice, without any legal consequences or ramifications. The legal exclusion of Jews from the Nazi German state rendered their lives 'bare', akin to the *homo sacer* of ancient Rome, and the concentration camp became a space of exception, where the rule of law was suspended. For many scholars, Agamben has become an invaluable conceptual scaffold to think about the condition of the refugee.[9] The refugee has become the archetypal modern-day *homo sacer*, the paradigmatic subject of contemporary sovereign power.

Other scholars have applied Agamben's work even more liberally, using it, for example, in the context of categories as broad as 'the poor'. It has even become another way of denoting the 'excluded'. This, however, tends to play down the degree to which states, through their sovereign powers, *produce* bare life. Thus, it is not that migrants are excluded – on the outside – but that the matrices of state power shape a particular political space which migrants occupy, and where their room for manoeuvre, in multiple senses, is compromised. When they broach this space and become 'illegal', 'irregular', or 'undocumented' they challenge the state's authority, thus becoming "a permanent and incorrigible affront to state sovereignty and the power of the state to manage its social space" (De Genova 2010: 39).

There are evident differences between the refugee – who Agamben chooses as emblematic of bare life – and the labour migrant, and particularly the regular or documented labour migrant. There are also, however, similarities that are much more than merely incidental. To begin with, the labour migrant is subject to regulation and control, an object of governmentality where individuals find themselves and their behaviours shaped, controlled, even dominated by the state and its policies. Second, the labour migrant is, like the refugee, a biopolitical subject: "those who can be regulated and governed at the level of population in a permanent 'state of exception'" (Owens 2009: 568). The processes of control that are set out later in this chapter with regard to labour migrants in Singapore and Thailand, and the way that migrants in both countries are treated as different – exceptional – from citizens reveals these resonances with Agamben's refugees.

In his book *Red tape: bureaucracy, structural violence, and poverty in India* (2012), Akhil Gupta aligns the premature and unnecessary death of many millions of poor people in India to the notion of the *homo sacer*. He calculates that there have been 140 million "excess deaths" since independence, more than two million annually (2012: 5). India's poor are palpably not excluded in the same manner as the Jews in Nazi Germany or, indeed, refugees more latterly. They are not excluded from political participation; they have rights and, in that sense, cannot be equated to the *homo sacer* as outlined above. For Gupta, "the paradox of the violence of poverty in India is that the poor are killed despite their inclusion in projects of national sovereignty and despite their centrality to democratic politics and state legitimacy" (2012: 6). The *de facto* operation of the bureaucratic polity in India produces the structural violence that leads to the premature death of large numbers of Indians.[10]

In using the term 'structural violence', Gupta is drawing on Galtung's (1969) influential paper in the *Journal of Peace Research*. Galtung makes a distinction between personal violence (where there is an actor or perpetrator) and structural violence (where there is no actor). Galtung is concerned not to overwork the word 'violence', and therefore also refers to 'social injustice'. For the purposes of this chapter, 'structural injustice' is preferred because it is less incendiary but, unlike social injustice, highlights the institutions and policies (the structures) that produce and sustain injustice (see Calder 2010; Ingram 2012). Galtung argues that when we think of violence as necessarily intended then we may fail to see how structures can also lead to violence (Galtung 1969: 172). Personal violence *shows*; it has visibility. "Structural violence is silent, it does not show" (p. 173). Injustice works in the same manner: there are personal injustices, which show, and structural injustices, which are silent.[11]

The power of seeing the irregular migrant as *homo sacer* is clear; it so intensely highlights their vulnerability and the degree to which this is institutionally or structurally mandated.[12] As Kitiarsa (2014: 3) argues with regard to Thai construction workers in Singapore, they are separate and separated from the sociocultural, economic and legal structures that frame their existence at home while, as noncitizens in Singapore, do not have access to the parallel structures that govern the citizens of the country where they reside. However, this focus on the structural vulnerability of the migrant is also the approach's weakness because it either denies or underplays the agency of the migrant. Migrants, even when they have few rights and very little power, do have *some* room for manoeuvre.

Ethnographic studies reveal, as discussed later in this chapter, that irregular migrants are not without autonomy and agency. We need, therefore, both to understand how structures create and perpetuate vulnerability but also, at the same time, how vulnerable subjects are able autonomously to shape their lives in the face of structural, as well as personal, injustice. Just as James Scott (1985) highlighted the everyday weapons of resistance of the poor in his famous study of the Malaysian village of Sedaka, so undocumented migrants have their own powers and weapons of resistance, all be they constrained and partial. Lee writes:

> Examining the workspace of private households where female migrants work as domestic workers and where labor laws and regulations are indefinitely suspended, in this essay I argue that, while these laboring spaces relate to [Agamben's] camp as the undocumented workers are stripped of juridico-political rights and reduced to a state of exploited bare life, the conception of camp lacks a dynamic account of power relations to address the complex agency of migrant subjects as they negotiate their daily workspace.
>
> (Lee 2010: 57–58)

Empirically, the binary in Agamben's work that separates those with political rights and citizenship from those with no rights (bare life) is problematic. Most transnational migrants are not without rights even while they are without citizenship. This is what Lee (2010: 59) calls the "third space of citizenship". Whereas Agamben's paradigmatic modern concentration camp state strips the inmates of their political rights, making them bare, but following political and judicial order, the experience of transnational migrants is to find that their rights are denuded rather than expunged (McNevin 2013). Furthermore, and as noted above and explored later in this chapter, migrants, whether documented or undocumented, are not without agency. They entertain a panoply of dissident practices, oppositional acts and subversive discourses, some quite overt but most low profile and everyday (see p.116).

There is a final point to make in introduction, before turning to the empirical discussion. At one level, it is clear that globalization and capitalism shape the processes and outcomes discussed above. The fact of growing mobility and migration, and the ways in which migrant labour sojourners are implicated in and insinuated into national development projects, are quite clearly tied up with broader currents of economic transformation. But, and this is the challenge, the texture of migrants' engagement with work and their places of work varies tremendously; many migrants are far from being 'unfree', and national contexts also differ considerably. In this debate, details and empirics matter and generalizations and theoretical positions generated deductively get us only so far. As McNevin insists (2013: 199), "without grounding theory production in concrete migrant struggles, conscious of the particular histories and diverse contexts that shape specific claims, we are unlikely to make theoretical advances on the gap that exists between existing analytics and emergent subject formations". Table 4.3 provides a compendium of papers beyond those discussed below that deal with international migrants and their position in different countries of Southeast Asia.

Table 4.3 Transnational migrants in Southeast Asia: a compendium of studies

Country of origin	Country of destination	Form of employment	Status	Source
Cambodia	Thailand	Fishermen	Undocumented	Derks (2010b)
Cambodia	Thailand	Child workers	Undocumented	Sankharat (2013)
Indonesia	Malaysia	Domestic service	Undocumented	Killias (2010)
Indonesia	Malaysia	–	Documented and undocumented	Nielsen and Sendjaya (2014)
Indonesia, Philippines	Brunei	Domestic service	Documented	Zirwatul Asilati *et al.* (2000)
Indonesia, Philippines	Singapore	Domestic service	Documented	HRW (2005)
Myanmar	Thailand	Factory work	Documented and undocumented	Arnold and Pickles (2011); Kusakabe and Pearson (2010); Pearson and Kuskabe (2012); MAP (2012)
Myanmar	Thailand	Domestic work	Documented and undocumented	HRW (2010a)
Myanmar	Thailand	Factory and sex work, agriculture	Trafficked	Meyer *et al.* (2014)
Philippines	Singapore	Fishermen	Trafficked	Yea (2012
Philippines	Hong Kong, Taiwan	Domestic work	Documented and undocumented	Lindio-McGovern (2004)
Thailand	Singapore	Construction work and sexual services	Documented and undocumented	Kitiarsa (2008, 2014)
Vietnam	Malaysia	Low-skilled work in the garment, textiles, electronic assembly and wood-based fabrication industries	Documented	Lê (2010)
Vietnam	Southeast Asia	–	Trafficked	Bélanger (2014)

Migrant rights and wrongs in Singapore and Thailand

Singapore and Thailand, as noted, lie at the epicentres of insular and mainland Southeast Asia's human resource economies respectively. In Thailand, as many as three million transnational migrants from Cambodia, the Lao PDR and Myanmar fill the interstitial economic spaces that have been created by the socio-economic processes that have transformed the country over the last half-century, constituting as much as 10 per cent of the Thai workforce (HRW 2010a: 19; and see Table 4.1). What is remarkable is that until comparatively recently, the need for low-skill and low-wage labour, especially in the more physically taxing, dangerous and degrading sectors of the economy, was met from domestic sources and especially by migrants from the impoverished Northeastern region. For decades, millions of north-easterners made the annual pilgrimage, usually in the dry season, from their parched fields to work as pedicab and taxi drivers, construction labourers, in slaughterhouses and rice mills, and as cooks and maids, especially in Bangkok and the provinces surrounding the capital. While this flow continues, today the opportunities on the very lowest rungs of the employment ladder tend to be filled by transnational migrants from neighbouring Cambodia, Laos and Myanmar. In the 1980s, Thailand was one of the region's major labour-exporting countries; it is now a net labour-importing country, with this shift from net labour exporter to importer occurring in short order from the late 1980s when Thailand was one of the world's fastest-expanding economies.[13]

Singapore, too, was once a place that met its own labour needs. In 1970 the non-resident population of the country was less than 3 per cent and the foreign workforce numbered under 21,000. By 2010 it had risen to 26 per cent, and in 2013 reached 29 per cent (Figure 4.1). The flows of low-skill, low-wage migrants

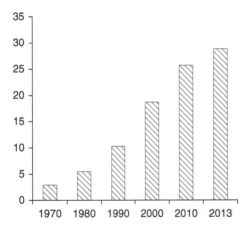

Figure 4.1 Non-resident population of Singapore (per cent, 1970–2013)

Source: http://www.singstat.gov.sg/publications/publications_and_papers/population_and_population_structure/population2013.pdf.

to Singapore are mainly from Indonesia, Malaysia, Myanmar, the Philippines and Thailand, and also from China and South Asia. In addition, there is a parallel current, but much smaller, of 'foreign talent', mainly from the countries of the global North, although China and India are also important sources. It is thought that unskilled workers make up around 80 per cent of the total migrant workforce (Devasahayam 2010: 47).[14] In 2007 Singapore's foreign workforce numbered 900,800; in 2013 it was 1,296,800, constituting around 40 per cent of the total workforce (Figures 4.2 and 4.3).[15]

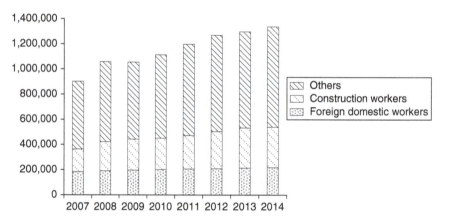

Figure 4.2 Singapore's foreign workforce, 2007–2014

Note: all date to year end, except 2014 (end of June).

Source: Ministry of Manpower statistics (http://www.mom.gov.sg/statistics-publications/others/statistics/Pages/ForeignWorkforceNumbers.aspx).

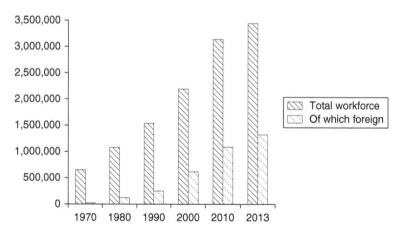

Figure 4.3 Singapore workforce, 1970–2013

Source: data extracted from MoM 2014.

Thailand has made the transition from labour exporter to net labour importer; Singapore has moved from close to self-sufficiency in terms of labour to becoming highly dependent on migrant workers. In both Singapore and Thailand there exists quite extensive legislation to manage and control migration flows. This is because of the twin fears that migrants of the wrong sort and in the wrong numbers might either have negative economic effects and/or negative social effects. Migrants are popularly seen, and not just in these two countries of course, as exerting downward pressure on wages and competing to take jobs from nationals. As Pearson and Kusakabe say, "there is the widely held view in Thailand that 'alien' workers bring little or no benefit to the economy … threatening the employment and well-being of Thai citizens" (2012: 42 and 43). In similar vein, the Singapore government's 2013 White Paper on population states that "we cannot allow in unlimited numbers of foreign workers. …We do not want to be overwhelmed …. Too many foreign workers will also depress wages" (GoS 2013: 42). Thus, migrants in both countries tend to be channelled into particular sectors and activities: a small number of skilled professionals to fill employment gaps at the high end, and then a much larger number to take on the 3D (Dirty, Dangerous and Demeaning [or, sometimes, Difficult]) or 3L (Low pay, Low skill, Long hours) jobs at the bottom of the employment hierarchy (Table 4.4). Jim Glassman (2007) writes of Thailand's 'spatial fix' following the economic crisis of 1997 in which capital has exploited the lower production costs of Thailand's margins – away from high-cost Bangkok and surrounding provinces – as a way of maintaining competitiveness and profits in lower-wage, lower-value-added products. Although Glassman does not address this feature in his paper, a critical logic in the spatial fix he describes is the ability of manufacturers to use cheap migrant labour from Myanmar.

In Singapore, as one might expect given the city state's reputation, we find a carefully and finely calibrated policy context that structures and manages migration. These policies are segmented according to sector, and to skill and salary levels. For example, employers of Foreign Domestic Workers (FDWs, or 'helpers') have to pay a monthly 'FDW levy' of S$265 per month, a security deposit of

Table 4.4 Migrant working patterns in Singapore and Thailand

Singapore	Thailand
Construction	Agriculture
Domestic work	Construction
General labouring	Domestic work
Manufacturing	Fish and seafood processing
Sex work	Fishing
Shipbuilding	General labouring
Unskilled services (gardening, cleaning)	Low-skill manufacturing (footwear, textiles and garments)
	Restaurant and shop assistant employment
	Sex work

S$5,000, while the workers themselves are required to undergo a medical test within 14 days of arrival (including pregnancy, STD and HIV tests) and every six months thereafter. They are not permitted to be accompanied by dependents, are prohibited from becoming pregnant or having a child while holding a work permit, and are also prohibited from marrying Singapore residents or permanent residents without approval from the Controller of Work Passes (see Box 4.1). Unskilled workers, unlike skilled professionals, are essentially denied the possibility of citizenship (Devasahayam 2010). They are 'guest' workers, and the intention is that they should remain guest workers. In the case of Malaysia, workers are also not permitted to be accompanied by their families and should they lose or leave their jobs they become, overnight, undocumented (irregular) migrants facing arrest and deportation, making it almost impossible for them to bring a case for unfair dismissal or a grievance against an employer to court. In Singapore, the country's employment laws provide three sets of standards and rights: one for the local population; one for skilled migrant workers; and a third for unskilled migrant workers. Entitlements for each are different, and entitlements are least for the last.

Box 4.1 Regulating domestic workers in Singapore

PART VI

CONDITIONS TO BE COMPLIED WITH BY FOREIGN EMPLOYEE ISSUED WITH WORK PERMIT

Employment

1   The foreign employee shall work only for the employer specified and in the occupation and sector specified in the work permit.

2   Where the foreign employee whose occupation as stated in the work permit is that of a "domestic worker", the foreign employee shall only perform household and domestic duties and reside at the employer's residential address or residential premises as stated in the work permit and visit pass.

3   Except for a foreign employee whose occupation as stated in the work permit is that of a "domestic worker", the foreign employee shall reside at the address indicated by the employer to the foreign employee upon the commencement of employment of the foreign employee and shall inform the employer about any subsequent self-initiated change in residential address.

4   The foreign employee shall undergo a medical examination by a medical practitioner registered under the Medical Registration Act (Cap. 174) as and when directed by the Controller.

5   The foreign employee shall report to the Controller as and when required by the Controller to do so.

Conduct

6   The foreign employee shall not go through any form of marriage
     or apply to marry under any law, religion, custom or usage with a
     Singapore citizen or permanent resident in or outside Singapore, with-
     out the prior approval of the Controller, while the foreign employee
     holds a work permit, and also after the foreign employee's work permit
     has expired or has been cancelled or revoked.
7   If the foreign employee is a female foreign employee, the foreign
     employee shall not become pregnant or deliver any child in Singapore
     during and after the validity period of her work permit, unless she is
     a work permit holder who is already married to a Singapore citizen or
     permanent resident with the approval of the Controller.
8   The foreign employee shall not be involved in any illegal, immoral or
     undesirable activities, including breaking up families in Singapore.
         (Extracted from the application form for foreign domestic workers
             downloaded from the Ministry of Manpower's website at
         http://www.mom.gov.sg/Documents/services-forms/passes/WP_
                                         Appln_Form_for_FDW.pdf)

Legislation is designed not just to manage and control migration but also, ostensibly, to protect migrants from abuse and exploitation. These twin sets of aims – of control/management on the one hand and care/protection on the other – while not necessarily incompatible often, in practice, conflict. Attempts to protect migrant 'rights', particularly when they are also part of a parallel enterprise to 'manage' migrants, lead to migrant 'wrongs'. This may be unintentional but, in a sense, it is inevitable.

Migrant rights[16]

In Thailand, no doubt stung into action by sustained international criticism, a number of new laws were introduced from the late 1990s ostensibly to protect workers from abuse and exploitation. In principle, migrant workers enjoy the same protections and privileges under Thai labour laws as do Thai nationals.[17] In addition, Thailand is a signatory to most international human rights treaties which protect non-citizens residing within the territory of Thailand, as well as its own citizens.[18] Thailand's Labour Protection Act (1998) applies equally to nationals and migrants; it seeks to protect workers' interests, sets a minimum wage, an eight-hour working day, overtime work only with the employee's consent, one day off in seven, paid sick leave, maternity leave, overtime pay, and various protections against hazardous working, among other protections and guarantees. In practice, the LPA rarely seems to apply to migrant workers, even when they are documented. Most migrants are unaware of the provisions of the Act and employers often exploit this fact. The other important piece of legislation is the Alien

Employment Act (2008) which sets out what work can be undertaken by non-Thai workers and where it can be performed. The Act provides broad parameters for search and undocumented workers face stiff penalties if caught, including imprisonment for up to five years. In addition to these national pieces of legislation, provincial decrees are also influential in shaping migrants' engagement with work, life and officialdom. Because these tend to have a national security emphasis, they can be particularly draconian in the way that they limit migrants' rights, and their application not infrequently appears arbitrary.

Until 2004, the registration system for migrant workers in Thailand was both opaque in its formulation and inconsistent in its application. In 2004 the Thai government permitted, for the first time, registration not through employers but through the government's own offices and over 1.2 million migrants from Myanmar, Cambodia and the Lao PDR took advantage of this opportunity, of which 814,000 were also awarded temporary ID cards and work permits. In addition – and in this regard, unlike Malaysia and Singapore – dependents could register, and some 93,100 children of migrants under 15 were so registered. The Thai government also drew-up separate agreements with the governments of Cambodia, the Lao PDR and Myanmar in 2002 and 2003 to improve the management and regularization of migration. These bilateral MoUs require the verification of a migrant's nationality whereupon travel documents are issued by the migrant's country of origin. Thai immigration then provides a visa which allows travel across the country, without restriction.

It has been suggested by the ILO (Pearson *et al.* 2006) and Human Rights Watch (HRW 2010a), however, that far from protecting workers, these laws play an important role in *explaining* abuse. As Derks says, "human-rights abuses are related not only ... to the absence of the law (that is, the lack of rule of law, weak state structures, and corruption) but also to the actual workings of the law" (2013: 221).[19] This links to the second of the paradoxes outlined above.

As is so often the case with transnational labour migrants and migration, there are latent contradictions in many governments' policies and practices as they pursue the impossible task of balancing the needs of the economy with public fears and security concerns. This is evident in the case of Singapore. While the Republic's borders are assiduously policed and policies fine-tuned to economic needs and security concerns, it has been argued for some years (e.g. Yeoh *et al.* 1999, Devasahayam 2010) that when it comes to the everyday living arrangements of low-skilled migrant workers, the state has been surprisingly disconnected and seemingly unconcerned. While, as explored later, this has changed due to pressure and criticism from groups in Singapore and internationally, so long as migration 'management' issues embedded in a political-economy mode of thinking dominate the state's approach, so the needs and interests – their rights – of workers will be subordinated to those of employers, and those of employers to the state. Policies are crafted to deliver a migrant workforce that will, on the one hand, contribute to Singapore's economic progress and, on the other, do so in a manner that will not be disruptive to the smooth functioning of Singapore society (Yeoh and Annadhurai 2008: 549). The rights of migrants tend to be downplayed.

This is reflected in Singapore in the debate over whether FDWs should be legally entitled to a day off a week. Singapore is one of the few countries where this is not currently legally mandated. The Ministry of Manpower, in a set of FAQs regarding weekly rest days for FDWs, states: "It is time to take a step forward by amending our legislation to improve the employment conditions of FDWs, while providing flexibility to employers and FDWs who wish to accept monetary compensation in-lieu of their rest day".[20] But while this policy adjustment was broadly welcomed by activists, even here we see the careful balancing of the city state's economic needs with internationally accepted best practice with the addition of the rider *"while providing flexibility to employers and FDWs who wish to accept monetary compensation in-lieu of their rest day"*. Given the balance of power between FDWs and employers, coupled with the predominant motivation for working away from home in the first place – namely, to generate income – it is hard to imagine that such a negotiation can be carried out in a balanced and equitable manner. It has been argued that the Ministry of Manpower's policy is, in effect, a 'signalling measure' put in place to appease growing pressure and criticism from local and international NGOs (Platt *et al.* 2013: 14).[21]

Whatever the reasons for the riots in Little India at the end of 2013 noted above, the government's immediate, forthright, multi-faceted response to them is indicative of the fact that in this instance the careful regulation of the migrant workforce broke down. But, transnational migrant work is not merely a political-economic arrangement or strategy. As Yeoh *et al.* say (1999: 133), "the buying and selling of domestic labor is not simply an economic transaction governed by the market but a socio-cultural relation between individuals, negotiated at many levels, including the everyday world of the household".

This brief summary of legislation and policies pertaining to migrant workers in Thailand and Singapore hints at the tensions that exist between the need to protect migrant workers on the one hand and, on the other, three other critical logics that underpin a country's engagement with its migrant workforce, and the policies that exist. These are: national security interests, economic and development interests, and social order interests. These logics are reflected in the laws themselves but of greater interest is how the legislation is enacted in practice, on the ground. It is here that we see how legal and policy frameworks are implemented, and how these come to be personalized, by which I mean how individual migrants experience the migration regime first hand. An additional important element in this experience is how wider society engages with their guest worker population, where issues of difference importantly come into play. The sometimes appalling conditions that migrant workers face, and the abuses they suffer, are often easier for host populations to accept because migrants are different (see, e.g. Arnold and Pickles 2011: 1613–4).

It is these contradictions that explain the migrant 'wrongs' that are so vividly recounted in many reports by NGOs and international bodies. It is important to note, however – and this is why tallying up the 'costs' and 'benefits' of migration to arrive at some balanced viewpoint is fruitless – that rights generate wrongs. It is through the governing of migration ever more assiduously, often under the banner of migrant rights, that migrants become biopolitical objects of control. From this emerges an additional set of problems and issues beyond those that the extension of rights aims to address.

Migrant wrongs

It is commonly thought that the way to protect migrants is by 'regularizing' their presence in a country – to move them from irregular/undocumented/illegal to regular/documented/legal. This, it is assumed, will then draw them into the mainstream, shield them from abuse, and cloak them in the protective umbrella of the state's labour laws and employment acts.

Much of the attention paid to migrant work and workers has focused on irregular or undocumented migration and trafficking, and especially child trafficking (see Huijsmans and Baker 2012). In both instances this is often associated with prostitution. The answer to the more egregious forms of exploitation that arise in such contexts is seen to involve regularizing the process (see below). What studies of transnational migration show, however, is that unfree labour, a form of modern-day bonded labour (Derks 2010a), can exist even in the context of fully documented and regularized movements. It is here, not at the murky edges of the migration industry but at its core, that we see the true extent of injustice. Such contract labour migrants are unfree in several respects: they are often bound by large debts owed to recruitment agencies; they are tied to an employer who often takes possession of their travel (and identification) documents;[22] they rarely have freedom of movement; and their legal protections are of a second order compared with citizens (see Piper 2010: 406). The dilemma that it raises is that the challenge is more intractable than simply calling for more or better legislation; it even goes beyond asking that these laws are implemented and policed; it asks more fundamental questions about the nature of the economic and social processes that underpin the flows of people and capital, and the work that entails.

An ILO report stated that Thailand's "registration policy is one of control on all fronts; controlling the number of migrant workers, controlling their movements and controlling any perceived damage they might do to the Thai workforce and national security" (Pearson *et al.* 2006: 9). It is through such controls that migrant labour becomes unfree and, therefore, open to abuse by employers who appreciate fully their migrant workers' lack of manoeuvre (Derks 2013). As Killias says in the context of the regularization of undocumented Indonesian domestic workers in Malaysia, "it is actually questionable whether state intervention has improved migrant workers' access to better working conditions, better wages, and justice" (2010: 911). Free labour is associated with undocumented, irregular migration; unfree (or modern day bonded) labour is associated with documented, regular migration. The act and process of regularizing migration and migrants involves disciplining labour, thus making their labour unfree. It is for these reasons that Piper (2010: 407) argues that we need to distinguish between free/unfree migration and free/unfree labour. Unfree migration with free labour might be a more attractive and empowering option than free migration and unfree labour.

For Pearson *et al.* (2006: xxiv) in their ILO report *The Mekong challenge: underpaid, overworked and overlooked*, "Laws and policies [in Thailand] play a significant role in how employers treat migrant workers" and the "absence of labour protection laws to protect the rights of workers in some of these sectors certainly facilitates their exploitation". For Derks (2013: 220–1), however, it is not the absence of laws and policies that is the issue, but rather their presence. In the introduction to their 2010 report on the abuse of migrant workers in Thailand, Human Rights Watch state:

> In interviews in Thailand from August 2008 to May 2009 and in follow-up research through January 2010, we found evidence of widespread violations of the rights of migrant workers from Burma, Cambodia, and Laos. The violations are not limited to one or two areas but range the entire length of the country from the Thai-Lao border gateway towns in Ubon Ratchathani to the seaports on the Gulf of Thailand to remote crossroads in areas on the Thai-Burma border. Many types of abuses are either embedded in laws and local regulations, such as restrictions on freedom of movement, or are perpetrated by officials, such as extortion by the police.
>
> (HRW 2010: 2)

A very similar position to that of Derks is postulated by Devasahayam in her work on migrant and migration policies for FDWs in Singapore. She argues (2010: 48) that Singapore's Employment of Foreign Manpower Act which regulates conditions of employment while, in theory, it protects workers by permitting employees to report infractions, actually puts in place a regime of management and better surveillance, rather than a system of protection.

Most egregious of all, however, is human trafficking and what is sometimes termed 'modern-day slavery'. While the numbers may be small in the context of the wider issue discussed above, the presence of such working practices and conditions in twenty-first century Southeast Asia demands our attention.[23] Migrants from Cambodia (Derks 2010b), Myanmar (Meyer *et al.* 2014), the Philippines (Yea 2012) and Vietnam (Bélanger 2014) are enticed, through deception, into domestic, factory and plantation work, and into the deep-sea fishing industry. Studies report a litany of practices which are common to almost all studies: deception, coercion, debt bondage, non-payment of salary, arbitrary salary deductions, forced work and forced overtime, and physical, verbal and mental abuse.[24] The Singapore government has managed to deflect criticism of its failure to control the trafficking of Filipino men into the long-haul fishing industry by claiming that they have no jurisdiction over the matter, as the offence occurs out at sea, in international waters (Yea 2012).[25] There is no doubt that the abuses are real, continuing and shocking. Whether they can be counted as 'modern-day slavery', as many anti-trafficking activists would wish – because slavery is such a special category – is more contentious. Davidson, for example, asks what distinguished the abuses suffered by trafficked women and men, from those who "are forced to work in appalling conditions by economic circumstances or other impersonal forces" (2010: 256). Do they face 'unfreedoms' that are qualitatively different from those of trafficked labour?

Migrant resistance

The fact that states seem so often to fail in their attempts to control migration and manage and track migrants, demonstrably shows that migrants work around the laws that have been put in place, resist or avoid the employers who abuse and exploit them, and occasionally confront the host societies that demean them. How do migrants, especially undocumented migrants, enact their 'rights' in the context of relative rightlessness and embedded unfreedoms?

Political activity by migrants or on behalf of migrants in Europe, the United States, Australia and Hong Kong has been quite marked and, sometimes, successful (see Edkins and Pin-Fat 2005; Ellerman 2010; McNevin 2013; Owens 2009). In Southeast Asia, while it is by no means absent – especially in Singapore[26] – such activity has been less pronounced and successful. This is not to say that migrant actions are lacking; it is just that they are low key, low profile, subversive rather than overt, and everyday.

Derks' studies (2010b, 2013) of Cambodian migrants in Thailand suggest that resistance mainly takes the form of evasion, rather than any attempt overtly to challenge employers or go against government policies. Workers use their ability to move – which, of course, is constrained through regularization – to escape from employers who are abusive or who do not pay wages on time or in full. Derks does recount some episodes of collective action on the part of migrant workers when trawlermen have 'downed tools' and staged labour boycotts, but she notes that such actions are rare and, furthermore, usually largely fruitless. Much more common is migrants job-hopping until they find an employer who meets what they regard as acceptable standards of behaviour. Also common are minor criminal acts on the part of migrant trawlermen; the stealing of trash fish, for example, to sell privately to top-up their low pay. It is in these ways that migrants claw back just a little agency and exert some power that challenges employers' tendencies towards exploitation and the state's attempts at control and management. Many of these minor acts of resistance, however, require that the migrant evades the state: by entering Thailand illegally, working and earning illegally, and travelling across the country illegally. Through these multiple illegal acts, however, migrants give up their right to rights; but, at the same time, it is by reneging on such official rights that a space for empowerment and action is opened up, and a route to alternative rights.

The room for manoeuvre of foreign (female) domestic workers in Singapore would seem to be even more constrained that it is for Derks' Cambodian fishermen in Thailand. Their immobility is heightened by their containment within the private space of the home, the regulating practices of the Singapore state and the disciplining practices of the employer, along with their constructed status as noncitizens (Yeoh and Huang 2010: 221). Certainly, it seems that domestic workers, isolated as they are on a day-to-day basis in private houses, not infrequently working seven days a week, find less scope – and perhaps less courage – to resist and challenge their conditions of work and employment. Even so, FDWs do answer back, refuse to undertake certain jobs, use social media to network with other FDWs, and take opportunities to use the family phone and relax when they are alone. Recourse to flight – simply leaving their employer – which is common in Thailand is much harder in Singapore because workers' entry to the country is dependent on employment and Singapore is policed so much more effectively than is Thailand. Nonetheless, instances of FDWs simply up-and-leaving do occur (Yeoh and Huang 2010: 233–4).

It is partly, perhaps, because of the particularly vulnerable position that FDWs occupy that NGOs and faith-based and other civil society groups in Singapore have been particularly active in campaigning for their interests. This gained real momentum following the shocking death of a 19-year-old Indonesian domestic worker at the hands of her male employer in 2002 while neighbours and other family members did nothing. "From the marginal position and near-invisibility of just a few years ago", Yeoh and Annadhurai (2008) wrote, "transnational domestic worker issues have gained much more prominence [in Singapore] and the current civil society landscape pertaining to these workers has become more variegated" (p. 555).

At the end of 2005, Human Rights Watch released a report entitled *Maid to order: ending abuses against migrant domestic workers in Singapore* (HRW 2005). The report detailed a myriad of abuses: deaths, forced confinement, low and unpaid wages, restricted communication, poor working conditions, lack of rest days, excessively long hours of work, illegal deployment to multiple homes, inadequate living accommodation, physical and sexual abuse and mistreatment, food deprivation, verbal abuse and threats, restrictions on freedom of movement, restrictions on religious freedom, and restrictions on reproductive and marriage rights. (Note the similarity here with those abuses and infractions listed in the context of trafficked workers, above.) While the report welcomed some of the steps that had been taken by the government, it also claimed that:

> These initiatives … do not go far enough. Singapore needs to do more to address the underlying inequities and lack of protection that result in widespread abuse. … In a country well-known for strictly enforcing laws to promote order and efficiency, the failure to provide adequate and equal protection to an entire class of workers is an anomaly and undermines the rule of law.
>
> (HRW 2005: 5–6)

A more recent report by Human Rights Watch on the status of domestic workers across Asia and the Middle East positively noted that "Singapore stands out as a country that has vigorously and successfully prosecuted employers and recruiters who physically abused domestic workers" (HRW 2010b: 4). It also, however, made the point that "of the countries surveyed here, only Singapore has made no movement to amend their labor laws to include domestic workers" (p. 15).

The government has defended its position partly on the grounds that the market mechanism should be allowed to set domestic workers' wages and partly on the basis that patrolling employment conditions (hours worked, days off, and so forth) is not practicable when FDWs live and work in a home setting. This is a surprising abrogation of responsibility by a state which, in so many other ways, manages to insinuate its way into the personal lives and everyday living of its citizens. As this book argues throughout, leaving economic processes and arrangement that have important social implications and outcomes to 'the market' is deeply problematic.

Governing rights

There is some scope for resistance, as outlined above. But it is important to ask the question whether this is more narrowly drawn in illiberal than in liberal political contexts. In other words, what does the varying nature of political regimes in Southeast Asia mean for the expression and articulation of migrant rights?

In liberal regimes, Ellerman (2010: 409) argues, a critical space for resistance is created by the "self-imposed curtailment of [the liberal state's] coercive powers". Essentially, undocumented migrants have the opportunity to protect themselves through identity stripping – through destroying their identity documents, even mutilating their fingertips so that they cannot be identified. This act of resistance is born of desperation and is premised on the paradox, unique to liberal states, that it "is those individuals with the weakest claims against the liberal state…who are able to constrain its exercise of sovereignty" (p. 409). This, of course, challenges Agamben's view that it is the very absence of the state's recognition of a person's citizenship that makes them 'bare'.[27] Liberal states are constitutionally bound as well as internationally required (as they are usually signatories to international human rights conventions) to protect human life and not to deport people who might face torture or a reasonable threat to their lives. If their identities are uncertain then liberal states cannot easily resort to deportation. What, though of non-citizens in illiberal regimes, which include Singapore and Thailand – indeed, all the countries of the region with the possible exception of the Philippines? The evidence is while everyday acts of resistance carried out in the workplace, at a personal level, might have some traction, those that seek to challenge state policies are almost always, and inevitably, unsuccessful.

Conclusion: viewing the economy in the round

The previous chapter of this book made the point that rapid growth has generated new types and forms of poverty and that we therefore need to pay careful attention to the articulation of particular types of living and classes of people with neoliberal economic expansion. An important part of this examination pays attention to the role of transnational migration in sustaining economic growth and underpinning the 'miracle' economies of the region.

Economic growth in the countries of Southeast Asia that receive large numbers of transnational migrants – namely Brunei Darussalam, Malaysia, Singapore and

Thailand – has been importantly founded on flows of cheap labour from neighbouring countries, as well as further afield. Transnational migrants constitute some 50 per cent of Brunei Darrusalam's workforce, 40 per cent of Singapore's, 25 per cent of Malaysia's, and 10 per cent of Thailand's workforces. These are very significant numbers. Indeed, they are so large that it is possible to argue that the recent and continuing expansion of these countries' economies has been founded on flows of such labour, and this in turn can be seen inscribed in the working and employment conditions they face.

These migrants do not enjoy the same remuneration as do the citizens of the countries where they work. This is partly because they are restricted to the very poorest-paid work although even when they do the same work, the evidence is that they are typically paid significantly less.[28] When politicians claim that poverty has been eradicated (see p. 55), they are not including these transnational migrants in their calculations. The incomes of these migrants are not recorded in national statistics and their poverty, therefore, goes unreported. But it is the poverty of these new poor who, in a real sense, have helped to make the old poor, non-poor. Consider the numbers: Malaysia, in 2010, had a population of 600,000 living below the $2 poverty line; in the same year there were more than 3 million transnational migrant workers, five times the number of recorded poor. In Thailand, in 2010, there were 6.6 million poor, and perhaps 3.5 million migrants. While not all migrants' incomes would necessarily place them below the poverty line, the evidence is that they are usually among the poorest paid of workers and, if there is a minimum wage, frequently receive wages that fall beneath this level (see Table 4.2).

'Made in Malaysia', 'Made in Singapore' and 'Made in Thailand' become, given the level of transnational migrant work and their contribution to the economy only a partial reflection of the people behind the production statistics. Textiles from Malaysia should have sewn into their hems 'Made in Malaysia, Produced by Vietnamese', tins of seafood from Thailand might be labelled with 'Produced in Thailand, Fished by Cambodians and Burmese', and young men and women in Singapore stamped with 'Born in Singapore, Raised by Filipinos'.

That transnational migration for the majority of workers raises their incomes and supports livelihoods at 'home' is its major justification. It is viewed as broadly developmental at an individual and household level and, often, also at a national level when countries come to rely on the substantial flows of foreign exchange that such migration can generate.[29] But when workers are injured or die in workplace accidents, when they are routinely abused by their employers, and when receiving states seem more intent on exploiting the labour of these workers than protecting their rights, then the developmental argument becomes increasingly questionable.

To point out that transnational migrant workers in Southeast Asia are vulnerable and open to abuse is hardly novel; it has been extensively documented. Furthermore, it is not just a Southeast Asian affliction but is echoed, time and again, across the world. The abuse of migrants is, moreover, scarcely a new phenomenon. In the 1860s, Mark Twain wrote this of Chinese migrant labourers in California:

I have seen Chinamen abused and maltreated in all the mean, cowardly ways possible to the invention of a degraded nature, but I never saw a policeman interfere in the matter and I never saw a Chinaman righted in a court of justice for wrongs thus done to him.

(Quoted in Chang 2014: 79)

To be sure, we have seen in Singapore and Thailand incremental improvements in the legislative framework, following sometimes intense domestic and international criticism. The Singapore state, for example, has amended the Penal Code to raise the penalties imposed on abusive employers; the minimum age of FDWs has been increased to 23 years; employment contracts have been standardized; and agencies and employers are now more carefully and stringently checked. Even so, centre stage still lies the Singapore government's "primordial interest in maximizing economic benefits while minimizing [the] social and economic costs" of employing FDWs and other migrants (Devasahayam 2010: 55).[30] Devasahayam continues:

Protection of human and worker rights … let alone the empowerment of FDWs, is given the least priority, with scant exceptions, leaving women migrants to either fend for themselves or be left to suffer a series of disadvantages in their employment in Singapore. Moreover, whatever few protection measures are in place, it is worth highlighting that they are yet to be seriously implemented hand in hand with empowerment measures.

(Devasahayam 2010: 55)

This chapter has sought to highlight, however, not just that abuses occur, but to explain *why* they occur.

What, at first glance, may appear perplexing is that notwithstanding very significant extensions to the legislative frameworks in both Singapore and Thailand, ostensibly designed to protect migrant workers from abuse and exploitation, both continue – and at a wide level. Appreciating this legislative failure requires that we view international labour migration in terms of the neoliberal context that underpins and drives the process. Wages are poor and conditions are dangerous because they need to be so in the context of neoliberal growth; regulations are put in place because migrants are needed, but not wanted; and laws that might protect workers are either lacking or poorly policed because the conditions in which migrants work are not of central public anxiety and therefore of political concern. Moreover, as Grugel and Piper (2011) argue in general terms, there are a series of barriers to the effective governance of migrants' rights. This is partly because of the complex transnational governance of such rights, partly because in many receiving countries there is no culture of migrant rights, and partly because activist organizations find their room for action curtailed in various ways. Most important of all, however, is the way in which governments have been intent on strategically narrowing the definition of 'exploitation', 'victimhood' and 'trafficking' to only the most egregious examples. In this way, everyday or banal exploitation is pushed to the margins of attention, and processes of capitalist accumulation can continue unhindered.

This chapter has focused resolutely on transnational migrants and their experiences in destination sites. But migrants have families, are embedded in households and communities, and are citizens of their countries of origin. The following chapter tracks back to focus on the family, household and community implications of the spatial, social and economic transformations of which migration is just one – albeit an important – part.

Further reading

The UNDP's downloadable *Human Development Report 2009*, on the theme of migration and development, provides a good global overview of migration trends and flows. For Southeast Asia in particular, see the papers by Kelly (2011) and Kaur (2010); the latter author also provides a good summary of state policies towards migrants in Malaysia, Singapore and Thailand.

Many studies of undocumented transnational migrants use Agamben's work as a theoretical scaffold. For a general critical analysis of this tendency, see Lee (2010). Rajaram and Grundy-Warr's (2004) paper represents an important early study (drawing on evidence from Australia, Malaysia and Thailand). Also see Owens (2009) and De Genova and Peutz's (2010) edited volume *The deportation regime*.

For the human angle on migrant work and workers, documents produced by campaigning organizations are often the most vivid. See, for example, Amnesty International on migrant workers in Qatar (2013) and Malaysia (2010), and Human Rights Watch on domestic workers in Singapore (HRW 2005), and more widely in Asia and the Middle East (HRW 2006, 2010b). Human Rights Watch (HRW 2010b) and the ILO (2006) also provide good and hard-hitting for reports on the status of transnational migrants in Thailand and the IOM has produced a report on the trafficking of fishermen in Thailand (IOM 2011). In 2014 the *Guardian* newspaper published an account of 'slave' conditions on Thailand's trawlers, with an accompanying short film (see http://www.theguardian.com/ global-development/2014/jun/10/-sp-migrant-workers-new-life-enslaved-thai-fishing and http://www.theguardian.com/global-development/video/2014/jun/10/ slavery-supermarket-supply-trail-prawns-video). All these reports are downloadable. The 2014 World Slavery Index report from the Walk Free Foundation can be downloaded from http://www.globalslaveryindex.org/.

For empirically grounded academic studies of international labour migrants in Thailand see Derks (2010a, 2013) on Cambodian migrants, and Pearson and Kusakabe (2012), Kusakabe and Pearson (2010) and Arnold and Pickles (2011) on Burmese migrants in Thailand. There is a wealth of work on domestic contract workers in Singapore, especially by Shirlena Huang and Brenda Yeoh (Huang *et al.* 2012; Yeoh and Annadhurai 2008; Yeoh and Huang 2010; Yeoh *et al.* 1999). There is relatively little, by comparison, on male contract workers in Singapore, although the work of Kitiarsa (2008, 2014) is an exception and Sallie Yea has a book forthcoming entitled *Precarious men: banal exploitation, labour migration and human trafficking in Singapore*. Also see Yea's (2012) report on Filipino fishermen trafficked through Singapore. Finally, for studies of migrant rights see the work of Nicola Piper (2009a, 2009b, 2010).

Notes

1 There are also significant forced migrations due to war, civil conflict, natural disasters and government policy. These, however, do not match in terms of numbers those who move for 'voluntary' reasons.
2 The full IOM definition can be accessed at http://www.iom.int/cms/en/sites/iom/home/about-migration/key-migration-terms-1.html#Irregular-migration.
3 While the IOM tries in this way to decriminalize undocumented migration, migrants tend to form a disproportionately large part of the prison population. Ramachelvam (2008, quoted in Kaur 2010: 13) points out that while 33 per cent of Malaysia's prison population are foreign nationals – many migrants – they commit just 3 per cent of crimes.
4 Status hierarchies in Thailand are not just linked to the Thai/non-Thai binary. Gullette (2013) and McCargo (2013) show how Bangkokians are often contemptuous of the rural 'masses'.
5 Following the release of a *Guardian* newspaper exposé (see http://www.theguardian.com/global-development/2014/jun/10/-sp-migrant-workers-new-life-enslaved-thai-fishing) of slave conditions on Thailand's trawlers, a Thai friend and academic wrote to me saying: "I was speechless with this. The thing that sticks in my throat is that many Thais do not see this as a big problem. It might be because the victims are Burmese and Cambodian migrants; for many Thais, it's ok to just close their eyes and ignore it".
6 For studies of migrants and migration in Southeast Asia that use Agamben's work see Rajaram and Gundy-Warr (2004), Owens (2009), De Genova and Peutz (2010), McNevin (2013), Kitiarsa (2014) and Derks (2010a, 2013).
7 Agamben quotes Pompeius Festus: 'The sacred man [*homo sacer*] is the one whom the people have judged on account of a crime. It is not permitted to sacrifice this man, yet he who kills him will not be condemned for homicide' (1998: 71).
8 Used here in the political science sense of state power shaping human's natural lives.
9 In *Means without end*, Agamben (2000: 14–25) makes the refugee the ultimate biopolitical subject:

> What is new in our time is that growing sections of humankind are no longer representable inside the nation state – and this novelty threatens the very foundations of the latter. Inasmuch as the refugee, an apparently marginal figure, unhinges the old trinity of state-nation-territory, it deserves instead to be regarded as the central figure of our political history.
>
> (pp. 20–21)

10 Gupta writes:

> The extremely poor could be a perfect example of what Agamben means by homo sacer in that their death is not recognized as a violation in any respect: not a violation of a norm, a rule, a law, a constitutional principle, not even perhaps of the idea of justice. Does not providing food, clothing, shelter, and healthcare to someone who is obviously in dire need represent killing?
>
> (2012: 17)

11 Sargeson (2013) sees land expropriation in China as structural violence, but unlike Galtung does not view it as silent, nor does she see its perpetrators as invisible. They may be multiple and the process may be multi-scaled and iterative but the agents of harm, she argues, are readily identifiable.

12 A special issue of the *Asian Journal of Social Science* (Vol. 38, No. 6, 2010) is couched around the concept of 'bonded labour'. Bonded labour has tended to be seen as 'unfree' and therefore as a form of forced labour or trafficking. However, in reality there are gradations along the spectrum from slavery at one end to free labour at the other (Derks 2010a, b).

13 Although there is still a significant flow of Thai workers to Singapore, East Asia (Japan, South Korea, Taiwan) and the Middle East. In 2011 the total number of Thai workers deployed overseas numbered 147,600; of these, 11,500 were employed in Singapore, 34,300 in the Middle East, and 70,900 in East Asia (Huguet *et al.* 2012: 4).

14 It is worth noting that for Singapore there is a wealth of academic – and activist – work on foreign domestic workers (who are almost entirely female) and comparatively little on foreign workers in the construction industry (who are almost entirely male). This is mainly because it is much harder for researchers to access the latter group, contained as they often are within gated, company-owned dormitories.

15 This was not planned. Yeoh *et al.* (1999: 117) some 15 years ago stated that "in the long term, the state aims to restructure the economy to manage without such a high dependence on immigrant workers, both skilled and unskilled". Since then the number of foreign workers has more than doubled. The most recent population White Paper (2013) states, again, that while "we … continue to need a significant number of foreign workers to complement the Singaporean core in the workforce … We must rely less on foreign labour" (GoS 2013).

16 For a sustained engagement with transnational migrant rights, see the work of Piper and Grugel (Piper 2008, 2009a, 2009b, 2010; Grugel and Piper 2011).

17 Exceptions to this being the right to establish or lead a labour union, which are denied to migrants (HRW 2010a: 20).

18 These include the International Covenant on Civil and Political Rights (ICCPR), the International Covenant on Economic, Social and Cultural Rights (ICESCR), the International Convention on the Elimination of all Forms of Racial Discrimination (ICERD), and the Convention against Torture and Other Cruel, Inhuman or Degrading Treatment or Punishment (Convention against Torture). Thailand has also ratified many of the ILO Conventions, including Convention No. 182 on the Worst Forms of Child Labour, ILO Convention No. 138 on Minimum Wage, and ILO Conventions No. 29 and No. 105 on Forced Labour. (Sourced from ILO 2006 and HRW 2010a.)

19 This mirrors the debate over the root causes of extensive dispossession in Cambodia discussed in the previous chapter (see p. 68).

20 Downloaded from: http://www.mom.gov.sg/Documents/foreign-manpower/FAQs%20 on%20weekly%20rest%20days%20for%20FDWs.pdf.

21 In a sample of some 200 Indonesian FDWs in Singapore, Platt *et al.*'s (2013: 44) work reveals that around 30 per cent of respondents received a day off each week from their employers, 31 per cent did not, and the remainder had one day a fortnight off, or less. This work was completed in late 2012, however, just before the new day-off policy was adopted.

22 Pearson and Kusakabe (2012: 89) say that the retention of migrants' travel documents by factory owners among their survey sample of Burmese workers in Thailand was 'routine'.

23 The 2014 Global Slavery Index report (Walk Free Foundation 2014) states that the governments of Brunei, Malaysia and Singapore should be doing more, given their wealth, while Indonesia and Thailand 'appear to have strong responses on paper, but these are often poorly implemented, or are hampered by high levels of corruption' (p. 23). Officials in Cambodia, Laos and Myanmar, as well as in Thailand, are 'complicit' in

the smuggling of undocumented migrants, some of whom then become trafficking victims (p. 93).

24 Physical abuse is normally inflicted by employers; sometimes it is state-orchestrated. In 2009 the Malaysian government released figures showing that between 2002 and 2008 some 35,000 migrant workers were caned, often for quite minor misdemeanours (see Amnesty International 2010, Nielsen and Sendjaya 2014). Illegal entry, for example, can lead to a penalty of six strokes of the *rotan,* the thin wooden cane that is used for such purposes.

25 Yea writes:

> [Filipino] men [trafficked through Singapore] were variously subjected to excessive working hours, no days off, extremely substandard living conditions, including inadequate food, lack of treatment for injuries and sickness, lack of protective gear whilst working, and enforced isolation – sometimes for years – on the vessels. Further, many participants' recounted experiences of physical and psychological abuse by the captain or senior officers on the vessels. Apart from conditions on board, the study found that men were universally deceived during the recruitment process, with the nature of deception including agreements concerning remuneration, working conditions and, in some cases, deception about the actual job that was to be performed in/ through Singapore.
>
> (2012: 8–9)

26 See, for example, the website of TWC2 (Transient Workers Count Too) at http://twc2.org.sg/.

27 In contending that modern-day detention camps like Guantanamo Bay cannot be equated with Hitler's concentration camps, Ellerman writes:

> [I]n liberal democracies even exceptional state power is bounded. In detention centers, aspects of the normal legal order are suspended, but the rule of law is not abolished. Rather, in liberal polities, zones of marginalization are places where the legal order is partially abrogated and replaced with a lesser set of constitutional and statutory protections.
>
> (2010: 413)

28 See the following blog on Singapore's bus drivers' strike – the first for many years – which involved bus drivers from mainland China: http://blogs.wsj.com/searealtime/2013/08/26/the-strike-that-rattled-singapore-a-wsj-investigation/.

29 This is true, for example, of the Philippines and Nepal where international remittances constitute 10 and 28 per cent of GDP respectively (World Bank data).

30 The 2013 White Paper of the Government of Singapore sets out the logic very clearly. The role of migrant workers is:

> Providing flexibility to businesses during upswings, while buffering Singaporean workers from job losses during downturns. Foreign manpower has provided the flexibility for businesses to capitalise on economic upswings and capture growth opportunities when they arise. Foreign workers also provide a buffer for Singaporean workers during recessions.
>
> (GoS 2013: 41)

References

Agamben, G. (1998). Homo sacer*: sovereign power and bare life.* Stanford, CA, Stanford University Press.

Agamben, G. (2000). *Means without end: notes on politics.* Minneapolis, University of Minnesota Press.

Amnesty International (2010). *Trapped: the exploitation of migrant workers in Malaysia.* London, Amnesty International.

Amnesty International (2013). *The dark side of migration: spotlight on Qatar's construction sector ahead of the World Cup.* London, Amnesty International.

Arnold, D. and J. Pickles (2011). "Global work, surplus labor, and the precarious economies of the border." *Antipode* 43(5): 1598–1624.

Azim, P. (2002). "The ageing population of Brunei Darussalam: trends and economic consequences." *Asia-Pacific Population Journal* 17(1): 39–54.

Bélanger, D. (2014). "Labor migration and trafficking among Vietnamese Migrants in Asia." *The Annals of the American Academy of Political and Social Science* 653(1): 87–106.

Calder, T. (2010). "Shared responsibility, global structural injustice, and restitution." *Social Theory and Practice* 36: 263–290.

Chanda, R. (2012). Migration between South and Southeast Asia: overview of trends and issues. ISAS Working Paper. Singapore: 140.

Chang, J. (2014). *Empress Dowager Cixi: the concubine who launched modern China.* London, Vintage Books.

Davidson, J. O. (2010). "New slavery, old binaries: human trafficking and the borders of 'freedom'." *Global Networks* 10(2): 244–261.

De Genova, N. (2010). The deportation regime: soveignty, space, and the freedom of movement. *The deportation regime: sovereignty, space, and the freedom of movement.* N. De Genova and N. Peutz. Durham, NC and London, Duke University Press: 33–65.

De Genova, N. and N. Peutz, Eds. (2010). *The deportation regime: sovereignty, space, and the freedom of movement.* Durham, NC and London, Duke University Press.

Derks, A. (2010a). "Bonded labour in Southeast Asia: introduction." *Asian Journal of Social Science* 38(6): 839–852.

Derks, A. (2010b). "Migrant labour and the politics of immobilisation: Cambodian fishermen in Thailand." *Asian Journal of Social Science* 38(6): 915–932.

Derks, A. (2013). "Human rights and (im)mobility: migrants and the state in Thailand." *Sojourn: Journal of Social Issues in Southeast Asia* 28: 216+.

Devasahayam, T. W. (2010). "Placement and/or protection? Singapore's labour policies and practices for temporary women migrant workers." *Journal of the Asia Pacific Economy* 15(1): 45–58.

Edkins, J. and V. Pin-Fat (2005). "Through the wire: relations of power and relations of violence." *Millennium – Journal of International Studies* 34(1): 1–24.

Ellermann, A. (2010). "Undocumented migrants and resistance in the liberal state." *Politics & Society* 38(3): 408–429.

Friedman, T. (2005). *The world is flat: a brief history of the globalized world in the 21st century.* London, Penguin Books.

Galtung, J. (1969). "Violence, peace, and peace research." *Journal of Peace Research* 6(3): 167–191.

Gardner, A. M. (2010). Engulfed: Indian guest workers, Bahraini citizens, and the structural violence of the Kafala system. *The deportation regime: soveignty, space, and the freedom of movement.* N. De Genova and N. Peutz. Durham, NC and London, Duke University Press: 196–223.

Glassman, J. (2007). "Recovering from crisis: the case of Thailand's spatial fix." *Economic Geography* 83(4): 349–370.

GoS (2013). *A sustainable population for a dynamic Singapore.* Singapore, National Population and Talent Divison, Government of Singapore.

Grugel, J. and N. Piper (2011). "Global governance, economic migration and the difficulties of social activism." *International Sociology* 26(4): 435–454.

Gullette, G. S. (2013). "Rural–urban hierarchies, status boundaries, and labour mobilities in Thailand." *Journal of Ethnic and Migration Studies* 40(8): 1254–1274.

Gupta, A. (2012). *Red tape: bureaucracy, structural violence, and poverty in India.* Durham, NC, Duke University Press.

Hewage, P., C. Kumara and J. Rigg (2011). "Connecting and disconnecting people and places: migrants, migration, and the household in Sri Lanka." *Annals of the Association of American Geographers* 101(1): 202–219.

HRW (2005). *Maid to order: ending abuses against migrant domestic workers in Singapore.* New York, Human Rights Watch.

HRW (2006). *Swept under the rug: abuses against domestic workers around the world.* New York, Human Rights Watch.

HRW (2010a). *From the tiger to the crocodile: abuse of migrant workers in Thailand.* New York, Human Rights Watch.

HRW (2010b). *Slow reform: protection of migrant domestic workers in Asia and the Middle East.* New York, Human Rights Watch.

Huang, S., B. S. A. Yeoh and M. Toyota (2012). "Caring for the elderly: the embodied labour of migrant care workers in Singapore." *Global Networks* 12(2): 195–215.

Huguet, J., A. Chamratrithirong and C. Natali (2012). *Thailand at a crossroads: challenges and opportunities in leveraging migration for development.* Bangkok and Washington DC, International Organization for Migration and Migration Policy Institute.

Huijsmans, R. and S. Baker (2012). "Child trafficking: 'worst form' of child labour, or worst approach to young migrants?" *Development and Change* 43(4): 919–946.

ILO (2006). *The Mekong challenge: underpaid, overworked and overlooked – the realities of young migrant workers in Thailand,* Vol. 1. Bangkok, International Labour Organization. Downloaded from: http://www.ilo.org/wcmsp5/groups/public/@asia/@ro-bangkok/documents/publication/wcms_bk_pb_67_en.pdf.

Ingram, D. (2012). "The structural injustice of forced migration and the failings of normative theory." *Perspectives on Global Development & Technology* 11(1): 50–71.

IOM (2011). *Trafficking of fishermen in Thailand.* Bangkok, International Organization for Migration.

Jalilian, H. and G. Reyes (2012). Migrants of the Mekong: wins and losses. *Costs and benefits of cross-country labour migration in the GMS.* H. Jalilian. Singapore, Institute of Southeast Asian Studies: 1–117.

Kaur, A. (2010). "Labour migration in Southeast Asia: migration policies, labour exploitation and regulation." *Journal of the Asia Pacific Economy* 15(1): 6–19.

Kelly, P. F. (2011). "Migration, agrarian transition, and rural change in Southeast Asia." *Critical Asian Studies* 43(4): 479–506.

Killias, O. (2010). "'Illegal' migration as resistance: legality, morality and coercion in Indonesian domestic worker migration to Malaysia." *Asian Journal of Social Science* 38: 897–914.

Kitiarsa, P. (2008). "Thai migrants in Singapore: state, intimacy and desire." *Gender, Place & Culture* 15(6): 595–610.

Kitiarsa, P. (2014). *The 'bare life' of Thai migrant workmen in Singapore.* Chiang Mai, Thailand, Silkworm Books.

Kundu, A. (2009). Urbanisation and migration: an analysis of trend, pattern and policies in Asia. Human Development Reports Research Paper 2009/16 (April). New York, United Nations Development Programme.

Kusakabe, K. and R. Pearson (2010). "Transborder migration, social reproduction and economic development: a case study of Burmese women workers in Thailand." *International Migration* 48(6): 13–43.

Lê, T. H. (2010). "A new portrait of indentured labour: Vietnamese labour migration to Malaysia." *Asian Journal of Social Science* 38: 880–896.

Lee, C. T. (2010). "Bare life, interstices, and the third space of citizenship." *Women's Studies Quarterly* 38(1): 57–81.

Li, M. (2012). "Making a living at the interface of legality and illegality: Chinese migrant workers in Israel." *International Migration* 50(2): 81–98.

Lindio-McGovern, L. (2004). "Alienation and labor export in the context of globalization." *Critical Asian Studies* 36(2): 217–238.

McCargo, D. (2013). The last gasp of Thai paternalism. *New York Times*, 19 December.

McNevin, A. (2013). "Ambivalence and citizenship: theorising the political claims of irregular migrants." *Millennium – Journal of International Studies* 41(2): 182–200.

MAP (2012). *Regular rights: do documents improve migrants' lives?* Chiang Mai, Thailand, MAP Foundation.

Martin, P. 2009. Migration in the Asia-Pacific region: trends, factors, impacts. Human Development Reports Research Paper 2009/32 (August), United Nations Development Programme.

Meyer, S. R., W. Courtland Robinson , N. Abshir, A. A. Mar and M. R. Decker (2014). "Trafficking, exploitation and migration on the Thailand-Burma border: a qualitative study." *International Migration*, doi: 10.1111/imig.12177

MoM (2014). *Labour force in Singapore, 2013*. Singapore, Ministry of Manpower.

Newland, K. (2009). Circular migration and human development. Human Development Reports Research Paper 2009/42 (October). New York, United Nations Development Programme.

Nielsen, I. and S. Sendjaya (2014). "Wellbeing among Indonesian labour migrants to Malaysia: implications of the 2011 Memorandum of Understanding." *Social Indicators Research* 117(3): 919–938.

Owens, P. (2009). "Reclaiming 'bare life'? Against Agamben on refugees." *International Relations* 23(4): 567–582.

Pearson, E., S. Punpuing, A. Jampaklay, S. Kittisuksathit and A. Prohmmo (2006). *The Mekong challenge: underpaid, overworked and overlooked – the realities of young migrant workers in Thailand*. Geneva, International Labour Organization.

Pearson, R. and K. Kusakabe (2012). *Thailand's hidden workforce: Burmese migrant women factory workers*. London and New York, Zed Press.

Peters, R. (2012). "City of ghosts." *Critical Asian Studies* 44(4): 543–570.

Piper, N. (2008). "The 'migration–development nexus' revisited from a rights perspective." *Journal of Human Rights* 7(3): 282–298.

Piper, N. (2009a). "The complex interconnections of the migration–development nexus: a social perspective." *Population, Space and Place* 15(2): 93–101.

Piper, N. (2009b). "Temporary economic migration and rights activism: an organizational perspective." *Ethnic and Racial Studies* 33(1): 108–125.

Piper, N. (2010). "All quiet on the Eastern front? Temporary contract migration in Asia revisited from a development perspective." *Policy and Society* 29(4): 399–411.

Platt, M., B. S. A. Yeoh, G. Baey, K. C. Yen, T. Lam, D. Das and M. Ee (2013). Financing migration, generating remittances and the building of livelihood strategies: a case study of Indonesian migrant women as domestic workers in Singapore. Working Paper 10. Singapore, Asia Research Institute, National University of Singapore.

Rajaram, P. K. and C. Grundy-Warr (2004). "The irregular migrant as *homo sacer*: migration and detention in Australia, Malaysia, and Thailand." *International Migration* 42(1): 33–64.

Sankharat, U. (2013). "Cambodian child migrant workers in the Rong Kluea market area in Thailand." *Asian Social Science* 9(11): 24–32.

Sargeson, S. (2013). "Violence as development: land expropriation and China's urbanization." *The Journal of Peasant Studies* 40(6): 1063–1085.

Scott, J. (1985) *Weapons of the weak: everyday forms of peasant resistance.* New Haven, CT, Yale University Press.

UNDP (2009). *Human Development Report 2009: Overcoming barriers – human mobility and development.* New York, United Nations Development Programme.

Walk Free Foundation (2014). *The Global Slavery Index 2014.* London, Walk Free Foundation.

World Bank (2009). *World Development Report 2009: reshaping economic geography.* Washington DC, World Bank.

Yea, S. (2012). *Troubled waters: trafficking of Filipino men into the long haul fishing industry through Singapore.* Singapore, Transnational Workers Count Too (TWC2).

Yea, S. (forthcoming). *Precarious men: banal exploitation, labour migration and human trafficking in Singapore.* Manoa, University of Hawaii Press.

Yeoh, B. S. A. and K. Annadhurai (2008). "Civil society action and the creation of 'transformative' spaces for migrant domestic workers in Singapore." *Women's Studies* 37(5): 548–569.

Yeoh, B. S. A. and S. Huang (2010). "Transnational domestic workers and the negotiation of mobility and work practices in Singapore's home-spaces." *Mobilities* 5(2): 219–236.

Yeoh, B. S. A., S. Huang and J. G. Iii (1999). "Migrant female domestic workers: debating the economic, social and political impacts in Singapore." *International Migration Review* 33(1): 114–136.

Zhao, Y. (1999). "Leaving the countryside: rural-to-urban migration decisions in China." *The American Economic Review* 89(2): 281–286.

Zirwatul Asilati bte Hj, M., S. E. Tan and S. Tan Phek (2000). "Foreign housemaids in Negara Brunei Darussalam: an analysis of a secondary labour market." *Borneo Review* 11(1): 1.

5 Building the neoliberal family
Dislocated families, fragmented living, fractured societies?

Introduction

In the 1990s, it was not uncommon to find political leaders and policy-makers in Asia, and even some scholars, suggesting that the region's economic transformation would not be accompanied by the same social shocks and perturbations that had come to afflict Western countries – or that, at least, was the way it was often perceived and presented.[1] Asian societies, for a range of often ill or only partially thought-through reasons, were considered to be different and would therefore be insulated from and resistant to such problematic social developments. This tended to be viewed through the lens of Asian culture and society. Asian values made Asia exceptional:

> Asian Values does not simply justify one or another Asian exception, but also opens space to think critically about the fact that *broadly shared Asian realities confound accepted wisdom about the cultural requirements for – and social consequences of – modernization*. ... Asian characteristics are often invoked to turn accepted wisdom about development, social order, and authority upside down. ... [there is a] push by Asian Values supporters to expose and overturn the culturally specific implications of much accepted dogma in the social sciences.
>
> (Jenco 2013: 254, emphasis added)

Nowhere, arguably, has the case for Asian exceptionalism had more purchase than with regard to the family and family relations. It is in the resilience of Asian family structures, values and norms in the face of rapid economic transformation where we find, so it has been suggested, the Asian difference being most obviously manifested (see Yi 2013: 253). As Martin writes, for example, "it has been an article of faith in Asia and the Pacific that the family will care for its respected elderly and not abandon them as the West is perceived to have done" (1989: 627).

Debates about the resilience of the Asian family have not, however, fully come to terms with the way in which the mechanics of economic transformation would re-engineer societal arrangements and structures and, in turn, social and cultural norms. Falling fertility rates, an ageing population, growing levels of migration and mobility, the entry of women – especially young, unmarried women – into the non-farm workforce, rising levels of education, smaller families, declining terms of trade between the farm and non-farm sectors, all this and more have had enormous societal, livelihood and economic implications. The status quo, as it were, even while familial ties, obligations and responsibilities may have remained strong, has sometimes been impossible to sustain.

To be sure, Asian societies will be transformed in ways that are distinct from transition paths in the West, but it is clear that change they will, and not infrequently in ways and directions that are viewed by the political mainstream as problematic. Furthermore, the rapidity and nature of these changes have often been a surprise to many social scientists. In the early 1990s, for example, few scholars expected there to be such a thorough-going opening up of national space in East Asia to transnational migration; and rather earlier, even fewer thought that fertility rates would decline as steeply as they have. Like much else in the recent transformation of Asia, these came as something of a surprise. To appreciate how these wider structural changes have impacted on the household we need to shift our focus from the minutiae of Asian culture and pay attention, instead, to the societal outcomes of the economic forces at work. It is true that the articulated norms of *the* family often remain strong, even if these are idealized and sometimes problematically promoted by the state, but the reality is that the family has had to adapt to radically new conditions. In what light we view these changes, as the chapter will explore, is not straightforward. Divided families are one social 'cost' of the new opportunities that exist. Accessing these opportunities plays an important role in lifting individuals and households out of poverty, not to mention driving national economic expansion. Doing so may also empower women and the young. At the same time, however, there may be a loss of individual and community well-being, and an erosion of livelihood resilience. It is the assessment of these mixed and sometimes problematic processes and outcomes with which this chapter concerns itself.

Problematizing the modern Asian household

The years since the turn of the century have seen a proliferation of terms to try and account for the new household forms that are emerging in Asia. This tendency, in itself, provides some indication of the manifold challenges that are seen to be facing the household and family in Asia (and more widely).

Scholars, policy-makers and practitioners have written about, for example: "left-behind children" (Hoang and Yeoh 2012) and "absentee mothers/fathers"; a "care deficit" and the emergence of "global care chains" (Kusakabe and Pearson 2010); "global householding" (Douglass 2006, 2012), "translocal householding" (Nguyen 2014) and "astronaut households" (Waters 2002); the "transnational family", "transnationally split households" and "transnational motherhood" (Piper 2008); "distance mothering" (Kusakabe and Pearson 2013), "absent mothering" and "remote parenting" (Locke *et al.* 2012: 71); the "wife-worker" paradox and "liberal familiarism"; "split-apart" households (Parreñas 2005a: 19);

"visiting marriages" (Locke *et al.* 2012: 71); and "empty nests" (Nguyen 2014: 19). While these terms address themselves to a range of issues, whether they be the geographical fragmentation of households, the separation of children from their parents, or support for the elderly, they deal at root with the same core question: how does the (Asian) family 'care' now, and will it – and how will it – care in the future?

More often than not, the terms listed in the last paragraph also carry with them negative connotations even though it is entirely plausible that some of the processes they highlight might bring with them some significant positive effects. For example, the movement of women to waged employment out of the home can be empowering and status enhancing. It may be viewed by individual married women as a way of escaping an abusive relationship, or of furthering their careers. And most obviously, migration often brings additional income into the household. Nonetheless the tendency in the literature, and even more so in policy documents, has been to focus on the assumed socially harmful and corrosive effects of these changes, and the political dilemmas that arise from them. This is a challenge for individual families and wider society, but also for the state. Writing of the dramatic and unexpected growth of global householding, for example, Douglass suggests that it represents a

> challenge to the nation-state as the basic socio-cultural and political unit of the world system ... [and] ...weakens state-centred ideologies of the family, such as the idealisation of gender relations circumscribed by Confucianist values in the family which are metaphorically linked to the government and its leader as 'father' of the nation.
>
> (Douglass 2006: 441)

Global householding and the transnational family

The household is, in most Asian societies, the basic social unit. Classically, it was a 'co-residential dwelling unit', defined by the spatial proximity – the propinquity – of its membership (see Rigg 2012: 171–176). Notions of 'living under one roof' (Evans 1991) or 'eating from the same cooking pot' (Annan *et al.* 1986; Holtz *et al.* 2004) are representative of this view of the household. Such an approach focuses not so much on the constitutive social fundamentals of the household but on their material, spatial manifestation. The reason why the household as a co-residential dwelling unit worked in definitional and operational terms in Asia was not because the household *had* to be so, but because it *was* so. (While also recognizing that in some societies it was never so.) Arising from this is a further important normative characteristic of the household: it was also co-residential, because it *should* be so. Indeed, normative support for co-residence continues even while its actual manifestation is often on the decline.

Over the last four decades a gap has opened up between the essence of the household as a social unit and as an ideal, and its spatial expression. The key social and economic functions of the household are:

- sharing labour and managing resources;
- pooling production and incomes;
- meeting the existential and other needs of household members;
- bearing, raising and, increasingly, educating children;
- caring for the elderly;
- reproducing the family and the household.

In Asia, these social and economic activities, responsibilities and requirements used to be quite closely interleaved in spatial terms. They were also often spatially coincident with the family. What you saw, in a sense, is what you got.[2] As the last chapter revealed, this is no longer the case. The household now operates, socially and economically, across space, between rural and urban and, sometimes, transnationally. It is the latter which has led to prominent academic work on 'global householding' and the 'transnational family'.

The terms 'global householding' and 'transnational family' are closely intertwined; indeed, they can be regarded as complementary. Global householding occurs where the "formation and sustenance of households is increasingly reliant on the global movement of people and transactions among household members originating from or residing in more than one national territory" (Douglass 2006: 423; and see Yeoh *et al.* 2014). The emphasis here is on the material functioning of the household and how migration and mobility – across national boundaries – requires the household as a unit of production and consumption to operate in new ways. The transforming of the noun (household) into a verb (householding) highlights the fact that the household is a social unit in flux, adapting and adjusting to changing circumstances.

The transnational family and familyhood refers to families that "live some or most of the time separated from each other, yet hold together and create something that can be seen as a feeling of collective welfare and unity, namely 'familyhood', even across national borders" (Bryceson and Vuorela 2002: 3). As Bryceson and Vuorela remark, such families are an "elusive phenomenon – spatially dispersed and seemingly capable of unending social mutation" (p. 3). This term, then, emphasizes the emotional and social essence of the family (and household). Like global householding, it also pays attention to how the family adapts in the light of spatial separation across national borders.

The focus on transnational movements is important because it picks-up on a number of recent and important developments in human mobility. It is also problematic, however, because it means that national movements and their implications are at risk of being sidelined and overlooked. As noted in the last chapter (see p. 95), more – indeed, far more – Asians are living in households which are separated across national space than there are those which are divided transnationally. This much larger group equally requires the household and family to be reconsidered and redefined in both material and emotional/social terms. In response, there are a range of additional terms – beyond global householding and the transnational family – that have come into recent use. Scholars now write, for example, of "shadow" (Rigg 2003), "multi-sited" (Padoch *et al.* 2008;

Rigg and Salamanca 2011) and "trans-local" (Brickell and Yeoh 2014) households, dependent on and sustained in a manner that has created new "livelihood footprints" (Rigg 2005).

One question which this overview of these two key terms – global *householding* and transnational *families* – raises is whether we should be writing about 'households' or 'families'. The term family, after all, highlights kinship and not propinquity and therefore might get around some of the problematics raised here concerning the stretching of the household over space and how we deal with this in definitional terms. In this chapter, however, household is preferred to family for two reasons.[3] First, it extends the social unit under investigation beyond kin, a necessary qualification given the non-kin household members who are becoming critical to social reproduction, such as domestic workers. And second, it more easily permits us to connect the socio-cultural and the politico-economic.

The care puzzle

These changes to the nature of the household raise a puzzle – and provide the outlines of a key policy challenge. The puzzle is as follows. The emergence of these new spatial household forms has been driven by the need and the desire to engage with the capitalist economy so as to generate income and elevate consumption. For many migrants, the social (and existential) reproduction of the household is founded and dependent on migration. There is also no question, as earlier chapters in this book have elaborated, that in material terms Southeast Asians are 'better off' today than they have ever been. Even the invisible migrant poor discussed in the last chapter are, in the most part, better off materially because of their migration. This also sometimes feeds through into better health (see, for example, Lu 2013 on Indonesia) and education (Garza 2010: 16–17) profiles of the family members who are left in the places of origin. But, and herein lies the paradox and the challenge, in securing material progress there has emerged the question of whether the household is beginning to fracture and fail in terms of its ability to deliver on its very *raison d'être* – of social reproduction beyond the material. This is occurring as a result of the economic forces that have reshaped households and their operation, and which have delivered prosperity.

The reshaping of the contemporary Asian household reveals the intense interweaving of production and reproduction (Locke, Seeley and Rao 2013). As Linh, a Vietnamese migrant and one of Locke *et al.*'s (2012: 73) respondents succinctly put it: "If I want to provide for them [my children], I have to migrate. But when I migrate I cannot take care of them" (2012: 73). For Locke *et al.* (2012: 65), therefore, there are "problematic contradictions and severe psychological pressures for women [migrants] trying to balance domestic and productive roles and identities". Taking care of the family in material and existential terms sometimes comes at the expense of taking care of the family in social terms. Production *for* the family rubs uneasily up against the reproduction *of* the family. Marketization and reform has provided greater scope for women to engage in productive work, but domestic responsibilities often remain largely unchanged (Vu and Agergaard 2012).

It is suggested here that there are two key elements to building an understanding of household formation and functioning in developing Asia. One pays attention to Asia's reproductive revolution: essentially, the dramatic fall in fertility rates across the East Asian region over the last three decades. The second focuses on the re-spatializing of household production and reproduction due to rising levels of migration and mobility. It is these, combined, which have played a large part in shaping the new household forms that have emerged, and the tensions, opportunities and accommodations that have resulted and which are continually being negotiated and renegotiated. The wider point is that the household is not an inert social category that maintains its coherence untroubled and untrammelled by the currents of history. Households are caught up in the development process, as well as contributing in important ways to that process. The household is very much a work in progress.

Asia's reproductive revolution

> When I first began studying Asia's fertility and family planning efforts 33 years ago, neither I nor other serious observers expected such rapid fertility declines to occur on that continent ...
>
> (Freeman 1995: 3)

I have written at length elsewhere about Asia's fertility decline (Rigg 2012: 143–178), and the surprise of that decline – reflected in Freeman's quote above from the mid-1990s. Here fertility decline provides only the backcloth for the later discussion, so I will limit myself to setting out the empirics and the implications for the nature, structure and size of Asian households.

As Table 5.1 shows, total fertility rates (TFRs) in Southeast Asia more than halved between 1960 and 2012, and if we exclude the unusual case of Timor Leste, then TFR rates have fallen by close to two-thirds over the period. Most countries in the region have TFRs that are at less than replacement rates, and the same is also true of all of the countries of East Asia. How and why this has occurred, whether due to the efficacy of state-led family planning policies or ideational change as a result of 'modernization' – or for some other reason or combination of reasons – is not my concern. Here, the concern is on the implications for the functioning of the household. As Jones (2007: 453; and see Jones and Leete 2002: 122) writes, Asia's fertility transition has been "one of the most fundamental and consequential developments in Pacific Asia in the last half of the twentieth century" and it will "vitally affect prospects for the way [their populations] will live in the twenty-first century and beyond".

Most obviously, rapidly falling TFRs will lead to a correspondingly rapid ageing of the population (assuming no large-scale immigration), accentuated by rising life expectancy. In addition, and necessarily so without the emergence of new extended household forms, household (and family) size will decline. Dependency rates will also rise as the demographic dividend comes to an end, but old-age

Table 5.1 Fertility decline in Southeast and East Asia, 1960–2012

Country/region	Total fertility rate						
	1960	*1970*	*1980*	*1990*	*2000*	*2010*	*2012*
Developing Asia & Pacific	5.83	5.54	3.20	2.73	*1.82*	*1.86*	*1.85*
Southeast Asia							
Brunei Darussalam	6.49	5.75	4.25	3.53	2.40	*2.05*	*2.01*
Cambodia	6.97	6.48	5.69	5.62	3.75	2.97	2.89
Indonesia	5.67	5.47	4.43	3.12	2.48	2.43	2.37
Lao PDR	5.96	5.97	6.28	6.15	4.19	3.29	3.11
Malaysia	6.19	4.87	3.79	3.52	2.83	*2.00*	*1.98*
Myanmar	6.05	5.96	5.00	3.42	2.43	*2.00*	*1.96*
Philippines	7.15	6.26	5.18	4.32	3.81	3.15	3.08
Singapore	5.45	3.09	*1.74*	*1.87*	*1.41*	*1.15*	*1.29*
Thailand	6.15	5.60	3.39	2.11	*1.68*	*1.44*	*1.41*
Timor-Leste	6.37	5.92	4.77	5.34	7.11	5.60	5.30
Vietnam	6.35	6.47	5.05	3.56	*1.98*	*1.82*	*1.77*
East Asia							
China	5.76	5.47	2.71	2.51	*1.51*	*1.65*	*1.66*
Hong Kong SAR, China	5.16	3.42	*2.05*	*1.27*	*1.04*	*1.13*	*1.29*
Japan	*2.00*	2.14	*1.75*	*1.54*	*1.36*	*1.39*	*1.41*
Korea, Rep.	6.16	4.53	2.83	*1.59*	*1.47*	*1.23*	*1.30*
Korea, Dem. Rep.	4.58	4.33	2.68	2.29	*1.99*	*2.00*	*2.00*

Source: http://data.worldbank.org/indicator/SP.DYN.TFRT.IN?page=5&cid=GPD_11

Notes: total fertility rate (TFR) represents the number of children that would be born to a woman if she were to live to the end of her childbearing years and bear children in accordance with current age-specific fertility rates. It is thus forward-looking, but on the basis of current levels of fertility.
TFRs in *italic* are below the replacement level, which is taken to be 2.1, although it will vary slightly between countries. The listed 2000 figure for Singapore is 2001 data.

dependency (65+ years) will replace child dependency (<15 years).[4] In addition, the countries of Asia are experiencing an increase in delayed or late marriage, and a rise in singlehood especially among educated women. One of the consequences is that men, and this is particularly true of less well-educated men, are finding marriage partners harder to come by. This has led to a minor explosion in international marriage migration as women from poorer countries – such as from China, the Philippines, Thailand and Vietnam – make up for this spousal shortfall in the richer countries of the region (Japan, Singapore, South Korea and Taiwan), and beyond (Australia, Europe, USA) (Jones 2010). Across Asia there has been a growth in female labour force participation rates, especially in the non-farm sector, and a geriatrification or greying of farming as the older generations remain in the countryside. All of these trends are circularly interlinked, in a cascade of cause, effect, and cause.

Migration and the resultant spatial reworking of the household has, often, accentuated these effects of falling fertility.

Generalizing the Asian household migration transition

The layered transformation in the nature of the household – in terms of its spatiality (footprint), constitution (in gender and generational terms) and functioning (in economic and socio-emotional respects) – has, it is tentatively suggested, a characteristic temporal signature. As ever, there are dangers with generalizing complex processes shaped by the particularities of geography, history and culture, but we can see four quite distinct phases in Asia's household/migration transition story. We can also attach periodicities to these shifts, although it makes more sense – and here the argument becomes even more Rostovian in tenor – to tie them to stages in the industrialization/development process. A significant health warning should be attached to these periodicities, but they do serve to highlight two points: that migration and household forms are linked, and that they are also shaped by the exigencies of the development process, particular though it is, country-by-country.

- *Peri-industrial*: in this early 'stage', migration streams were both limited (on the whole) and dominated by men with the result that, if the men were married, wives were 'left behind'.[5] Locke *et al.* (2012: 71) claim, for example, that male migration of this form, known as 'visiting marriages', has a long history in Vietnam, especially in the north. It is rooted, as it is elsewhere in the region, in notions of the husband as breadwinner. The early left-behind literature often entertained the working assumption that the left-behind were, by definition, female for the simple reason that migrants were male. The classic Vietnamese visiting marriage always had the husband as the visitor.
- *Early-industrial*: from the 1980s, migration streams became gradually – but significantly – more feminized. This coincided with Southeast Asia's export-oriented industrialization and the growing demand for labour to (wo)man the garment, footwear and electronics factories of the region. Most of these migrants were young and unmarried. They were 'dutiful daughters' migrating for the sake of the family who were able to move because they were free of reproductive responsibilities that would tie them to home, and where the former socio-cultural restraints on female mobility were easing.[6] The literature from this era tends to focus not so much on those left behind by this process, but on the poor working conditions that such young women faced, and their exposure and susceptibility to exploitation by factory management.
- *Middle-industrial*: during the 1990s the migration story took another twist. Increasingly, married women were migrating (or re-migrating) to work, leaving behind their children and, sometimes, their husbands as well. While men's absence has traditionally been justified in terms of gendered discourses of the male breadwinner, and this often continues to be the case, female migration (by both single and married women) became increasingly permissible because of an emergent discourse of the dutiful daughter/martyr mother that encompassed productive as well as reproductive work, with a consequent opening up of the moral envelope of acceptable practice. In Thailand (Pearson

and Kuskabe 2012; Kusakabe and Pearson 2013) and Vietnam (Locke *et al.* 2012), the trope of the young, unmarried migrant daughter has come to have less and less purchase.[7]

- *Late-industrial*: the latest wrinkle to the household-migration-development story is the long-term absence of migrants from their natal villages, leaving their ageing parents as well as their children who are raised by their left-behind grandparents. The periodicity of migration has shifted from seasonal circulation where absence and non-farm work were inter-locked with return and farm work; to sojourning, where absence extends over several years but with return (especially for women migrants) for child raising; to long-term absence where return is often assumed but not certain. As Locke *et al.* (2012: 86) write of migrants in Vietnam, "the 'window of opportunity' for many low-income migrants may well extend to a lifetime of chronic migration or urban poverty despite their current sacrifices". Whether absence equates to family and rural abandonment is contentious.

Given the way it is set out here, the impression is of a uni-linear, staged transition model, where patterns of migration are linked to modernization. What is important to note, however, is that individuals, families and households navigate this transformation process in a variety of ways. So, while it is helpful to view the process taking a particular form over time, because it directs our attention to the ways that development, migration/mobility and household form interplay and change, the implications for social and spatial relations are highly diverse.

In the early migration years, migrants were in the minority and the left-behind was another way of writing about non-migrants. These were two quite distinct groups. Some people moved, and some did not and it was also possible to segment these groups according to gender, generation and class (wealth). Current second-generation migrants have not infrequently themselves been left behind, are leaving behind their own children, and may well end up also struggling to look after their ageing parents while they continue to remain absent from the natal household (see Rigg *et al.* 2014; Locke *et al.* 2012: 69). Migration, until quite recently the exception rather than the rule, has become increasingly normalized. Not only has it become normalized; it has also become extended from temporary sojourning to long-term absence. Asia and Asians are truly living in an age of migration.

The China Health and Nutrition Survey (CHNS) records that the proportion of children in China living in households with migrant members more than tripled over less than a decade, from 11 per cent in 1997 to 39 per cent in 2006. The figures for children with migrant parents were 5 per cent in 1997 and 28 per cent in 2006 (de Brauw and Mu 2011: 89). The 2004 Vietnam migration survey found that 54 and 46 per cent of women migrants to Hanoi and Ho Chi Minh were married, and that 82 per cent of those married at first move had at least one child (Locke *et al.* 2012: 64).[8] In Thailand, the proportion of children being raised by grandparents with *both* parents absent quadrupled from 2 per cent in 1986 to 8 per cent in 2006 (Jampaklay *et al.* 2012: 1). The proportion of the elderly (defined as aged 60 years or over) living alone in Thailand almost doubled from

4.3 per cent in 1986 to 8.4 per cent in 2011, and the proportion living alone or with their spouse only, increased by an even greater extent over the same period from 11.1 per cent to 25.7 per cent (Knodel *et al.* 2013). Across the Asian region, then, propelled by intensifying capitalist relations, we see migration dividing more and more families to such an extent that mobility has become a key explanatory entry point for understanding many of the important development outcomes of the twenty-first century.

The key question, of course, is: 'So what?' Is this something for governments and societies to be concerned about?

The caring household? Caring for the 'left-behind'

> A growing crisis of care troubles families in the developing world. By care, I refer to the labor and resources needed to ensure the mental, emotional, and physical well-being of individuals.
>
> (Parreñas 2005a: 12)

The new household forms noted above have, potentially, profound implications for how the household functions in caring terms. It is also worth noting that some states in the region – notably Vietnam (and also China) – have withdrawn state-provided social support just as these changes to the household have taken root. Vietnam's Law on Family and Marriage institutionalizes the family as the moral and legal basis for care provision, while de-emphasizing the role of the state in social protection (Nguyen 2014). In other countries, such as Singapore, the state has also been at pains to avoid taking on the responsibility for familial support even as fertility falls and the scope for the household to do so declines.[9] Here, and to a lesser extent in other countries of the region, the costs of care are internalized within the household. Where family members are unavailable to take on caring responsibilities, usually because they are in full-time work, then these roles are carried out by a migrant care worker (Douglass 2014). Public transfers to care for those aged 65 years and older are negligible in Indonesia, the Philippines and Thailand. Indeed, in the latter two countries the elderly collectively actually pay more in taxes than they receive in benefits; the net transfer flow is from the elderly to the non-elderly (Mason and Lee 2011: 4). As Table 5.2 shows, East and Southeast Asia have very different old-age support profiles to those that are characteristic of Europe and the USA, with familial transfers and asset-based real-locations playing a much more significant role than public transfers. Whether this approach to the funding of elderly care can be maintained with falling fertility and the growing political power of the elderly is a critical area of current policy debate. As Douglass (2012: 12) writes:

> These [demographic trends in Southeast Asia] are bringing an impending crisis in the respective national economies as the labor force has already begun to dramatically shrink, dependency ratios are rising, and welfare systems are becoming more difficult to publically finance in their rapidly ageing societies.

Table 5.2 Supporting the elderly: a generalized regional typology of resource flows

	Public transfers	*Asset-based reallocations*	*Familial transfers*
Europe and the USA	High (~50+ per cent)	Significant (~30–40 per cent)	Negative or small (–10 to +20 per cent)
East Asia	Significant (~25–50 per cent)	Significant (~25–50 per cent)	Significant (~25–50 per cent)
Southeast Asia	Negative or negligible (–10 to +10 per cent)	High (~50+ per cent)	Significant (~25–50 per cent)

Source: data summarized from Mason and Lee (2011: 5).

Note: asset-based reallocations are the drawing down of savings and assets accrued by the elderly during their working lives.

Both popularly and often in terms of policy, there is an assumption – which is sometimes also reflected in academic studies – that the new household forms described here place intolerable pressures and burdens on the family. This is reflected in Parreñas's quote at the start of this section, taken from her study of transnational Filipino migrant children. As noted, the terms themselves have negative overtones: the 'left-behind', a 'care deficit', 'distance' or 'absent mothering', and 'remote parenting', for instance. The actual evidence, however, is more equivocal that these terms might suggest (see Locke *et al.* 2014; Liu 2014) and some studies argue (e.g. Parreñas 2005a; Ye *et al.* 2013). Spatial and social fragmentation *are* occurring, but the implications of this for the family are contingent on a range of factors including, for example, the presence of kinship support networks, whether migration is for survival or accumulation, the ability of families to devise strategies to deal with parental absence, the presence and nature of state- and community-support systems, the cultural histories and contexts that shape family relations, and whether absence is of mothers/wives, fathers/husbands, or both. Locke *et al.* (2014) who examine migration and marital separation/divorce in Vietnam, while they recognize that "absences from husband or wife undoubtedly strained marital relations", also claim that "these strains do not lead in any straightforward way to divorce or separation" (p. 279). In writing this, however, the authors are highlighting that in low divorce societies like Vietnam where the stigma of formal separation is high, simply recording divorce rates may not adequately reflect or record the level and extent of martial disruptions brought about, at least in part, by spatial separation.

The methodological difficulty with connecting migration and these household and family outcomes is that migration itself is selective, and so the comparison of migrants and non-migrants may simply reflect prior differences between the two groups (see Antman 2012). To provide a pair of examples: if transnational migration is relatively costly and therefore restricted to the better-off, is the higher educational status of migrant children an outcome of migration or merely of the greater prior prosperity of migrants in the first place? Likewise, if married women are more likely to leave their families to take up employment as domestic workers if they have strained marital relations, is subsequent separation or divorce a result of migration? Although long-run longitudinal studies get around this problem of omitted-variable (unobserved variable) bias, many studies that connect migration with health, educational and other outcomes do not adequately recognize that the causal factors that drive migration may also play a significant role in shaping its outcomes.

Accumulation with social fragmentation

It was noted in Chapter 3 that accumulation has often occurred in Asia *without dispossession* (see p. 61). It is this, however, that has underpinned some of the key social consequences of economic transformation. Development may have occurred without dispossession, but it has often occurred *with social fragmentation*.

The massive, recent epochal shift of the Chinese rural population to urban work, an estimated 230 million in 2009 (Lui 2010 cited in Ye *et al.* 2013: 1119), has taken place while the large majority have maintained familial, emotional and financial links with their rural homes. It is for this reason that they have been termed 'phantom farmers' by some scholars (Rawski and Mead 1998) or, more popularly, 'peasant workers' (*nong min gong*) (Ye *et al.* 2013). In China it has been estimated that there are 58 million left-behind children, 47 million left-behind wives (and, one imagines, also a large number of left-behind husbands), and 45 million left-behind elderly (Ye *et al.* 2013: 1119).

Figure 5.1 illustrates the sort of household form that is becoming increasingly common in developing Asia. This multi-sited household is based on field research in a village in the Northeastern Thai province of Mahasarakham undertaken in 2008 (see Rigg and Salamanca 2011 for further details). In this instance, Mrs Kesanee, a widowed grandmother (aged 59 at the time of interview) lives alone with her two grandchildren, aged 7 and 15 years, whom she raises. Her daughter and son-in-law, the parents of these two children, live in Bangkok some 450 km to the south-west and they return only periodically. They do, however, regularly remit money to meet childcare and other costs. Mrs Kesanee's other living child, a son, is married and lives in Phetchabun, 300 km to the west. He also returns only occasionally to visit his mother in Mahasarakham. We see here an example, at least on paper, of 'left-behind children', 'absentee mothers/fathers', 'distance mothering' and the 'elderly alone'. In the village in question this sort of living arrangement is far from exceptional. It is important to point out, however, that Mrs Kesanee is not poor; her children remit considerable sums. Her care in the existential sense is met; but whether care in the broader sense is achieved, is less certain.

The same economic and social forces that shape Kesanee's predicament also explain the caring context that Phan faces, some 800 km to the north-east of Mahasarakham, in rural north Vietnam. Phan is a 68-year-old widow who cares for her 91-year-old mother-in-law. She explained to Nguyen:

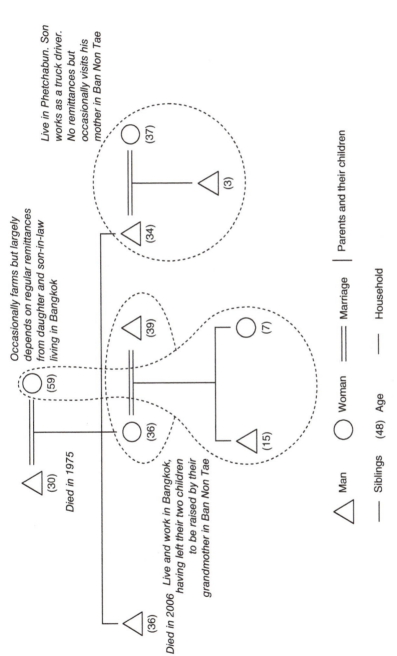

Figure 5.1 Distance caring and left-behind children and elderly in Northeast Thailand

Source: based on field undertaken by the author and Albert Salamanca in 2008. Also reproduced in Rigg and Oven (2015).

In the past everyone was poor, but there were people around. If something happened or if there was a family event you just needed to shout and the whole village would come. Now there are hardly any young people at home – only old people and children. It's depressing.

(Nguyen 2014: 19)

The fact that new household forms are rapidly emerging in Asia is clear and indisputable. This is also, as noted, a source of concern among policy-makers and in the media. But is this concern justified and how is it manifested?

Left-behind children

Of all the social effects of migration, the most problematic is seen to be the effect of parental absence, and especially that of the mother, on children left behind. Much as inequality is linked to a range of negative outcomes, from the educational to the mental (see p. 26), so some studies suggest that this is also true for left-behind children. There is substantial and growing evidence that left-behind children suffer in a range of ways, from the mental to the educational and nutritional. While studies from Southeast Asia are generally fewer and less robust, we can impute the likely pattern of effects from studies undertaken in China.

A key data source for China is the longitudinal China Health and Nutrition Survey (CHNS) undertaken by the Carolina Population Center at the University of North Carolina at Chapel Hill and the National Institute of Nutrition and Food Safety at the Chinese Center for Disease Control and Prevention.[10] Survey rounds, to date, have been undertaken in 1991, 1993, 1997, 2000, 2004 and 2006 across nine provinces. The survey covers 4,400 households and over 26,000 individuals and includes data on individual health, nutrition and socio-economic status; in addition, migration status can be identified from the household roster.

Drawing on this survey, de Brauw and Mu (2011: 96) found a strong positive relationship between having a migrant parent and underweight older – i.e. aged 7–12 years – children.[11] The authors link this outcome to the fact that children with migrant parents spend longer on chores and are more likely to work. They are, they conclude, relatively less cared for; parental absence leads to a care deficit. This conclusion that the left-behind frequently have higher workloads is supported by other studies (see Mu and van de Walle 2011; Chang *et al.* 2011; Ye and Pan 2011).[12] There is also evidence from China that left-behind children are more prone to depression and anxiety. Research undertaken in 2009 in China's Hubei province (He *et al.* 2012) among 590 left-behind children and 285 control children, for example, found strong evidence that the left-behind were at greater risk of depression.

A study that has attempted to record all the manifold effects of migration on left-behind children is that of Ye and Pan (2011), who interviewed 400 left-behind children and 200 non-left-behind children across five provinces in China (Anhui, Henan, Hunan, Jiangxi and Sichuan). The authors conclude that China's "economic prosperity has been achieved at a heavy social cost" (p. 375) in the guise of millions of incomplete families:

[C]hildren who are left behind in the rural communities have paid a high price for these economic benefits [of migration]. … In summary, many of the impacts of parent migration for children may be defined as negative …. These children not only shouldered heavy labor burdens in housework, farm work, and caring for other family members but also suffered from psychological pressures and even the risks of misbehavior and abnormality. They have less time for play and study. Migration impacts their emotional security and associated personal development in terms of behavior, personality, and education potential.

(2011: 374)[13]

Their data show that children of migrant households carry a heavier burden of farm work and housework (echoing de Brauw and Mu's study) (Figures 5.2a, 5.2b), face additional difficulties in sourcing support for their studies (Figure 5.2c), and experience a decline in parental attachments (Figure 5.2d).

For the countries of Southeast Asia, studies tend to have smaller samples and are more qualitative in approach. Nonetheless, conclusions similar to those of the China studies noted above are evident, as set out in Table 5.3. We see in studies from the Philippines, Thailand and Vietnam the negative effects of parental absence on the children left behind and the care deficit that results. Jampkalay's longitudinal study of parental absence on children's education in Thailand's Kanchanaburi province found that the long-term (>2 years) absence of mothers impacted negatively on children's educational prospects. Parreñas's book *Children of global migration* provides a hard-hitting account of the effects of absence on children left behind in the Philippines. Barbara, a 19-year-old college student who had been looking after her two younger brothers from the age of 13 while her mother was away, explained to Parreñas:

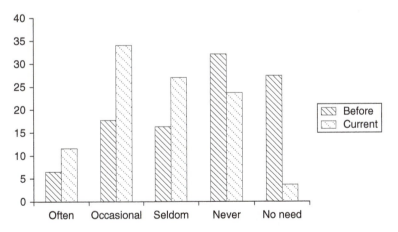

Figure 5.2a Differentiated rural childhoods in China: frequency of participation in farm work, before and during migration (% children surveyed)

Source: data extracted from Ye and Pan 2011: 365.

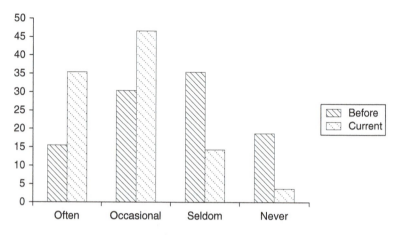

Figure 5.2b Differentiated rural childhoods in China: frequency of participation in housework, before and during migration (% children surveyed)

Source: data extracted from Ye and Pan 2011: 365.

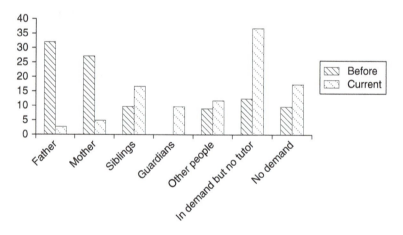

Figure 5.2c Differentiated rural childhoods in China: children's tutor before and during migration (% children surveyed)

Source: data extracted from Ye and Pan 2011: 368.

I had a very difficult time when my mother left. I am the oldest and I had to take over her work at home. I had a hard time adjusting and juggling my studies with my housework. ... Before my mother left I did not have to do anything when I got home from school. ...I would play with friends before I headed home. ... [Mom] helped me with my homework. Well, that stopped... Now my grades are not so good anymore. It is because sometimes I cannot study because of all the housework that I have to do.

(Parreñas 2005a: 110; and see Parreñas 2001)

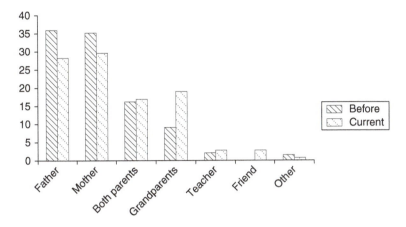

Figure 5.2d Differentiated rural childhoods in China: children's rankings on the most
important person in their life (% children surveyed)

Source: data extracted from Ye and Pan 2011: 372.

There is a good deal of evidence, then, to suggest that migration and long-term parental absence can create a care deficit and lead to emotional strain, depression and schooling failure for the children left behind. Most studies, qualitative (Parreñas 2005a) and quantitative (Cortes 2013), also unequivocally show that a mother's absence has greater negative consequences than a father's absence. This is not, it should be added, because the remittances (cash transfers) are less, but because the care deficit is greater, and this deficit is harder and less likely to be filled. Flexible familyhood and various creative adaptations (see Section 5.4, below) can go some way to bridging the spatial gap and filling the emotional vacuum but studies show that such strategies are usually only partially successful. When mothers are absent, adaptive caring is unlikely fully to fill the care deficit (Table 5.4).

The evidence is not all one-sided, of course, and it is important not to discount or underestimate the effects of increased income on the wider household. After all, the over-riding motivation for migration, whether domestic or transnational, is usually financial. We also know from well-being studies from the region (see http://www.welldev.org.uk/) that notwithstanding the importance of measuring and assessing development in new, more holistic ways, economic and financial factors loom very large indeed in most migrants' minds and justifications. As John Kenneth Galbraith famously put it, "Wealth is not without its advantages and the case to the contrary, although it has often been made, has never proved widely persuasive" (quoted in Economist 2012). The income that can be generated from migration can boost children's life chances through investment in education. This has also been shown, for example, in studies from the Philippines and Thailand. Perhaps the study that goes furthest in highlighting the positive effects of migration on children who are left behind, and which are seen to more than mitigate

Table 5.3 Migration and children left behind: Southeast Asian country studies

Country	Survey dates	Negative effects on children left-behind	Points to note	Source
Philippines	1992–2007	The study shows that mothers' absence has a larger negative effect on educational outcomes than fathers' absence. The author postulates that this is not due to differing levels of remittances but lower levels of parental care (time)	Study focuses on mothers' absence, with fathers' absence as a control. It is not possible to conclude that educational attainment would be higher in the absence of migration	Cortes (2011)
Philippines	1996	The children of migrants are shown to face problems in terms of school achievement and social adjustment. These vary according to how the parenting void is filled; when fathers are absent, mothers take up the slack; when mothers or both parents are absent, other relatives substitute for the absent parent(s). "The single most important finding in the survey is that the absence of the mother has the most disruptive effect in the life of the children" (p. 237)	Survey of 709 children in 39 schools in Metro Manila, Bulacan, Quezon and Rizal in four groups: mother absent, father absent, both parents absent and both parents present	Battistella and Conaco (1998)
Philippines	2000–2002	Takes an ethnographic approach to detail the mental, emotional, and physical effects of absent mothers on left-behind children	Interviews with 69 young adults who have grown up in transnational households, and 31 guardians	Parreñas (2005b)
Thailand	2010–2011	"Issues for concern" include left-behind children's behaviour (drinking, life satisfaction) although the study concludes that the findings "are not alarming in terms of the impact of parental migration on children's physical and psychological health" (p. 98)	The study found no significant deterioration of left-behind children's well-being in terms of school performance, weight, and their psychological well-being	Jampaklay et al. (2012)
Thailand	2000–2003	The study of 2,576 children aged 13–18 years showed that the long-term (>2 years) absence of mothers has a negative impact on left-behind children's education	The long-term absence of fathers does not appear to impact negatively on children's education. Rather than remittances being used to invest in and extend education, parental migration seemed to increase the probability of children leaving school early and migrate themselves	Jampaklay (2006)
Vietnam	2008–2010	Children take on more domestic and agricultural tasks in their migrant mothers' absence, are more likely to play truant from school, and say that they receive less care	Survey of 121 households and interviews with 35 migrant wives	Vu and Agergaard (2012)
Vietnam	2009	Anxiety and emotional damage; emotional distance from absent parent(s)	Wider kin network can ameliorate some of the negative effects; absence does not imply abandonment	Hoang and Yeoh (2012)

Table 5.4 Caring and failing to care

Absent mother	
↓	
Care deficit	*Adaptive caring*
Reflected in:	*Reflected in:*
• Reduced emotional support • Commodification of parental bonds • Reduced parental guidance • Reduced parental time	• Use of ICTs and other technologies to maintain regular contact • Paid-for care • Care by father • Support from other kin • Older siblings (especially daughters) taking on caring responsibilities
Leading to:	*Leading to:*
• Additional housework for child left behind • Truancy from school • Reduced school performance • Heightened levels of anxiety and depression • Feelings of 'abandonment' • Under- or malnutrition	• Intense distance mothering • Alternative caring strategies • Gender boundary crossing by father
↓	
Left-behind child	

the negative, is Bryant's (2005) UNICEF report drawing on data from Indonesia, the Philippines and Thailand.[14] He comes to two main conclusions. First, that the economic benefits of migration feed through into better health and schooling outcomes for migrants' children; and second, that the social costs of migration are substantially mitigated by the role of the extended family. In other words, that the care deficit discussed earlier is largely met by other family members. Thus Bryant argues that:

> the evidence to date suggests that these children [of migrants] do not, on average, suffer greater social and economic problems than their peers. This is because migration is generally an effective way for households to alleviate poverty, and because extended families help fill the gaps left by the absent parents. … Migration of parents is likely to cause the most good or do least harm when there are few other options for boosting household income, and when extended families step in to help.
>
> (2005: 23)

Since Bryant's summary report of the state of knowledge was released in 2005, however, more data have become available. While the debate over the costs/benefits of migration remains contentious, and methodological difficulties (noted above) and data gaps are significant, the ramifications of parental absence have become clearer. Children are often under-protected and less assiduously supervised and cared for; they have to take on adult tasks and responsibilities with daughters often caring for their younger siblings; they are more prone to emotional and psychological stress; and broader patterns of socialization may be compromised (Garza 2010).

Left-behind wives and husbands

Most studies of labour sojourning in Asia that have paid attention to the impacts on source communities have focused on left-behind wives (and children). This made sense when the labour flows were mostly male, as they were during much of the 1970s and 1980s. From the 1990s, however, migration streams have become increasingly feminized (Piper 2008). In the 1970s, for example, women represented just 15 per cent of the Filipino international migrant labour force; by 2010 they made up 55 per cent of new hires (Cortes 2013). Indeed, between 1992 and 2010, recruitment of male overseas Filipino workers outnumbered females for just three of those 19 years (Cortes 2013).

The reasons for this shift are not of central concern here, but they link to the hiring practices of firms and the nature of the employment opportunities available in the industrial economies of the region, the gender-selective effects of mechanization on labour demand in rural areas, and the loosening of social restrictions and cultural norms regarding female migration. This means that in many cases there are as many left-behind husbands as there are left-behind wives.

Husbands and wives left behind are viewed very differently and face different challenges and dilemmas. In Vietnam, for example, while wives who remain in the countryside when their husbands migrate are viewed locally as 'left behind', when it is husbands who remain they are said to have 'sent their wives' to the city (Locke *et al.* 2012: 75). The guiding role of the male household head as breadwinner, even when it is the wife who plays the main role in winning the bread, is clear in such local discourses. Whether, however, this can adequately disguise the loss of the husband's relative income-earning and livelihood-sustaining role is questionable. How left-behind husbands may self-identify themselves and negotiate the transition, partial though it may be, from breadwinner to homemaker, is fraught. This is particularly evident in work from the Philippines.

Work on left-behind husbands in the Philippines shows how gender conventions persist even while gender roles are transformed. Parreñas (2005a: 92) calls this the "gender paradox": women's paid work outside the household challenges the ideology of their domesticity and yet women's continuing (even intensified) caring responsibilities reinforces such an ideology.[15] Some gender boundaries are quite easily, albeit not painlessly, traversed; others remain seemingly impervious to change. Few of Parreñas's Filipino left-behind fathers took on caring responsibilities in the absence of their wives; this was instead left to daughters and extended kin, as discussed above. Some, rather than facing the possibility of taking on domestic work, left altogether once their wives had migrated, "in the process completely avoiding the possibility that women's work would become part of their daily routine of family life" (2005a: 101). The terms that Parreñas uses reflects her view of their respective tendencies: absentee fathers; martyr moms; dutiful daughters; and over-extended kin.

This situation recorded for the Philippines is not always echoed in other countries, and changing roles can sometimes be quite neatly accommodated. In north Vietnam, for example, Nguyen (2014) records how middle-aged men who had stayed at home in Nam Dinh while their wives were working away described themselves as 'goalkeepers'. The use of a masculine, sporting analogy in itself is notable. Further, such men depicted themselves as successfully juggling and fulfilling several important tasks – managing the household, caring for parents and children – which signified, for them, no reduction in their status: "As 'the goalkeeper'", Nguyen writes, "they live up to the ideal of manhood as the protector of the family's hierarchy [and] morality" (Nguyen 2014: 15).

The elderly alone

> While parents are alive, one must not travel afar. If one must, one's whereabouts should always be made known.
>
> *(Analects, Book II: Li Ren 19)*

Almost all the countries of East Asia are experiencing a rapid decline in total fertility rates (see Table 5.1) and face an ageing population. Just as left-behind children are a source of concern, even alarm, so too is the growing number of older adults living alone. Traditionally, older generations were supported by their younger kin-folk through an intergenerational 'bargain' wherein at least one child would remain co-resident or would live very close by their ageing parent(s). With heightened levels of migration and falling fertility, however, this is becoming harder to sustain as a matter of course and there has occurred a marked increase in the numbers of elderly living alone. The terms used tend to reflect how this trend is viewed. Reports that speak of 'abandonment' depict the elderly as victims, their children – or wider society – having failed in their duty of care. If reference is made, instead, to the elderly as living 'alone' or 'solo', these terms are less negatively loaded. Here the emphasis is on how the elderly continue to be supported and support themselves even while their children may be absent (see Zimmer *et al.* 2007: 5–6; Knodel and Saengtienchai 2007).

States are reluctant to take on the responsibility – and therefore the cost – of caring for the elderly, doing their utmost to ensure that adult children bear this burden. Yet patterns of migration in the region, which underpin the logics of capitalist accumulation, present two real dilemmas. First of all, the nature of migration where the elderly remain in rural areas creates a spatial care deficit: the adult children who might care for their parents are not available directly to take on this task. Second, community-based caring is also fragmenting, for a range of reasons.

Just as there continues to be normative support for co-residence across Asia, among the public and in terms of government pronouncements and policies, this is also true of co-residence of older parents with their children. Against this, however, for many of the reasons described here, there has been a marked fall in many countries in Asia in the proportion of persons aged 60 or over living with their children. In Thailand, co-residence with children for the over-sixties fell from 77 per cent in 1986 to 57 per cent in 2011 (Knodel *et al.* 2013: x).

For the moment at least, it seems that the triple challenge of an ageing population, falling fertility and dispersed living arrangements is being met. In Thailand, for which we have some of the best data sets,[16] while a growing proportion of the elderly are not living with their children, just 9 per cent live in single-person households (Knodel *et al.* 2013: 20, and see UNDP 2010). Furthermore, the elderly continue to find support in extended kinship and community networks, children often live close by if not in the same house, grandchildren take on the role of carer when children are absent, and technology has increased contact even in the absence of close physical proximity. For these reasons, some scholars have challenged the notion that the elderly are being 'abandoned'. In Thailand, for example, HelpAge concluded the following based on Knodel *et al.*'s (2013) report: "[T]he Thai people are doing their best to maneuver through unprecedented social and economic change and they continue to lean on strong cultural traditions" (Knodel *et al.* 2013: 86). In a related, slightly earlier study from Thailand, also led by Knodel, a similar conclusion is reached:

> Contrary to claims embodied in much of the discourse about the rural elderly in the developing world, extensive rural to urban migration of adult children has not led to the widespread desertion of 'left-behind' elderly parents in Thailand. Rather the relationships between rural parents and their geographically dispersed children have changed in ways consistent with the 'modified extended family' perspective common in discussions regarding elderly parents in developed countries. This is undoubtedly the most significant implication of our study, and provides a very different theoretical perspective with which to view the impact of migration, and indeed social change more generally, than the more common modernisation framework that underlies most of the assertions of declining elderly welfare in the third world.
>
> (Knodel and Saengtienchai 2007: 207–8)

Liu (2014) explores the creative adaptation of divided rural families and support for the elderly in northern China through 32 life history interviews with multiple generations across nine households in one village. Her core argument is that we should look not at migration and the spatial separation that results from migration, imputing certain outcomes from the process, but at the webs of social relations that may be problematic even in the absence of migration and may be maintained even while family members are absent.[17] She highlights the resilience and flexibility of families as they search for ways to maintain relations across space and sustain the collective welfare of the household. Her research "shows that the way in which migration affects care and support for older people is dependent upon the relations between older parents and adult children prior to and during migration" (2014: 311).

While families in many contexts may have shown considerable creativity in addressing the challenges of caring for the elderly in the context of changing householding, looking ahead, the demographic forces at work across Southeast and East Asia are necessarily going to exert considerable pressure on family living arrangements, not least for the elderly. When total fertility rates are below replacement levels (see Table 5.1) and when economic necessity requires distant living, the traditional family safety net for the elderly will become harder to sustain. Currently, most elderly have large families to support them, even when (some) children are absent; that will not be the case for those currently in their fifties and sixties. In Thailand, for example, 44 per cent of 50–54 year-olds have two or fewer children (Knodel and Saengtienchai 2007: 208). We know that this proportion will rise for subsequent generations. Along with the demographic inevitability of thinning families, a second caveat that Knodel and Saengtienchai (2007) raise in their study is the question of how current strategies of caring will deal with the elderly during the final stages of life when frailty and health may require daily personal assistance (Knodel and Saengtienchai 2007: 208). With fewer children to go around, a growing need to build livelihoods away from home, a thinning community support network, and a state that has been reluctant, hitherto, to take on such caring roles, it is easy to conclude that something has to give.

Maintaining and developing relations across space

The 'left-behind' thesis is often underpinned by the assumptions that, first, these developments are problematic and, second, that they are difficult to address. In other words, that the contradictions noted above – that the search for material well-being (prosperity) has had, as one of its necessary corollaries, non-material ill-being (emotional and relational poverty) – are impossible to reconcile. That might, indeed, be true when looked at in isolation. But while children may be left behind, parents absent, and grandparents left, often quite literally, holding the baby, this is rarely abandonment. A central theme in studies of global householding and the transnational family is the continuing commitment of absentee mothers, fathers, daughters and sons to their families and, often, also to their communities. The question is whether this commitment is sustainable given the forces at work.

Certainly, there are real ructions and frictions in this negotiated process but it would be highly surprising if families and individuals did not find novel ways to address the problems that emerge. Just as multi-sited households materialized out of the particular developmental demands presented to families by contemporary change – essentially, how to build sustainable livelihoods in the late twentieth and early twenty-first centuries – so the challenges of maintaining familial relations across space have led to further creative adaptations.

Most obviously, migrants remit income to maintain the natal family in the place of origin. This, often, is the very *raison d'être* for such moves, and the ability for a portion of the family/household to remain in their place of origin, usually the countryside, is contingent on some parts of the social unit leaving. More intractable, though, are the demands that separation has on social reproduction.

In theory and frequently in practice, the information and communications technology (ICT) revolution enables distant family members to remain in touch in a manner that would have been unthinkable, even in the 1990s.[18] Social media, cheap international calls, Skype, FaceTime and the ubiquity of the mobile phone have all made it increasingly cheap and easy to remain in touch, sometimes almost daily, across national boundaries and great distances (Parreñas 2005b). Intense mothering-from-a-distance has been made possible by the ICT revolution. The Philippines was the texting (SMS) capital of the world from the late 1990s into the early years of the new millennium, although now other forms of communication are preferred. This is not just limited to voice communication; Skype, FaceTime and other technologies have permitted virtual face-to-face contact.

In some instances, however, employers exert tight control by restricting access to the internet, banning the ownership or use of mobile phones, and limiting communication. This is a particular problem when female domestic workers live with their employers. Hoang and Yeoh (2012) quote the husband of one of their Vietnamese migrant-mothers working as a domestic helper in Taiwan:

> She contacts us [her husband and 12 year-old daughter] two of three times a year because her employer does not allow her to use the phone … He does not allow her to buy a mobile phone … He is afraid the she would run away to work illegally if she has a phone … each time she gets in touch, she has to ask him for permission …
>
> (Quoted in Hoang and Yeoh 2012: 316)

While in the studies discussed so far the migrant worker is spatially separated from their family, this need not always be the case. Kusakabe and Pearson (2013; and see Pearson and Kusakabe 2012) surveyed the childcare strategies of 283 Burmese female migrants in three sites in Thailand. These migrants all had their first child while working in Thailand; some had had two children, and a handful three, giving 330 children in total. All were less than six years of age. Figure 5.3 shows the range of childcare strategies adopted by these migrants. Some 40 per cent had their child cared for in Myanmar, while 34 per cent invited parents to Thailand to take on caring responsibilities. This was possible in border towns like Mae Sot where state surveillance is less intense, and the border porous. It was much more difficult in Bangkok. What is evident in this study are the difficulties migrant mothers face in constructing childcare strategies in a work context that pays little heed to motherhood and its needs, and two states – Thailand and Myanmar – where the former attempts to regulate migrants and their activities and the latter seeks to take control of their earnings. Kusakabe and Pearson (2013: 974) conclude:

> Migrant workers, who lack citizenship and entitlements in their place of destination, face limited options and resources for delivery and care of young children. The migrant workers juggle the restrictions and control of the two states – the Thai state that tries to control their reproduction as well as their mobility, and the Burmese state that tries to control their remittances by imposing arbitrary taxes on families back home.

Pearson and Kuskabe's work highlights one particular aspect of the new household and family forms discussed in this chapter, namely the way in which migration, marriage, livelihoods and child-rearing have become, in recent years, ever more intimately interleaved. The trope of the unmarried female migrant – the dutiful daughter – of the 1980s no longer has the empirical purchase that it did. The care chain, whether global or national, has become more complex as biological reproduction and socio-economic production are co-constituted in new ways.

Migration represents a rupture and therefore a challenge to established gendered and generational arrangements. Absence also poses a challenge to wider societal assumptions about 'normal' living. Even in the Philippines, where there are said to be some nine million children growing up away from their mothers, fathers or both parents, the nuclear Filipino family is considered the 'right' family (McKay 2012). Absent mothering is viewed by many with disapprobation (Parreñas 2005a: 43).

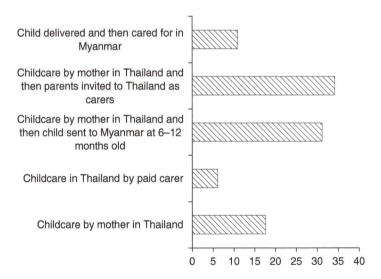

Figure 5.3 Caring strategies of Burmese migrant workers in Thailand

Source: data extracted from Kusakabe and Pearson 2013: 968.

Caring or failing to care? Sustaining the neoliberal family

It is easy enough to dramatize the implications of the family and household revolution set out in this chapter. That increasing numbers of children will be cared for by others than their parents; that rising numbers of elderly are living alone, 'abandoned' by their children; that relationships are fraying as married couples are forced to live apart; and that the state seems unwilling to fill the care-deficit that has emerged, and which is widening. This is a partial and selective reading of the processes underway and their effects.

The case for migration, and especially transnational migration, normally rests on the greater economic returns that can be generated by travelling to work overseas. While instances of deception and trafficking are more common than often assumed, the large majority of migrants do achieve their aim of securing better paid work. This does sometimes feed through into better education and health profiles, notwithstanding the omitted variable problem noted earlier in this chapter. In many communities, it is those who cannot move, whether for social or economic reasons, who face the gravest challenges. Furthermore, there is no doubting that families devise ingenious ways to deal with parental absence. Assumptions about the 'left-behind elderly' also need to be challenged. Just because a woman or man achieves the age of 65 does not make them suddenly, on the stroke of midnight, unproductive – a burden on their family, the state and on wider society, unable to care for themselves. Just as childhood is being extended by lengthening years in education, the working age at the other end of the demographic profile is being extended as people stay healthier for longer, work for longer and are also able to care for themselves for longer.

But, and like so much when it comes to development, if we focus our attention on the economic drivers and outcomes of these new household forms and the processes that have shaped them, then we almost inevitably arrive at a positive conclusion: that they are livelihood-enhancing, income-raising and poverty-reducing. This has been a common feature of approaches to migration, for example. In the World Bank's 2009 *World Development Report: reshaping economic geography*, the chapter on migration barely touches on the issues of concern in this chapter. The report proposes, for example, that "for the communities left behind, internal migration is critical for overcoming poverty and smoothing household consumption ... [and is] an important 'pathway out of poverty' for rural households that can no longer rely solely on agriculture for their livelihood" (World Bank 2009: 166).[19] Is this all there is to it, and all that we need to be concerned about?

If we widen out perspective to the well-being of communities, households, families and individuals, and especially those who are more vulnerable, namely children and the elderly, then the balance of the ledger – if that is an appropriate way to view it – begins to shift and what to some analysts seems so self-evident that it is not even a point of conjecture, becomes a matter for reflection.

Shaping the neoliberal family

> We [have] become increasingly unsatisfied with a mere description of miserable situations of migrant workers and their left-behind family members .... We cannot help asking, why do the majority of peasants have to suffer? Why do they have to migrate and why could migration not bring them wealth instead of aged, injured and unhealthy bodies? We heard frequently during the fieldwork from the investigated peasants that 'we will be better off when our children grow up'. However, when we looked back into the history and looked forward, what we observed was migration as rite of passage – generations of migration without radical changes in households and rural communities.
>
> (Ye *et al.* 2013: 1138)

This chapter has argued that transformations in Southeast Asian societies, and more particularly in the Southeast Asian household and family, can only be understood through the lens of economic change and the shaping forces of neoliberalism. Capitalist accumulation is dependent on patterns of labouring that require people to move and families and households to become divided over space. Households cannot meet their needs without adopting such new household forms. These pressures extend to individual migrants and their families where economic necessity requires people to move, and yet for the migrant, moving makes it far harder to support their wider family in various non-material ways (see Myerson *et al.* 2010). Leaving is essential to the maintenance of the family unit in livelihood terms given growing land shortages, rising needs and the decline in the relative returns to farming, and yet leaving also, as discussed here, contributes to the partial dissolution of the household and, by extension, often the community as well (see Rigg *et al.* 2008).

With this in mind, it is – at the same time – the failures and the successes of development-as-modernization which underpin the processes discussed here. Securing material well-being in marginal locations is often impossible; development has simply failed to make adequate and sufficient inroads into such areas, where populations remain marginalized from the mainstream. Development has provided alternatives, but these are situated in other places. It is the failure, then, to provide *in situ* means to meet people's needs that explains their search for *ex situ* alternatives. Tania Murray Li's monograph (Li 2014: 169–73) on upland Central Sulawesi makes just this point. There were few local opportunities and few jobs; people had to move in order to find work beyond the meagre possibilities for wage employment available locally. The wrinkle in this story, however, was that the mobility of the Lauje was constrained by their lack of education and poor facility in Bahasa Indonesia. When they did venture out to Kalimantan or Malaysia their experience of work was rarely uplifting, and hardly ever developmental. They were poorly paid at best, and regularly cheated.

Frequently, studies of the family and household have emphasized the primacy of individual decision-making, stressing the agency of women and men in the context of the barriers and opportunities that lie before them. What should be evident, however, from this and earlier chapters, is that social fragmentation is underpinned by structural inequalities. To be sure, individuals struggle, often successfully, to build better lives for themselves and their families, but the form and direction that these struggles take are shaped by higher-order forces. The fact, for example, that married migrants only rarely are able to travel with their partners and children; the deepening inequalities that have forced people to look elsewhere for work; and the inability to sustain a reasonable livelihood in rural areas. We must not lose sight of these structural inequities even as we marvel at the ingenuity and flexibility of ordinary Southeast Asians.

Douglass (2014: 445), who coined the term "global householding", in a recent paper leaves the reader with the following questions:

- In the future, how will new generations care for ever-larger superannuated populations?
- How can capitalism find an alternative to its dependence on the household to absorb its crises and to have and raise children?
- How can [capitalism] continue to depend on household consumption as the principal driver of higher-income national economies?
- Can the corporate economy producing home robotics, instant food, personal services and home delivery adequately replace the household's internal division of labour to carry out daily household reproduction as households dwindle in size to just one person per residential unit, as they are in much of today's urban world?
- When a person loses a job or is mentally distressed, can social services compensate for the needed welfare or psychological support that families can no longer provide?

These are all questions that this chapter has touched on. The answers, however, are far from clear, whether nationally or regionally. What is clear, however, is that the rapid modernization of Southeast Asia's economies has had – and will continue to have – consequences for the structure and functioning of families and households, consequences that raise uncomfortable questions for states that have sought to minimize their responsibilities.

Further reading

For perhaps the fullest review paper of the social effects of migration on source communities and families, see Ye *et al.* (2013). This paper focuses mainly on China, although it does extensively document work from other countries. Bear in mind that it takes a strongly negative view of the effects of migration on families. Piper's (2008) paper on the feminization of migration and its effects on social development provides a broad, Asian perspective on the issues of concern in this chapter.

For work on global householding see Douglass (2006) for his seminal paper and Douglass (2012) for a forward-looking and region-wide reflection on what this means for Southeast Asian economy and society. The key source for the transnational family is the introductory chapter to Bryceson and Vuorela's (2002) edited volume *The transnational family: new European frontiers and global networks* (although none of the chapters deals directly with Asia).

Discussions of falling total fertility rates in Asia and their implications are well covered in the literature. For clear overviews see the work of Gavin Jones (2007, 2010), the downloadable and concise study by Mason and Lee (2011), and my own discussion (Rigg 2012).

For studies of the challenging of caring and building and sustaining the neoliberal family see the following: Locke *et al.* (2012) and Hoang and Yeoh (2012) on Vietnam; and Parreñas (2001, 2005a, 2005b) and Cortes (2013) on the Philippines. For studies of ageing, see Liu (2014) on China and the work of Knodel and colleagues on Thailand (Knodel and Saengtienchai 2007; Knodel *et al.* 2013).

Notes

1 'West' is used here, rather than North or global North, because the division is often seen in such studies as cultural and societal, rather than geographical.

2 It was this that underpinned the 'village study' of so many anthropologists, sociologists and geographers. It rested on the assumption that the village – as a geographical settlement – would be a world unto itself, a window into the totality of social and economic relations that existed among and between the populations of that settlement. (See Rigg and Vandergeest 2012.)

3 Some studies (e.g. Liu 2014 for China) use family and household interchangeably on the grounds, it seems, that the members of a household are, more often than not, kin and therefore family.

4 There are two important caveats to note here. First, the 'working-age population' is defined as people aged 15–64; in most Asian countries, education extends beyond 15 years of age. Second, people aged over 64 years often continue to work and are not dependent. The latter point is linked to the absence of guaranteed state pensions across much of the region such that many people cannot, literally, afford to stop working. It is also an inheritance of the past when people did not 'retire' and fulfilled a productive function for much of their lives.

5 There are (as always) exceptions to this, such as the long-distance female traders of Laos (see Walker 1999).

6 This sometimes occurred in apparent opposition to state policies. In Malaysia, for example, the New Economic Policy introduced at the beginning of the 1970s aimed to create a *male* Malay working class; the working class that actually emerged was, in fact, more female than male (Rigg 2012: 174).

7 With the result that the 'dutiful daughter' is increasingly metamorphosing into the 'martyr mother'.

8 These data on the marital status of female migrants match those for men: 46 per cent of male migrants to both Hanoi and Ho Chi Minh City were married.

9 In 1995 the Singapore government introduced the Maintenance of Parents Act. This Act "allows Singapore residents aged 60 years and above – who are unable to provide for themselves – to claim maintenance from their children who are capable of supporting them, but are not doing so". See http://app.maintenanceofparents.gov.sg/Pages/Home.aspx.

10 Details of the survey and downloadable data sets can be accessed from http://www. cpc.unc.edu/projects/china.
11 The study also found a less strong relationship between migrant status and overweight younger children.
12 Although Mu and van de Walle (2011) found that while wives took on additional farm work when their husbands were absent, the reverse was not the case – there was no evidence of men having a higher workload.
13 Joe Zhang who returned to the Chinese village of his childhood writes that "China's traditional social fabric has become shredded – and the disintegration is most obvious in the countryside, where families are falling apart, crime is soaring and the environment is killing people" (Zhang 2014).
14 This report, it should be noted, was released in 2005 and is based on limited and scattered data, especially for Indonesia and Thailand. Since then – as referenced in this chapter – a large number of additional studies have been published.
15 Vu and Agergaard (2012: 116) outline a similar paradox in Vietnam: "We suggest that by 'doing family', migrant women are negotiating gender roles and relations without openly confronting the patriarchal family ideals while also being able to exploit their increases in power in an acceptable manner".
16 Targeted national socio-economic surveys of the elderly have been undertaken in 1986, 1994, 1995, 2002, 2007 and 2011.
17 This is a slightly more sophisticated rendering of Bryant's (2005) point that the role of the extended family goes a considerable way to mitigating the effects of parental absence on children left behind.
18 The speed with which some technologies have made the transition from sporadic to ubiquitous is worth highlighting. In Hoang and Yeoh's paper on transnational familyhood in Vietnam published in 2012 (and based on 2009 interviews), the authors depict a country where telecommunication costs are high, mobile ownership low, computer ownership even lower, and awareness of ICT technology minimal. They write: "the transformational power of affordable international phone calls … has yet to have an impact on many migrant families we studied in Vietnam" (2012: 315). Based on my own work on migrants in Hanoi, I don't think this would have been the case had the interviews been carried out just four years later.
19 In a section entitled "Labor mobility: learning from a generation of analysis", the same World Bank report states:

> Migrants who move to cities, to leading areas, or to leading countries are rarely disconnected from their home places. Most migrants maintain strong and active links with their home communities and send remittances. And they do much more than remit capital. They send back information and technical assistance, and when a place is ready, they often bring back ideas, knowledge, expectations of good governance, and links to leading markets.
>
> (2009: 159)

Writing of migration in this manner gives the process a Panglossian glow.

References

Annan, A., D. W. T. Crompton, D. E. Walters and S. E. Arnold (1986). "An investigation of the prevalence of intestinal parasites in pre-school children in Ghana." *Parasitology* 92: 209–217.
Antman, F. M. (2012). The impact of migration on family left behind. IZA Discussion paper no. 6374. Bonn, Institute for the Study of Labor.
Battistella, G. and M. C. G. Conaco (1998). "The impact of labour migration on the children left behind: a study of elementary school children in the Philippines." *Sojourn: Journal of Social Issues in Southeast Asia* 13(2): 220–241.

Brickell, K. and B. S. A. Yeoh (2014). "Geographies of domestic life: 'householding' in transition in East and Southeast Asia." *Geoforum* 51: 259–261.

Bryant, J. (2005). Children of international migrants in Indonesia, Thailand, and the Philippines: a review of evidence and policies. Innocenti Working Paper 2005/5 Florence, Italy, Innocenti Research Centre, UNICEF.

Bryceson, D. and U. Vuorela (2002). Transnational families in the twenty-first century. *The transnational family: new European frontiers and global networks*. D. Bryceson and U. Vuorela. Oxford, Berg: 3–30.

Chang, H., X.-Y. Dong and F. MacPhail (2011). "Labor migration and time use patterns of the left-behind children and elderly in Rural China." *World Development* 39(12): 2199–2210.

Cortes, P. (2013). "The feminization of international migration and its effects on the children left behind: evidence from the Philippines." *World Development* 65: 62–78.

de Brauw, A. and R. Mu (2011). "Migration and the overweight and underweight status of children in rural China." *Food Policy* 36(1): 88–100.

Douglass, M. (2006). "Global householding in Pacific Asia." *International Development Planning Review* 28(4): 421–445.

Douglass, M. (2012). Global householding and social reproduction: migration research, dynamics and public policy in East and Southeast Asia. ARI Working Paper Series. Singapore, Asia Research Institute.

Douglass, M. (2014). "Afterword: global householding and social reproduction in Asia." *Geoforum* 51: 313–316.

Economist (2012). "The real wealth of nations." *The Economist*, 30 July.

Evans, A. (1991). "Gender issues in rural household economics." *IDS Bulletin* 22(1): 51–59.

Freeman, R. (1995). *Asia's recent fertility decline and prospects for future demographic change*. Asia-Pacific Population Research Reports. Honolulu, East-West Center.

Garza, R. D. l. (2010). Migration, development and children left behind: a multidimensional approach. Social and Economic Policy Working Paper. New York, UNICEF, Division of Policy and Practice.

He, B., J. Fan, N. Liu, H. Li, Y. Wang, J. Williams and K. Wong (2012). "Depression risk of 'left-behind children' in rural China." *Psychiatry Research* 200(2–3): 306–312.

Hoang, L. A. and B. S. A. Yeoh (2012). "Sustaining families across transnational spaces: Vietnamese migrant parents and their left-behind children." *Asian Studies Review* 36(3): 307–325.

Holtz, T. H., S. Patrick Kachur, J. M. Roberts, L. H. Marum, C. Mkandala, N. Chizani, A. Macheso and M. E. Parise (2004). "Use of antenatal care services and intermittent preventive treatment for malaria among pregnant women in Blantyre District, Malawi." *Tropical Medicine & International Health* 9: 77–82.

Jampaklay, A. (2006). "Parental absence and children's school enrolment." *Asian Population Studies* 2(1): 93–110.

Jampaklay, A., P. Vapattanawong, K. Tangchonlatip, K. Richter, N. Ponpai and C. Hayeeteh (2012). *Children living apart from parents due to internal migration (CLAIM)*. Bangkok, Institute for Population and Social Research, Mahidol University.

Jenco, L. (2013). "Revisiting Asian values." *Journal of the History of Ideas* 74(2): 237–258.

Jones, G. W. (2007). "Delayed marriage and very low fertility in Pacific Asia." *Population and Development Review* 33(3): 453–478.

Jones, G. W. (2010). Changing marriage patterns in Asia. Working Paper Series No. 131. Singapore, Asia Research Institute.

Jones, G. W. and R. Leete (2002). "Asia's family planning programs as low fertility is attained." *Studies in Family Planning* 33(1): 114–126.

Knodel, J. and C. Saengtienchai (2007). "Rural parents with urban children: social and economic implications of migration for the rural elderly in Thailand." *Population, Space and Place* 13(3): 193–210.

Knodel, J., V. Prachuabmoh and N. Chayovan (2013). *The changing well-being of Thai elderly: an update from the 2011 survey of older persons in Thailand.* Chiang Mai, HelpAge International East Asia/Pacific Regional Office.

Kusakabe, K. and R. Pearson (2010). "Transborder migration, social reproduction and economic development: a case study of Burmese women workers in Thailand." *International Migration* 48(6): 13–43.

Kusakabe, K. and R. Pearson (2013). "Cross-border childcare strategies of Burmese migrant workers in Thailand." *Gender, Place & Culture* 20(8): 960–978.

Li, T. M. (2014). *Land's end: capitalist relations on an indigenous frontier.* Durham, NC and London, Duke University Press.

Liu, J. (2014). "Ageing, migration and familial support in rural China." *Geoforum* 51: 305–312.

Locke, C., N. T. N. Hoa and N. T. T. Tâm (2012). "Struggling to sustain marriages and build families: mobile husbands/wives and mothers/fathers in Hà Nội and Hồ Chí Minh City." *Journal of Vietnamese Studies* 7(4): 63–91.

Locke, C., J. Seeley and N. Rao (2013) Migration, reconfigurations of family relations and social (in)security: an introduction, *Third World Quarterly* 34(10): 1872–1880.

Locke, C., N. T. T. Tâm and N. T. N. Hoa (2014). "Mobile householding and marital dissolution in Vietnam: An inevitable consequence?" *Geoforum* 51: 273–283.

Lu, Y. (2013). "Household migration, remittances and their impact on health in Indonesia." *International Migration* 51: e202–e215.

McKay, D. (2012). *Global Filipinos: migrant lives' in the virtual village.* Bloomington, Indiana University Press.

Martin, L. G. (1989). "Living arrangements of the elderly in Fiji, Korea, Malaysia, and the Philippines." *Demography* 26(4): 627–643.

Mason, A. and S. H. Lee (2011). Population aging and economic progress in Asia: a bumpy road ahead? *Asia Pacific Issues.* Honolulu, East-West Center: 99.

Mu, R. and D. van de Walle (2011). "Left behind to farm? Women's labor re-allocation in rural China." *Labour Economics* 18, Supplement 1: S83–S97.

Myerson, R., Y. Hou, H. Tang, Y. Cheng, Y. Wang and Z. Ye (2010). "Home and away: Chinese migrant workers between two worlds." *The Sociological Review* 58(1): 26–44.

Nguyen, M. T. N. (2014). "Translocal householding: care and migrant livelihoods in a waste-trading community of Vietnam's Red River Delta." *Development and Change* 45(6): 1385–1408.

Padoch, C., E. Brondizio, S. Costa, M. Pinedo-Vasquez, R. R. Sears and A. Siqueira (2008). "Urban forest and rural cities: multi-sited households, consumption patterns, and forest resources in Amazonia." *Ecology and Society* 13(2), Art. 2.

Parreñas, R. S. (2001). "Mothering from a distance: emotions, gender, and inter-generational relations in Filipino transnational families." *Feminist Studies* 27(2): 361–390.

Parreñas, R. S. (2005a). *Children of global migration: transnational families and gendered woes.* Stanford, CA, Stanford University Press.

Parreñas, R. S. (2005b). "Long distance intimacy: class, gender and intergenerational relations between mothers and children in Filipino transnational families." *Global Networks* 5: 317–336.

Pearson, R. and K. Kusakabe (2012). "Who cares? Gender, reproduction, and care chains of Burmese migrant workers in Thailand." *Feminist Economics* 18(2): 149–175.

Piper, N. (2008). "Feminisation of migration and the social dimensions of development: the Asian case." *Third World Quarterly* 29(7): 1287–1303.

Rawski, T. G. and R. W. Mead (1998). "On the trail of China's phantom farmers." *World Development* 26(5): 767–781.

Rigg, J. (2003). *Southeast Asia: the human landscape of modernisation and development.* London, Routledge.

Rigg, J. (2005). *Living with transition in Laos: market integration in Southeast Asia.* London, RoutledgeCurzon.

Rigg, J. (2012). *Unplanned development: tracking change in Asia.* London, Zed Books.

Rigg, J. and A. Salamanca (2011). "Connecting lives, living, and location." *Critical Asian Studies* 43(4): 551–575.

Rigg, J. and P. Vandergeest, Eds. (2012). *Revisiting rural places: pathways to poverty and prosperity in Southeast Asia.* Singapore and Hawaii, Singapore University Press and Hawaii University Press.

Rigg, J. and K. Oven (2015) "Building liberal resilience? A critical review from developing rural Asia." *Global Environmental Change* 32: 175–186.

Rigg, J., S. Veeravongs, L. Veeravongs and P. Rohitarachoon (2008). "Reconfiguring rural spaces and remaking rural lives in Central Thailand." *Journal of Southeast Asian Studies* 39(3): 355–381.

Rigg, J., B. Promphaking and A. Le Mare (2014). "Personalizing the middle-income trap: an inter-generational migrant view from rural Thailand." *World Development* 59(7): 184–198.

UNDP (2010). *Thailand human development report 2009: human security, today and tomorrow.* Bangkok, United Nations Development Programme.

Vu, T. T. and J. Agergaard (2012). "'Doing family': female migrants and family transition in rural Vietnam." *Asian Population Studies* 8(1): 103–119.

Walker, A. (1999). *The legend of the golden boat: regulation, trade and traders in the borderlands of Laos, Thailand, China and Burma.* Richmond, UK, Curzon Press.

Waters, J. L. (2002). "Flexible families? 'Astronaut' households and the experiences of lone mothers in Vancouver, British Columbia." *Social & Cultural Geography* 3(2): 117–134.

World Bank (2009). *World Development Report 2009: reshaping economic geography.* Washington DC, World Bank.

Ye, J. and L. Pan (2011). "Differentiated childhoods: impacts of rural labor migration on left-behind children in China." *The Journal of Peasant Studies* 38(2): 355–377.

Ye, J., C. Wang, H. Wu, C. He and J. Liu (2013). "Internal migration and left-behind populations in China." *The Journal of Peasant Studies* 40(6): 1119–1146.

Yeoh, B. S. A., H. L. Chee and T. K. D. Vu (2014). "Global householding and the negotiation of intimate labour in commercially-matched international marriages between Vietnamese women and Singaporean men." *Geoforum* 51: 284–293.

Yi, C.-C. (2013). "Changing East Asian families: values and behaviors." *International Sociology* 28(3): 253–256.

Zhang, J. (2014). The disintegration of rural China. *The New York Times*, 28 Nov.

Zimmer, Z., K. Korinek, J. Knodel and N. Chayovan (2007). *Support by migrants to their elderly parents in rural Cambodia and Thailand: a comparative study.* New York, Population Council.

6 The poverty of sustainable development in Southeast Asia

Economic growth, the environment and people's lives

The environmentalism of the poor – because they are (not) worth it

At the end of December 1991, then chief economist of the World Bank, Lawrence Summers, wrote an internal memo setting out the logic of polluting poor countries (Box 6.1). The memo ends by claiming that

> the problem with the arguments against [allowing] more pollution in [less-developed countries] (intrinsic rights to certain goods, moral reasons, social concerns, lack of adequate markets, etc.) could be turned around and used more or less effectively against every Bank proposal for liberalization.

When the memo was leaked, Brazilian Secretary of the Environment Jose Lutzenburger replied to Summers:

> Your reasoning is perfectly logical but totally insane . . . . Your thoughts [provide] a concrete example of the unbelievable alienation, reductionist thinking, social ruthlessness and the arrogant ignorance of many conventional 'economists' concerning the nature of the world we live in . . .
>
> (Accessed from: http://www.counterpunch.org/1999/06/15/
> larry-summers-war-against-the-earth)

Box 6.1 A dirty little secret exposed?

DATE: December 12, 1991
TO: Distribution
FR: Lawrence H. Summers
Subject: GEP

'Dirty' Industries: Just between you and me, shouldn't the World Bank be encouraging MORE migration of the dirty industries to the LDCs [less-developed countries]? I can think of three reasons:

1) The measurements of the costs of health impairing pollution depend on the foregone earnings from increased morbidity and mortality. From this point of view a given amount of health impairing pollution should be done in the country with the lowest cost, which will be the country with the lowest wages. I think the economic logic behind dumping a load of toxic waste in the lowest wage country is impeccable and we should face up to that.

2) The costs of pollution are likely to be non-linear as the initial increments of pollution probably have very low cost. I've always thought that under-populated countries in Africa are vastly UNDER-polluted, their air quality is probably vastly inefficiently low compared to Los Angeles or Mexico City. Only the lamentable facts that so much pollution is generated by non-tradable industries (transport, electrical generation) and that the unit transport costs of solid waste are so high prevent world welfare enhancing trade in air pollution and waste.

3) The demand for a clean environment for aesthetic and health reasons is likely to have very high income elasticity. The concern over an agent that causes a one in a million change in the odds of prostate cancer is obviously going to be much higher in a country where people survive to get prostate cancer than in a country where under 5 mortality is 200 per thousand. Also, much of the concern over industrial atmosphere discharge is about visibility impairing particulates. These discharges may have very little direct health impact. Clearly trade in goods that embody aesthetic pollution concerns could be welfare enhancing. While production is mobile the consumption of pretty air is a non-tradable.

The problem with the arguments against all of these proposals for more pollution in LDCs (intrinsic rights to certain goods, moral reasons, social concerns, lack of adequate markets, etc.) could be turned around and used more or less effectively against every Bank proposal for liberalization.

(Source: http://www.whirledbank.org/ourwords/summers.html)[1]

While defenders of the memo have claimed either that it was meant ironically or that Summers was logically correct (e.g. Johnson *et al.* 2007), the reality is that this is just the way that the environment-development process *has* operated in much of the poorer world.[2] Moreover it is a within-country and not just a between-country phenomenon. Poor(er) countries and poor(er) people have felt the burden of pollution and environmental degradation because, in a crude sense, they are worth it. What the furore over the memo also highlighted was a wider debate: over the relationships between development, poverty and the environment. In their book on the political ecology of Cambodia's transformation, Milne and Mahanty write the following:

If we consider Cambodia's economic growth alone, then what appears to emerge is an outstanding success story in human development: higher average incomes, improvements in infrastructure, increased exports and rising life expectancy. ... However, macro-economic indicators provide only one crude measure of a country's development ... [and] ... it is in the environmental domain that some of the most profound changes and challenges of economic development are seen.

(Milne and Mahanty 2015: 3)

Development and sustainable development

There is no doubt that the countries considered in this book have achieved development. Whether this can also be counted as *sustainable* development, in the classic environmental sense of the word, is more questionable. It is worth restating the problematic – but most commonly quoted – definition of sustainable development from the World Commission on Environment and Development's *Our common future*. The report defined sustainable development as "development that meets the needs of the present without compromising the ability of future generations to meet their own needs" (WCED 1987: 43).

There are two critical components to this definition: first, the implied potential trade-offs between (economic) development and environment; and second, the focus in the definition on inter-generational equity. For critics of the WCED's definition, it is better as a slogan than as a basis for theory (Adams 1990: 3). Adams (2009, p. xvii) writes, dismissively, that "the rhetorical vagueness of that master phrase [sustainable development] has made it too easy for hard questions to be ignored, stifled in a quilt of smoothly crafted and well-meaning platitudes".

This chapter is not aimed at critically reviewing sustainable development either as a concept (see Adams 2009; Imran *et al.* 2014) or as a process in Southeast Asia (see Parnwell and Bryant 1996); the literatures on both are extensive. There is little evidence that either modes of production or approaches to consumption in the countries of Southeast Asia have made substantial progress towards sustainability since the publication of *Our common future* almost three decades ago. Where it might *appear* that individual countries have taken some steps in this direction – perhaps best reflected in controls over logging in some countries – this often disguises, as elaborated below, an off-shoring or leakage of these processes to neighbouring countries. To date at least, the growth logic or paradigm that underpins development has not been challenged to any serious and meaningful degree in the Southeast Asian region. As McNeill and Wilhite (forthcoming) write in a book on sustainable development and the emerging economies:

In brief, the outlook for sustainable development now looks worse than ever. ... The record shows that innumerable international conferences have achieved very little in response to the challenge of sustainable development – despite evidence of increased urgency as the scientific evidence of climate change becomes overwhelming.

This pessimism is common and widespread.[3] In Southeast Asia (and other parts of the global South) it arises because of a pair of interconnected dilemmas that show little evidence of being reconciled. To begin with, there is the dilemma of whether there exists a feasible alternative to the market-based approach to ameliorating poverty through growth. There is, after all, no equal to the market-based economic growth model when it comes to combatting poverty, and the growth case for Southeast Asia seems irrefutable, as earlier chapters have explored. In the opening page of *The growth report: strategies for sustained growth and inclusive development*, the World Bank sets out the case for market-led growth observing that, while growth is not an end in itself, it does "make it possible to achieve other important objectives ... [and] ... can spare people *en masse* from poverty and drudgery ... Nothing else ever has" (World Bank 2008: 1). Why would any government or society wish to tinker with or turn its back on such a self-evidently successful strategy?

The second dilemma concerns the market-based, neoliberal approach to growth, where monetary value is attached to labour and resources. Only by valuing nature and the environment can it be protected; but it only becomes so valued in a market context which drives economic growth with negative consequences for the environment. More concisely, there is no policy space for an alternative environmental paradigm.

Not surprisingly, then, many environmentalists working in the global South find themselves caught in something of an impasse. There often seems to be no alternative to the current dominant system of market-based growth; and such an approach is ill-suited to furthering an environmental agenda. This issue will be returned to in the final chapter in the context of a broader consideration of development means and ends.

Multiple paths of environmental transition

In a series of review papers of the neoliberal nature literature, the geographer Noel Castree (2008a, 2008b, 2009) asked what light this literature might shine on the following questions:

- Why are market approaches [to nature] being adopted serially?
- How are they implemented and enacted?
- What effects are they having?
- How ought they be judged?

This chapter attempts to address – if not answer – these questions by looking at a series of such market-based approaches as they have been applied across the Southeast Asian region. This is, in part, to bridge the gap between the theory of neoliberal nature and the reality of neoliberalism and the intersections between nature/environment and development; or, to put it another way, between what is sometimes known as neoliberalism as a generic category and 'actually existing neoliberalisms' as diverse but very real experiences.

Across much of the global South, and not least in Southeast Asia, natural resource extraction has both accelerated and become increasingly globalized. There are, self-evidently, particularities of time and place when it comes to understanding environment–development dilemmas in the region. It is also possible to identify, however, wider processes that give these dilemmas shape and direction, including policies of economic and trade liberalization, export production and promotion, and spatial integration (Elmhirst and Resurreccion 2014). The cases discussed later in this chapter thus show both important specificities that we need to recognize and seek to understand, but also commonalities the identification of which is equally, if not more valuable. A word of warning, however: at first glance the environmental dilemmas discussed here appear to echo those of the 1980s. The upshot is that it is easy to suppose that little has changed. This would be wrong, a point that is returned to in the final section of the chapter.

In the 1990s, before the Asian financial crisis and at the height of the Southeast Asian growth 'miracle' there was, seemingly, ample evidence of the environmental costs of rapid economic growth. The region's environmental crisis emerged from the policies pursued and, just as importantly, from those *not* pursued. As Bryant and Parnwell wrote at the time in the introduction to their book *Environmental change in South East Asia: people, politics and sustainable development*, "perhaps more than anywhere else in the developing world, the contradictions between environment and development, economic growth and environmental conservation, are visible" in the region (1996: 2; and see Hart-Landsberg and Burkett 1998: 103). It has long been recognized that the costs of modernization has an environmental face and the destruction of forests and degradation of land, the loss of biodiversity and extinction of species, and the pollution of air and water courses, have profound consequences for certain social and geographical groups. In this way, such cases became the leitmotifs of critical development scholars seeking to challenge the very basis of the region's economic 'miracle' and the terms on which it was gauged and assessed.

Environmental optimists, however, came to see these sorts of environmental outcomes – or costs – not as products of development, but as legacies of underdevelopment. This was central, of course, to the sustainable development discourse as it was embraced and reworked by institutions such as the World Bank. Rather than being the oxymoron that its critics proposed (see Brown 2011; Adams 2009), sustainable development was a case of win–win where market-led development could actually solve, rather than create, environmental problems.[4] 'Liberal' or 'market environmentalism', reflected in the greening of the World Bank, shows to highlight what has been argued to be the "compatibility of environmental concern, economic growth, the basic tenets of a market economy, and a liberal international order" which has become "common wisdom among many policy makers, diplomats, and a large number of nongovernmental organizations throughout the world" (Bernstein 2001: 3). Where the neoliberality of sustainable development lies is in its seeming ability to turn a problem into an opportunity for profit: sustainable development, then, has provided a space for capital not only to make a profit from polluting the world, but then also from cleaning it up (Bakker 2009: 1782).

Liberal environmentalism drew succour from environmental transition theory, reflected in the Environmental Kuznets Curve (EKC). This led some scholars to postulate – and to hope – that market-led development itself would actually solve the environmental problems that were emerging with market-led development. More specifically, that with growing affluence, awareness and education, society's concern for the environment would grow, that this would place pressure on governments to respond to public and media concerns, and with a reduced need to pursue development 'at all costs', stronger and more robust environmental controls and regulations would be enacted and, importantly, policed.[5] Industry would also respond creatively to market incentives and develop innovative solutions to environmental problems. A virtuous cycle of growth with sustainability would be set in train.

While theoretically enticing the environmental transition curve in reality takes multiple shapes depending on the environmental concern under investigation (Goklany 1995: 436; Jahan and Umana 2003: 63; Stern 2004; and see Figure 6.1). Experience tells us that some environmental challenges, such as access to clean drinking water, are addressed easily and early in the modernization process; others, such as dealing with airborne pollutants in urban areas, tend to get resolved

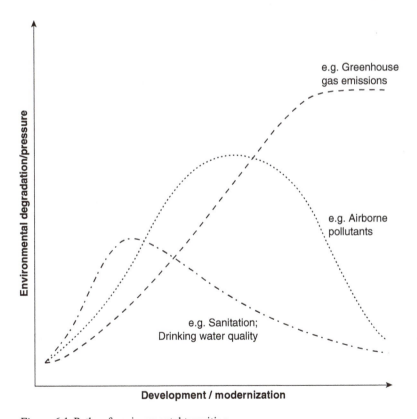

Figure 6.1 Paths of environmental transition

rather later; and there are also some environmental challenges which would seem to increase with modernization and so far have shown little evidence of being resolved, the most obvious of which is greenhouse gas emissions. It is not just, however, that the EKC takes different shapes according to the pollutant or challenge under consideration. As with the sustainable development trope, there are a series of other more intractable issues,[6] three of which are relevant for the later discussion in this chapter.

First, some environmental processes may be irreversible, reaching a tipping point or ecological threshold from which recovery is highly costly, and possibly impossible. Climate change might fall into this category (see Lenton 2012 on Arctic climate tipping points). Second, growing trade and economic integration has meant that countries can follow growth strategies in which the environmental costs of economic expansion are off-shored. (This is the logic of the Summers memo.) And third, the EKC takes no account of the within country distribution of the social and economic costs of environmental degradation. The first of these concerns focuses on the temporalities of environmental processes and change; the second on their spatialities; and the third on their social distribution.

Since the 1990s, Thailand and Vietnam have shown quite substantial net gains in forested area.[7] A logging ban was introduced in Thailand at the end of the 1980s (as that country achieved middle-income status, thus conforming to the environmental transition model), while in Vietnam, forest-conservation policies were substantially strengthened in the early 1990s. These policies partially 'solved' the problem of Thailand and Vietnam's rapidly declining and denuding forest resource. In 1998, China also introduced a logging ban, and this likewise led to a fall in rates of logging nationally (McCarthy 2014: 2). But, at the same time, these national success stories accentuated the self-same problems facing neighbouring Cambodia, the Lao PDR and Myanmar, as continuing demand for tropical hardwoods in China, Thailand and Vietnam led to the displacement – or leakage – of logging, often by Chinese, Thai and Vietnamese firms, across international borders (see Figure 6.2). As Copeland and Taylor (2004: 65) conclude in their extensive review of the evidence of links between trade policy and the environment:

> With the increased integration of the global economy, it has become difficult to ignore the international consequences of domestic environmental policy regulation. And with rising concern over environmental quality both at home and abroad, an assessment of how trade policy affects the environment has become unavoidable.[8]

We see this reflected at a regional level in Southeast Asia, where wealthier countries have been able to transfer or displace land use demands to neighbouring, poorer states. Positive readings of forest transitions in China, Thailand or Vietnam, then, have to be seen against – and in direct relation to – more deleterious transitions in countries like Cambodia, the Lao PDR and Myanmar. In reviewing the statistical evidence of the leakage of logging pressures from one country to

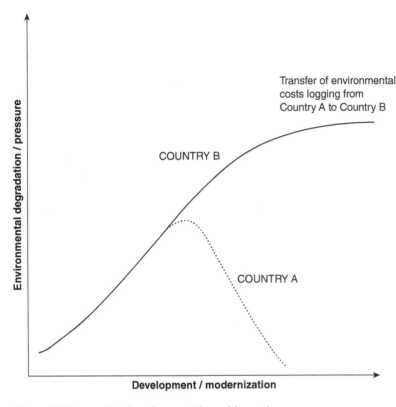

Figure 6.2 Transnational environmental transition paths

another, Meyfroidt *et al.* (2010: 20917) write that the "international timber trade ... creates illusory images of conservation by preserving forests in accessible, affluent political jurisdictions while extracting natural resources from remote places with permissive or poorly enforced environmental policies". In Cambodia, a substantial portion of the loss of some 7 per cent of the country's forest cover in the decade between 2002 and 2012 has been attributed to the conversion of forested state land largely to agriculture under Economic Land Concessions (ELCs). A significant proportion of this was likely land degraded due to activities during the 1990s. At the end of 2012, the Cambodian government had granted or reserved over 2.6 million hectares of land to private companies under the ELC scheme (ADHOC 2013: 9). This amounted to 14 per cent of the country's total land area.

The discussion above highlights one of the key shortcomings of many of the more optimistic readings of environmental trends in Southeast Asia: the tendency to take the nation state as the unit of analysis. This takes our attention away from both the within-country and between-country distribution of environmental outcomes (effects, costs). Problems tend to be produced, experienced, governed, addressed, measured and recorded at the country scale. Yet, increasingly, Asia's development is regional and global, and this goes beyond the role of trade. In order to understand fully the environmental costs of growth and the environmental victories in one country we need to look to other places. From rubber concessions in the Lao PDR to the disposal of electronic waste in Malaysia and the 'haze' across Indonesia, Malaysia and Singapore, these problems are evidence of the cross-border transmission and reproduction of environmental problems. Just as there is a new geography of poverty (see p. 4), so there is also a new geography of the environment.

The focus on the nation state as the unit of analysis not only ignores the international transmission of environmental costs, it also overlooks the within-country distribution of environmental processes and their externalities. Looking at the impact of resource extraction on indigenous groups in three Latin American countries with very different political contexts – Bolivia, Ecuador and Peru – Bebbington and Bebbington (2011) unearth a similar slate of effects in each place. They state that:

> Value is taken from certain spaces and distributed to others. The spaces that bear the brunt of the externalities generated by extraction are in the vicinity of the wells, mines, pipelines and smelters, and in none of these three countries are environmental safeguards and regulations handled with the seriousness necessary to offset the risk that today's sites of extraction will be tomorrow's sites of contamination and reduced viability. Meanwhile benefits and opportunities accrue in other spaces – in departmental and national capitals and more generally in areas of demographic concentration.
>
> (p. 142)

Their paper raises questions of spatial as well as social justice. In the 1980s, Harold Brookfield and Piers Blaikie wrote of the "desperate ecocide" of the poor (Blaikie and Brookfield 1987) and more recently, Blaikie *et al.* have noted that "limited resources will generate pressure for '*desperate ecocide*', driven by a combination of marginalization through government policy or through encroachment of more politically powerful groups in the reconstruction process, dispossession, and lack of alternative livelihood sources" (2005: 6, emphasis in original).[9] The key point here, and this will be illuminated in the later discussion, is that development will not smoothly and unproblematically deliver better environmental conditions in the manner that environmental transition theory posits. Indeed, often quite the reverse. Environmental transitions are highly uneven, they are usually profoundly local and, often, also highly personal. Furthermore, the character of these effects needs to be tied to the very nature of the development process and the policies and logics that underpin it.

Neoliberal development and the environment

It has been suggested that while in the global North environmental issues tend to be framed in terms of conservation, in the global South it is poverty which provides the theoretical and practical cornerstone for discussions of the environment (Lawhon 2013). This division is valuable as a didactic starting point, but in Southeast Asia we see a conflation of conservation and poverty-driven environmentalism. Neoliberalism offers a link between the two. Bakker (2009: 1784) usefully provides a tabulation of the environmental targets for neoliberalism, or neoliberal natures (Table 6.1). These provide a set of 'hooks' on which to hang the cases that follow.

The chapters in this book so far have set out how market-led growth, and the very *success* of such growth, has created a series of new development problematics. There is an important environmental component to this process. As McCarthy and Prudham write, "neoliberalism is also an *environmental* project, and ... it is *necessarily* so" (2004: 277, emphases in original). That neoliberalism should have environmental permutations is inevitable (Bakker 2009: 1782).

Neoliberal nature can be seen to exist in two ways. To begin with, the exploitation of nature becomes justified and explained through the logic of neoliberalism. This was the thrust of Summers' memo: the export of pollution to poor(er) countries is explained and justified in economic terms. Simply put, poorer countries have a comparative advantage when it comes to hosting polluting industries. The

Table 6.1 Neoliberalizing nature: targets and tactics

Target	Tactic	Case discussed in the chapter
Institutions (rules, norms, laws)		
Property rights	Marketization	Rights to sand in Cambodia
Trade rules	Liberalization	Sand mining in Cambodia
Pricing	Commercialization	Park management in the Wakatobi National Park, Sulawesi
Governance (decision-making practices)		
Regulatory frameworks	Deregulation and reregulation	Elimination of shifting cultivation in the Lao PDR
Resource management	Private sector participation	Land concessions and enclosure in the Lao PDR
Decision-making authority	Devolution to non-governmental actors	Recognition of customary land rights in Kalimantan
Accountability mechanisms	Client–provider substitutes for citizen–representative relationship	–
Socionatural actors		
Environmental pollution	Ecological fix	Climate change and the adaptable neoliberal subject
Human bodies	Alienation	Minority ('tribal') peoples in Indonesia and the Lao PDR
Government agencies	Corporatization	–
Conventional resources	Privatization, accumulation by dispossession	Land in Indonesian Borneo and Laos converted to rubber and oil palm

Source: adapted from Bakker (2009).

second way of thinking about the production of neoliberal nature is through the way that ordinary people are seen to be market responsive. This is evident, for instance, in debates over climate-change adaptation. In this way, debates over neoliberal nature are personalized in the guise of the inherently adaptable neoliberal environmental subject.

Many of the key processes outlined so far in this book – for example, enclosure, accumulation by/without dispossession, commoditization and market integration – are not only representative of the neoliberal project but they also have environmental consequences and ramifications. The character of environmental change in Southeast Asia, in other words, is closely tied to neoliberalism and the landscapes and environmental processes and outcomes that we see across the region are shaped, intentionally and unintentionally, by the neoliberal project. What is often lost in the generalities of debates over the global environmental crisis is that neoliberalism – the market – does not just either accentuate or ameliorate (depending where you stand) elements of this crisis, but remakes, as well as re-engineers, the very environmental context itself.

New commodities come into being under the aegis of neoliberalism. Uncommodified realms of the natural world become commodified and, as a result, become resources to be enclosed, guarded, stolen, bought, sold and accumulated (Nevins and Peluso 2008). Most clearly this is land but it also extends to many other things, such as water, wildlife, reef fish or, more broadly, nature. Arising from this, and second, the social relations that underpin the production, management and distribution of these new commodities also changes. And finally, it brings new actors – or 'stakeholders', as they are often termed – into the frame: the state and various commercial and corporate entities, for example. This leads us to consider the environmental rudiments of the structural violence impelled by marketization.

The environmentalism of the poor and the poverty–environment nexus

In his book *Slow violence and the environmentalism of the poor* (2011), Nixon writes that "by slow violence I mean a violence that occurs gradually and out of sight, a violence of delayed destruction that is dispersed over time and space, an attritional violence that is typically not viewed as violence at all" (p. 2). He links slow violence to Galtung's structural violence (1969; and see p. 104 this volume) but emphasizes the temporality of violence wherein its gradualism can be such that it becomes decoupled from its roots (2011: 11). The result is that we lose sight of how and why the poor face the environmental dilemmas they do – and the causalities that lead to this state of affairs. That the cause and the effect are separated out over time is, to be sure, part of the reason why the culprit and victim are difficult to connect; this is compounded, however, by a geography that also disconnects cause and effect over space, as some of the vignettes that follow show.

There is a story of structural violence to recount, and this is important in seeing why, at a high level of abstraction, the forms of development pursued in Southeast Asia often have such disturbing and distressing environmental outcomes. These, however, are never inscribed in singular ways, and this requires us to ask questions about the particular qualities of different places and different peoples (Ireland and McKinnon 2013). Sand mining in Cambodia, for example, while it can be understood through adopting an international political economy of the environment approach, is played out between and within coastal Cambodian settlements in quite particular ways. After all, not all the households in Koh Sralao, a Cambodian village affected by sand mining, discussed later in this chapter, were forced to leave their homes and pursue a livelihood elsewhere. Not everyone in Tania Li's account (2014) of the spread of cacao in Sulawesi was displaced; some undoubtedly benefited. Finally, the forces of neoliberalism and the crimes of globalization, as they are sometimes termed, are not just 'out there'. Li writes this of the process of land enclosure in the Lauje highlands from the 1990s:

> In 1990, Lauje highlanders didn't have a word in their language equivalent to the English term 'land'. By 1998 the word *lokasi* … was in common use. It referred to land as a unit of space that was interchangeable with other units, individually owned, and freely bought and sold. The new word signalled the emergence of new practices and relations. These were not shifts the highlands planned. They didn't hold neighbourhood meetings or talk about the need to create lokasi. Land-as-lokasi was a by-product of highlanders' decision to plant tree crops …. The effect was enclosure: the permanent withdrawal of plots of land from the highlanders' commons.
>
> (2014: 84)

Most policy-makers studiously avoid viewing – and certainly of writing about – environmental dilemmas in terms of structural violence. Instead they prefer to write about the poverty–environment nexus or, sometimes, the poverty–development–environment nexus. At a basic level, this is viewed as a two-way relationship: the environment is important for the sustaining of livelihoods in many developing countries; a degraded environment will therefore increase the vulnerability, reduce the resilience and undermine the livelihoods of people and, especially, poorer people. At the same time, poverty will – as Blaikie *et al.* suggest in the quote above – leave people with little choice but to degrade their environment (Jahan and Umana 2003: 59). Poverty is accentuated by environmental decline, and environmental decline is accelerated by poverty.

The manner in which the poverty–environment–development nexus is framed by most institutions and multi-lateral agencies is through the lens of environmental transition theory, justified by the logic of sustainable development. It is poverty which creates environmental problems and, therefore, addressing poverty through market-led growth will help to solve those problems. This is evident, for example, in the World Bank Development Research Group's discussion of the poverty–environment nexus in Cambodia, Laos and Vietnam (Dasgupta *et al.* 2005; DECRG 2002). Having identified that the north of Laos harbours high levels of environmental degradation and high levels of poverty, the authors "conclude that the poverty–environment nexus appears to be strongly defined for the Lao PDR, and that the potential synergy between poverty alleviation and environmental poli-cies is high" (DECRG 2002: 27; and see Dasgupta *et al.* 2005). If only it was that simple.

It has been Third World political ecology that has gone furthest in illuminating the centrality of neoliberalism to environmental change and, more particularly, the way that this impacts on vulnerable groups in society. It is the poor who are the casualties of the violence of environmental changes shaped and driven by neolib-eralism and fast capitalism. In light of this, we should be wary of interventions and policy prescriptions that assume that because poverty and environmental degrada-tion are often co-present, that addressing the former through growth-enhancing policies will automatically solve the latter. They may be co-present but they do not operate hand-in-hand.

Cases of market-based environmental violence in Southeast Asia

The four cases of environmental violence that follow aim to flesh out the discussion so far in the following ways. To start with, all the cases show the quite particular ways that environmental dilemmas work their way out in each instance. There is a specific geography to the environment–development relationship that requires a degree of interpretative specification at the local level. At the same time, however, and second, these local level geographies of the environment also require, if they are to be understood as more than just local-level resource conflicts, to be contextualized against the wider processes that have played an important role in shaping the con-ditions that lead to tension and conflict. These processes are often intimately tied to the nature of the development process. How each of the case studies is illustrative of the key themes addressed in this chapter is set out for clarity's sake in Table 6.2.

Table 6.2 Making the case

	Climate change adaptation	Land enclosures in Laos	Sand mining in Cambodia	Subak and the Green Revolution in Bali
Commodity-making		✓	✓	
Trans-boundary environmental dilemmas	✓		✓	
Off-shoring of environmental costs			✓	
Structural environmental violence		✓	✓	✓
Social (in)justice	✓	✓	✓	
Environmental temporalities	✓		✓	
Poverty–environment nexus		✓	✓	
Adaptable neoliberal subject	✓			✓
New technologies and expert knowledge		✓		✓

Climate change in Southeast Asia and the adaptable neoliberal subject

Vietnam, the Philippines, and parts of Malaysia, Indonesia and Thailand have been identified as countries and regions that face particularly severe climate change-related hazards (Table 6.3). The challenge of climate change, in Southeast Asia and beyond, has focused attention on the scope for 'adaptation' and this, in turn, on the vulnerability and resilience of social groups and natural systems to climate change. Pelling (2011: 6) makes a valuable distinction between "forward looking" and "backward looking" adaptation. The latter pays attention to the capacities of systems to cope with disturbances or shocks. These are the attributes that make communities, for example, resilient in the face of an environmental stress. Forward-looking adaptation focuses on adaptive capacity and seeks to assess the degree to which a community is adapted to future disturbance. Underpinning interest in adaptation is the notion of the adaptable environmental subject.

The 'adaptable Southeast Asian subject' rests on the belief that societies and individuals in Southeast Asia – and beyond – have the capacity to adapt their behaviour in the face of climate change. This is linked to what is known as autonomous adaptation; the conviction that people and societies can adapt to risks, in this instance environmental risks associated with climate change, without outside intervention (Forsyth and Evans 2013). The notion of the adaptable neoliberal environmental subject brings together two currents of work that are often viewed as lying in opposition: the populist and the neoliberal. The populist current emphasizes the creativity of local people and the power of local knowledge and technologies; the neoliberal current pays attention to the responsiveness of populations to market forces and economic stimuli. While they are sometimes uneasy bedfellows, both see local populations as inherently knowledgeable, responsive

Table 6.3 Climate hazard hotspots and dominant hazards

Climate-change hotspots	Dominant hazards
Vietnam	
Northwestern Vietnam	Droughts
Eastern coastal areas of Vietnam	Cyclones, droughts
Mekong region of Vietnam	Sea-level rise
Thailand	
Bangkok and its surrounding area in Thailand	Sea-level rise, floods
Southern regions of Thailand	Droughts, floods
Philippines	
The Philippines	Cyclones, landslides, floods, droughts
Malaysia	
Sabah state in Malaysia	Droughts
Indonesia	
Western and eastern area of Java Island, Indonesia	Droughts, floods, landslides, sea-level rise

Source: adapted from Yusuf and Francisco (2009: 6).

and adaptable. Critics of this thesis, such as Felli and Castree (2012), maintain that such a view on adaptation is a 'neoliberal fix'.

The idea of the adaptable neoliberal subject has two weaknesses. First, it represents a subtle reworking of the logic underpinning the poverty–environment nexus which, in turn, echoes the underlying tenets of liberal environmentalism. In this instance, the two-way relationship outlined earlier in this chapter, where a degraded environment creates poverty and poverty degrades the environment, is replaced by a one-way relationship: climate change threatens livelihoods requiring the poor (and the non-poor) to adapt. Second, it makes invisible the respective roles of economic inequality, unequal social relationships, exploitative political positionings, and inefficient institutional systems in exposing people to climate change and shaping their adaptive capacities. As O'Brien (2009) discusses, adaptation priorities not infrequently represent the values of privileged groups of stakeholders who occupy the higher ground of decision-making. The politics of adaptation, and the politics of *needing* to adapt, are pushed to the margins, out of sight. This is a point that Forsyth and Evans (2013) make in their study of autonomous adaptation among Karen smallholders in Mae Hong Son in Thailand. The belief in the autonomously adaptive peasant farmer pays insufficient attention to "pre-existing structures of social vulnerability" and the barriers and constraints that vulnerable groups face in their efforts to exert their agency (2013: 64). Adaptation, then, cannot be understood as an individual response to a stimuli or threat; it is situated in the relations that structure and govern society.

This is not to downplay and devalue the inventiveness of the poor and the marginalized. Their lives, after all, are often a continual and continuing adaptation performance where they bob-and-weave to survive in an uncertain and unfair world. As Bankoff *et al.* (2003) argue, the "discourse on vulnerability to climate change – like much technocratic work that arises from the collision between science and people – underplays the agency of 'ordinary' people, seeing them as 'victims' of events and actions orchestrated from other scales". Vulnerable people in exposed places with difficult livelihoods are knowledgeable and often far from powerless. Even so, the slow (and sometimes not-so-slow) environmental violence that this chapter explores may be such that the adaptation practices of the past are either insufficient or ill-suited to the demands of the present. This opens up the risk of a disjuncture or adaptation deficit (Tschakert and Dietrich 2010) when autonomous adaptation is inadequate to the task that people and societies face. We can see this at work in two summary examples of climate change-driven adaptation, drawn from Thailand and Vietnam.[10]

The injustices of flooding in Thailand

In October–November 2011, Thailand experienced its most serious floods in recent memory; many analysts put their severity down to climate change. The floods led to 730 deaths and affected 1.6 million hectares of land with a loss of a quarter of the main-season rice crop. Almost 10,000 factories employing 660,000 workers had to temporarily close, and the total bill was put at US$46 billion or equivalent to 13 per cent of GDP in 2011 (Promburom and Sakdapolrak 2012: 18). Not everyone, however, was equal when it came to the Thai state's response to the floods. Certain areas, occupations and classes were privileged, namely: the Central Plains generally and central Bangkok in particular; industrial and service sector activities rather than agriculture; and the Bangkok elite over poor classes and, especially, migrants from rural areas. The 2011 floods illustrated that, as far as the Thai government and bureaucracy were concerned, some people, some occupations and some areas were more important or valuable than others. Questions of social, spatial and occupational justice therefore arise.

In a sense the decisions that the Thai government took were eminently logical and understandable. Lebel *et al.* (2011) have termed this tendency 'elite capture' by which

> flood and disaster management are organized in such a way that it makes it easy for elites to deploy experts and technical tools in ways that serve their interests and not those of less politically empowered and socially vulnerable groups.
>
> (p. 52)

Such elites became *de facto* protected and/or compensated classes, while non-elites have the expectation of adaptation thrust upon them. The institutions that govern responses to climate change in Thailand reflect power relations and asymmetries, and therefore class interests (Lebel *et al.* 2010: 353). The logic of the logic, so to speak, of such patterns of response is indubitably linked to geometries of power. Only very occasionally do these geometries become twisted out of shape.

Adaptive farmers in Vietnam under conditions of market reform

Vietnam, since the mid-1980s, has made the transition – through the policies encapsulated in *doi moi* ('renovation') – from a centrally planned to a market economy. It has also, and this is directly linked to this first transformation, made the transition from being one of the poorest countries in Asia, to middle income. These two transitions make clear and highlight the limitations of taking backward-looking adaptive practice as an indicator of forward looking adaptive capacity. They also emphasize the importance of seeing adaptive capacity against the backdrop of marketization and its effects (Table 6.4).

Adaptive practice in Vietnam in the 1970s and 1980s was based on collective systems and action, and common property. Close to two-thirds of the population were poor, and yet we can identify a good deal of adaptive practice and resilience in the face of environmental threats. In the Vietnam case therefore, it is not possible to read-off from past poverty an equal level of vulnerability to climate change or other environmental hazards. Indeed, there is reason to think that even in the context of rising incomes and falling poverty, some marginal groups are *more* vulnerable today than in the meagre past. While the modernization of the agricultural sector in Vietnam through the policies of *doi moi* has undoubtedly led

Table 6.4 Forward- and backward-looking vulnerability and adaptation in Vietnam

Backward-looking		Forward-looking	
Vulnerability	*Adaptive practice*	*Vulnerability*	*Adaptive capacity*
Narrow livelihoods	Collective support structures	Market liberalization	Widening of opportunities beyond traditional livelihoods
Few opportunities	Common property	Undermining of collective support mechanisms	Rising incomes
Limited scope for mobility	Relative equality combined with the re-distribution of wealth and resources	Widening inequalities (gender and inter-personal) – collective security versus individual prosperity	Growing scope for mobility
	Collective action	Privatization of collective resources and common property	Improving education and skills

→ → → *Doi moi* (renovation) → → →
→ → → Rising incomes and material wealth → → →

Source: adapted from Adger (1999).

to truly impressive aggregate increases in output,[11] the combination of marketization, chemicalization and mechanization, fuelled by debt, has "led to a vicious circle of induced systemic fragility through engineered landscapes, reduced agrobiodiversity, and weakened social networks, knowledge and skills" (Fortier and Tran Thi Thu Trang 2013: 82; and see Beckman 2011). The country's market-based mode of agricultural modernization has left it more exposed – and less resilient – to climate change. The key argument here is that vulnerability has been *induced* by the policies adopted. This is because state and commune safety nets have been partially dismantled; market individualization has replaced community cooperation, assistance and mutual support; and inequalities at multiple levels (regional, inter-personal, gender) have widened.

This is exemplified in the example of Giao Thuy in North Vietnam's Nam Dinh province where mangrove destruction has amplified environmental risks (Adger *et al.* 2002, Adger 2000). Adger *et al.* conclude that while their results indicate rising incomes and well-being for some in the context of transforming livelihoods, a newly marginalized social group is also emerging in the process who will have "great difficulty adjusting to [the] new 'rules of the game' in contemporary Vietnam" and who are poorly placed to cope with emerging environmental (and demographic) stresses (2002: 365).

How policy interventions, risk and livelihoods are linked can be seen in Beckman's (2011; and see Beckman 2006) study of adaptation to environmental change in central Vietnam's Quang Tri province. Essentially, Beckman argues – and he is not alone in this – that a series of policy interventions by the Vietnamese government have rendered forest-dependent communities more vulnerable by reducing the flexibility that used to be built into their livelihood systems (Table 6.5). Resettled in valley bottom sites in the mid-1970s, they became exposed to floods and could less easily supplement agriculture with the collection of forest products. From the early 1990s, a major programme of watershed management and refor-estation was introduced, alienating the forest still further as a livelihood resource. With land holdings declining, villagers had little choice but to take advantage of the government agricultural extension programme to intensify production, using new seeds and chemical inputs. Flood risk became amplified, culminating in the disastrous floods of 1999. By 2010, villagers, while in some respects living more comfortable lives with better access to schools, clinics and roads (p. 38), were also more exposed to environmental hazards, had less room for livelihood manoeuvre in the face of such hazards, and were at the same time in far greater debt and therefore exposed to the risks of price and market fluctuations.

What these examples from Thailand and Vietnam show is that while a hazard or a risk may, indeed, be climate change-induced or related, the vulnerability of people in the face of the hazard is tied to structural factors, which often need to be viewed in historical perspective and against the backdrop of the policies that may, at the same time, have lifted them out of income poverty. Moreover,

Table 6.5 Policy-produced vulnerability and environmental exposure in Vietnam

Policy interventions	*Resettlement of upland forest communities in valley sites*		*'Programme 327': Watershed management; reforestation of hill slopes; agricultural intensification programme*		
Livelihood	Diverse and flexible forest-based livelihoods	→	Paddy-rice farming on river banks	→	Intensification of rice production through use of high-yielding varieties and high levels of chemical input
Risk/ vulnerability context	Meagre living; resilient livelihoods	→	Rice-farming dependent; shortage of land; exposed to flood risk	→	Debt-funded farming; vulnerable to seasonal crises and price fluctuations
Timeline	*c.*<1970	1976	*c.*1980	1992	*c.*2010

Source: Information extracted from Beckman (2011).

their resilience in terms of response is also importantly shaped by the sorts of structural constraints discussed in earlier chapters. Migrants from rural areas laid-off from their factory work in the Central Plains of Thailand had little or no job protection and, in most cases, their only recourse was to return to their rural homes where land holdings were often too small to sustain a living. Farmers embracing the opportunities offered by Vietnam's policies of economic reform and marketization were, at the same time, creating for themselves new modalities of vulnerability. The adaptable Southeast Asian subject may have only limited scope for manoeuvre when her or his resilience in the face of climate change has been compromised and narrowed by these processes of market-led development. Development processes, therefore, both expose people to climate change risks and, at the same time, compromise their ability to adapt in the face of such risks. They also, and this is important, boost growth, raise incomes and reduce poverty.

Enclosing the commons in mainland Southeast Asia

In the uplands of mainland Southeast Asia (and the abutting highland areas of China), over a million hectares of land have been converted to rubber plantations, with the expectation that this will expand a further four-fold by 2050 (Fox *et al.* 2014: 3). While some of this conversion is being undertaken by smallholders, the majority involves large-scale commercial concessions, mostly controlled by Chinese, Thai and Vietnamese corporations and capital. Of the countries where this is occurring, it is most pronounced in the Lao PDR.

As described in Chapter 3 (see p. 63), the Lao uplands that have been enclosed for rubber were neither unused nor unpopulated. We see in this process of dispossession, enclosure and conversion the poverty–development–environment nexus at work. Where it differs from the last example is in the separation of cause from effect such that the root causes of environmental change are shielded from view.

The Lao state's view of environmental change in the uplands of the Lao PDR, and not infrequently multilateral agencies' as well, is one where shifting cultivation is the cause and the minorities are the culprits as well as the victims. Traditional systems of upland living are portrayed as primitive, livelihoods as necessarily fragile and meagre, and modes of production as inherently environmentally destructive. As a UNDP report on an integrated rural development project in the highlands of the Lao PDR put it: "The main type of agriculture in the district is shifting cultivation, which provides only a marginal subsistence and is, as far as the Hmong variant is concerned, extremely destructive to the forest and hence to restoration of soil fertility" (1986: 5). The United Nations Environment Programme concurred with this view in their state of the environment report, saying that "shifting cultivation [in the Lao PDR] remains one of the major factors [for] the depletion of forest land" (UNEP 2001: 39; see also Forsyth and Walker 2008: 76–84). With this three-fold justification – that such systems are primitive, unproductive and environmentally destructive – eradicating shifting cultivation has been a central policy initiative of the Lao government since the early days of the revolutionary government in 1976 (Souvanthong 1995: 19; Rigg 2005), and

Figure 6.3 'The route to a new life': land settlement in the hills of Laos

it continues to drive land settlement in the country (Figure 6.3). The same policy, underpinned by the same beliefs and assumptions, has also been evident in the uplands of Thailand and Vietnam.

This entrenched view of the uplands and uplanders has been critiqued on a range of grounds, developmental, political and socio-cultural (see Rigg 2012: 88–92). With regard to the discussion here, the environmental logic has also been challenged as simplistic and excessively narrow in its identification of causality (see e.g. Rambo *et al.* 1995; Santasombat 2003; Chamberlain and Phomsombath 2002; ADB 2001; Laungaramsri 2000; Baird 2010; Lindeborg 2012; La-orngplew 2013). To be sure, shifting cultivation on limited land with short fallows can – and does – lead to soil erosion, land degradation, declining yields and compromised livelihoods. The real question that needs to be asked, however, is why do minorities find themselves squeezed onto and working smaller and smaller plots? This has not, hitherto, been the case. To answer this question we need to look not at methods of shifting cultivation, but at the instrumentalities of the state and market-led development, namely:

- attempts by the state to capture the uplands in the interests of national development;
- attempts by capital to capture the uplands in the interests of capital accumulation.

Both start with dispossession, as outlined in Chapter 3, and this has environmental ramifications. Rigg and Salamanca (forthcoming) set out the case of a village of resettled minority households in the district of Phonexay in northern Laos'

Luang Prabang province. With a mix of minority Khmu and Hmong households, resettlement had forced households to degrade their land in a manner not dissimilar from Piers Blaikie's (see above) ecocide of the poor. Originally shifting cultivators, these minority households were resettled by the government supposedly to control the negative environmental impacts of shifting agriculture. They arrived at their lowland location in the late 1980s. Between their original settlement in 1988 and 2012 the village grew from sixteen to forty-three households. They had farms and gardens located in the lowlands, near a river, but the land area available for cropping was limited and much of it increasingly exposed to flooding. Their ability to fallow fields after a season of cropping was impossible, and fields were cultivated year-round. This change necessitated tree crops being replaced with corn, sesame, Job's tears (a type of grain) and other annual crops, which are poor at absorbing runoff, accentuating the effects of flooding. Other potentially available land had been claimed by influential absentee farmers who were able to secure certificates for their land through their connections to state officials.

What this example from the Lao PDR shows is that the poverty–environment nexus in this instance is intimately associated with the comparatively powerless positioning of upland minorities in Lao society; the manipulations of their lives by the state in the 'interests' of national development; and certain problematic assumptions about the nature of minorities' 'primitive' modes of living. This is a theme that ripples through many studies of upland farming, livelihoods and policy in the country (see e.g. Lestrelin and Giordano 2007; Lestrelin 2010; Lestrelin *et al.* 2012a, 2012b). Deepening intra-village inequalities have also created the conditions where a subset of the village in Phonexay District has found their vulnerability accentuated, even while others have used unequal systems of access to gain control over land. Behind much of this, in turn, is the way in which market-based reforms in the Lao PDR and the opening up of the country to foreign commercial interests has shaped the wider context of accumulation. Villagers are competing over resources because wider processes have led them to become settled in places where land is scarce, even while hundreds of thousands of hectares are allocated to commercial estate farming. As Piers Blaikie wrote in his seminal book *The political economy of soil erosion*, "a principal conclusion of this book is that soil erosion in lesser developed countries will not be substantially reduced unless it seriously threatens the accumulation possibilities of the dominant classes" (1985: 147).

The environment–development–poverty nexus is often presented in a manner that is reminiscent of the 'growth is good for the poor' argument (see p. 6 this volume). In fact, however, levels of poverty are highest where swidden systems have been most "traumatised" (ADB 2001: xv). Such trauma is increasingly associated with the operation of the market and the impacts and effects of government policies. In their study of Ban Lak Sip in Luang Prabang province, Lestrelin *et al.* (2012b: 73) note the link between rural development policy on the one hand and land degradation on the other; rather than addressing the problems of soil erosion and land degradation, policies are causing and exacerbating these problems. They conclude: "Looking at the broad picture, by creating conditions where the maintenance of short cropping and long fallow periods is impossible, rural development policy contributes itself to the poor reputation of shifting cultivation and is thus self-legitimizing". The easy, lazy conclusion may be to view shifting cultivation as poverty-creating, thus legitimating policies of sedenterization. Detailed studies would lead one to a rather different conclusion: that it is the way in which such systems have been twisted by the market and the state that explains, more often than not, the concentration of poverty among swidden farmers. This is reminiscent of Nixon's slow violence and the environmentalism of the poor where the root causes of environmental conflict are partially obscured.

Also evident in the experiences of the hill and forest peoples across mainland and island Southeast Asia is the intersection of citizenship and the environment – sometimes termed environmental (or ecological) citizenship (Latta and Wittman 2010: 114; Latta 2007a, 2007b). To date, environmental citizenship has focused on the question of how green, or environmental attitudes can be cultivated and promoted amongst the citizenry. A second way in which the term is used, and this is how it is seen to be particularly relevant here, is with regard to how rights to the environment (land, water, resources) are enclosed and appropriated. This enables us to connect environmental citizenship and environmental justice (Latta 2007b: 385–6). Environmental justice is, at heart, about distributional justice: who gets what, why and how. It therefore links to a number of themes discussed in earlier chapters: dispossession, social exclusion, inequality and, of course, citizenship itself. We see in the experiences of the hill and forest people of Southeast Asia all these factors at play.

It does not follow, it should be stressed, that environmental justice can be equated with environmental sustainability. It is entirely plausible that a more environmentally just outcome may be a 'worse' one environmentally. This, of course, is one of the key justifications that has driven efforts across mainland Southeast Asia to sedentarize hill peoples and eradicate shifting cultivation.

What we see in this process of enclosure for rubber in the Lao PDR is not just dispossession and potential immiseration even when aggregate incomes are rising, but also the imposition of an official, formalized landscape of control and ownership onto a vernacular one. It is the fissures that emerge during this process that provide, not infrequently, the space for extraction. Moreover, this is a theme which can be seen repeated in many other areas of Southeast Asia – the forests of Kalimantan and Irian Jaya, for example – where neoliberal tendencies for management, control and valuation come into contact with indigenous or local systems.

Urano's (2010, 2014) study of the spread of oil palm in East Kalimantan shows how state recognition of customary tenure has actually weakened, rather than strengthened farmers' land rights, making it easier for large-scale estates to take control of villagers' land. In one of her study sites

> the company took advantage of the local hierarchical social structure, and obtained easy approval from elite members to advance and set up operations in a way that served the interests of the company at the cost of those of local populations.
>
> (2014: 21)

This was, in effect, a process of elite capture – something which has been identified time-and-again in studies of natural resource development. In her other research site, while strong local leadership thwarted company attempts to take their land, when villagers tried to use the state-sponsored Community-Based Forest Management (CBFM) programme to protect their land rights, this was undermined by wider forest policies that prioritized business interests over villagers' rights. The World Bank's evaluation of participatory development experience is instructive in this instance and indicates that Urano's study probably represents the norm, rather than the exception.[12] There is elite capture at one end of the equation, and there are participatory exclusions at the other (see p. 221).

Sand mining and coastal settlements: connecting livelihoods in Cambodia with global city ambitions in Singapore

Land-short, income-rich and with grand ambitions, Singapore has expanded its land area by reclamation since the 1960s by over a fifth. Land – in the guise of sand – has been sourced from Indonesia, Malaysia and Vietnam but as each country has come fully to appreciate the environmental costs of large-scale sand mining so they have banned the practice with the result that firms in Singapore have had, each time, to find alternative sources of supply. Cambodia became Singapore's largest supplies of sand after Indonesia banned the export of sand on environmental grounds in early 2007.[13]

Global Witness, a campaigning NGO, has critically and contentiously detailed in a series of publications the workings of the sand-mining industry in Cambodia (Global Witness 2010). In summary, Global Witness has contended that the sand-mining industry is manifested by the following problematic relationships and practices, or by their absence:

- close links between the issuing of sand-mining licenses and individuals close to the ruling Cambodian People's Party (CPP);
- lack of transparency in the issuing and regulation of licenses;
- awarding of concessions for mining within protected areas and close to vulnerable and valuable marine and coastal ecosystems;
- dredging without due regard to national legislation concerning best environmental management practice;
- absence of due diligence requirements by Singapore companies sourcing sand;
- failure of the Singapore government to monitor and regulate the sand trade, in conflict with its stated commitment to sustainable practices;
- systematic environmental governance failures at all levels in Cambodia;
- failure of the international donor community in Cambodia to respond or react and use their influence to pressure for change.

Shortly after the release of the report *Shifting sands* by Global Witness (2010), a spokesperson for the Cambodian government, said: "Their reports are always exaggerated, far beyond the imagination, and attack the Cambodian Government in order to try and bring political benefit to one of the smaller opposition parties" (quoted in Abdullah and Goh 2012: 2). The Singapore government likewise rejected accusations that it had not followed required procurement procedures. The Singapore Ministry of National Development, on its part, released a rebuttal to the Global Witness report stating that the Singapore government was committed to the protection of the global environment, does not facilitate the illegal export or smuggling of sand and that, in any case, sand is imported by private firms and not by the government (Abdullah and Goh 2012: 15–16). Notwithstanding the Singapore government's claims, it is widely assumed that substantial quantities of sand have been illegally imported into Singapore (see Franke 2014: 26).

The discussion here, however, is not aimed at examining the veracity or otherwise of these claims, although the extent to which Cambodia's extractive industries generally have been beset by rampant corruption and a lack of regulation and transparency is not without significance (Un and So 2009; Le Billon 2002; Milne and Adams 2012; Milne and Mahanty 2015; Sok 2014).[14] Nor is the focus here on the direct environmental effects of sand mining. Rather the intention is to focus on the effects of sand mining on poor, coastal communities, drawing on the work of Melissa Marschke (2012a, 2012b). Marschke has been working in the Cambodian coastal village of Koh Sralao since June 1998.

When Marschke first arrived she was 'awestruck' by the health and abundance of the mangrove forest, the abundance of wildlife and the pristine environment. No wonder, she thought, that so many people were migrating from other parts of the country to this resource rich coastline. Twelve years later, in 2010, she revisited the area to see a dozen or more large barges filled with sand. "I was told", she writes, that "people were leaving because of steep declines in the swimming crab population and high debt levels, thought to be linked with the sand mining operations that had been taking place near local fishing grounds since 2008" (2012b: 250).

Scientific evidence of the links between sand mining and resource degradation are hard to come by in the case of Koh Sralao. There is no baseline survey against which to measure trends and, in any case, no environmental impact assessment has ever taken place. But villages noticed a decline in the main crab species caught within weeks of sand mining commencing in the area in 2008. Livelihoods were compromised and, for the first time since Marschke had begun working in the village a decade earlier, abandoned homes (Figure 6.4) could be seen, with one-quarter of households leaving the village between 2009 and 2010:

[T]he tipping point for most villagers appears to have been the sand mining activities. Crab stocks were perceived to have declined significantly between 2008 and 2010, debt levels seemed to have increased, and people had left the village. There was little that villagers could do in terms of sustainable resource management when outside business interests with high-level connections decided to operate in their fishing grounds. In 12 years this area had gone from attracting migrants to being a village whose very future was in question.

(Marschke 2012b: 267)

Figure 6.4 Abandoned house, Koh Sralao, Cambodia (2010)

Source: Melissa Marschke.

Marschke notes that had she left Koh Sralao in 2007 or 2008 and not returned she would have departed with a sense that there had been modest gains and that families were on a gradual upward trajectory in terms of their livelihoods. But two years later she was concluding, in contrast, that "marginalization and immiseration is the norm" for villagers (2012a: 75). Sand mining, she argues, has been key to this transformation from a situation of gradual improvement to a context of widespread immiseration.[15]

In itself and against the larger scheme of things, it might seem that the case of Koh Sralao is neither remarkable nor particularly important. But it is the former which belies the latter. It is the fact that such micro-studies are so common which make them so very important. They are not isolated and unusual examples of environmental governance failures which run against the grain of success; they are numerous, common and therefore reflective of the *normal* operation of the economic and political systems in place. The marginalization and immiseration of villagers in Koh Sralao, driven by environmental decline, is repeated thousands of times across Southeast Asia from the rice villages of northern Vietnam (Scott 2012) and coastal settlements in protected areas of Sulawesi in Indonesia (Clifton 2013a, 2013b), to upland minority settlements in the Lao PDR (Baird 2010; Lestrelin 2010; Lestrelin *et al.* 2012a, 2012b). Village committees in this area of coastal Cambodia have sent petitions to national government departments, protested peacefully in the local town of Koh Kong, and drawn on their informal networks to share their experiences of what is happening. They suffer the costs of sand mining and receive none of the benefits and yet have been unable to shift the direction that development has taken. 'Agency' for these fisherfolk is distinctly limited and constrained. Furthermore, the experience of Koh Sralao is not an exception; it is emblematic of development in such fragile and marginal political, social and environmental contexts.

This case of sand mining in Cambodia shows the ways in which environmental dilemmas have to be seen, and increasingly so, in terms of the wider regional context and the national exigencies that drive and shape development. Franke (2014) applies world-systems theory to understanding Singapore's imports of sand from peripheral (Cambodia, Vietnam)[16] and semi-peripheral (Indonesia, Malaysia) states. She concludes by suggesting that the "economic growth and development of Singapore [has come] at the expense of environmental problems in the countries which are found below Singapore in the core/periphery hierarchy" (2014: 35). 'Cheap growth' in Singapore, she contends, has come at the expense of society, economy and environment in sand exporting countries like Cambodia.

Disruptive technologies in Bali

The Indonesian island of Bali's irrigation associations or societies, known as *subak*, have probably received more attention than any other institution of water management in Southeast Asia, dating from the first arrival of the Dutch in the late nineteenth century (Figure 6.5). *Subaks* are irrigation or water management societies where religion, ritual, resource management and farming come together. Numbering around 1,500 individual societies, *subaks* have been in operation for

Figure 6.5 Rice terraces, Bali

some 1,000 years and continue to play an important role in both rice agriculture and Balinese society (Jha and Schoenfelder 2011). Indeed, they have become exemplars of culturally embedded, community-based and sustainable natural resource management (MacRae and Arthawiguna 2011). They have also been reproduced in other areas of Indonesia where Balinese have settled (e.g. through the transmigration scheme).

Despite – or perhaps because of – this detailed attention, there are continuing and sometimes quite heated differences of opinion between scholars regarding the constitution and operation of *subaks*.[17] These controversies tend to coalesce around the linked issues of solidarity, governance and autonomy. In essence, these boil down to the questions of the degree to which *subaks* in Bali enjoy administrative autonomy; how this is governed and achieved (locally, harmoniously, at the supra-*subak* level ...); and who are the key actors in the process and the structures that underpin it (religious leaders, state officials, *subak* members ...). For MacRae and Arthawiguna:

> Wet-rice cultivation [in Bali] is undergoing something of a crisis. The problems are multiple: shortages of land and water, environmental problems resulting from decades of petrochemical fertilizer and pesticide use, and a growing imbalance between rising costs of inputs and low prices for produce, exacerbated by a rapidly rising cost of living.
>
> (2011: 11)

In writing this they are highlighting a series of resource, economic and environmental issues including land and water shortages, shifting terms of trade against farming, and technology-induced environmental decline. We can add to these, competition from alternative livelihoods and a loss of interest in rice farming among the younger generation. It is the environmental facets of agrarian change which are of interest here and this is most closely associated with the work of anthropologist Stephen Lansing (1987, 1991; Lansing *et al.* 2005; Lansing and de Vet 2012).

The clash between technology, farm 'governance' and environment in Bali's *subaks* came to a head during the high point of the extension of the Green Revolution during Indonesia's New Order (see Lansing 1991).[18] The argument is two-fold, one part concerning the nature of the governance of the Green Revolution (i.e. the manner of its dissemination), and the second the nature of the technology involved. As regards the first, it is suggested that this has been top-down, bureaucratic and one-dimensional: the extension by the state of a single technology package regardless of local conditions, cultural and environmental (see p. 218 and Table 7.5). The second criticism concerns the technology package itself where generalized seeds, bred in other contexts, are combined with high levels of chemical inputs. The result, to critics of the Green Revolution such as Lansing, was that pest attacks increased as synchronized irrigation schedules choreographed carefully using diverse seed stocks were replaced by the uniform planting of single varieties (Lansing and de Vet 2012: 454–6). Lansing concludes his discussion of the Green Revolution in Bali in his seminal 1991 monograph *Priests and programmers* with the following:

> [B]y the mid-1980s, Balinese farmers had become locked into a struggle to stay one step ahead of the next rice pest by planting the latest resistant variety of Green Revolution rice. Despite the cash profits from the new rice, many farmers were pressing for a return to irrigation scheduling by the water temples to bring down the pest populations. But to foreign consultants at the Bali Irrigation Project, the proposal ... was interpreted as religious conservatism and resistance to change. The answer to pests was pesticide, not the prayers of priests. Or as one frustrated American irrigation engineer said to me, 'These people don't need a high priest, they need a hydrologist'.
>
> (p. 115)

The poverty of sustainable development

> [N]otions of peak oil; the 'race' to buy up fertile agricultural land across the planet (often referred to as land grabbing); the competition for new and old precious minerals (such as rare earths, phosphate), in turn strongly linked to the growing demand from China and the other rapidly industrializing countries; accelerated deforestation especially in tropical regions; and the rapid exploitation and threat of extinction of many commercial fisheries including those of various cod and tuna species. These signs of environmental crises are more and more interpreted as being global and interdependent in nature ...
>
> (Sonnenfeld and Mol 2011: 772)

There has been a tendency in geographical studies of environmental dilemmas in recent years to emphasize the geographical and historical specificities of each case in question, and to avoid analytical abstraction and generalization.[19] This has been valuable in challenging the universalizing and reductionist tendencies in some of the earlier literature and, to be sure, the devil *is* often in the detail. But, taken to the extreme, this can sideline attempts at identifying the rhymes that are critically important if environment–society relations and their transformation under the influence of global economic change are not continually to be discounted as exceptional. As Sonnenfeld and Mol imply in the extract above, the environmental dilemmas – or crises – that face different parts of Southeast Asia, and in many different ways, do rhyme.

Perhaps the most distinctive feature of environment–development dilemmas in the new millennium in Southeast Asia is their transnational character, as several of the cases recounted here show. In mainland Southeast Asia this has been carefully engineered in the guise of the ADB's Greater Mekong Subregion (GMS). The GMS programme, encompassing the five countries of mainland Southeast Asia along with China,[20] was launched in 1992 and formally adopted as a strategic framework of ASEAN in 2001. The programme's five key thrusts embrace infrastructure linkages, cross-border trade and investment, private sector participation in development, human resource development and sustainable use of the subregion's shared natural resources (Rigg and Wittayapak 2009). A key debate has been how the balance of power between the different members of the GMS can be seen reflected in development processes and outcomes, not least environmental.

While the use of world systems theory and unequal environmental exchange[21] to explain the export of environmental pollution and pressures from one country (rich) to another (poor) is tempting – particularly given evidence like Summers' memo – this is, in itself, too simple. Receiving countries have environmental policies, however flawed; international and domestic NGOs and media highlight especially egregious cases of environmental ruin; there are international norms in some areas of environmental policy that countries and companies are expected to subscribe to, no matter what their 'level' of development; and companies themselves are not immune to calls that they take their global environmental responsibilities seriously. We can see this at work, for example, in the case of sand mining in Cambodia. That said, there is also little doubt that there is an unequal environmental exchange, which can be seen in the examples discussed in this chapter.[22] As an ADB report on upland–lowland relations in the GMS observed, and which also resonates at a country level, a "power imbalance leads to a fundamental inequity in the flow of ecological goods and services between the uplands and lowlands" (ADB 2000: 5).

At times, environmental struggles are couched in terms of equity – that groups suffering from environmental degradation should have that degradation valued, and that they should receive 'fair' compensation for such degradation. This is akin to 'playing the game', while ensuring that the costs and benefits are better apportioned. One such effort that reflects a mainstream approach to environmental management is payments for environmental services, giving primacy to economic valuations, returns and incentives. In his study of environmental management in the Wakatobi National Park in southeast Sulawesi, Clifton (2013a, 2013b) notes the way that the tendency to stress economic interventions and incentives is out of step with the priorities of the historically marginalized, indigenous Bajau communities. He argues that this "underlines a lack of understanding of Bajau history or culture and an unwillingness to adapt programmes to suit the Bajau context, which will continue to limit the effectiveness of any participative, knowledge-based or interpretative incentives" (2013a: 86). A second issue concerns elite capture of compensation, particularly acute in those contexts where local governance is weak (Clifton 2013b). In other instances, struggles focus less on seeking fair compensation than on contesting and resisting extraction on cultural or political grounds citing, for example, minorities' rights over the resources in question or their cultural significance which should take precedence over any economic valuation (Martinez-Alier 2014).

A key question that lurks behind the environmental vignettes presented in this chapter is why, given Southeast Asia's growing prosperity and bearing in mind the 'logic' of the EKC, has it proved impossible, to date, to shift policies in a significant manner towards modes of production and consumption that are more sustainable? This is more surprising still when we consider that people on the front line of the environment in Southeast Asia are becoming 'environmental subjects'. I use this term in the same vein as Agrawal (2005: 162), to mean people who care about the environment. Sometimes this is reflected in growing environmental activism at a local level and, where that is politically problematic or difficult – such as in Cambodia – in activism which is embedded in campaigning at an international level.

There are four factors to consider. To begin with – and this has been said before – the neoliberal capitalist model of economic growth is fundamentally founded on economic expansion. There is almost no room or scope for policies that challenge this core principle. Second, the continued integration of the global economy provides space for countries to pursue what might appear to be environmentally sustainable development strategies through off-shoring the environmental costs of growth so that, from a domestic standpoint, progress is being made. Third, governments see their role, above all else, as delivering continuing and growing prosperity to their citizens. This is, moreover, what citizens expect. Singapore is said to have a 'prosperity consensus' (Ismail and Shaw 2011); so too with the other countries of the region. Former President Suharto of Indonesia was only forced to resign in 1998, after over three decades in power, in the wake of the country's *krismon* (monetary crisis). With the collapse of Indonesia's economy, Suharto could no longer reasonably claim to be *Bapak Pempangunan*, or the Father of Development. In light of this it is none too surprising that, time-and-again, policies that might compromise the key goal of economic expansion are avoided or watered down. Furthermore, the ever-rising minimum acceptable standard of living means an ever-rising global social metabolism with growing energy and natural resource use (Martinez-Allier 2014). And finally, many of those groups and individuals suffering from resource extraction and environmental decline are poor and/or politically marginalized, with little power or scope fundamentally to alter the trajectory of development. Taken together, this conjunction of impediments makes, it is suggested, sustainable development all but impossible.

Further reading

There are scores of studies of sustainable development in the global South, but for a general book see the latest edition of Bill Adams' *Green development* (2009). On the EKC, Stern's highly cited (2004) paper is a good summary by an economist. For more theoretical and critical views of neoliberalism and the environment see Castree's series of papers (2008a, 2008b, 2009) and Bakker's (2009, 2010) reviews.

For a summary of debates over the environment–poverty nexus in mainland Southeast Asia, see Dasgupta *et al.* (2005).

As regards the specific cases outlined here, for more detail on debates over climate change adaptation and resilience see Lebel *et al.* (2010, 2011) for flood risk in Thailand, and Adger *et al.* (2002) and Beckman (2011) for farming and environmental risk in Vietnam. Upland policy and environmental degradation in the Lao PDR is well reflected in Lestrelin and colleagues' papers (Lestrelin 2010; Lestrelin and Giordano 2007; Lestrelin *et al.* 2012a, 2012b). For trans-boundary resource dilemmas see Marschke's (2012a, 2012b) work on sand mining and coastal communities in Cambodia, as well as the Global Witness (2010) report on the topic. Franke looks more widely at sand imports to Singapore, applying world-systems theory to elucidating the underpinning structural factors. The best known work on Bali's *subaks* is that of Lansing (1987, 1991; Lansing and de Vet 2012) but also see alternative viewpoints in a special issue of the journal *Human Ecology* 40(3) 2012.

Notes

1   There has been some debate about whether the memo as quoted here was doctored before it was made public; it has been suggested that the intended ironic tenor of the memo was lost through careful editing. See Johnson *et al.* (2007).
2   Defenders of the Summers memo (see e.g. Johnson *et al.* 2007) continue to note the inherent and, as they see it, irrefutable logic of the argument. Citizens of poor countries have a low opportunity cost in hazardous waste. But this overlooks the way the most poor countries actually work, where property rights are disputed or poorly regulated, where corruption is common and where poorer groups do not, often, receive compensation for the pollution or environmental degradations that they suffer. It has also been said that the memo it was written by an intern, and not by Summers at all.
3   See, for example, the contributions in Hansen and Wethal (forthcoming).
4   In the introduction to its web pages on sustainable development, the World Bank states:

> Sustainable development recognizes that growth must be both inclusive and environmentally sound to reduce poverty and build shared prosperity for today's population and to continue to meet the needs of future generations. It must be efficient with resources and carefully planned to deliver immediate and long-term benefits for people, planet, and prosperity.
>
> (http://www.worldbank.org/en/topic/sustainabledevelopment)

To its critics, this illustrates the contradictions that lie at the heart of the institution's policies. Consider the final clause: development must "deliver immediate *and* long-term benefits for people, planet and prosperity" [emphasis added]. Cake today and cake tomorrow.
5   This perspective is reflected in Panayotou's 1993 working paper for the ILO (downloaded from http://www.ilo.org/public/libdoc/ilo/1993/93B09_31_engl.pdf) in which he writes:

> At low levels of development both the quantity and intensity of environmental degradation is limited to the impacts of subsistence economic activity on the resource base and to limited quantities of biodegradable wastes. As economic development accelerates with the intensification of agriculture and other resource extraction and the take off of industrialization, the rates of resource depletion begin to exceed the rates of resource regeneration, and waste generation increases in quantity and toxicity. At higher levels of development, structural change towards information-intensive industries and services coupled with increased environmental awareness, enforcement of environmental regulations, better technology and higher environmental expenditures, result in levelling off and gradual decline of environmental degradation.
>
> (p. 2)

6 For discussions of these see Panayotou (1993) and Stern *et al.* (1996).
7 Although what should count as forest is disputed (natural forest, or natural forest + plantations, for example) and this can lead to very different estimates of forest cover.
8 This is echoed in Stern's otherwise quite positive take on environmental trends with income growth (in connection with the EKC). He states that the outstanding research challenge is to identify the effects of trade on greenhouse gas emissions, observing that "rigorous answers to such questions are central to the debate on globalization and the environment" (2004: 1435).
9 Downloaded from: http://cmsassets.dev.getunik.net/iucn/downloads/ip_tsunami_risks_and_services_2.pdf.
10 These two examples are explored at greater length in Rigg and Salamanca (forthcoming).
11 In 2013 Vietnam was the world's second largest exporter of rice; at the tail end of the period of socialist reconstruction and development it was facing famine conditions in some areas.
12 This World Bank desk study reviewed more than 400 papers and reports.
13 Earlier, in 2003, Jakarta banned the export of sea sand. Singapore's Ministry of National Development was said to have been 'disappointed' by Indonesia's decision. Myanmar is also becoming an important source of sand.
14 Un and So (2009: 134) write:

> The exploitation of natural resources [in Cambodia], such as timber and land, has been awarded to business tycoons who are, among other things, financiers of the CPP [Cambodian People's Party] mass-based patronage politics. We argue the political use of natural resources has increased economic inequality and human rights abuses.

15 In mid-2014, researchers at the site reported that sand mining activities had ramped up again, except this time close to the community itself (500 metres from the village) and within the protected area (Melissa Marschke, personal communication and see https://melissamarschke.wordpress.com/2014/06/12/sand-mining-returns-dredging-for-every-last-grain-within-a-coastal-protected-area/).
16 Myanmar could be added to this list of peripheral states.
17 See, for example, the exchange of commentaries in *Human Ecology* 40(3) 2012.
18 'Green Revolution' is shorthand for the new rice technology embodying high-yielding seeds, high levels of chemical inputs (pesticides and herbicides) and, for some scholars, the use of machines.
19 This is also a point that Bakker (2009: 1785) makes.
20 The GMS encompasses: Cambodia, China (originally Yunnan province only, but since 2005 also including Guangxi Zhuang Autonomous Region), the Lao People's Democratic Republic, Myanmar, Thailand, and Vietnam.
21 This is closely allied to mainstream environmentalism's discussion of 'externalities' wherein environmental costs incurred in one place can be devolved to another.
22 Mol, in his study of China's economic ascent and Africa's environment writes:

> [W]e do see ongoing environmental destruction by Chinese companies in Africa as well as at home. In that sense, and in absolute figures, China's rapidly expanding and ascending economy is continuing resource extraction and environmental degradation in peripheral economies, along lines asserted by most World-Systems Theory scholars. On the other hand, Chinese companies and operations in Africa also increasingly have come to be influenced by environmental normativity, far more than European and US TNCs were when they operated in peripheral regions in the 19th and first half of the 20th centuries.
>
> (2011: 792)

References

Abdullah, F. and A. T. Goh (2012). *The dirty business of sand – sand dredging in Cambodia.* Singapore, Lee Kuan Yew School of Public Policy at the National University of Singapore.

Adams, W. M. (1990). *Green development: environment and sustainability in the Third World.* London, Routledge.

Adams, W. M. (2009). *Green development: environment and sustainability in a developing world*, London, Routledge.

ADB (2000). *Poverty reduction and environmental management in remote greater mekong subregion watersheds.* Manila, Asian Development Bank. Phase II: Draft Final Report.

ADB (2001). *Participatory poverty assessment: Lao People's Democratic Republic.* Manila, Asian Development Bank.

Adger, W. N. (1999). "Social vulnerability to climate change and extremes in coastal Vietnam." *World Development* 27(2): 249–269.

Adger, W. N. (2000). "Institutional adaptation to environmental risk under the transition in Vietnam." *Annals of the Association of American Geographers* 90(4): 738–758.

Adger, W. N., P. M. Kelly, A. Winkels, L. Q. Huy and C. Locke (2002). "Migration, remittances, livelihood trajectories, and social resilience." *Ambio* 31(4): 358–366.

ADHOC (2013). *A turning point? Land, housing and natural resources rights in Cambodia in 2012.* Phnom Penh, Cambodia, ADHOC.

Agrawal, A. (2005). "Environmentality: community, intimate government, and the making of environmental subjects in Kumaon, India." *Current Anthropology* 46(2): 161–190.

Baird, I. G. (2010). "Land, rubber and people rapid agrarian changes and responses in Southern Laos." *Journal of Lao Studies* 1(1): 1–47.

Bakker, K. (2009). "Neoliberal nature, ecological fixes, and the pitfalls of comparative research." *Environment and Planning* A 41(8): 1781–1787.

Bakker, K. (2010). "The limits of 'neoliberal natures': debating green neoliberalism." *Progress in Human Geography* 34(6): 715–735.

Bankoff, G., G. Frerks and D. Hilhorst (Eds) (2003). *Mapping vulnerability.* London, Earthscan.

Bebbington, A. and D. Humphreys Bebbington (2011). "An Andean avatar: post-neoliberal and neoliberal strategies for securing the unobtainable." *New Political Economy* 16(1): 131–145.

Beckman, M. (2006). *Resilient society, vulnerable people: a study of disaster response and recovery from floods in Central Vietnam.* PhD, Swedish University of Agricultural Sciences.

Beckman, M. (2011). "Converging and conflicting interests in adaptation to environmental change in central Vietnam." *Climate and Development* 3(1): 32–41.

Bernstein, S. (2001). *The compromise of liberal environmentalism.* New York, Columbia University Press.

Blaikie, P. (1985). *The political economy of soil erosion in developing countries.* Harlow, UK, Longman.

Blaikie, P. and Brookfield, H. (1987). *Land degradation and society.* London, Methuen.

Blaikie, P., S. Mainka and J. McNeely (2005). The Indian Ocean tsunami: reducing risk and vulnerability to future natural disasters and loss of ecosystem services. IUCN Information Paper. Gland, Switzerland.

Brown, K. (2011). "Sustainable adaptation: an oxymoron?" *Climate and Development* 3(1): 21–31.

Bryant, R. L. and M. J. G. Parnwell (1996). Politics, sustainable development and environmental change in South-East Asia. *Environmental change in South East Asia: people, politics and sustainable development.* M. Parnwell and R. Bryant. London, Routledge: 1–20.

Castree, N. (2008a). "Neoliberalising nature: the logics of deregulation and reregulation." *Environment and Planning* A 40(1): 131–152.

Castree, N. (2008b). "Neoliberalising nature: processes, effects, and evaluations." *Environment and Planning* A 40(1): 153–173.

Castree, N. (2009). "Researching neoliberal environmental governance: a reply to Karen Bakker." *Environment and Planning* A 41(8): 1788–1794.

Chamberlain, J. R. and P. Phomsombath (2002). *Poverty alleviation for all: potentials and options for peoples in the uplands*. Vientiane, SIDA.

Clifton, J. (2013a). "Compensation, conservation and communities: an analysis of direct payments initiatives within an Indonesian marine protected area." *Environmental Conservation* 40(3): 287–295.

Clifton, J. (2013b). "Refocusing conservation through a cultural lens: improving governance in the Wakatobi National Park, Indonesia." *Marine Policy* 41: 80–86.

Copeland, B. R. and M. S. Taylor (2004). "Trade, growth, and the environment." *Journal of Economic Literature* 42(1): 7–71.

Dasgupta, S., U. Deichmann, C. Meisner and D. Wheeler (2005). "Where is the poverty–environment nexus? Evidence from Cambodia, Lao PDR, and Vietnam." *World Development* 33(4): 617–638.

DECRG (2002). *The poverty–environment nexus in Cambodia, Lao PDR and Vietnam*. Development Research Group of the World Bank, World Bank.

Elmhirst, R. and B. P. Resurreccion (2014). Introducton. *Gender, environment and natural resource management: new dimensions, new debates*. R. Elmhirst and B. P. Resurreccion. London, Earthscan: 3–20.

Felli, R. and N. Castree (2012). "Commentary: neoliberalising adaptation to environmental change – foresight or foreclosure?" *Environment and Planning* A 44: 1–4.

Forsyth, T. and A. Walker (Eds) (2008). *Forest guardians, forest destroyers: the politics of environmental knowledge in Northern Thailand*. Seattle, WA, University of Washington Press.

Forsyth, T. and N. Evans (2013). "What is autonomous adaption? Resource scarcity and smallholder agency in Thailand." *World Development* 43: 56–66.

Fortier, F. and T. Thi Thu Trang (2013). "Agricultural modernization and climate change in Vietnam's post-socialist transition." *Development and Change* 44(1): 81–99.

Fox, J. M., J.-C. Castella, A. D. Ziegler and S. B. Westley (2014). Rubber plantations expand in mountainous Southeast Asia: what are the consequences for the environment? *Asia Pacific Issues*. Honolulu, East-West Center. 114.

Franke, M. (2014). When one country's land gain is another country's land loss . . .: the social, ecological and economic dimensions of sand extraction in the context of world-systems analysis exemplified by Singapore's sand imports. Working Paper No. 36/2014. Berline, Institute for International Political Economy.

Galtung, J. (1969). "Violence, peace, and peace research." *Journal of Peace Research* 6(3): 167–191.

Global Witness, G. (2010). *Shifting sands: how Singapore's demand for Cambodian sand threatens ecosystems and undermines good governance*. London, Global Witness.

Goklany, I. (1995). "Strategies to enhance adaptability: technological change, sustainable growth and free trade." *Climatic Change* 30(4): 427–449.

Hansen, A. and U. Wethal (Eds) (forthcoming). *Emerging economies and challenges to sustainability: theories, strategies, local realities*. London, Routledge.

Hart-Landsberg, M. and P. Burkett (1998). "Contradictions of capitalist industrialization in East Asia: A critique of 'flying geese' theories of development." *Economic Geography* 74(2): 87–110.

Imran, S., K. Alam and N. Beaumont (2014). "Reinterpreting the definition of sustainable development for a more ecocentric reorientation." *Sustainable Development* 22(2): 134–144.

Ireland, P. and K. McKinnon (2013). "Strategic localism for an uncertain world: A post-development approach to climate change adaptation." *Geoforum* 47: 158–166.

Ismail, R. and B. J. Shaw (2011). Future proofing the intelligent island? Singapore resilience as 'tahan lasak' or 'exceedingly hardy'. First World Sustainability Forum, 1–30 November. Downloaded from: www.sciforum.net/conference/wsf/paper/614/download/pdf.

Jahan, S. and A. Umana (2003). "The environment–poverty nexus." *Development Policy Journal* 3: 53–70.

Jha, N. and J. Schoenfelder (2011). "Studies of the Subak: new directions, new challenges." *Human Ecology* 39(1): 3–10.

Johnson, J., G. Pecquet and L. Taylor (2007). "Potential gains from trade in dirty industries: revisiting Lawrence Summers' memo." *Cato Journal* 27(3): 397–410.

Lansing, J. S. (1987). "Balinese 'water temples' and the management of irrigation." *American Anthropologist* 89(2): 326–341.

Lansing, J. S. (1991). *Priests and prgrammers: technologies of power in the engineered landscapes of Bali.* Princeton, NJ, Princeton University Press.

Lansing, J. S. and T. de Vet (2012). "The functional role of Balinese water temples: a response to critics." *Human Ecology* 40(3): 453–467.

Lansing, J. S., L. Pedersen and B. Hauser-Schäublin (2005). "On irrigation and the Balinese state." *Current Anthropology* 46(2): 305–308.

La-orngplew, W. (2013). Living under the rubber boom: market integration and agrarian transformations in the Lao Uplands. PhD, Durham University.

Latta, A. (2007a). "Environmental citizenship." *Alternatives Journal* 33(1): 18–19.

Latta, A. (2007b). "Locating democratic politics in ecological citizenship." *Environmental Politics* 16(3): 377–393.

Latta, A. and H. Wittman (2010). "Environment and citizenship in Latin America: a new paradigm for theory and practice." *Revista Europea de Estudios Latinoamericanos y del Caribe / European Review of Latin American and Caribbean Studies* (89): 107–116.

Laungaramsri, P. (2000). "The ambiguity of 'watershed': the politics of people and conservation in Northern Thailand." *Sojourn: Journal of Social Issues in Southeast Asia* 15(1): 52–75.

Lawhon, M. (2013). "Situated, networked environmentalisms: a case for environmental theory from the south." *Geography Compass* 7(2): 128–138.

Le Billon, P. (2002). "Logging in muddy waters: the politics of forest exploitation in Cambodia." *Critical Asian Studies* 34(4): 563–586.

Lebel, L., P. Lebel and R. Daniel (2010). "Water insecurities and climate change adaptation in Thailand." *Community, Environment and Disaster Risk Management* 5: 349–372.

Lebel, L., J. Manuta and P. Garden (2011). "Institutional traps and vulnerability to changes in climate and flood regimes in Thailand." *Regional Environmental Change* 11(1): 45–58.

Lenton, T. (2012). "Arctic climate tipping points." *Ambio* 41(1): 10–22.

Lestrelin, G. (2010). "Land degradation in the Lao PDR: discourses and policy." *Land Use Policy* 27(2): 424–439.

Lestrelin, G. and M. Giordano (2007). "Upland development policy, livelihood change and land degradation: interactions from a Laotian village." *Land Degradation & Development* 18(1): 55–76.

Lestrelin, G., J.-C. Castella and J. Bourgoin (2012a). "Territorialising sustainable development: the politics of land-use planning in Laos." *Journal of Contemporary Asia* 42(3): 581–602.

Lestrelin, G., O. Vigiak, A. Pelletreau, B. Keohavong and C. Valentin (2012b). "Challenging established narratives on soil erosion and shifting cultivation in Laos." *Natural Resources Forum* 36(2): 63–75.

Li, T. M. (2014). *Land's end: capitalist relations on an indigenous frontier.* Durham, NC, Duke University Press.

Lindeborg, A.-K. (2012). Where gendered spaces bend: the rubber phenomenon in northern Laos. PhD, Uppsala University.

McCarthy, J. and S. Prudham (2004). "Neoliberal nature and the nature of neoliberalism." *Geoforum* 35(3): 275–283.

McCarthy, S. (2014). Democratic change and forest governance in the Asia Pacific: implications for Myanmar. *Asia Pacific Issues* 112. Hawaii, East-West Centre.

McNeill, D. and H. Wilhite (forthcoming). Making sense of sustainable development in a changing world. *Emerging economies and challenges to sustainability: theories, strategies, local realities.* A. Hansen and U. Wethal. London, Routledge.

MacRae, G. and I. W. A. Arthawiguna (2011). "Sustainable agricultural development in Bali: is the subak an obstacle, an agent or subject?" *Human Ecology* 39(1): 11–20.

Marschke, M. (2012a). *Resource governance at the margins: fish, trees and life in coastal Cambodia.* Ottawa, University of Ottawa Press.

Marschke, M. (2012b). Koh Sralao village, Cambodia: living at the margins. *Revisiting rural places: pathways to poverty and prosperity in Southeast Asia.* J. Rigg and P. Vandergeest. Singapore and Honolulu, NUS Press and University of Hawaii Press: 250–268.

Martinez-Alier, J. (2014). "The environmentalism of the poor." *Geoforum* 54: 239–241.

Meyfroidt, P., et al. (2010). "Forest transitions, trade, and the global displacement of land use." *PNAS* 107(49): 20917–20922.

Milne, S. and B. Adams (2012). "Market masquerades: uncovering the politics of community-level payments for environmental services in Cambodia." *Development and Change* 43(1): 133–158.

Milne, S. and S. Mahanty (2015). The political ecology of Cambodia's transformation. *Conservation and development in Cambodia: exploring frontiers of change in nature, state and society.* S. Milne and S. Mahanty. Abingdon, Oxford, Routledge: 1–27.

Mol, A. P. J. (2011). "China's ascent and Africa's environment." *Global Environmental Change* 21(3): 785–794.

Nevins, J. and N. L. Peluso (2008). Introduction: commoditization in Southeast Asia. *Taking Southeast Asia to market: commodities, nature, and people in the Neoliberal age.* J. Nevins and N. L. Peluso. Ithaca, NY and London, Cornell University Press: 1–24.

Nixon, R. (2011). *Slow violence and the environmentalism of the poor.* Cambridge, MA, Harvard University Press.

O'Brien, K. L. (2009). Do values subjectively define the limits to climate change adaptation? *Adapting to climate change: thresholds, values, governance.* W. N. Adger. Cambridge, Cambridge University Press: 164–180.

Panayotou, T. (1993). Empirical tests and policy analysis of environmental degradation at different stages of economic development. Working Paper, Technology and Employment Programme. Geneva, International Labour Office.

Parnwell, M. and R. Bryant (Eds) (1996). *Environmental change in South East Asia: people, politics and sustainable development.* London, Routledge.

Pelling, M. (2011). *Adaptation to climate change: from resilience to transformation.* London, Routledge.

Promburom, P. and P. Sakdapolrak (2012). 'Where the rain falls' project. Case study: Thailand. Results from Thung Hua Chang District, Northern Thailand. Report no. 7. Bonn, Institute for Environment and Human Security (UNU-EHS), United Nations University.

Rambo, A. T., R. R. Reed, L. T. Cuc and M. R. DiGregorio (Eds) (1995). *The challenges of highland development in Vietnam.* Honolulu, Hawaii, East-West Center.

Rigg, J. (2005). *Living with transition in Laos: market integration in Southeast Asia.* London, RoutledgeCurzon.

Rigg, J. (2012). *Unplanned development: tracking change in South East Asia.* London, Zed Books.

Rigg, J. and C. Wittayapak (2009). Spatial integration and human transformations in the Greater Mekong sub-region. *Re-shaping economic geography in East Asia.* Y. Huang and A. M. Bocchi. Washington, DC, World Bank: 79–99.

Rigg, J. and A. Salamanca (forthcoming). Adaptation to climate change in Southeast Asia: developing a relational approach, *Routledge handbook of the environment in Southeast Asia.* P. Hirsch. London, Taylor & Francis.

Santasombat, Y. (2003). *Biodiversity: local knowledge and sustainable development.* Chiang Mai, Regional Center for Social Science and Sustainable Development (RCSD).

Scott, S. (2012). Land displacement and livelihood marginalization through 'townification' in a Northern Vietnamese village. *Revisiting rural places: pathways to poverty and prosperity in Southeast Asia.* J. Rigg and P. Vandergeest. Singapore and Honolulu, NUS Press and Hawaii University Press: 269–283.

Sok, S. (2014). "Limited state and strong social forces: fishing lot management in Cambodia." *Journal of Southeast Asian Studies* 45(2): 174–193.

Sonnenfeld, D. A. and A. P. J. Mol (2011). "Social theory and the environment in the new world (dis)order." *Global Environmental Change* 21(3): 771–775.

Souvanthong, P. (1995). *Shifting cultivation in the Lao PDR: an overview of land use and policy initiatives.* IIED Forestry and Land Use Series No. 5. London, International Institute for Environment and Development.

Stern, D. I. (2004). "The rise and fall of the environmental Kuznets curve." *World Development* 32(8): 1419–1439.

Stern, D. I., M. S. Common and E. D. Barbier (1996). "Economic growth and environmental degradation: the environmental Kuznets curve and sustainable development." *World Development* 24(7): 1151–1160.

Tschakert, P. and K. A. Dietrich (2010). "Anticipatory learning for climate change adaptation and resilience." *Ecology and Society* 15(2).

Un, K. and S. So (2009). "Politics of natural resource use in Cambodia." *Asian Affairs, an American Review* 36(3): 123–138.

UNDP (1986). *Muong Hom integrated rural development project: irrigated rice schemes.* Vientiane, Lao PDR, UNDP.

UNEP (2001). *State of the environment 2001: Lao PDR.* Bangkok, United Nations Environment Programme.

Urano, M. (2010). *The limits of tradition: peasants and land conflicts in Indonesia.* Kyoto, Japan, Center for Southeast Asian Studies, Kyoto University.

Urano, M. (2014). "Impacts of newly liberalised policies on customary land rights of forest-dwelling populations: a case study from East Kalimantan, Indonesia." *Asia Pacific Viewpoint* 55(1): 6–23.

WCED (1987). *Our common future: report of the World Commission on Environment and Development.* Oxford, Oxford University Press.

World Bank (2008). *The growth report: strategies for sustained growth and inclusive development.* Washington, DC, World Bank.

Yusuf, A. and H. Francisco (2009). *Climate change vulnerability mapping for Southeast Asia.* Singapore, Economy and Environment Program for Southeast Asia.

7 The politics of poverty and development

Branch and root

The political lacunae of modernization and development

Ultimately, all development is political. Attempts by governments and assorted agencies to suggest otherwise and imagine that development can be treated as an apolitical technocratic exercise are fundamentally and profoundly flawed. The politics of development starts from the very pinnacle of the development industry in the guise of how development funds are allocated by multilateral (such as the World Bank and the UNDP) and bilateral (for example, USAID, SIDA, AusAid and DFID) development agencies. From there down, all interventions are exercises in politics. From whether to subsidize or support farm production, where to draw the poverty line, whether and at what level to provide a safety net for single mothers, how to decide on the balance between centralization and decentralization, and whether and how to welcome foreign investment – all these decisions reflect a careful and deeply political balancing of interests. Financial resources are finite, capacities are partial, expertise is limited and interests are different and divided, while needs are limitless. Groups, whether they are ministries, expert advisors, foreign investors, non-governmental organizations, or citizens compete for attention and for funds.

This chapter is not about the higher reaches of politics. It is about the personal and community politics of development. It is about how high-level politics becomes inscribed at the local and personal scales and how, just occasionally, the local shapes other arenas of politics. It is, therefore, about the everyday politics of development.

While the chapter is careful not to ignore the agency of ordinary people, it also seeks to show how and why groups in society are pushed to the margins of power and decision making. It is one thing to note with awe and respect the myriad, inventive ways in which the poor and excluded get by in often tightly constrained circumstances; it also important, however, to ask why they are poor and excluded in the first place and why they do not have a 'right' to development but instead simply be thankful for the crumbs left to them from the table of prosperity. William Easterly in his book *The tyranny of experts* writes:

> The conventional approach to economic development, to making poor countries rich, is based on a technocratic illusion: the belief that poverty is a purely technical problem amenable to such technical solutions as fertilizers, antibiotics, or nutritional supplements. ... The technocratic illusion is that poverty results from a shortage of expertise, whereas poverty is really about a shortage of rights.
>
> (2013: 6–7)

Development is no neutral, politics-free enterprise where the good will of governments and the technical skills of experts can be brought together in an unproblematic effort to achieve material progress and eradicate poverty. Every step of the way, there is a politics to development.

The structural politics of development

Much of the debate about poverty concerns itself with how poverty is manifested and who suffers, and the purposeful interventions that might 'address' poverty. It tends not to reflect on the social and political processes and relations that create these conditions and attributes in the first place.[1] The debate over poverty, therefore, is arguably one step removed from the real nub of the question and until this is addressed, indeed if it can be, then poverty will remain intractably present even in the fastest-growing countries. This requires us to focus on the politics of entitlement that facilitate or empower people to access and secure development.

Green and Hulme (2005: 870) illustrate the importance of access with reference to a notional widow-headed household in South Asia, where the absence of a male spouse has a marginalizing effect. She lacks resources and is therefore poor but the "social casting of widows as second-class citizens, and the associated processes of asset stripping, is politically institutionalised within customary, statutory, and common law systems that licence and perpetuate such processes of impoverishment". This point is similar to Sen's (1981) seminal argument that famine is not about lack of food, but about lack of access to food. Poverty is, to be sure and in a proximate sense, manifested in a lack of income and therefore more widely, of material resources. But we also need to ask why an individual, household or community lacks access to those resources or that level of income in the first place. To link the discussion here back to the last chapter: why do upland minority groups in the Lao PDR so often find themselves dispossessed of their land? What are the development logics and justifications that permit this to happen (see p. 180 this volume)?

A concern for access or entitlement to resources, then, requires us not to examine the 'characteristic' features of the poor in terms of their human capacities and material assets, but to dig deeper and to consider the structural constraints, social relations and cultural norms that make people poor and perpetuate this condition. Work on social capital has tended to emphasize the positive attributes of social networks and institutions, rather than paying attention to those negative aspects that might contribute to the production and reproduction of poverty. As Cleaver says, drawing on Bourdieu, "the chronically poor engage in social and institutional life on adverse terms; they are less able to negotiate the 'right way of doing things,' to create room for manoeuvre, to shape social relationships to their advantage rather than others" (2005: 895). The poor are less able to play the system because of their entrenched structural disadvantage; they are also more dependent on playing the system because of their lack of assets. The need of the poor, and especially the chronically poor, for agency is acute; but their ability to exercise agency is often constrained and compromised. This may be because, for example, they are disabled; because a household is female-headed; because they lack the proper residency registration; because they lack citizenship; or because they belong to an ethnic minority. As Chapter 3 explored, when it comes to understanding why these groups are poor is primarily not a question of economics, not even a question of income or access to resources: it is a question of social position and political access.

It might seem reasonable to imagine that the shift to participatory approaches and the emphasis on social movements as vehicles for development and poverty alleviation might address some of these concerns. Robert Chambers, a leading proponent of efforts to put the 'last, first' (see Chambers 1983, 1997), in a 50-page working paper (Chambers 2010) which presents a new people-centred paradigm of development, does not once use the words 'politics' or 'political'. And yet participatory approaches are far from being politics-proof. A major review of participatory projects undertaken by the World Bank concludes:

> On balance, the review of the literature finds that participants in civic activities tend to be wealthier, more educated, of higher social status (by caste and ethnicity), male, and more politically connected than nonparticipants. This picture may partly reflect the higher opportunity cost of participation for the poor. It also appears, however, that the poor often benefit less from participatory processes than do the better off, because resource allocation processes typically reflect the preferences of elite groups. Studies from a variety of countries show that communities in which inequality is high have worse outcomes, especially where political, economic, and social power are concentrated in the hands of a few.
>
> (Mansuri and Rao 2013: 5)

This conclusion echoes that of Bebbington and colleagues who, drawing on research in Peru and South Africa, describe social movements as never only movements of the poor and rarely movements *for* the poor (Bebbington *et al.* 2010). Even when their concerns are directly connected to poverty, leaders of social movements often resist being labelled in terms of movements "of the poor" (p. 1320) because of the fear that political concerns will be reworked by the state into developmental concerns, becoming instrumentalized and depoliticized in the process.

The World Bank review mentioned above (Mansuri and Rao 2013) assessed the development outcomes of some US$85 billion allocated by the Bank to local participatory development between 2002 and 2012. Its overall conclusion: results have been disappointing. The standard reasons to explain this failure are because interventions have been inefficient, distorted by corruption, insufficiently supported, rely on inappropriate technology, and so forth. From such reasoning the answers that emerge are to improve interventions: to target them more effectively, to widen participation, to reduce corruption, to alter the technology mix, or to provide additional support, for example. For radical scholars, however, the structural (class) roots of poverty cannot be addressed by simply improving and fine-tuning delivery systems. Hickey argues that "many states remain in thrall of capital, adopting a discourse of poverty reduction that is used to legitimate socially and environmentally damaging processes of capital accumulation" (Hickey 2010: 1150).

The everyday politics of development

There has been a burgeoning of interest in the 'everyday' across the social sciences. From geography (Flint 2002; Rigg 2007) to urban studies (Elsheshtawy 2010; Kelbaugh 2000) and international political economy (Hobson and Seabrooke 2007a; Widmaier 2009) the everyday is, seemingly, everywhere. Each disciplinary field and subfield uses the term in its own way but there are several currents that tend to run through all these literatures.

Most obviously, the everyday demands that scholars focus on the quotidian and mundane, the everyday activities that constitute life and living for most people, most of the time.[2] Thus attention is paid to the informal, conversational and prosaic – to the everyday – rather than to the formal, official and atypical.

Second, a focus on the everyday constitutes an alternative view into the nature of mass–elite interactions and the direction and shape of change. Particularly in politics and political economy, there has been a tendency to see mass–elite interactions operating in one direction, from the elite to the masses as political decisions are communicated and enacted 'downwards'. An everyday approach opens up the possibility that it might work the other way round as well, and that there are sites of agency in the local and the everyday to which we should pay attention (Elias and Rethel, forthcoming). Hobson and Seabrooke define everyday agency as "acts by those who are subordinate within a broader power relationship but, whether through negotiation, resistance or non-resistance, either incrementally or suddenly, shape, constitute and transform the political and economic environment around and beyond them" (2007b: 15–16). Linked to this is the recognition of the possibility of change in other arenas, from the economic to the institutional and social, working 'up' from the everyday decisions and actions of individuals to the national and global contexts. Thus, Hobson and Seabrooke (2007b: 2) say that their book aims to "reveal not simply everyday actors but, more importantly, the manifold ways in which everyday actions can transform the world economy".

Third, there is an emphasis in studies of the everyday on taking an inductive or grounded approach to studying and interpreting the world. Research is framed not in terms of grand theories but more pragmatically in terms of 'problems' (Widmaier 2009: 956). Understanding these problems demands that attention is paid to the values and emotions that underpin behaviours and actions, and not just to the structures that may frame them.

Finally, paying attention to the everyday often requires a narrow, as well as a personal perspective. Politics, for example, becomes issue based (Seabrooke 2011: 458). This may occur through individual, quotidian acts but we can also see it in the actions of social movements and advocacy groups who have, often, quite narrowly framed agendas.

How does this feed into the politics of development in Southeast Asia? Certainly there is a case for looking at how the development project, as a technocratic enterprise in managing change, enters the development space of people's lives; therefore, how development as a mode of planning and control becomes personalized, and the tensions that inevitably arise between the science of domination and the arts of resistance. To be sure, many development 'interventions' – the word itself is instructive of how development is seen to operate (it enters and intervenes in people's lives) – are welcomed: schools, power, health clinics, roads, irrigation, clean water, new seeds, extension services … but few such interventions are received without pause for thought, or without some groups or individuals seeking to twist or mould them to their own benefit. And there are also some interventions, of course, that are actively resisted. Resistance tends to occur not because the technologies and infrastructures of modernization are not welcomed – far from it – but because their allocation, implementation and distribution are felt to be 'unfair'. It is at this interface between the development project and the subjects/objects of development, then, that the politics of development emerges and it is this which provides the canvas for the chapter.

A 'right' to development?

The Declaration on the Right to Development was adopted by the United Nations in 1986. Seven years later, in 1993 at the World Conference on Human Rights in Vienna, the Right to Development (RTD) was declared a universal and inalienable right (Sengupta 2000, 2004). The key articles of the Declaration on the Right to Development in terms of the discussion here (emphases added) are:[3]

> Declaration on the Right to Development (4th December, 1986)
>
> Article 1.1 The right to development is an *inalienable human right by virtue of which every human person and all peoples are entitled to participate in, contribute to, and enjoy economic, social, cultural and political development*, in which all human rights and fundamental freedoms can be fully realized.
>
> Article 2.1 The *human person is the central subject of development* and should be the active participant and beneficiary of the right to development.
>
> Article 2.3 *States have the right and the duty to formulate appropriate national development policies* that aim at the constant improvement of the well-being of the entire population and of all individuals, on the basis of their *active, free and meaningful participation in development and in the fair distribution of the benefits* resulting therefrom.
>
> Article 4.2 Sustained action is required to promote more rapid development of developing countries. As a complement to the efforts of developing countries, *effective international co-operation is essential in providing these countries with appropriate means and facilities to foster their comprehensive development.*

These articles highlight four aspects of the Declaration: (i) that the individual, not the country, is the central development subject; (ii) that states have the responsibility to put in place development policies that aim to develop the entire population; (iii) that the distribution of development should be fair; and (iv) that the wider international community, as well as individual states, has a responsibility for the achievement of the RTD.

Self-evidently, almost than three decades on from the Vienna conference, there are many millions of people in Southeast Asia who still do not enjoy the basic rights that the Declaration professed to be 'universal'. The fact, however, that the Declaration's achievement still lies some way in the future is not surprising. It was aspirational and there was always the realization that resource constraints would delay its achievement, and in the poorest countries of the world that would be by several decades. The issue, rather, is whether there is the political commitment, in the shape of structures and processes, for the achievement of the RTD. As Sengupta elaborates in his analysis of the Declaration's various articles, "it is the responsibility of States to *create the conditions* for realizing the Right to Development, not actually to realize it" (2000: 564, emphasis in original). It is in this respect that an argument can be made for non-compliance, rather than for the non-achievement of the RTD. The elements of this processual and structural approach might be a commitment to meaningful participation, equal opportunity, fair distribution, and full respect for cultural, political and social rights.

In the years since the signing of the Declaration in 1986, however:

> '[G]lobalization' has devalued sovereign equality and stripped states of economic and administrative policy instruments essential to medium- and long-term development planning. The authority of the United Nations has declined. Private global capital flows have displaced official development assistance as the major source of external finance. Market criteria of profitability have trumped social criteria in the provision of public good directly affecting the wellbeing of people. International inequalities have escalated. Commodity prices continue to fall. Finance has been privileged at the expense of productive activity and countries open to capital inflows have borne the full economic, social, and human costs of adjustment to ever more frequent and serious financial and economic crises.
>
> (Levitt 2003: 542)

The implication of Levitt's series of contentions is that the very nature of neoliberal development ('globalization') makes difficult, if not impossible, the achievement of the Right to Development. That it is *global* processes and structures, as much as national ones, wherein lies the impediment to its achievement (see Rajagopal 2013: 896). Above all else, however, the Declaration on the Right to Development emphasizes the primacy of the achievement of human development at the level of the individual (see Article 2.1) (Fukuda-Parr 2012: 842). What Levitt's paper does not do – and admittedly does not seek to do – is to ask questions that connect the individual's RTD with global structures and processes, namely: how do such global structures and processes come to rest at the individual level, and with what effects? And why and how does the operation of the (global) market economy retard the achievement of the RTD?

It is the work of Amartya Sen which has been most influential in bringing a 'right to development' perspective to our understanding of the development process. The UNDP's first *Human Development Report* in 1990 drew very heavily on Sen's capability approach and his ideas of 'development as freedom' (Sen 1999; Gasper 2002; Corbridge 2002). Sen's work was also important in framing the 1995 Human Development Report, which focused on gender and women's agency and the right to development (Desai 2001). More recently, Sen's trenchant comparison of development achievements in China and India shows his desire to think beyond the aggregate and the economic. For most observers, China has achieved development far beyond that attained in India. But "if our focus is on a comprehensive comparison of the quality of life in India and China", Sen suggests, then "we have to look well beyond the traditional social indicators, and many of these comparisons are not to China's advantage" (Sen 2011).[4] With an authoritarian system of government, there is "little recourse or remedy when the government leaders alter their goals or suppress their failures". The famine brought about by China's Great Leap Forward (1959–62) in which scores of millions died is one such case, as is the systematic attempt to erase the memory of the 1989 massacre of pro-democracy demonstrators in Tiananmen Square.[5]

We can think 'beyond' development as economic growth in two ways, and both bring the politics of development to the fore. Following Sen, we can think of development as much more than the achievement of material prosperity on the basis of economic expansion. It is this which underpins his questioning of whether China has achieved – in developmental terms – so much more than India in recent decades. In addition, however, we can pay attention not to the aggregate story but to the personal experiences of individuals and individual experiences of particular policy interventions, for example. This is not so much to foreground agency, but to see how generalized policies have markedly differentiated outcomes.

Dreams, aspirations and rights: the politics of poverty

> Politics are, or ought to be, nothing else than the application of thought and effort to the wellbeing of the community; and nowadays it is apparent to even the most cynical of public men that much thought and effort must be promptly devoted to the problems incidental to poverty, if grave mischiefs are to be avoided. ... let the community recognise that it has a corporate duty towards the most unfortunate – towards the crippled combatants who are helpless, more or less, in the struggle with the strong. Let it apply the great power of its corporate wealth and corporate organising power to make life at least tolerably human for those who, if left to their individual energies, would go under altogether, to our harm as well as their own.
>
> (BMJ 1890: 965)

At the end of the day, poverty is the consequence of a society's failure to collectively take responsibility for ensuring the economic security of its citizens. ... The focus on individualism in poverty research has impoverished our understanding of this persistent social problem. As long as debates about poverty are more about the poor than about the state and society, poverty will continue to haunt the progress of affluent Western democracies. Poverty is truly a political problem.

(Brady 2009: 181)

Almost 120 years separates these two quotes. The first, from 1890 and extracted from a short piece in the *British Medical Journal*, reflects on poverty in England. The second is taken from the concluding paragraph of David Brady's book *Rich democracies, poor people*, on the puzzle of the persistence of poverty in affluent democracies. Both argue that addressing poverty is primarily political. Both also make the point that poverty, while experienced individually must be addressed collectively.

The politics of poverty can be seen, at its simplest level, in rates of absolute poverty across the Southeast Asian region: it is clear that they do not correspond neatly to levels of income (measured in terms of purchasing power parity) (Figure 7.1). Indonesia, the Philippines and Vietnam have roughly the same proportion of the population living on less than $2-a-day, but significantly different levels of per capita income. Moreover, if poverty was measured in relative terms – as a percentage share of the median income – as it is in most rich countries,[6] then these differences would be starker still (Table 7.1). Indeed, it seems that the richer and more prosperous a country is, the higher its *relative* poverty. These differences reflect, as Chapter 2 argued, a set of *political* choices about how to allocate resources. And this allocation is not only because the poor have little political power and voice, although these issues are surely important, but is linked to certain beliefs about how poverty relates to economic growth, and how economic growth is best achieved. We can, therefore, view poverty as political in structural, ideological *and* institutional terms.

Key questions, such as whether to have a poverty line in the first place, where to draw that line, how to count the poor and who counts as poor and, finally, how poverty – so measured – should be addressed (or ameliorated), all these are political questions, as well as being technical challenges (see pp. 55–59). Being poor is certainly no fiction, but who is counted as poor is a political art, sometimes masquerading as a science. Poverty is political in a second sense: the poor themselves usually have little power, voice and influence. They tend not to belong to political parties, they have lower levels of education, they are rarely unionized, they are disconnected from the mainstream, and they often live in isolated and remote places.[7]

And beneath these politico-technical questions is the fundamental issue of why people are poor in the first place. Do we view poverty as a personal failure, explained and understood at the individual level; or do we interpret the production of poverty as arising from the structural inequalities in society that are a product

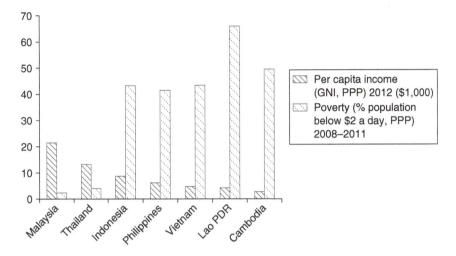

Figure 7.1 Poverty and per capita income

of a particular mode of development (p. 61)? The neoliberal take on poverty tends to assume that 'a rising tide lifts all boats' – that ensuring the rapid expansion of the economy in aggregate terms is the best means to help the poor, because they too benefit from national growth. And, as a corollary, that market liberalism is the best means to ensure growth in the first place. From this emerges the seemingly inescapable conclusion that market-led growth, embodied in the policies of neoliberalism, is not only the best but the *only* answer to poverty.

The only countries in Southeast Asia not to have national poverty lines are Brunei Darussalam and Singapore (Ng 2013). This should be viewed – and the position may well change[8] – for a combination of reasons covering need and ideology. As to the first, both countries are wealthy and the poorest people residing in each are, in the main, non-citizens. Political pressure to engage with the poverty agenda from the grassroots has, to date, therefore been muted. Singapore's meritocratic system has also created a view, especially among the elite, where poverty comes to be viewed as a personal failure rather than as a societal responsibility (Bellows 2009: 39).

Brunei Darussalam and Singapore are two of Southeast Asia's wealthiest countries; some of the poorest countries in the region also had no poverty lines until quite recently, but for rather different reasons. In a 1989 report prepared by the Government of Laos (GoL 1989) setting out the development needs of the country, for example, there is no mention of poverty – but there is a great deal of discussion of underdevelopment. This surprising oversight was largely ideological: as a Socialist nation, the Lao PDR could have no poverty, because the poor are a class created by capitalism. A second reason was more prosaic: there were no systematic data that could be used to calculate a poverty line and thereby identify and count the poor. The first national expenditure and consumption survey (known as

Table 7.1 Poverty, income and inequality

| | Per capita income (GNI, PPP) 2012 | Head count absolute poverty (%) 2008–11 | | Percentage share of income (or consumption) that accrues to specified income group | | | | Quintile ratio |
		$1.25-a-day (PPP)	$2-a-day (PPP)	Bottom 10%	Bottom 20%	Bottom 40%		
Singapore	71,900	–	–	1.9	5.0	14.4		12.0
Malaysia	21,430	0.0	2.3	2.6	6.0	13.2		11.3
Thailand	13,270	0.4	4.1	2.8	6.8	17.3		7.1
Indonesia	8,750	16.2	43.3	3.2	7.3	18.0		6.6
Philippines	6,170	18.4	41.5	2.8	6.8	15.4		8.3
Vietnam	4,780	16.9	43.4	3.2	7.4	18.9		5.9
Lao PDR	4,170	33.9	66.0	3.3	7.6	18.9		5.9
Cambodia	2,690	18.6	49.5	3.5	7.9	19.3		6.1

Sources: ADB key indicators (2013); World Bank databank (http://data.worldbank.org/).

Notes: GNI per capita based on purchasing power parity (PPP). Headcount poverty rates (PPP) and share of income/consumption based on latest year available; Cambodia (2009), Indonesia (2011), Lao PDR (2008), Malaysia (2009), Philippines (2009), Thailand (2010), Vietnam (2008). Singapore data are from 1998 (latest available from both UN and World Bank). The quintile ratio is the ratio of the total income/expenditure of the top (richest) 20% of the population to the bottom (poorest) 20%. Quintile ratios from ADB (2012) and Bhaskaran et al. (2012).

LECS I) was only conducted in 1992/93 and covered fewer than 3,000 households across 147 villages, itself a thin basis for any robust, national calculation of poverty (Rigg 2005: 73).

The politics of poverty in the Lao PDR

We can see in the Lao PDR the way that when, in the end – and presumably pressured by international agencies and advisors (which has its own politics) – the government did decide to grasp the nettle and embrace the poverty agenda they were careful to frame it in a way that was distinctive. They were particularly keen to differentiate the language, and by implication the production of poverty in Laos from poverty in neighbouring Thailand, even though the countries have mutually intelligible languages. The official term for poverty in Lao is *thuk nyak* (suffering + difficult), and the term was only formally officially adopted in 2002 (Chamberlain and Phanh Phomsombath 2002: 62). In embracing *thuk nyak* the government was putting some etymological and definitional distance between poverty in Laos and poverty in Thailand. *Thuk* is the Buddhist term for suffering and, as Chamberlain and Phanh Phomsombath say, is closer to mental than to physical suffering. Significantly, the Lao authorities decided to pair *thuk* with *nyak* and in so doing avoided using the most likely alternative pairing, of *thuk + chon*. *Chon*, as in *yaak chon*, is the Thai word for poverty and is closer to meaning 'destitute' than the less extreme and grinding 'difficult'. 'Destitution' is produced through the workings of the capitalist economy; 'difficult' is closer to a natural state of meagre living that can be seen to be an inheritance of the past (Evans 1995), and which the government of the Lao PDR was, of course, in the business of eradicating as it civilized its population, and especially its upland minorities living in a state of so-styled 'backwardness'.

It has been argued that poverty in the Lao PDR – and the same argument can be extended to *all* the countries of the region – has been both produced and ameliorated by policies of development (Rigg 2005). If policies are political, then poverty is political. This applies not just to the rate of poverty (as mentioned above and discussed in more detail in Chapter 4 in relation to inequality), but also to the shape or texture of poverty.

Table 7.2 uses the LECS 3 data to take several 'cuts' through the poverty cake. We can see here that the poor are concentrated in rural areas, that they tend to live in upland areas with limited road access, and that many belong to one of the country's minorities. With these data in mind, much development policy in Laos has focused on connecting marginal, upland peoples with the mainstream by bringing the market to the uplands – through building roads – and by bringing the people to the market – through resettlement. Both approaches to addressing the perceived poverty problem in Laos have been highly controversial, and especially the latter.[9] While the effects of road-building (whether it can be viewed as poverty-reducing, poverty-accentuating, or poverty-reconstituting)[10] and resettlement are contested, there is a deeper politics connected with how the state views certain styles of living, and the policies that have emerged.

Table 7.2 Slices through the poverty cake in the Lao PDR, 2002–3

	% of national population	*Incidence of poverty (headcount, %)*
Geographical 0		
National poverty rate	–	33
Geographical 1		
Vientiane capital region	–	15.7
Northern region	–	34.5
Central region	–	27.9
Southern region	–	33.5
Geographical 2		
Urban	23	19.7
Rural	77	37.6
Geographical 3		
Lowland	57.5	28.2
Midland	17.5	36.5
Upland	25.0	43.9
Geographical 4		
No rural road access	–	21.7
Seasonal rural road access	–	27.9
All-weather rural road access	–	9.7
Ethnic		
Lao-Thai	66.6	25.0
Mon-Khmer	20.6	54.3
Hmong-lu Mien	8.4	40.3
Chine-Tibet	3.3	45.8
Other	1.1	48.4
Social		
Male-headed households	94.9	31.0
Female-headed households	5.1	28.0

Sources: data are from the LECS 3 (Lao Expenditure and Consumption Survey), extracted from Chamberlain (2006: 22) and Phomtavong (2010).

The notion of backwardness, of people 'living in the past', and the denial of common time that goes with such tropes is central to the modernization agenda. It is because people lack certain things that they are defined as poor; and these things are often the material products of modernization. Laos' second Participatory Poverty Assessment (PPA), coordinated by the ADB and the National Statistics Centre, highlights the on-going debate between practitioners, officials and academics regarding whether people living traditional lives can be counted as poor:

> [U]sing conventional means of measuring poverty is unlikely to provide a complete picture. 'Subsistence affluence', a term often used to describe conditions in the Pacific islands is not out of place in Laos. Even the term 'subsistence', often misconstrued as 'backward' or 'lacking surplus', can be seen in a positive light, especially where traditional livelihood systems are still in place. That is to say, so-called subsistence agriculture is not equated

with poverty in the minds of villagers, because their economies are carefully designed to preserve what they regard as 'quality of life'.

(Chamberlain 2006: 17)

In his influential paper on the Thai notion of *siwilai* – to be 'civilized' – Winichakul (2000: 529) notes that it has two broad, but related, meanings.[11] It means to be refined in terms of dress, language, manner, conduct and etiquette; and it also means developed or modern in the sense of material progress (similar to the Thai word *charoen*). Those who were not *siwilai* were considered, in the late nineteenth and first half of the twentieth centuries in Siam (Thailand), to fall into one of two camps. The hill peoples or *khon pa* (people of the forest) were not *siwilai* because they were barbaric and, to many at the time, also therefore uncivilizable. *Chao ban nok*, rural folk, were uncivilized because they were backward but might become civilized if they could be developed. The second of these meanings retains its development potency, even if the first has not.[12] In effect, the geography, language and politics of *siwilai* have been superseded by that of poverty.

The desire for modernity is not just an imposition of the elite. It is common currency. Even when prosperity, as it is for many in Laos, "is a dream of the future rather than lived reality", this makes the yearning for development no less urgent (Singh 2012: 26; and see High 2014). The identification of the poor, whether this is based on income or on consumption, is linked to material progress. A lack of material progress, so defined, therefore delineates the poor. There have been numerous attempts to 'go beyond' income as a measure of poverty development, but these tend to fall foul of the fact that for many poor people, poverty *is* about income and material progress. What one generation may lack quite happily, the next generation will find a failure to consume deeply degrading. Adam Smith's observation that a non-impoverished life is about being 'able to appear in public without shame' (Sen 2000: 4) highlights that we need to look not just at the achievement or performance of a certain consumption level (or style), but the social context within which it is embedded. Singh describes the connection between national policies of poverty amelioration through development, and personal projects of prosperity-building through embracing modern living in her work on the Nakai plateau in central Laos' Khammouane Province. She writes of the

> melding of official discourses of national 'development' (*kan patthana*), in the form of poverty eradication and rural development, and popular aspirations for 'prosperity' (*khuam chaleun*), in the form of personal wealth. The disjunction between the two is elided since national development is seen as the means to achieve, and a justification of, personal prosperity.
>
> (Singh 2009: 754)

When people fail in their efforts to achieve prosperity, and remain poor, this is experienced as a personal failure. But we need to understand this as reflecting a particular articulation of the development-as-modernization project, which reflects a set of political decisions that can be tracked 'back' through a series of stages, and which have policy outcomes. For Chamberlain:

> It is clear that poverty is caused by external events over which villagers have no control. Although development policies that involve relocation … may be well-intentioned, their poor implementation has contributed to adverse effects …. As was seen … commercialized agriculture presents many problems, and the majority of enterprises suggested by villagers have already been tried and failed because of a variety of factors, and it is mainly the non-poor villages that have benefited from activities that involve credit and debt.
>
> (2006: 53–54)

What we can see here with regard to poverty is an agenda that is shot-through with politics, from top to bottom (see Table 7.6). Of course there is an individualized outcome to poverty, however we measure it, whatever we call it, and whether we choose to define it at all. But in tracking poverty through to individualized experiences we need to keep in mind the development project that has defined poverty as something to be 'tackled' in the first place, how the problem is so defined, and the policies that are put in place for poverty's amelioration. Some manifestations of poverty count, in official parlance, and others do not. Similarly, some individuals count more than others. Lund (2011: 901), in his review of land settlement in the Lao PDR, sets out the degree to which what might appear at first blush to be development policy aimed at poverty alleviation, is part of a political project:

> Despite obvious failures, patchy implementation and many instances of non-compliance with government [land] policy, the contingent government-donor collaboration made resources, such as rhetoric (development goals, decrees, legislation, etc.), technical expertise, money and violence lodged with different institutional actors, come together and cohere. Therefore, while the land reform purported to grant land rights to people with the sanction of government, it also represented government's claim to institutional control over land. This started to change people's political subjectivities: the authority to grant rights to land inserted government into the lives of people.

What the discussion here points to, and which has been a leitmotif of the book, is that what appears in aggregate terms to be so positive and clear – economic growth, poverty alleviation, land settlement, road-building – becomes less positive and less clear when we come to examine the process or the policy in detail. It has been said before but is worth saying again: the devil truly is in the detail. Understanding that detail is crucial, and can be seen through the lens of oil palm in Southeast Asia.

Oil palm: a walk on the dark side?

> A Godsend for some, a malediction for others, oil palm development gives
> rise to contrasting opinions.
>
> (Feintrenie *et al.* 2010: 381)

Oil palm (*Elaeis guineensis*) and rubber (*Hevea brasiliensis*) are the crops of the moment in Southeast Asia. The three largest – by far – global producers of palm oil are Southeast Asian countries, and Southeast Asian countries also occupy the top four spots for rubber (Table 7.3). Between them, it is these two crops which have driven one the most remarkable land use changes of recent decades. In 1967, the area of oil palm in Indonesia amounted to little more than 100,000 ha. In 2000, the area planted to the crop was around 4.2 million ha; ten years later, in 2010, it had reached 8.4 million ha. Along with its rapid spread, however, oil palm has attracted increasing criticism and concern due to the negative effects it is seen to be having on people and environments. As Rist *et al.* say (2010: 1010), "oil palm has been accused of negatively affecting human health, destroying cultural heritage and leading to the loss of autonomy and self-sufficiency, in addition to impoverishment as a result of debts and low wages". The speed and extent of oil palm expansion has also raised environmental concerns about its impact on forest loss, forest ecosystems and biodiversity, and on global climate change (Lee *et al.* 2014a, 2014b).

The crop itself, however, would seem to be a route to a better life for impoverished rural populations. In many of the areas where oil palm has been planted there are both few other opportunities available and a keen desire among the local population to earn additional income. The development imperative in such areas is strong.[13] To put it another way, the right to development is as yet unrealized for many marginal Indonesian rural inhabitants and the gift of oil palm seems an appropriate and generous one.

To fuse this desire for development and the opportunities that oil palm would seem to offer, the Indonesian government established Nucleus Estate and Smallholder (NES) schemes in the late 1970s. These were seen as a way of

Table 7.3 Oil palm and rubber in Southeast Asia, global rank by production (2012)

Palm oil		*Rubber*	
Country, rank by production	*Production (Mt)*	*Country, rank by production*	*Production (Mt)*
Indonesia	23,672,000	Thailand	3,500,000
Malaysia	18,785,030	Indonesia	3,040,400
Thailand	1,600,000	Malaysia	970,000
Colombia	966,900	Vietnam	863,773
Nigeria	940,000	India	805,000

Source: FAOSTAT (http://faostat.fao.org/site/339/default.aspx).

bridging the need for financial and technical support on the one hand, which individual smallholders could not access, and the requirements of estate companies for labour and land on the other (Table 7.4). Farmers voluntarily transferred a portion (around 10 ha) of their land to an palm oil estate company and, in return, were allocated 2 or 3 ha of planted land which they could either manage themselves or request that the company manage on their behalf.[14] The NES scheme, in other words, was an attempt to circumvent the relatively high thresholds for engagement in oil palm production by linking smallholders to agribusiness through the good offices of the state. Thousands of relatively poor smallholders were therefore able to engage in oil palm production, which they would never have been able to do without such support. The NES scheme ran through to the mid-1980s, since when it has been replaced by the similar KKPA scheme (Table 7.4).

It is clear that there is a puzzle in the oil palm tale. In agronomic and economic terms, oil palm would seem like an ideal crop to bring development and prosperity

Table 7.4 Forms of oil palm plantations in Indonesia

Name	*Form*	*Dates*
Nucleus Estate and Smallholder (NES) scheme or *Perkebunan Inti Rakyat* (PIR)	Joint venture between estate companies and local smallholders. Later, transmigrant-based schemes were introduced with some costs borne by the Indonesian state. Land allocated 70:30 between smallholders and core estates	1977–1985
Perkebunan Besar Swasta (PBS)	Plantation company dominated in which workers could be hired	1980s–mid-1990s
Primary Cooperative Credit for Members scheme or *Koperasi Kredit Primer untuk Anggota* (KKPA).	Similar to the PIR scheme where a company and smallholders work in partnership; smallholders are grouped into cooperatives and land is entrusted to the company. The company plants, supervises and harvests the crop and smallholders receive a proportion of the land back, usually in the ratio 20:80 or 30:70. The company's share (70–80%) is termed the 'nucleus' and the smallholders' share the 'plasma'	Late 1980s–2000
Independent smallholders	Consisting of wealthier smallholders with 2–10 ha of oil palm	
Plantation revitalization scheme	State and private estates in which smallholders provide land and are included in the scheme with typically 20% of land allocated to smallholders	2006–

Sources: information extracted from Feintrenie *et al.* (2010); McCarthy *et al.* (2012).

to marginal people and places. Yields and returns are generally higher than other alternative crops, labour demands are low, it can be planted on degraded land, and it can be harvested year-round. Yet time-and-again the human development outcomes belie the crop's apparent appeal and potential.

To understand why such an apparently enviable crop should so often be presented in negative terms we need, as McCarthy (2010: 823) says, to unpick and interrogate the terms on which cultivators are incorporated and integrated into the global oil palm system. There is no *a priori* reason why oil palm should be deleterious to rural livelihoods; indeed there are broadly 'successful' instances that can be presented to make the case for the crop. It is also clear that in individual settlements, oil palm brings mixed blessings, with some households apparently benefiting and others seemingly losing out. To understand the balance of effects and outcomes we need to ask questions not of the crop, but of the manner of its extension and management, the way in which poorer farmers come to grow the crop, and why and how global and national imperatives become imprinted at the local level, not infrequently to the detriment of the poor. In other words, we need to interrogate how the Right to Development (and the Gift of Development) becomes distorted in the process of its transmission and promotion.

The first point to note is that to grow oil palm as a smallholder, without the support of an estate, requires considerable resources. Its successful and profitable cultivation is therefore largely limited, without state support structures, to better-off smallholders. It is, as McCarthy (2010: 826) says, "a rich farmer's crop". The NES scheme was, in theory (and not infrequently in practice), a means by which this impediment could be overcome through the integration of the needs of smallholders and those of the estate companies. Since Indonesia's liberalization (from 1998) and decentralization (from 2001) following the Asian financial crisis, however, this bargain that the state sanctioned and made possible, has broken down. The liberalization of the Indonesian economy has, in effect, marginalized poorer farmers and farm workers within the oil palm economy. With the progressive withdrawal of state support they can no longer take advantage of the benefits that the oil palm economy can bestow (McCarthy 2010: 825–6), and the politics of production has turned against poorer smallholders. How does this happen? It is McCarthy and colleagues' work (McCarthy 2010; McCarthy and Cramb 2009; McCarthy and Zen 2010; McCarthy *et al.* 2012) that provides the most detailed account of how such a promising crop has sometimes ended up proving so destructive of rural livelihoods.

To start with, it is necessary to understand the ways in which foregoing inequality drives further differentiation in the oil palm system. In many oil palm areas, land is either collectively owned or land ownership rights are 'fuzzy' – unclear and insecure. This creates a space of opportunity that the rich and well-connected can exploit. When local governance is weak and headmen unscrupulous this space is amplified still further. In their study of Tanjung Jabang in Sumatra's Jambi province, McCarthy *et al.* (2012: 559) identify an 'irreversible' transfer of land from marginal to rich(er) smallholders and outside entities:

In this new milieu, village lands that were previously owned collectively were privatized and transferred through informal payments to third parties. These dynamics – shaped by power laden relationships within the district – created a transitional situation that supported rapid agrarian differentiation. ... Large numbers of prosperous oil palm farmers emerged with the expansion of intermediate size oil palm landholdings under the control of influential village and district actors. Meanwhile, large numbers of poor farmers and landless laborers were losing less productive rubber gardens. As in other cases, processes of accumulation by some are accompanied [by the] dispossession of others.

(McCarthy *et al.* 2012: 560; and see Gillespie 2012)

This process operates through interactions at a range of scales. At an inter-personal level, wealthier smallholders found that through their 'generosity' to poorer smallholders[15] – through making loans at times of personal crisis, for example – they were able to accumulate land.[16] At the intra-village level, key institutions of settlement governance, such as cooperatives, were often dominated by wealthier and better connected villagers who were then able to use their positions of local authority to gain control over land. These households were also able to access the credit that is critical to successful oil palm cultivation. Liberalization further exposed smallholders to economic shocks and with no safety net to protect them many in this remote field site in Jambi were encouraged to sell their land, whether to meet a debt or pay for a child's wedding. In 2004, there were only a handful of landless farmers in the area but five years later, in 2009, some 30 per cent of villagers were landless. While in theory the democratization and decentralization that followed Indonesia's *krismon* (monetary crisis) should have made local government more accountable to local people, patronage politics and collusion has probably worsened (McCarthy and Zen 2010 and see Varkkey 2012, 2013).

When smallholders work with plantation companies under a 'partnership' model (see Table 7.4), a second set of rather different problems emerges, reflective of the power and knowledge imbalances between the villagers and the plantation company. McCarthy *et al.* (2012) explore this with reference to field work in the West Kalimantan district of Sanggau. Here the company managed to convince the district authorities to permit them to establish their estate on the basis of an 80:20 landholding arrangement, where local Dayaks would relinquish their land and receive just 20 per cent back as their share in the partnership. This was the smallest proportion permitted under national law. Villagers were then 'socialized' into giving up their land, although many believed it was being lent rather than transferred in perpetuity. McCarthy *et al.* (2012: 560) write that "clearly the absence of effective forms of villager representation and deliberation in the consent process, together with the co-option of village leaders and the lack of forceful guidelines and supervision, contributed to this lack of clarity". This is a theme that Rist *et al.* (2010) also explore in their comparison of sites, also from Jambi and Kalimantan. Farmers do not read and cannot understand the contracts they have signed; and they do not know the debt they have incurred to the company or how it was arrived at. Promises made by government and company officials are not delivered, particularly commitments to community development. Land has been 'stolen' or grabbed by companies or allocated by government officials. They write:

> Several factors emerged repeatedly across the study locations as sources of conflict following plantation development; the clarity of the contracts signed with companies, weak local governance, the failure of companies to meet either contractual or perceived obligations, lack of clarity over land tenure prior to plantation development and changing land values.
>
> (Rist *et al.* 2010: 1017)

Finally, at an international level, it has been claimed that one of the reasons that oil palm has continued to spread notwithstanding concerns about its social and environmental impacts has been due to a well-financed and 'aggressive' public relations campaigns by the industry (e.g. the Malaysian Palm Oil Council) to persuade the consuming public that the concerns of environmentalists are wilful and ill founded (Koh and Wilcove 2009).

We can see in the case of oil palm in Indonesia, then, how some of the general points made by Levitt (2003) in her reflection on the Right to Development in an era of globalization (see above) become grounded in places and people's lives. Under liberalization, the Indonesian state has largely withdrawn from its previous role as an arbiter between companies and smallholders, acting as a developmental state at the local level. The policy instruments necessary to guard villagers against more egregious forms of exploitation have been removed or diluted. Companies are in a much stronger position to insist on the strictest market criteria for their involvement. And all this is set against the context of widening inequalities and not-nearly-good-enough governance (see Grindle 2004, 2007). The irony is that, for Indonesia, "despite the shift away from highly criticized, top-down models associated with the earlier period, the terms under which smallholders engage with oil palm under an apparently decentralized and more democratic regime in general have significantly deteriorated" (McCarthy *et al.* 2012: 563). Smallholders find themselves part of the oil palm economy, but either incorporated on highly unfavourable – even adverse – terms, or simply excluded, sometimes through dispossession (see p. 61 this volume).[17]

What is important to note as regards this chapter is that oil palm's dark sub-text is about politics and power, at all levels. It is about:

- the abrogation of the central role of the state in a liberalization era;
- how decentralization has opened up new avenues for collusion;
- the latitude that companies enjoy to shape relations and engagement with smallholders greatly to their advantage;
- the scope for local officials and some villagers to accumulate wealth at the expense of marginal smallholders.

So, if we want to know how a crop with such potential to deliver the gift and achieve the right to development failed – for many – to do either, we need to pay attention to how oil palm has been introduced and taken up, the roles of the institutions and individuals who have governed its management, and the texture of the social and economic relations that provide the canvas for its cultivation (McCarthy 2010: 827).[18]

Development projects and development subjects: the science of domination and the arts of resistance

In a pair of important books, James Scott (1985, 1990) sets out the resistance case. In *Weapons of the weak* (1985) he draws on fieldwork in the Malaysian village of 'Sedaka' to detail the myriad ways that poor peasants 'get by' – through, for example, foot-dragging and shirking, thieving and pilfering, smear and defamation, lying and deception, and evasion and circumvention. *Domination and the arts of resistance* (1990) focuses more specifically on the 'hidden transcripts' that serve to challenge and undermine the public transcripts of the order of things. In this second book, Scott pays attention to language, and more particularly to gossip, rumour and innuendo and the ways that the poor and marginalized can use language to provide an alternative interpretation of events, systems or individuals. Both books have inspired a wealth of work from Southeast Asia and beyond, as well as a good many critiques. Although in *Weapons of the weak* Scott makes a sometimes heart-warming case for the agency of the poor it would, as Scott himself admits, "be a grave mistake ... to overly romanticise the 'weapons of the weak'" (1985: 29). The weapons that lie to hand for the poor, marginal and excluded in no way match those of the rich and powerful, be they individuals, companies or states.

So, set against the resistance arts of the weak is the science of domination. The use of 'arts' and 'science' to describe these two modes of operation highlights the nature and tendencies of each. Resistance arts tend to be individualized, informal, non-official, oral, unrecorded, hard-to-measure and hard-to-pin-down, and utilize soft methods and approaches. The science of domination, on the other hand, is normally based on group interventions and is formal, official, written, statistical and measured, and utilizes hard methods and approaches (Table 7.5). This is akin to Chambers' (2010) distinction between development that emphasizes 'people' and development that pays attention to 'things'. For him, "many of the errors and failures of development policy and practice have stemmed from the dominance of the things paradigm" (2010: 13).

The two cases discussed above, namely the poverty agenda and project in the Lao PDR and oil palm in Indonesia, reveal the *political* point of contact between the arts of resistance and the science of domination. On the one hand, we have the blueprints of the development project, inscribed by experts and reflected in planning documents and policies; on the other, the everyday and mundane, informed by local knowledge and acted out by individuals and communities. The blueprints of development and their implementation reflect political beliefs, choices and actions. This covers, for example: key strategic questions such as whether to pursue a market-based approach to development and whether that should be

Table 7.5 The arts of resistance and science of domination: forms and approaches

	Resistance: arts and people		Domination: science and things	
	Arts	People	Science	Things
Form	Diverse	Evolving, open	Standardized	Pre-set, closed
	Decentralized	Decentralized	Centralized	Centralized
	Unofficial	Holistic	Official	Reductionist
	Diverse, diffuse	Diverse, local	Unified	Standardized, universal
	Informal	Varied basket	Bureaucratic	Fixed package
	Self-generated		Imposed	
	Demanded		Supplied	
	Software		Hardware	
	Episodic		Structural	
	Spoken		Written	
Approach	Non-statistical, unmeasurable	Participation	Statistical, measurable	Planning
	Non-material	Enabling	Material	Instructing
	Cultural	Empowering	Economic	'Motivating'
	(Fe)male	Partners, actors	Male	Beneficiaries
	Demand-focused	Demand-pull	Output-driven	Supply-push
	Bottom-up	Bottom-up	Top-down	Top-down
	Vernacular	Capabilities	Professional	Uniform, infrastructure

Source: 'people' and 'things' adapted from Chambers (2010:12).

softened or mediated by social policies to protect the weak and the vulnerable; sectoral policy decisions regarding whether to target lagging regions or to support rural livelihoods; as well as specific policies and the manner of their grounding in particular places and people's lives.

From gifts to rights: the politics and Politics of development

From time-to-time, the politics of development becomes the Politics of development: development failures and successes that have their roots in local experiences and actions can be seen reverberating at the national level. Thailand's long-running political impasse stretching from the ousting of former Prime Minister Thaksin Shinawatra by a *coup d'état* in September 2006 through to the 'creeping' *coup* of May 2014 is one such instance.

Thaksin Shinawatra's great success lay in making Thailand's rural population and, especially the rural poor, think – and believe – they had a Right to Development beyond their role as low-wage labour in Thailand's industrialization or as marginal semi-peasants providing cheap food to support this process (see Glassman 2010). The introduction of the 30-baht-a-visit universal health care scheme[19] was not only, if could be argued, the act of a consummate (populist) politician but also reflected the realization, for the first time, by Thailand's political elite that the country's rural population had as much right to the fruits of growth as the urban classes who hitherto had largely benefited. This is not to say, of course, that there was no 'development' prior to this moment; but development was regarded as a gift from the state to a grateful populace, not as an obligation on the part of the state. Indeed, rather the reverse – the people were obliged to the state. As Vandergeest writes in his study from southern Thailand:

> Local officials [in Thailand] phrased development as the government's gift to the people. The language of the gift, used in this way, is not neutral; it is an act of power incurring obligation. In this case, the obligation is released through the donation of land and labour. The policy of mobilizing labour in this way, 'for the common good' on 'development' projects, remained relatively unchanged [from the 1930s] until the 1970s. ... Rural development should be reclaimed and maintained as a right, against an increasing tendency to define public expenditures of all sorts as gifts which governments have the right to discontinue at their will.
>
> (Vandergeest 1991: 428, 441)

There are obvious wrinkles in this characterization of the gift/right diptych, but it highlights that development always entails subtle, and sometimes not so subtle, political manoeuvrings.

At roughly the same time as Thaksin was coming to dominate Thai politics, the development debate in the country was taking a novel turn with the espousal of *sethakit phorpiang* or the 'sufficiency economy' (SE) from the late 1990s.[20] The significance of the sufficiency economy is reflected in the central place it has occupied in successive Thai national development plans. Since the Eighth Plan (1997–2001), the sufficiency economy has been both the organizing framework and the philosophical inspiration for the Thai state's view of what form and direction development should take (see Unger 2009: 140; UNDP 2007; NESBD 2011; and http://eng.nesdb.go.th/). While the sufficiency economy is defined extremely (and unhelpfully) broadly (see Hewison 2008), the Eleventh Five-Year National Development Plan (2012–16) states that the "heart of this [sufficiency] Philosophy is 'human development' toward well-being based on sufficiency, moderation, reasonableness, and resilience" (NESDB 2011; see also UNDP 2007).

Thaksin's politically inspired RTD and the sufficiency economy, which is also highly politicized, both have a rural development rationale. It is not going too far to say that every Thai villager will have heard of *sethakit phorpiang,* and many will tacitly lend their support to its credo that emphasizes local knowledge, *in situ* living and livelihoods, traditional lifestyles, production for consumption not for sale, and communitarian values. Rarely, however, do villagers go further than this and actually *follow* the sufficiency credo. The fact that it is so closely associated with the King of Thailand also provides it with a kudos that it would not otherwise enjoy. In a study of three villages in Northeast Thailand's Khon Kaen province in 2012–13, we found that far from embracing a lifestyle mediated by *phor* ('enough'), 8 out of 10 households were in debt, to an average of over 100,000 baht ($3,500); three-quarters of household heads, at some point, had had to leave the village to find work; each household had at least one member absent; and almost every household owned a TV and a motorbike and approaching one half of households also owned a vehicle (see Rigg *et al.* 2014). Walker (2012: 222) sees the sufficiency economy and political society (by which he means, drawing on the work of Partha Chatterjee, a modern 'middle-income' peasantry) as being the antithesis of each other: one moralistic and local, the other pragmatic and non-local. The villages in the Khon Kaen study were also very 'Red' in the sense that seemingly everyone supported the *Phua Thai* party, at the time led by Thaksin's sister, Yingluck Shinawatra.

We see here, then, some of the general issues discussed in this chapter reflected in three villages: an enthusiastic embracing of development as prosperity in material terms; an engagement with alternative development, but often only discursively; a growing sense, with attendant political ramifications, of individuals' right to development; and a frustration with the ways in which the fruits of growth become allocated spatially, sectorally and socially. Thailand's political impasse, at its most elemental, can be seen to represent a continuing struggle between the claims of the rural 'masses' for an RTD and an urban elite's desire to maintain its control over development and the wealth that it generates. The sufficiency economy masquerades as a culturally sensitive and locally rooted approach to development but, in fact, has been shaped by the urban elite: "Thai social critics who have taken up the sufficiency discourse have rephrased the economic and political desires of the rural and urban poor as simple greed, which itself was a product of capitalism" (Elinoff 2014: 92). Unger (2009) views the sufficiency economy as a means to indigenize capitalism according to the norms of the urban elite. The rural 'masses', increasingly sophisticated and worldly wise, are fighting their corner while their opponents' efforts to thwart them represent, in the words of Duncan McCargo, "the last gasp of Thai dynastic paternalism" (McCargo 2013). What is important to note for the discussion here is that this political conflict is a dispute over development: its shape, nature, location, and what it has delivered or failed to deliver.

Civil society, political society and the politics of development

It was the perceived failure of top-down, expert-led and managerialist approaches to development that led, in the 1980s, to the embracing of participation, a process by which the subjects of development ('stakeholders') could shape, influence and share control of development initiatives. By the early 1990s, participation in development had been mainstreamed and become a new orthodoxy. As noted earlier, between 2002 and 2012 the World Bank allocated US$85 billion to local participatory development projects, part-and-parcel of the participatory turn in development project management (Mansuri and Rao 2013). The belief was that development which empowered local communities, that decentralized control, and that permitted and enabled participation would be more effective and sustainable than top-down, expert-led approaches. Central to this was the belief that embracing and utilizing the power of civil society – composed of non-state associational entities such as women's groups, water-use associations and credit unions – might be the route to not necessarily more, but certainly better, development. This hope, as so often the case, has not delivered on its promise.

There has been a great deal of critical reflection on participatory development.[21] The focus here is on two particular, and closely linked, aspects of this critique: participatory exclusions (see Agarwal 2001; Beard and Cartmill 2007; Resureccion *et al.* 2004: 522) and participatory capture (Dasgupta and Beard 2007; Lund and Saito-Jensen 2013). One question underpins each. With regard to participatory exclusions: 'Are local systems of management socially inclusive and equitable with respect, for example, to women and ethnic minorities?' And, following this, with regard to participatory (or elite) capture: 'Do participatory development initiatives tend to become captured and controlled by local elites for their own benefit?'

Part of the problem with participatory development may lie with the very idea of civil society. Civil society has its roots in Western thinking and experience, and scholars from the global South have long wondered about its application to non-Western societies. Partha Chatterjee, in particular, has questioned the utility of civil society as a catch-all and coined the term 'political society' to describe "a domain of institutions and activities ... lying between civil society and the state" (1998: 61).[22]

The risk of participatory development is that it *conceals* the power relations that are always present, in every society. These are deep-seated, and embedded in norms that are hard to shift. A second risk is that participatory development initiatives lead to the lie that it is possible to have a development-without-politics. Participation gives development initiatives the cloak of community consensus: 'the people have agreed'; 'the community has decided'. This gives the impression not only of community agreement regarding a particular project or policy (thus disguising participatory exclusions) but it also partially absolves the state from its responsibilities. In their review of over 400 papers and books assessing the World Bank's experience of participatory development, Mansuri and Rao conclude that

> the evidence suggests that the people who benefit tend to be the most liter-
> ate, the least geographically isolated, and the most connected to wealthy and
> powerful people. Participation thus appears to affect the distribution of ben-
> efits in ways that suggest that capture is often not 'benevolent' or altruistic.
>
> (2013: 6)

The presence of participatory exclusions with the outcome of participatory capture directs our attention to the local politics of development. Highlighting the deficiencies of participation and the difficulties of making participation 'work' in an inclusive manner, however, is not reason to abandon the effort. As one would expect, studies show that it is complicated. Lund and Saito-Jensen (2013) note in their study of two forestry-related participatory initiatives in India and Tanzania, for example, that participatory capture is not a permanent state of affairs and that over time disadvantaged groups organized themselves, resisted elite capture, and became more effective in staking their claims. They also stress the need to distinguish between elite capture of decision making and elite capture of benefits. The former need not necessarily result in the latter. Dasgupta and Beard (2007) in their study of elite capture in Indonesia's Urban Poverty Project (UPP), while they did identify such an outcome, also found that elites were accountable to the community and so were not completely free to act to their own benefit alone.

Conclusion

> What a democratic system achieves depends greatly on which social conditions become political issues.
>
> (Sen 2011: 5)

We can consider this statement of Amartya Sen's in the context of the development questions facing Singapore, the country of Southeast Asia that, on the face of it, needs development least:

- Why does Singapore have no poverty line?
- What sustains the country's meritocratic logic in the face of widening income inequalities?
- What is the relationship between inequality and social cohesion?
- How are Singapore's army of poorly paid migrant workers viewed in everyday political terms?
- How do the institutions of government and society reproduce class/income stratifications?
- Who and what social groups are excluded from mainstream Singaporean society, and why?
- What are the links between Singapore's 'prosperity consensus' and its 'poverty consensus'?

These are all important development questions and they could be asked, with some adjustment, of any country. But they are not, mainly, questions of a technical nature – although they do require an appreciation of the technical complexities of, for example, drawing a poverty line or understanding the nature of social exclusion. They are *P*olitical questions. The politics of development does not just, however, require that we examine the decisions that state's make and the policies that emerge, and in that way seek to understand the distribution and articulation of political power. There is also a *p*olitics of development at the level of civil society, and community and household relations, as the discussion of participatory development in the previous section noted. Simply handing development over to 'local people', means that another arena of politics comes to the fore.

The chapter opened with the statement that 'all development is political'. Table 7.6 maps this out, for didactic purposes, with regard to poverty. The development agenda itself is political; the belief that market fundamentalism and the Washington Consensus are the best means of raising living standards and

Table 7.6 Tracking the politics of the poverty agenda

	Agenda	Political reflection
Rationalizing	Development agenda	Market fundamentalism and the growth agenda
		Growth → poverty alleviation
		Allocation of resources between sectors and spaces
		Personal versus structural explanations for poverty
	Political agenda	Voice and importance of the poor, politically
		The poor and socially excluded's Right to Development
		Notions of 'backwardness', especially for ethnic minorities, and the problematics of traditional living
Constructing, defining, identifying	Poverty agenda	Whether to have a poverty line
		How to define the poor
		The language of poverty
		What indicators define the poor
		Where to draw the poverty line
		What unit of analysis to use (individual or family/household)
		What interventions to prioritize
Experiencing	Local agenda	Prosperity as common currency
		Participatory exclusions
		Participatory capture

reducing poverty; a commitment to social safety nets and university health care; the political acceptance of a certain level of inequality and the relative poverty that thus results; whether the poor have a Right to Development. All these issues and questions cannot be reduced to and viewed as technical questions requiring technical answers. Each issue requires a consideration of the trade-offs, distributional effects, allocative implications and power geometries that help to explain both the decisions taken, and their outcomes. All these matters are deeply political.

The puzzle is that most of us know this instinctively. And yet the message conveyed is that development is about 'getting the fundamentals right', about the application of science, technology and expert knowledge, and the fine-tuning of policies. Section 10 of the World Bank's Articles of Agreement, which were drawn up at Bretton Woods in July 1944, under the sub-heading 'Political Activity Prohibited', states:

> The Bank and its officers shall not interfere in the political affairs of any member; nor shall they be influenced in their decisions by the political character of the member or members concerned. Only economic considerations shall be relevant to their decisions, and these considerations shall be weighed impartially...[23]

William Easterly monitored the speeches of World Bank President Robert Zoellick during the period of the Arab Spring and noted that "he never used the word *democracy* in any of its normal variants" (2013: 327, emphasis in original). The World Bank Press Office confirmed that this was because of Section 10 of the Articles of Agreement. Politics is not just ignored by many development experts; for some, it *has* to be ignored.

There is, however, a further puzzle, one that connects the reality of people's lives and aspirations; the development policies of states, the logics multilateral organizations and the actions of commercial firms; and the work of academics. The ends of development are rarely disputed by the subjects of development, however poor they might be. The failure of development for these poor is the failure of development. And the roots of that failure are usually political.

Further reading

The full text of the UN Declaration of the Right to Development can be downloaded from http://www.un.org/documents/ga/res/41/a41r128.htm. See Sengupta (2004) and Levitt (2003) for critical discussions of the RTD and, more widely, Amartya Sen's *Development and freedom* (1999) for the single most influential study that makes a case for the widening of the development frame to include freedom (or, rather, freedom*s*).

For recent book-length country and case study treatments of development in Southeast Asia that take a political angle to their considerations, see Walker (2012) on 'political peasants' in northern Thailand, Singh (2012) on forests, politics and the state in the Lao PDR, High (2014) on the politics of poverty in a village in southern Lao PDR, and Li (2014) on the spread and decline of cacao in Sulawesi, Indonesia.

For studies of 'old' and 'new' poverty in the Lao PDR see Rigg (2005), Chamberlain (2006) and Singh (2009). There is a vast recent literature on oil palm in Southeast Asia, and especially in Indonesia. For an overview of the region as a whole, see Cramb and Curry (2012) and the papers in this special issue of *Asia Pacific Viewpoint* (53[3] 2012). One of the most useful for the argument pursued here is McCarthy *et al.*'s (2012) grounded study from the provinces of Jambi, Riau and West Kalimantan.

For work on participatory exclusions and capture in Southeast Asia, Beard over the years has written a series of papers on such issues in Indonesia, often with an urban focus. See: Beard (2005 and 2007); Beard and Dasgupta (2006); Beard and Cartmill (2007); and Dasgupta and Beard (2007). The downloadable World Bank desk study of over 400 participatory projects by Mansuri and Rao (2013) provides a broad overview of the institutions experience with participation.

Notes

1   Hickey writes:

> [S]ome significant rethinking is required within international development regarding the forms of politics that are presumed to be pro-poor. In particular, and contrary to the current obsession with civil society, it appears that political society is the key arena for pro-poor politics.
>
> (2009: 474)

2   This is most obviously linked to the work of Henri Lefebvre (Kipfer *et al.* 2013).

3 Full Declaration downloadable from: http://www.un.org/documents/ga/res/41/a41r128. htm.

4 "The central point to appreciate here is that while economic growth is important for enhancing living conditions, its reach and impact depend greatly on what we do with the increased income. The relation between economic growth and the advancement of living standards depends on many factors, including economic and social inequality and, no less importantly, on what the government does with the public revenue that is generated by economic growth" (Sen 2011).

5 Sen has made the striking point that famines have never occurred in a functioning democracy "be it economically rich or relatively poor" (1999: 16).

6 In most rich countries the relative poor are those earning less than 50 per cent of the median income.

7 See Brady (2009) on the politics of poverty in the global North.

8 Following Hong Kong's introduction of a poverty line in 2013 there has been widespread discussion of whether similar steps should be taken in Singapore (see p. 55). In December 2011 the Acting-Director of the Department of Economic Planning and Development said that plans were afoot to establish a poverty line in Brunei (http:// bruneiembassy.be/jpke-plans-to-establish-poverty-line/).

9 For positive studies of the effects of road-building on poverty in the Lao PDR, see Warr (2006, 2008, 2010), and Phomtavong (2010); for more critical takes on road construction, see Rigg (2005) and Chareunsy (2012). Work on resettlement in the Lao PDR is very extensive indeed; see High (2008), High *et al.* (2009), Lund (2011), Petit (2008), Vandergeest (2003) and Evrard and Goudineau (2004). Also note that this debate links closely with that explored in the last chapter regarding the poverty-environment nexus and also the discussion of accumulation by dispossession in Chapter 4.

10 For discussions of the effects of roads on livelihoods and poverty, see Rigg (2002) and Rigg and Wittayapak (2009).

11 *Siwilai* is one of the earliest words transliterated into Thai from English, in the mid-nineteenth century. It can be used as an adjective, a noun or as a verb.

12 Although many officials and documents too readily elide 'minority' with 'backward'.

13 Rist *et al.* (2010: 1014) recount the following tale:

> In 2008 a respondent in Bungo district [in Jambi, Sumatra], along with fellow villagers, was about to sign a contract with an oil palm company handing over 10 ha of land in exchange for 2 ha of oil palm plantation and a small compensation in cash. He was told by field researchers that this deal was unfair and that he could get much better terms if he waited until the following year. The road was under construction and competition among companies was certain to increase when completed leading to better deals for the villagers. He did not want to listen arguing that he had been waiting for too long for a company to come. He said: 'I want to change my fate now! I own plenty of land which has no value. With oil palm I'll get a regular income, with the company doing all the work'.

14 Occasionally, farmers sell their land to the estate company and receive cash compensation, with no land allocated on the estate.

15 In his study from Jambi, for example, McCarthy (2010: 838) notes the way that households "suffering from a livelihood or family crisis, or unable to buy rice, [would] approach wealthy villagers to ask for rice". Land would be their guarantee and, if they were unable to repay their debt, they would lose their land.

16 In their economic analysis, Cahyadi and Waibel (2013) conclude that contract farming of oil palm discriminates against poorer smallholders.

17 Pye *et al.* (2012: 331) apply the notion of precarity discussed in Chapter 3 to migrant workers in Malaysia's oil palm sector. They write that the

permit system chains workers to a particular employer and subjects them to his arbitrary control; workers are 'trapped by the company' because the employer keeps their permit and passport. Workers have no right to choose or change their place of work or employer. ... leaving the permit-holding employer implies entering a state of illegality that can lead to arrest and corporal punishment.

18 An important topic not addressed in this section is the position of migrant labour in the oil palm sector. This links with the discussions in Chapters 3 (on precarity) and 4 (on the uncounted poor). Pye *et al.* write that the "precarious labour regime of the oil palm industry tries to deny people the right to marry, have children and live together as a family, reducing the migrant workers to their labour power" (2012: 341).
19 This was only the most notable of a series of such populist policies from the agrarian debt moratorium scheme to the 1 million baht-per-village fund (Phongpaichit and Baker 2004).
20 In fact the roots of the sufficiency economy can be tracked back to the 1980s, but it was only in the late 1990s, following the Thai economic crisis, that the ideology took on archetypal status. For papers on the sufficiency economy, see: Elinoff (2014), Walker (2012), Unger (2009) and Dayley (2011).
21 The intention here is not to provide a detailed account of these critical perspectives, but for more information see: Cooke and Kothari (2001), Cornwall (2003), Mohan (2001), Cleaver (2001) and Mohan and Stokke (2000).
22 Chatterjee writes:

I find it useful to retain the term civil society for those characteristic institutions of modern associational life originating in Western societies that are based on equality, autonomy, freedom of entry and exit, contract, deliberative procedures of decision making, recognized rights and duties of members, and other such principles.

(1998: 60)

See Mannathukkaren (2010) for a critique of Chatterjee's delineation of political society.
23 The full Articles of Agreement can be downloaded from: http://siteresources.worldbank. org/BODINT/Resources/278027-1215526322295/IBRDArticlesOfAgreement_ English.pdf.

References

ADB (2012). *Asian development outlook 2012: confronting rising inequality in Asia.* Manila, Asian Development Bank.
ADB (2013). *Key indicators for Asia and the Pacific 2013.* Manila, Asian Development Bank.
Agarwal, B. (2001). "Participatory exclusions, community forestry, and gender: an analysis for South Asia and a conceptual framework." *World Development* 29(10): 1623–1648.
Beard, V. A. (2005). "Individual determinants of participation in community development in Indonesia." *Environment and Planning* C 23(1): 21–39.
Beard, V. A. (2007). "Household contributions to community development in Indonesia." *World Development* 35(4): 607–625.
Beard, V. A. and A. Dasgupta (2006). "Collective action and community-driven development in rural and urban Indonesia." *Urban Studies* 43(9): 1451–1468.
Beard, V. A. and R. S. Cartmill (2007). "Gender, collective action and participatory development in Indonesia." *International Development Planning Review* 29(2): 185–213.

Bebbington, A. J., D. Mitlin, J. Mogaladi, M. Scurrah and C. Bielich (2010). "Decentring poverty, reworking government: social movements and states in the government of poverty." *The Journal of Development Studies* 46(7): 1304–1326.

Bellows, T. J. (2009). "Meritocracy and the Singapore political system." *Asian Journal of Political Science* 17(1): 24–44.

Bhaskaran, M., H. S. Chee, D. Low, T. K. Song, S. Vadaketh and Y. L. Keong (2012). Inequality and the need for a new social compact. *Singapore perspectives 2012: Singapore inclusive – bridging divides*. Singapore, Institute of Policy Studies, Lee Kuan Yew School of Public Policy, National University of Singapore.

BMJ (1890). "The politics of poverty." *The British Medical Journal* 1(1530): 965–966.

Brady, D. (2009). *Rich democracies, poor people: how politics explain poverty*. Oxford, Oxford University Press.

Cahyadi, E. R. and H. Waibel (2013). "Is contract farming in the Indonesian oil palm industry pro-poor?" *Journal of Southeast Asian Economies* 30(1): 62–76.

Chamberlain, J. R. (2006). *Participatory poverty assessment II*. Vientiane, Lao PDR, National Statistics Center, Lao People's Democratic Republic and Asian Development Bank.

Chamberlain, J. R. and P. Phomsombath (2002). *Poverty alleviation for all: potentials and options for peoples in the uplands*. Vientiane, Swedish International Development Agency (SIDA).

Chambers, R. (1983). *Rural development: putting the last first*. London, Longman.

Chambers, R. (1997). *Whose reality counts? Putting the first last*. London, Intermediate Technologies Publications.

Chambers, R. (2010). Paradigms, poverty and adaptive pluralism. IDS Working Paper 344. Brighton, UK, Institute of Development Studies.

Chareunsy, A. K. (2012). "Social hierarchy and the inequalities of access: evidence from rural Southern Laos." *Journal of Contemporary Asia* 42(2): 276–297.

Chatterjee, P. (1998). "Beyond the nation? Or within?" *Social Text* (56): 57–69.

Cleaver, F. (2001). Institutions, agency and the limitations of participatory approaches to development. *Participation: the new tyranny?* B. Cooke and U. Kothari. London, Zed Books: 36–55.

Cleaver, F. (2005). "The inequality of social capital and the reproduction of chronic poverty." *World Development* 33(6): 893–906.

Cooke, B. and U. Kothari (Eds) (2001). *Participation: the new tyranny?* London, Zed Books.

Corbridge, S. (2002). "Development as freedom: the spaces of Amartya Sen." *Progress in Development Studies* 2(3): 183–217.

Cornwall, A. (2003). "Whose voices? Whose choices? Reflections on gender and participatory development." *World Development* 31(8): 1325–1342.

Cramb, R. and G. N. Curry (2012). "Oil palm and rural livelihoods in the Asia-Pacific region: an overview." *Asia Pacific Viewpoint* 53(3): 223–239.

Dasgupta, A. and V. A. Beard (2007). "Community driven development, collective action and elite capture in Indonesia." *Development and Change* 38(2): 229–249.

Dayley, R. (2011). "Thailand's agrarian myth and its proponents." *Journal of Asian and African Studies* 46(4): 342–360.

Desai, M. (2001). "Amartya Sen's contribution to development economics." *Oxford Development Studies* 29(3): 213–223.

Easterly, W. (2013). *The tyranny of experts: economists, dictators, and the forgotten rights of the poor*. New York, Basic Books.

Elias, J. and L. Rethel (forthcoming). Southeast Asia and everyday political economy. *The everyday political economy of Southeast Asia.* J. Elias and L. Rethel. Cambridge, Cambridge University Press.

Elinoff, E. (2014). "Sufficient citizens: moderation and the politics of sustainable development in Thailand." *PoLAR: Political and Legal Anthropology Review* 37(1): 89–108.

Elsheshtawy, Y. (2010). "Little space, big space: everyday urbanism in Dubai." *The Brown Journal of World Affairs* 17(1): 53–71.

Evans, G. (1995). *Lao peasants under socialism and post-socialism.* Chiang Mai, Thailand, Silkworm Books.

Evrard, O. and Y. Goudineau (2004). "Planned resettlement, unexpected migrations and cultural trauma in Laos." *Development and Change* 35(5): 937–962.

Feintrenie, L., W. Chong and P. Levang (2010). "Why do farmers prefer oil palm? Lessons learnt from Bungo District, Indonesia." *Small-scale Forestry* 9(3): 379–396.

Flint, C. (2002). "Political geography: globalization, metapolitical geographies and everyday life." *Progress in Human Geography* 26(3): 391–400.

Fukuda-Parr, S. (2012). "The right to development: reframing a new discourse for the twenty-first century." *Social Research* 79(4): 839–864, 1084.

Gasper, D. (2002). "Is Sen's capability approach an adequate basis for considering human development?" *Review of Political Economy* 14(4): 435–461.

Gillespie, P. (2012). "Participation and power in Indonesian oil palm plantations." *Asia Pacific Viewpoint* 53(3): 254–271.

Glassman, J. (2010). "'The provinces elect governments, Bangkok overthrows them': urbanity, class and post-democracy in Thailand." *Urban Studies* 47(6): 1301–1323.

GoL (1989). Report on the economic and social situation, development strategy, and assistance needs of the Lao PDR. Prepared for the Asia-Pacific round table meeting concerning the improvement of the substantial new programme of action for the least developed countries. Geneva.

Green, M. and D. Hulme (2005). "From correlates and characteristics to causes: thinking about poverty from a chronic poverty perspective." *World Development* 33(6): 867–879.

Grindle, M. S. (2004). "Good enough governance: poverty reduction and reform in developing countries." *Governance* 17(4): 525–548.

Grindle, M. S. (2007). "Good enough governance revisited." *Development Policy Review* 25(5): 533–574.

Hewison, K. (2008). "Review of Thailand Human Development Report: sufficiency economy and human development." *Journal of Contemporary Asia* 38(1): 212–219.

Hickey, S. (2009). "The politics of protecting the poorest: moving beyond the 'anti-politics machine'?" *Political Geography* 28(8): 473–483.

Hickey, S. (2010). "The government of chronic poverty: from exclusion to citizenship?" *The Journal of Development Studies* 46(7): 1139–1155.

High, H. (2008). "The implications of aspirations." *Critical Asian Studies* 40(4): 531–550.

High, H. (2014). *Fields of desire: poverty and policy in Laos.* Singapore, NUS Press.

High, H., I. G. Baird, K. Barney, P. Vandergeest and B. Shoemaker (2009). "Internal resettlement in Laos." *Critical Asian Studies* 41(4): 605–620.

Hobson, J. M. and L. Seabrooke (Eds) (2007a). *Everyday politics of the world economy.* Cambridge, Cambridge University Press.

Hobson, J. M. and L. Seabrooke (2007b). Everyday IPE: revealing everyday forms of change in the world economy. *Everyday politics of the world economy.* J. M. Hobson and L. Seabrooke. Cambridge, Cambridge University Press: 1–23.

Kelbaugh, D. (2000). "Three paradigms: new urbanism, everyday urbanism, post urbanism – an excerpt from the essential common place." *Bulletin of Science, Technology & Society* 20(4): 285–289.

Kipfer, S., P. Saberi and T. Wieditz (2013). "Henri Lefebvre: debates and controversies 1." *Progress in Human Geography* 37(1): 115–134.

Koh, L. P. and D. S. Wilcove (2009). "Oil palm: disinformation enables deforestation." *Trends in Ecology & Evolution* 24(2): 67–68.

Lee, J., J. Ghazoul, K. Obidzinski and L. Koh (2014a). "Oil palm smallholder yields and incomes constrained by harvesting practices and type of smallholder management in Indonesia." *Agronomy for Sustainable Development* 34(2): 501–513.

Lee, J. S. H., S. Abood, J. Ghazoul, B. Barus, K. Obidzinski and L. P. Koh (2014b). "Environmental impacts of large-scale oil palm enterprises exceed that of smallholdings in Indonesia." *Conservation Letters* 7(1): 25–33.

Levitt, K. P. (2003). "The right to development: Sir Arthur Lewis Memorial Lecture." *Canadian Journal of Development Studies / Revue canadienne d'études du développement* 24(4): 541–555.

Li, T. M. (2014). *Land's end: capitalist relations on an indigenous frontier.* Durham, NC, Duke University Press.

Lund, C. (2011). "Fragmented sovereignty: land reform and dispossession in Laos." *The Journal of Peasant Studies* 38(4): 885–905.

Lund, J. F. and M. Saito-Jensen (2013). "Revisiting the issue of elite capture of participatory initiatives." *World Development* 46(6): 104–112.

Mannathukkaren, N. (2010). "The 'poverty' of political society: Partha Chatterjee and the People's Plan Campaign in Kerala, India." *Third World Quarterly* 31(2): 295–314.

Mansuri, G. and V. Rao (2013). *Localizing development: does participation work? A World Bank policy research report.* Washington DC, World Bank.

McCargo, D. (2013). The last gasp of Thai paternalism. *The New York Times*, 19 December.

McCarthy, J. (2010). "Processes of inclusion and adverse incorporation: oil palm and agrarian change in Sumatra, Indonesia." *The Journal of Peasant Studies* 37(4): 821–850.

McCarthy, J. and R. A. Cramb (2009). "Policy narratives, landholder engagement, and oil palm expansion on the Malaysian and Indonesian frontiers." *Geographical Journal* 175(2): 112–123.

McCarthy, J. and Z. Zen (2010). "Regulating the oil palm boom: assessing the effectiveness of environmental governance approaches to agro-industrial pollution in Indonesia." *Law & Policy* 32: 153–179.

McCarthy, J. P. Gillespie and Z. Zen (2012). "Swimming upstream: local Indonesian production networks in 'globalized' palm oil production." *World Development* 40(3): 555–569.

Mohan, G. (2001). Beyond participation: strategies for deeper empowerment. *Participation: the new tyranny?* B. Cooke and U. Kothari. London, Zed Books: 154–167.

Mohan, G. and K. Stokke (2000). "Participatory development and empowerment: the dangers of localism." *Third World Quarterly* 21(2): 247–268.

NESDB (2011). *Eleventh National Economic and Social Development Plan, 2012–2016.* Bangkok, National Economic and Social Development Board, Office of the Prime Minister.

Ng, I. Y. H. (2013). "Social welfare in Singapore: rediscovering poverty, reshaping policy." *Asia Pacific Journal of Social Work and Development* 23(1): 35–47.

Petit, P. (2008). "Rethinking internal migrations in Lao PDR: the resettlement process under micro-analysis." *Anthropological Forum* 18(2): 117–138.

Phomtavong, S. (2010). "The impact of rural road investment on poverty reduction in the Lao PDR." *Journal of Rural Problems* 46(3): 325–333.

Phongpaichit, P. and C. Baker (2004). *Thaksin: the business of politics in Thailand.* Copenhagen, Nordic Institute of Asian Studies.

Pye, O., R. Daud, Y. Harmono and Tatat (2012). "Precarious lives: transnational biographies of migrant oil palm workers." *Asia Pacific Viewpoint* 53(3): 330–342.

Rajagopal, B. (2013). "Right to development and global governance: old and new challenges twenty-five years on." *Human Rights Quarterly* 35(4): 893–909.

Resurreccion, B. P., M. J. Real and P. Pantana (2004). "Officialising strategies: participatory processes and gender in Thailand's water resources sector." *Development in Practice* 14(4): 521–533.

Rigg, J. (2002). "Roads, marketization and social exclusion in Southeast Asia. What do roads do to people?" *Bijdragen tot de taal-, land- en volkenkunde (Journal of the Humanties and Social Sciences of Southeast Asia and Oceania)* 158(4): 619–636.

Rigg, J. (2005). *Living with transition in Laos: market integration in Southeast Asia.* London, Routledge.

Rigg, J. (2007). *An everyday geography of the global South.* London, Routledge.

Rigg, J. and C. Wittayapak (2009). *Spatial integration and human transformations in the Greater Mekong Sub-region: re-shaping economic geography in East Asia.* Y. Huang and A. M. Bocchi. Washington DC, World Bank: 79–99.

Rigg, J., B. Promphaking and A. Le Mare (2014). "Personalizing the middle-income trap: an inter-generational migrant view from rural Thailand." *World Development* 59(7): 184–198.

Rist, L., L. Feintrenie and P. Levang (2010). "The livelihood impacts of oil palm: smallholders in Indonesia." *Biodiversity & Conservation* 19(4): 1009–1024.

Scott, J. C. (1985). *Weapons of the weak: everyday forms of peasant resistance.* New Haven, CT, Yale University Press.

Scott, J. C. (1990). *Domination and the arts of resistance: hidden transcripts.* New Haven, CT, Yale University Press.

Seabrooke, L. (2011). "Everyday politics and generational conflicts in the world economy." *International Political Sociology* 5(4): 456–459.

Sen, A. (1981). *Poverty and famines: an essay on entitlement and deprivation.* Oxford, Clarendon Press.

Sen, A. (1999). *Development as freedom.* Oxford, Oxford University Press.

Sen, A. (2000). Social exclusion: concept, application, and scrutiny. Social Development Papers No. 1. Manila, Asian Development Bank.

Sen, A. (2011). Quality of life: India vs. China. *New York Review of Books*, 12 May.

Sengupta, A. (2000). "Realizing the right to development." *Development and Change* 31(3): 553–578.

Sengupta, A. (2004). "The human right to development." *Oxford Development Studies* 32(2): 179–203.

Singh, S. (2009). "Governing anti-conservation sentiments: forest politics in Laos." *Human Ecology* 37(6): 749–760.

Singh, S. (2012). *Natural potency and political power: forests and state authority in contemporary Laos.* Honolulu, University of Hawai'i Press.

UNDP (2007). *Thailand human development report 2007: sufficiency economy and human development.* Bangkok, United Nations Development Programme.

Unger, D. (2009). "Sufficiency economy and the bourgeois virtues." *Asian Affairs, an American Review* 36(3): 139–156.

Vandergeest, P. (1991). "Gifts and rights: cautionary notes on community self-help in Thailand." *Development and Change* 22: 421–443.

Vandergeest, P. (2003). "Land to some tillers: development-induced displacement in Laos." *International Social Science Journal* 55(175): 47–56.

Varkkey, H. (2012). "Patronage politics as a driver of economic regionalisation: the Indonesian oil palm sector and transboundary haze." *Asia Pacific Viewpoint* 53(3): 314–329.

Varkkey, H. (2013). "Oil palm plantations and transboundary haze: patronage networks and land licensing in Indonesia's peatlands." *Wetlands* 33(4): 679–690.

Walker, A. (2012). *Thailand's political peasants: power in the modern rural economy.* Madison, University of Wisconsin Press.

Warr, P. (2006). "The impact of road development on poverty in the Lao People's Democratic Republic." *Asia-Pacific Development Journal* 13(2): 1–23.

Warr, P. (2008). "How road improvement reduces poverty: the case of Laos." *Agricultural Economics* 39: 269–279.

Warr, P. (2010). "Roads and poverty in rural Laos: an econometric analysis." *Pacific Economic Review* 15: 152–169.

Widmaier, W. (2009). "Economics are too important to leave to economists: the everyday – and emotional – dimensions of international political economy." *Review of International Political Economy* 16(5): 945–957.

Winichakul, T. (2000). "The quest for 'Siwilai': a geographical discourse of civilizational thinking in the late nineteenth and early twentieth-century Siam." *The Journal of Asian Studies* 59(3): 528–549.

8   More growth/less development?

We live in a world of unprecedented opulence .... And yet we also live in a world with remarkable deprivation, destitution and oppression. There are many new problems as well as old ones ... [and] many of these deprivations can be observed, in one form or another, in rich countries as well as poor ones.

(Sen 1999: xi)

One of the most heartening developments in recent years has been the broad progress in human development of many developing countries and their emergence onto the global stage: 'the rise of the South'.

(UNDP 2013: 1)

Introduction: questioning success

In his important book *Development as freedom* (1999), from which the first extract above is taken, Amartya Sen sought to move the development debate on from the notion that development is largely about the generation of economic growth and the reduction of income poverty. For Sen, notwithstanding unprecedented wealth and economic expansion, many people lack basic freedoms. These freedoms should not be seen either as barriers or enablers of development, but as *constitutive of development*. In this way, the question of whether, for example, certain political or social freedoms, or environmental regulations hinder or help the development process misses the point: they are central components of development.[1] They are ends as well as means of the development process. At the same time, wealth in the form of income is not, in itself, a development end: it is the means by which something valuable or useful is acquired that may contribute to well-being and human flourishing.[2]

In this way the development debate, at least as it has been followed by most states and multilateral agencies, has got the development challenge inverted:

- Economic growth and income are treated as development ends when they are the means to achieve development, both individually and nationally; while
- other components of development – such as education, human rights or environmental protection – are regarded either as means or as barriers to development, when they should (also) be viewed as ends.[3]

The assessment of countries' development success on the basis of their income levels, economic growth rates and levels of income poverty is certainly important. Income, after all, is often used as a proxy for development because the two not infrequently seem to correlate quite closely, particularly during the early stages of the development process. It was not caprice that led to this state of affairs. This, though, then deceives us into thinking that there are no significant omissions and oversights and that policies which generate growth and wealth will also, necessarily, engender development. When Jeffrey Sachs (2005) writes about the possibility of "ending poverty in our time" he is not only thinking about a particular manifestation of poverty (i.e. Poverty 1.0, see p. 8) but also a particular notion of what constitutes development. As earlier chapters in this book have argued, the challenge of eradicating Poverty 1.0, and in this sense 'making poverty history', has to a significant extent been achieved, or is on the route to being achieved, in many of the countries of the Southeast Asian region.

The Asian Development Bank has produced projections of extreme poverty in the Asian region through to 2030 which show that by that date Southeast Asia's poverty rate will stand at 0.8 per cent, amounting to some 5.5 million poor (ADB 2014: 33–4) (see Table 8.1). It is this that lies at the heart of the claim for developmental success in the region – the prospect of the effective eradication of poverty by around 2020.[4] But the development challenge, as this book has recounted, remains acute because development is about far more than income, and therefore cannot be read off from data on income poverty. This, of course, has been pointed out many times before – not least by Adam Smith in *An enquiry into the nature and causes of the wealth of nations* in 1776 – but it is surprising how often analyses of development end up being reductionist in just this manner.

The Commission on Growth and Development (note the linking of growth with development) states on the first page of its report that "Growth is not an end in itself" (p. 1), but then on the next page says that the "report identifies some of the distinctive characteristics of high-growth economies and asks how other developing countries can emulate them" (p. 2). Growth, the report argues, "makes it possible to achieve other important objectives of individuals and societies [and] can spare people *en masse* from poverty and drudgery. Nothing else ever has" (CGD 2008: 1).

The empirical evidence for the efficacy of the market mechanism in generating economic growth and material prosperity is hard to challenge. The second of the two quotations that starts this chapter is from the UNDP's *2013 Human development report* on the 'rise of the South'. The report notes how the development policies of some countries of the South are providing alternative approaches and visions of how to achieve development.[5] And it is certainly the case that the countries of Southeast Asia have played an important part in this rethinking of development, not least through the example that they have set, reflected in data such as those in Table 8.1. Heterodoxy in development strategies and policies is now broadly accepted by scholars and many governments (see Rodrik 2007; Rigg 2012), even if some agencies appear wedded to particular recipes. There are two important caveats to acknowledge, however.

First, market-based strategies of growth, even those that might be counted as hybrid, have particular developmental outcomes. Development would be different under a different growth regime even if the growth rate was the same. So, we need to ask not just the question 'What policies generate rapid growth?' (which is the question that the CGD report primarily addresses) but also, 'What developmental outcomes does growth under a particular policy regime produce?". As Chapter 3 explored, in important ways capitalist growth produces *new* forms and styles of poverty, which are often hard to see and isolate.[6] This leads us to the second caveat, which is that growth is a problematic proxy for development. It is quite possible that slower growth under one policy regime will result in more development than another which generates faster growth. The Indian state of Kerala famously shows a longer life expectancy, better health profile, greater gender equality and higher educational achievement than many other richer Indian states (Tharamangalam 2010; Meyer and Brysac 2011; but also see Venkatraman 2009 for a contrarian view). Cuba has also long been lauded as a country displaying a human development profile closer to high income countries. The achievements of Kerala and Cuba have been attained not because growth has been faster and incomes necessarily higher, but because of the policy decisions that have been taken. Moreover, it is not necessary to imagine that such policy differences are high level and strategic; they may be decisions taken – and choices made – within a policy framework that remains broadly market-oriented. Decisions are based partly on assumptions about the development and growth efficacy of different policies. The political status of different policies, however, is often just as important in shaping the policy framework adopted.

The development 'trap'

These two points set out the contours of a development 'trap'. To reiterate, the trap consists of the way in which growth and income poverty (their increase and decrease respectively) have become synonyms for development; and the way in which policies are treated in mainstream development practice as supporting and enabling market-led growth, as if such growth has particular outcomes largely independent of the policy environment. Policies shape the nature of growth and also its developmental outcomes.

There is a third element to the development trap and that concerns the way in which data become evidence which then informs and directs policy (aside from the politics of policy-making, as noted above). Tania Murray Li, drawing on the work of James Scott, calls this "rendering technical" (2007: 7). She writes:

> Two key practices are required to translate the will to improve into explicit programs. One is problematization, that is, identifying deficiencies that need to be rectified. The second is the practice I call 'rendering technical,' a shorthand for what is actually a whole set of [state] practices ...
>
> (Li 2007: 7)

We can see this at work in the poverty debate. The starting point for this is the identification of poverty as a problem requiring intervention and alleviation (where the politics of poverty is critical). Following this, the nature of poverty is defined and demarcated in income-centric and money-metric terms. This, in turn, becomes specified at a particular income level, informed by a certain identification of basic or minimum needs. The absolute or extreme poor are then conjured into existence, they are identified, and policies are constructed to lift them from their so-identified condition. The outcome is data such as those in Table 8.1.

For radical scholars, perhaps most notably Arturo Escobar, the 'development project was an invention of modernity' (2004: 15), and so too is the idea of the income poor (Escobar 1995). Less profound but, on balance, I think more significant is the way in which the 'extreme' or 'absolute' poor have become an object

Table 8.1 Extreme poverty and the extreme poor in developing Asia, 1981–2030

Developing Asia

	Extreme poverty at $1.25		Extreme poverty at $1.51[a]	
	Poverty rate (%)	Numbers living in poverty (billions)	Poverty rate (%)	Numbers living in poverty (billions)
Actual:				
1981	69.8	1.59	–	–
1990	54.7	1.48	–	–
2005	26.9	0.90	37.3	1.25
2010	20.7	0.73	30.5	1.08
Projected:				
2015	12.7	0.47	21.5	0.80
2020	5.8	0.22	11.7	0.45
2025	2.5	0.10	5.2	0.21
2030	1.4	0.06	2.5	0.10

Southeast Asia

	Extreme poverty at $1.25		Extreme poverty at $1.51	
	Poverty rate (%)	Numbers living in poverty (millions)	Poverty rate (%)	Numbers living in poverty (millions)
Projected:				
2015	6.5	39.23	14.9	85.04
2020	2.5	15.03	6.5	38.94
2025	1.3	8.05	2.7	17.06
2030	0.8	5.54	1.5	9.54

Source: ADB (2014).

Notes: [a] the $1.51 poverty line is the ADB's new 'extreme' poverty line.
The World Bank considers poverty to have been eradicated when the poverty rate falls below 3%.

of statistical argument. It is here that we really see the weaknesses of development orthodoxy and how the process of rendering technical is partial, ambiguous and therefore problematic. The extreme poverty line is usually taken to be $1.25 per day. Taking this figure, then in 1981 some 1.59 billion Asians were poor, or 70 per cent of the population. In 1990 the number was 1.48 billion, or 55 per cent. And by 2010, 0.73 billion Asians were poor, or around one-fifth of the population (Table 8.1).

The Asian Development Bank has, however, recently argued that "the extreme poverty line of $1.25 no longer works for Asia. It was largely based on African data and is also outdated. More recent data is needed" (ADB 2014: 5). The ADB then sets out the weaknesses of the World Bank's approach to arriving at the $1.25 poverty line, outlines the particular problems with its application to the Asian region, and arrives at a revised 'extreme' poverty line of $1.51. The poverty estimates that come from the application of the $1.25 and $1.51 lines are also provided in Table 8.1. Using the ADB's new (and apparently more appropriate) line, the number of extreme poor in developing Asia is 1.08 billion, rather than the 0.73 billion identified using the old line, in the process creating an additional 350 million people living in extreme poverty. These 350 million individuals, of course, experienced no change in their living conditions or experiences because of their reassignment as 'poor'. One can imagine the smart economists at the ADB, housed in their air-conditioned offices in Manila, pondering about that extra $0.01 which provides such a fiction of precision but which elides any real engagement with the poor and the causes of poverty.

To a degree this is unfair. The economists at the ADB are well aware of the assumptions and problems with this approach to measuring poverty but they are tied to taking such an approach by the nature of the Development project – which is to 'make poverty history'. The same report that realigned the extreme poor by arriving at a $1.51 poverty line also offers, right at the end of the discussion, the following observation:

> Until recently, poverty was measured using money-metric poverty lines. The fact that wellbeing is multifaceted means poverty is intrinsically multidimensional. Thus, money-metric measures do not provide a complete picture of well-being for either individuals or households. Other dimensions need to be taken into account. ... Empirical evidence is emerging that shows a lack of correlation between monetary income and other dimensions of human wellbeing. Non-monetary poverty tends to be more persistent than monetary poverty.
>
> (ADB 2014: 43)

This is not, as they say, rocket science, and most students of development are taught in their very first lectures that *economic growth + income ≠ development*.

How, then, do the countries of Southeast Asia match up when we compare, say, poverty rates or income per capita against other indicators of human wellbeing?

The visible trap: wealth, health and social development

In Southeast Asia the disparities between growth, income and development are not as striking as they are with regard to Kerala and Cuba, but they are significant nonetheless. Table 8.2 sets out income and health indicators for Indonesia, Malaysia and Vietnam. Vietnam is the poorest of the three countries in terms of per capita income – and by a significant margin – and yet it has the highest life expectancy. Vietnam's per capita income is about half the level of Indonesia's and yet it also has a lower income poverty rate whether measured at $1.25 or $1.51 per person per day.

Tables and data such as these can be used to explore differences between countries in terms of their development outcomes and to highlight inconsistences across different variables. Such tables and their contents, however, focus on the measurable and there is much, as this book has explored, which is not measurable, either because the data are not collected or because the variable is not susceptible to easy quantification. We can point, for example, to the effects of development transformations on the nature of the household and the family discussed in Chapter 5, or the wellbeing of migrants discussed in Chapter 4, or the structural violence visited on coastal communities in Cambodia raised in Chapter 6. Such discussions require that we ask questions of the meanings of data, and seek to uncover what has not been measured, for whatever reason be it technical or political.

Even when we think we have the data, there are complications as to what we read into those data. Ferguson (2013) has explored, in the context of southern Africa, what he calls *asocial* inequality. In using this term he is taking us from simple measures of inequality (such as those discussed in Chapter 2), to statements about *social* inequality. Social inequality implies, he argues, common membership of a social group. But inequality in twenty-first-century Southeast Asia is becoming increasing asocial. Ferguson writes that:

> By 'asocial', I mean here something quite specific. There are, of course, still identifiable and important links between the worlds of rich and poor, and if we insist (as social scientists tend to do) that every human relation is by definition a social one, then, of course, the sort of inequality I have in mind plainly *is* 'social'. But if we ask another question, namely whether inequalities are lived and experienced within the imaginary horizon of that nineteenth-century invention 'society' – whether inequality, that is, is conceived as a relation among the members of a morally binding membership group – then the answer, increasingly, is 'no'.
>
> (Ferguson 2013: 232–3)

Quite a number of the issues raised in this book connect with this idea of asocial inequality. International migrant labourers working in Brunei Darrusalam, Malaysia, Thailand and Singapore, for example, experience this sort of alienation and exclusion. We can extend this further to rural people dispossessed of their land, uplanders regarded as primitive by lowlanders, and workers living increasingly precarious lives under the pressures and exigencies of late capitalism. For

Table 8.2 Wealth and health in Indonesia, Malaysia and Vietnam

	Income/growth-related indicators					Human-development-related indicators					
	GNI per capita, PPP (current international $)	Poverty rate at $1.25 a day (PPP) (% of population)	Poverty rate at $1.51 a day (PPP) (% of population)	Income share held by lowest 10%	Gini coefficient of inequality	Life expectancy at birth, total (years)	Mortality rate, infant (per 1,000 live births)	Improved sanitation facilities (% of population with access)	Health expenditure, total (% of GDP)	Income share held by highest 10%	Maternal mortality ratio (per 100,000 live births)
	2013	2010	2010	2008–11	(as indicated)	2012	2012	2012	2012	2008–11	2013
Vietnam	5,030	16.9	22.4	3.2	0.356 (2008)	75.6	18.4	75	6.6	28.2	49
Indonesia	9,260	18.1	28.0	3.2	0.381 (2011)	70.6	25.8	59	3.0	30.6	190
Malaysia	22,460	0.0	0.4	1.8	0.441 (2009)	74.8	7.3	96	3.9	34.7	29

Sources: http://data.worldbank.org/indicator; ADB (2013, 2014).

these populations it is not so much that their income and security have relatively diminished against a backdrop of stagnant or rising inequality, but that they find themselves pushed to the margins of the morally binding social economy. Even when they are non-poor in absolute terms, their human flourishing is compromised such that it may be hard to consider such growth, development.[7]

There are policy implications to this observation, because it highlights the point that for Southeast Asia, where extreme poverty is fast being eradicated, development 'interventions' need to become attuned to – and adept at – addressing issues which are far less amenable to easy solution. Perhaps this was always the case, and it is has just become more obvious as the immediate challenge of addressing absolute poverty has receded. For Easterly:

> The conventional approach to economic development, to making poor countries rich, is based on a technocratic illusion: the belief that poverty is a purely technical problem amenable to such technical solutions as fertilizers, antibiotics, or nutritional supplements. ... The technocratic approach ignores...the real cause of poverty – the unchecked power of the state against poor people without rights. ... violations of the rights of real people is the moral tragedy of development today.
>
> (2013: 6)

Wealth, development and well-being: vignettes from Thailand and Vietnam

The data and observations above are generalized and aggregated. For individuals and households, development may play out in very different ways, as people make choices about the risks they are willing to take and demonstrate, in their actions, preferences and values. Just as reading off development from growth rates is problematic because of the way that it both distorts and omits, so assuming that national data on economic growth will somehow be reflected in individual experience is equally narrowing and distorting. We can see this at work in two vignettes from Thailand and Vietnam.[8]

The Thai study examined migration from three villages in the Northeastern region and its impacts on source settlements and households (see Rigg *et al.* 2014b; Le Mare *et al.* 2015). The fieldwork was conducted in 2012. The Vietnam research investigated the experiences of rural–urban migrants from the other end of the migration stream, interviewing migrants in Hanoi. These migrants and their experiences were then connected back to their natal households in rural contexts (see Nguyen *et al.* 2012; Rigg *et al.* 2014a). The fieldwork in this instance was undertaken in 2010.

Mr Viet, a *xe om* driver in Hanoi, was introduced in Chapter 3 (see Box 3.4). For the two decades from his arrival in 1990, Mr Viet had made his living in Hanoi even while his family remained in the countryside. Even in 2010, with more than 20 years of working in the city under his belt, he was still officially categorized as a 'temporary' urban resident, and lived in a small rented room with three other migrant men. His monthly income was such that he could not afford to bring his family to Hanoi but, at the same time, the land he owned in the village was not sufficient to provide sustenance and income to support his wife, mother and four children– a common state of affairs in the village. He could not afford to stay in the village but he also could not afford to bring his family with him to the city. It was not just his wife, children and widowed mother who kept him connected to the village; as the eldest son, Mr Viet felt a responsibility to maintain the patriline.

Like many millions of men and women across the world, Mr Viet had traded one sort of well-being – social – for another – economic.[9] The fact that he could not build and sustain an acceptable livelihood in his home village in the context of rising needs drove him to leave and make his living in Hanoi, only periodically returning home to see his family. This was the calculation he made and the decision he took, like hundreds of millions of other Asians.[10] Whether it was a choice, a constrained choice or a necessity can be debated. Others have remained and struggled to make a living in Xuan Truong, but many have left, and Mr Viet observed that his natal village is populated mainly by the elderly and the young.

This migration context is forged in a particular policy context. In the past, migration was limited by Vietnam's household registration system, the *ho khau* system. While this no longer prevents people moving from the countryside to urban centres, it influences *how* they engage with the urban. Other policies are now more important in helping to understand Mr Viet's presence in Hanoi: the introduction of the policies of *doi moi* (renovation) from the mid-1980s and the growth in employment opportunities in urban and peri-urban areas; the erosion of Vietnam's iron rice bowl and the de facto privatization of farming; the declining terms of trade between farming and non-farming; the gradual attrition in Vietnam's formerly quite finely woven state social safety net; and the widening in disparities between services and amenities provided in rural and urban areas. So while Mr Viet made the decision to leave his village for Hanoi with significant consequences for his well-being, this personal and family decision has to be seen against Vietnam's policy milieu. Policy choices at the national level, informed by received wisdoms at the international level, are important in explaining Mr Viet's predicament and his decision.

The study from Thailand provides a rather different insight. To be sure, the large majority of households in the three villages in Northeast Thailand where the study was conducted had migrant members, either current or returned. As in Vietnam, the continued existence of the villages was predicated on people leaving. In this case, however, most had returned and even though this may have led to a fall in absolute income because wage-earning opportunities were more limited in the village, many migrants were happy to return and live 'at home'. Out of 151 migrant villagers who we tracked, just 15 per cent were permanent labour outmigrants. The remainder had either returned or were intending to return.[11] There was a clear recognition that while opportunities for productive employment in the village and surrounding area were not great, the quality of life was much better than in Bangkok or abroad. Both men and women assessed their return to their natal village with enthusiasm, even joy. As one female respondent put it to us, 'now I have happiness more than suffering'. As in Vietnam, the reasons why villagers left in such numbers but also why they returned in close to the same numbers is explicable in terms of Thailand's policy context, set against the forces that characterize late capitalism (see Rigg, forthcoming). The reason why the large majority of migrants returned was because there was little security in working away; precarity characterized their migrant lives. Migration was virtually inevitable; but so too was return – and the background reasons for each were much the same.

A better capitalism?

It is important to recognize that these development outcomes, whether seen at a national aggregate level or in terms of the personal experiences of men and women like Mr Viet – have not just 'happened'. They have emerged because of a set of decisions that have been taken at national as well as international levels. Markets and market outcomes are not 'natural' but political, as Chapter 7 argued. Similarly, the 'spaces' of development and underdevelopment might be more accurately viewed as territories, in so far as they are crafted and demarcated by policy. As Stiglitz has argued with respect to inequality in the United States, "it is not the inexorable laws of economics that have led to America's great divide … but our policies and our politics" (Stiglitz 2014). This is an argument that has traction with respect to many other issues and in many other places. There is a necessity to evaluate and pass judgement on the market system as it exists and operates in different countries.

What does this mean for how we might understand the Development project across Southeast Asia? To understand this we need to refine the question slightly and ask the following:

• What understandings of progress were necessary to shape the development policies that we see enacted across the countries of Southeast Asia?

Development policies, in a real sense, can only come into being if we have an idea of what development is, and what we are trying to achieve by pursuing or enabling development. This then returns us to the two-pronged development trap noted above.

While the development experience in the region has, to date, been one defined by the growth-as-development orthodoxy, there are examples of, and possibilities for, building a better capitalism, even a better neoliberalism. The scholars who have done most to further this view, at least in the context of Southeast Asia, are Kathy Gibson and Julie Graham.

Alternative neoliberal spaces

The work of Katherine Gibson and Julie Graham,[12] drawing mainly on their work with colleagues in the Philippines (Gibson-Graham 2005, 2008; Gibson *et al.* 2010;

and see McKinnon *et al.* 2008), challenges the mainstream development project norm that "the only viable economy is a capitalist one and that the only dynamics that will produce economic development are those of capitalist productivity – production of commodities for the global market, capital accumulation and export led growth" (Gibson-Graham 2005: 12). In a separate paper, Gibson *et al.* (2010: 241) write that in their "view there has been disappointingly little rethinking beyond unidirectional logics of capitalist globalisation and development as 'motors' of rural transformation".

The 'diverse economy', as they call it, is an economy where the mainstream (i.e. market transactions, wage labour and capitalist enterprise) is allied to alternative economies such as those sketched out in Table 8.3. Their alternative economy is one where other means of production are valued, where divisions between different arenas of activities are broken down, and where policies and development transformations are not univalent and unidirectional but polyvalent and entertain the possibility of multiple transformation paths rather than a single transition trajectory (Gibson *et al.* 2010: 250).

This vision can be viewed as the alternative complement to the argument that Asia's research experience has been 'eclectic' (Wade 2004) or 'heterodox' (Rodrik 2007). Here the argument is that the region's development future can similarly be diverse and different.

Table 8.3 A diverse economy

	TRANSACTIONS	LABOUR	ENTERPRISE
MAINSTREAM ECONOMY	*Market*	*Wage*	*Capitalist*
	Alternative market	*Alternative paid*	*Alternative capitalist*
	Sale of public goods	Self-employed	State enterprise
	Ethical 'fair trade' markets	Cooperative	Green capitalist
	Local trading systems	Indentured	Socially
	Alternative currencies	Reciprocal labour	responsible firm
	Underground market	In kind	Non-profit
	Coop exchange	Work for welfare	
	Barter		
	Informal market		
	Alternative credit		
ALTERNATIVE ECONOMY	*Non-market*	*Unpaid*	*Non-capitalist*
	Household flows	Housework	Communal
	Gift giving	Family care	Independent
	Indigenous exchange	Neighbourhood work	Feudal/peasant
	State allocations	Volunteer	Slave
	Gleaning	Self-provisioning labour	
	Theft, poaching	Slave labour	

Source: Gibson-Graham (2005: 12).

Note: a fuller version of this table with examples from the Philippine field site can be found in Gibson *et al.* (2010: 246).

Growing fast and living well in Southeast Asia?

> If there is one number to which the rights of millions will be happily sacrificed, it is the national GDP growth rate.
>
> (Easterly 2013: 215)

In the main, Southeast Asians are living longer and healthier lives; they are also better educated and informed, more productive and – although this is open to dispute – have greater control over their lives. This book, however, has also set out a range of reasons to be cautious of excessive congratulation and wary of pushing the 'exemplar' status of the region too far. Furthermore, the reasons to be cautious are not diminishing as the region becomes more affluent, but multiplying.

There are not only many tens of millions of people who live below or close to the extreme poverty line, but the line itself is problematic for all that it overlooks and therefore undervalues. Measures of development that have as their starting point GDP and GDP per capita are failing, and increasingly so, to tell us much about development. This is particularly true after countries have made the transition from low to middle income, as most in Southeast Asia have done. Kubiszewski *et al.* (2013; and see Costanza *et al.* 2014) have tried to assess this growing mismatch between GDP and other measures of progress through a comparative study of 17 countries making up 53 per cent of the world's population (and including Thailand and Vietnam). They use the Genuine Progress Indicator (GPI)[13] to chart development more inclusively and on this basis conclude that "economic welfare at the global scale has not been improving since 1978" (Kubiszewski *et al.* 2013: 67). They continue:

> If we hope to achieve a sustainable and desirable future, we need to rapidly shift our policy focus away from maximizing production and consumption (GDP) and towards improving genuine human well-being (GPI or something similar). This is a shift that will require far more attention to be paid to environmental protection, full employment, social equity, better product quality and durability, and greater resource use efficiency (i.e., reducing the resource intensity per dollar of GDP).
>
> (2013: 67)

Individuals in Southeast Asia may not have access to the skills, data and technology to undertake the sort of analysis that Kubiszewski *et al.* perform, but many have a gut feeling that something is amiss: "In the past our life was hard but we lived in peace. Today we live comfortably but we suffer" (Promburom and Sakdapolrak 2012: 63).

A central reason for the divergence between economic growth and development that Kubiszewski *et al.* (2013) identify lies in the policies of market-led growth that have delivered the so-styled Asian miracle. Even more acutely, these policies have often done much to create the poor that the ADB identify, as well as many who are structurally and experientially poor, even if they are not income poor, that the ADB does not. From dispossessed peasants in the uplands of Laos and the forests of Indonesia, to factory workers making a precarious living in Hanoi and Phnom Penh or along the Thai-Myanmar border, to migrant labourers on the roads and in the homes of Singapore – these are the flotsam of Southeast Asia's rapid growth.

The important point is that while at times the stories can be recounted and interpreted as 'unintended consequences', in the main their production has been "a calculated decision, rationalized in terms of the greater good" (Li 2010: 80). It is necessary to acknowledge and take cognisance of the often problematic well-being consequences of the development policies that have been so successfully pursued across the region, and which have become development orthodoxy. These are the shadows of Southeast Asia's success.

Notes

1 Sen calls this the "Lee thesis", after Singapore's former Prime Minister Lee Kuan Yew (Sen 1999: 15).
2 See p. 11 on well-being and human flourishing.
3 It is often said that it is worth 'paying the price' of, say, environmental degradation or controls on freedom of expression, in order to achieve 'development' (by which it is meant, 'growth'). We can see this logic at work in the imposition of martial law in Thailand in May 2014. Martial law and all that it has entailed (including rounding up dissenters who have displayed the three-fingered mockingjay salute from *The Hunger Games* for 'attitude adjustment') is justified on the basis that it will bring stability, and stability will bring economic growth.
4 The World Bank considers poverty to have been eradicated when it falls below 3 per cent (ADB 2014: 3).
5 The 2013 HDR also states however that:

> even in the higher achieving countries, future success is not guaranteed. How can countries in the South continue their progress in human development …? This Report suggests four important areas to facilitate this: enhancing equity, enabling voice and participation, confronting environmental challenges and managing demographic change.
>
> (UNDP 2013: 5)

6 This is a theme that runs through Li's (2014) book on agrarian change in upland Central Sulawesi.
7 In China it has been suggested that it is harder for students from rural backgrounds to get into one of the elite universities today, than ever. The admissions officer at Tsinghua University was quoted in the *New York Times* as saying that the typical undergraduate is "someone who grew up in cities, whose parents are civil servants and teachers, go on family trips at least once a year, and have studied abroad in high school" (Gao 2014). Students from poor, rural backgrounds stand virtually no chance against the tutored children of the elite.
8 I also explore these two cases in Rigg (forthcoming).
9 While recognizing that this distinction is far from clear-cut.
10 'Hundreds of millions' is not an exaggeration to make a point.
11 There were also some marriage migrants, who are not included in the figure of 15 per cent.

12 The authors adopted the combined name J.K. Gibson-Graham in their co-written works.
13 "GPI starts with Personal Consumption Expenditures (a major component of GDP) but adjusts them using 24 different components, including income distribution, environmental costs, and negative activities like crime and pollution, among others. GPI also adds positive components left out of GDP, including the benefits of volunteering and household work. By separating activities that diminish welfare from those that enhance it, GPI better approximates sustainable economic welfare" (Kubiszewski *et al.* 2013: 58).

References

ADB (2013). *Key indicators for Asia and the Pacific 2013*. Manila, Asian Development Bank.

ADB (2014). *Key indicators for Asia and the Pacific 2014 – poverty in Asia: a deeper look*. Manila, Asian Development Bank.

CGD (2008). *The growth report: strategies for sustained growth and inclusive development*. Washington DC, World Bank.

Costanza, R. (2014). "Time to leave GDP behind." *Nature* 505(7483): 283–285.

Easterly, W. (2013). *The tyranny of experts: economists, dictators and the forgotten rights of the poor*. New York, Basic Books.

Escobar, A. (1995). *Encountering development: the making and unmaking of the Third World*. Princeton, NJ, Princeton University Press.

Escobar, A. (2004). "Development, violence and the new imperial order." *Development* 47(1): 15–21.

Ferguson, J. (2013). "Declarations of dependence: labour, personhood, and welfare in southern Africa." *Journal of the Royal Anthropological Institute* 19(2): 223–242.

Gao, H. (2014) "China's education gap." *The New York Times*, 4 September.

Gibson, K., A. Cahill and D. McKay (2010). "Rethinking the dynamics of rural transformation: performing different development pathways in a Philippine municipality." *Transactions of the Institute of British Geographers* 35: 237–255.

Gibson-Graham, J. K. (2005). "Surplus possibilities: postdevelopment and community economies." *Singapore Journal of Tropical Geography* 26(1): 4–26.

Gibson-Graham, J. K. (2008). "Diverse economies: performative practices for 'other worlds'." *Progress in Human Geography* 32(5): 613–632.

Kubiszewski, I., R. Costanza, C. Franco, P. Lawn, J. Talberth, T. Jackson and C. Aylmer (2013). "Beyond GDP: measuring and achieving global genuine progress." *Ecological Economics* 93: 57–68.

Le Mare, A., Promphaking, B. and Rigg, J. (2015). "Returning home: the middle-income trap and gendered norms in Thailand." *Journal of International Development* 27: 285–306.

Li, T. M. (2007). *The will to improve: governmentality, development, and the practice of politics*. Durham, NC and London, Duke University Press.

Li, T. M. (2010). "To make live or let die? Rural dispossession and the protection of surplus populations." *Antipode* 41: 66–93.

Li, T. M. (2014). *Land's end: capitalist relations on an indigenous frontier*. Durham, NC, Duke University Press.

McKinnon, K., K. Gibson and L. Malam (2008). "Introduction: critical and hopeful area studies – emerging work in Asia and the Pacific." *Asia Pacific Viewpoint* (49): 273–280.

Meyer, K. E. and S. B. Brysac (2011). "Kerala: multiple improbabilities." *World Policy Journal* 28: 60–69.

Nguyen, T. A., J. Rigg, T. T. H. Luong and T. D. Dinh (2012). "Becoming and being urban in Hanoi: rural–urban migration and relations in Viet Nam." *Journal of Peasant Studies* 39(5): 1103–1131.

Promburom, P. and P. Sakdapolrak (2012). 'Where the rain falls' project. Case study: Thailand. Results from Thung Hua Chang District, Northern Thailand. Report no. 7. Bonn, Institute for Environment and Human Security, United Nations University.

Rigg, J. (2012). *Unplanned development: tracking change in South East Asia.* London, Zed Books.

Rigg, J. (forthcoming). Policies and negotiated everyday living: a view from the margins of development in Thailand and Vietnam. *The everyday political economy of Southeast Asia: Economic cultures and global flows.* J. Elias and L. Rethel. Cambridge, Cambridge University Press.

Rigg, J., T. A. Nguyen and T. T. H. Luong (2014a). "The texture of livelihoods: migration and making a living in Hanoi." *The Journal of Development Studies* 50(3): 368–382.

Rigg, J., B. Promphaking and A. Le Mare (2014b). "Personalizing the middle-income trap: an inter-generational migrant view from rural Thailand." *World Development* 59(7): 184–198.

Rodrik, D. (2007). *One economics, many recipes: globalization, institutions, and economic growth.* Princeton, NJ and Oxford, Princeton University Press.

Sachs, J. D. (2005). *The end of poverty: economic possibilites of our time.* New York, Penguin Books.

Sen, A. (1999). *Development as freedom.* Oxford, Oxford University Press.

Stiglitz, J. E. (2014). Inequality is not inevitable. *New York Times*, 29 July.

Tharamangalam, J. (2010). "Human development as transformative practice: lessons from Kerala and Cuba." *Critical Asian Studies* 42(3): 363–402.

UNDP (2013). *Human Development Report 2013: the rise of the South.* New York, United Nations Development Programme.

Venkatraman, T. (2009). "The Kerala paradox." *Indian Journal of Economics and Business* 8: 43+.

Wade, R. (2004 [1990]) *Governing the market: economic theory and the role of government in East Asian industrialization*, Princeton, NJ and Oxford: Princeton University Press.

Index

Printed in the USA/Agawam, MA
November 5, 2015

625758.014